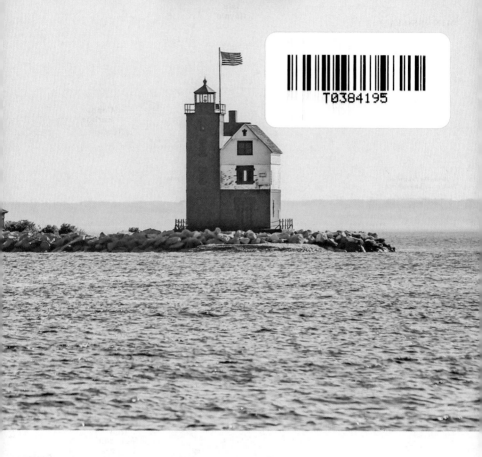

Michigan's
Upper Peninsula

PAUL VACHON

Contents

Lake of the Clouds at Porcupine Mountains State Park

Michigan's Upper Peninsula

Locals call Michigan's Upper Peninsula "the world above the bridge." Here you'll discover miles of freshwater coastline, hundreds of picturesque trails, and countless lakes, rivers, and waterfalls.

Brandishing a rustic, even austere terrain, the U.P. offers peace and solitude. The placid eastern portion, part of the Great Lakes plain, contrasts sharply with the more rugged western half. But each offers idyllic settings for camping, boating, and fishing. The dearth of human population allows wildlife to flourish, so there's a chance you'll see moose, black bears, red foxes, and white-tailed deer. Having a camera at the ready is an absolute necessity.

In many U.P. towns, descendants of European immigrants maintain traditions brought to America by their ancestors. The region's blend of heritage and warm hospitality is perhaps best experienced through the food. Be sure to try a Cornish pasty (a bread turnover filled with pork, chicken, or venison), a local favorite.

So, what doesn't the U.P. have? Crowds and congestion. Even the larger towns imbue a small-town feel. With a population density of just 19 people per square mile, Michigan's extreme north offers plenty of room to explore.

Welcome to America's northern paradise.

Presque Isle Park, Marquette

10 TOP
EXPERIENCES

1 Kayaking along **Pictured Rocks National Lakeshore** (page 248).

2 Hitting the trail (page 30), especially in Porcupine Mountains Wilderness State Park (page 147) and Isle Royale National Park (page 197).

3 Hitting the snow— the Upper Peninsula is tailor-made for almost any winter pastime (page 34).

6 Raising a glass on the **U.P. Wine Trail** (page 90) or at one of the many **breweries** (page 220).

7 Going on a romantic getaway to **Mackinac Island** (page 36).

8

9

10 Sailing through the **Soo Locks** (page 274).

Planning Your Trip

WHERE TO GO

The Straits of Mackinac

As the only physical connection between the two peninsulas, all the traffic from the Lower Peninsula funnels onto the 5-mile-long (8-km-long) Mackinac Bridge and into the great northern counterpart. The photogenic span prompts many travelers to stop with their cameras. **Mackinac Island,** established as a summer destination during the Gilded Age, endures as one of America's perfect getaways. Historic sites and state parks both on and off the island bring the region's bountiful history to life. Visit **Colonial Michilimackinac State Park** in Mackinaw City or **Fort Mackinac** on Mackinac Island for some fascinating exposure to this history.

Escanaba and the Lake Michigan Shore

The Lake Michigan shoreline makes for a pleasant drive, with dozens of waterfront stops and sandy beaches off US 2. The Garden Peninsula, which juts out into Lake Michigan, is home to **Fayette Historic State Park,** which memorializes the region's mining history. Continuing to the southwest, **Escanaba** and **Menominee** each offer their special appeal. An old mining town, Escanaba is in the midst of a rebirth. Don't overlook the city's waterfront, where you can tour the **Sand Point Lighthouse** and spend time in **Ludington Park.**

The Superior Upland

Without question, the number one highlight of the western U.P. is the majestic **Porcupine Mountains Wilderness State Park** (a.k.a. "the Porkies"). In summer, miles and miles of **hiking trails** lure visitors; in winter, the area's mountainous terrain and heavy snowfalls make **Ironwood** and its environs a top Midwest downhill skiing destination, offering a choice of many noteworthy **ski resorts.**

the Straits of Mackinac

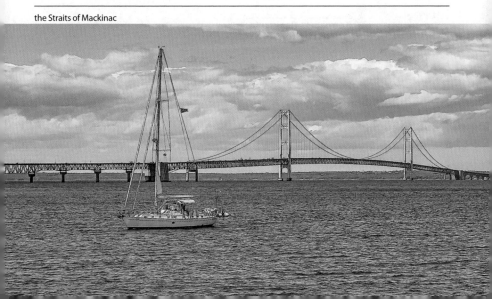

Keweenaw Peninsula and Isle Royale

As you journey up the Keweenaw Peninsula, the twin cities of **Houghton** and **Hancock** offer a cosmopolitan experience characteristic of college towns. Continuing north you'll find the historic town of **Calumet,** perhaps the most telling remnant from the glory days of Michigan's copper mining. You'll end your drive in **Copper Harbor,** mainland Michigan's "end of the road."

Sequestered by Lake Superior, the rugged **Isle Royale National Park** can be reached only by boat or plane. The quiet isolation of the island park offers the best fishing and kayaking in the U.P.—as well as a chance to see reclusive **moose** and **wolves.**

Marquette and the Lake Superior Shore

Lake Superior's southern shore offers some of the nation's most beautiful scenery: tough pines, stony beaches, and craggy rocks. Rent a **sea kayak** or take a boat tour to see the wonderful palette of colors on the formations at **Pictured Rocks National Lakeshore. Marquette** boasts a vibrant arts scene, a historic downtown, and tranquil **Presque Isle Park.** Situated on a picturesque bay, **Munising** is flanked by **Grand Island,** an offshore recreation area with unique hiking and camping options.

Whitefish Bay to the Lake Huron Shore

Whitefish Bay offers boaters welcome protection from a wildly unpredictable Lake Superior. The bay drains south into the St. Mary's River like a giant funnel, guiding ships through the **Soo Locks** that connect Lakes Superior and Huron, providing the Great Lakes with an essential shipping lane. A visit to these famous locks in **Sault Ste. Marie** offers a first-hand look at an engineering marvel. On the shore of Lake Huron, the **Les Cheneaux Islands** and **Drummond Island** remain remote, quiet destinations that are perfect for visitors seeking pleasure boating in a secluded setting.

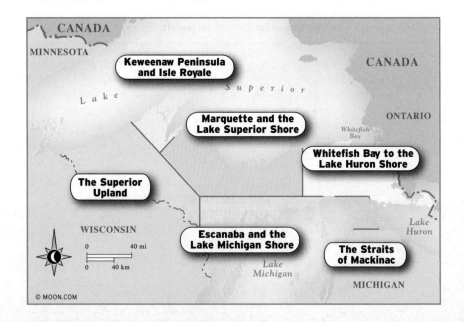

KNOW BEFORE YOU GO

When to Go

Summer is when nature is at its most vibrant. However, the weather can become especially hot and humid, with July being the most uncomfortable and bug-infested month. Try to time a camping trip before the mosquitoes and blackflies hatch, generally in mid-June, or go after mid-August. Hotel rates tend to spike around July 4 and Labor Day.

Autumn may be the very best time to visit—temperatures are mild, the bugs are gone, and fall colors put on a show that rivals New England's. Predicting the period of peak color is not an exact science, but it generally occurs around the fourth week of September. Colder temperatures begin to set in by late October.

Winter arrives in early December and usually lingers through March. For winter sports, February is the likeliest to ensure good snow cover. Planning a winter trip does require special attention to detail, as some restaurants and hotels close for the winter. For more on winter in the U.P., see page 298.

If you're able, avoid November and April, both of which are characterized by unpleasant gray skies and rain-snow-sleet mixtures. **Spring** doesn't begin until about mid-May at the earliest, and the shady pine forests of the U.P. can hold snow until Memorial Day or even later. Spring can be wonderful, with moderate temperatures, blossoming trees, and gushing waterfalls.

Transportation

The Upper Peninsula is accessible by any manner of transit, but for travel within the U.P., a **car** is an absolute necessity. **Public transportation is scarce** and rarely operates outside the larger cities. Distances throughout the U.P. are much greater than many people presume—it often takes hours to drive from one city to the next. Secondary roads are pretty rugged, so if you plan on venturing off the major routes, make sure

autumn in the Upper Peninsula

a narrow stream in the woods

your vehicle has **four-wheel-drive** and high clearance.

What to Pack

For many travelers to the Upper Peninsula, camping is the lodging of choice. In this case, it is essential to pack a **tent** and other necessities for traveling from campsite to campsite across the peninsula. Required outdoors staples include **bug spray with DEET,** sturdy shoes, and clothing for inclement weather. A small backpack for day trips or short hikes is also a good idea.

For other visitors, seasonal casual clothing and basic essentials are all that's necessary. Unless you plan to dine at one of Marquette's finer restaurants or enjoy a formal dinner at the Grand Hotel (several places on Mackinac Island have dress codes), dress clothing is unnecessary.

Purchasing a Michigan **Recreation Passport** is a wise investment. The annual pass allows access to any Michigan state park and offers savings at participating restaurants and stores.

If you decide to cross the International Bridge into Canada, you'll need a **passport** and/or other travel documents as determined by the US Department of Homeland Security.

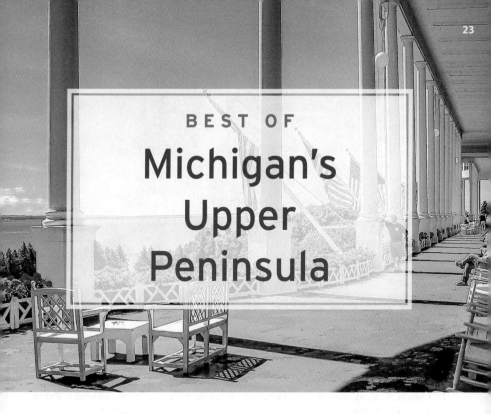

BEST OF
Michigan's Upper Peninsula

THE CHARMING EAST

On a map, the enormity of the Upper Peninsula can be deceptive. The unique qualities that give the U.P. its appeal are scattered over 30,000 square miles (77,700 sq km), 14 counties, and two time zones. If you only have a week and want to experience a bit of everything—without having to work too hard to do so—stick to the eastern half. Rustic hiking trails, breathtaking lake views, and charming small towns await you.

Day 1
Chances are you'll be arriving in **Mackinaw City,** the gateway to the U.P., after a very long drive from home. Check into a comfortable hotel room, enjoy a meal at one of the local restaurants, and take a bit of time to explore downtown. A respite like this is the perfect tonic for early vacation fatigue—one you'll thank yourself for later.

Day 2
If you plan on spending just one day on **Mackinac Island,** it's best to be a commuting visitor and return to your Mackinaw City lodgings at day's end. If you do this, catch an early ferry (7:30am is the first departure) to make the most of your day. Visit **Fort Mackinac,** take a captivating carriage ride past the lovely Victorian cottages along the **East Bluff,** then visit the **Governor's Residence** and the magnificent veranda at the **Grand Hotel.** A $10 per person charge allows

monarch at Mackinac Island Butterfly House

access to the veranda and the public areas of the hotel, and the experience is truly unforgettable. After lunch, take in a relaxing round of golf at **The Jewel** or spend some time at **Mackinac Island Butterfly House.** If you have a sweet tooth—and who doesn't?—pick up a wedge or two of world-famous Mackinac Island fudge at either **Murdick's Fudge** or **Ryba's.** Enjoy dinner on the island at the **Woods Restaurant** before returning to your lodgings on the mainland.

Day 3

Get an early breakfast at **Darrow's Family Restaurant;** you have a bit of a drive ahead of you. Cross the bridge and turn right just after the toll plaza to make a brief stop at **Straits State Park.** Here you can enjoy a breathtaking bridge view on the Upper Peninsula side. Next, head west along US 2. As you begin your trip from St. Ignace to Naubinway, you'll be treated to a pleasing panorama of the Lake Michigan shore, with St. Helena Island in the distance. There are many turnouts along this route, and with a good zoom lens and clear weather, you can get a

shot of the island's lighthouse. Continue on toward **Manistique** and stop for lunch at **Clyde's Drive-In No. 2** for a great burger and malt. After lunch, turn off onto M-149 and head to **Palms Book State Park** to see **Kitch-Iti-Kipi,** better known as "Big Spring." Continue on US 2, ending your day's sojourn in **Escanaba.** Have dinner at the **Ludington Grill.** Stay in any of the excellent chain hotels along US 2 or US 41.

Day 4

After breakfast in Escanaba at the authentic **Swedish Pantry,** head up M-35 toward Marquette, the Upper Peninsula's largest and most cosmopolitan city. Once you arrive, a stroll along the waterfront will be invigorating after time behind the wheel. Bring your camera so you can get some great shots of **Marquette Harbor Lighthouse,** a photogenic lighthouse on rocks located offshore. Grab lunch and spend the rest of the afternoon exploring the area, perhaps perusing junkyard art at **Lakenenland Sculpture Park** or viewing the sunset at **Presque Isle Park.** Choose from one of several excellent downtown

Waterfall Wonders

Scattered around the U.P. are no less than 300 sites of cascading water that punctuate its vast network of rivers and streams. Most require at least a short walk to reach, but the beauty that awaits you will make the effort worthwhile. While their sizes vary in terms of width and drop (the vertical height), virtually all of the falls are in idyllic tree-lined settings.

Spring is when the flow of water tends to be the strongest, as the runoff from the winter's snow and ice swells the rivers, allowing gravity to work its magic. In **summer,** trees that are in full bloom combined with the warm temperatures can make waterfall viewing an ideal daylong activity. But **autumn** is without question the most satisfying time to see waterfalls—taking in the cascading stream amidst patches of yellow, orange, and crimson is endlessly engaging. **Winter** is for the more intrepid visitor, but you'll be rewarded with solitude and unique beauty.

Be sure not to miss these beauties:

- **Bond Falls,** Paulding (page 137)

- **Presque Isle Falls,** Porcupine Mountains Wilderness State Park (page 152)

- **Tahquamenon Falls,** Paradise (page 264)

Best Scenic Drives

BROCKWAY MOUNTAIN DRIVE

Distance: *9 miles (14.5 km), 30 minutes*
Starting Point: *M-26 at Silver River Falls*
Ending Point: *Copper Harbor*
Without question the most spectacular drive in Michigan, this high-vista route offers an unmatched view of Copper Harbor and the rolling forests of the Keweenaw. Stop midway to soak in the panorama of Lake Superior.

US 2

Distance: *88 miles (142 km), 1.5 hours*
Starting Point: *St. Ignace*
Ending Point: *Manistique*
This stunning coastal drive hugs the Lake Michigan shoreline and offers a bevy of scenic turnouts and sandy beaches. A small detour takes you to a lighthouse viewpoint.

BLACK RIVER NATIONAL FOREST SCENIC BYWAY

Distance: *15 miles (24 km), 30 minutes*
Starting Point: *Bessemer*
Ending Point: *Black River County Park, along Lake Superior*
A wooded road that twists in tandem with the Black River, this drive links noteworthy attractions, including hiking trails and waterfalls, as it makes its way to the shores of Lake Superior.

MARSHLAND WILDLIFE DRIVE

Distance: *7 miles (11.3 km), 1 hour*
Starting Point: *Seney National Wildlife Refuge Visitor Center*
Ending Point: *Approximately 1 mile (1.6 km) south of starting point on M-77*
The route is short but packed with adventure! This one-way loop allows motorists to see Canada geese, common loons, and trumpeter swans—maybe even a deer—as it circles the wildlife refuge.

CURLEY LEWIS MEMORIAL HIGHWAY

Distance: *37 miles (60 km), 1 hour*
Starting Point: *M-123, 11 miles (18 km) south of Paradise*
Ending Point: *Sault Ste. Marie*
Following the curve of Lake Superior's Whitefish Bay, the drive is an attraction in itself, passing through the Hiawatha National Forest and offering views of the lake. Mission Hill Overlook is a worthwhile detour for sweeping views.

WESTERN SHORELINE DRIVE

Distance: *97 miles (156 km), 3 hours*
Starting Point: *Copper Harbor*
Ending Point: *Silver City*
While only portions of this drive hug the shoreline, the densely wooded route is peaceful and scenic, especially in autumn.

Fall Colors

Planning a fall color tour of Michigan's Upper Peninsula can be tricky, as the timing of peak colors is often unpredictable. While fall colors in the Upper Peninsula typically peak between **late September** and **early October,** a given year's weather conditions can either accelerate or delay their appearance.

The risk is that you'll arrive a week early and be met with a landscape of midsummer green, or you'll come too late and be greeted by a sea of bare trees. But the fortunate traveler is in for a real treat. If your timing is right, all you need to enjoy the glory of countless trees in their peak color is the will to get outside, whether it's on a hiking trail, in a kayak along the shoreline, or in a car on one of the main highways.

Visit **The Fall Color Blog** (www.fallcolorblog. com) for updates during the fall color season.

- One of the finest routes in the U.P. is the circle formed between **Eagle River** and **Copper Harbor** by US 41 and M-26, an hour-long 45-mile (72-km) loop. The scene is truly breathtaking, especially the section along US 41/Copper Country Trail Scenic Byway.

- The **Keweenaw Peninsula** from mid-September to early October showcases the best colors. A leisurely drive from Baraga to Copper Harbor (the base of the peninsula to the tip) is about 150 miles (241 km) and will take about three hours.

- The **Marquette-Negaunee-Au Train tour** will take you into the Huron Mountains on the way to Big Bay and back, as well as on a wider loop south and east of the city along M-35, US 41, M-94, and M-28. The trip is about 170 miles (274 km) and will take about three hours.

- Pure Michigan's website (www.michigan.org) lists 10 U.P. **fall foliage driving routes,** including stops along the way and detailed maps for each tour.

dining spots for dinner before spending the night in Marquette.

Day 5

Grab breakfast at **Donckers** before setting course on M-28 for **Munising** and **Pictured Rocks National Lakeshore.** Since the colorful rocks can only be seen from the water, book either a three-hour **boat tour** with Pictured Rocks Cruises or a **kayak tour** with Pictured Rocks Kayaking. Enjoy dinner at **Lake Superior Brewing Company** and stay the night in **Grand Marais;** renting one of the **Hilltop Cabins** will offer a great waterfront view.

Day 6

Grab a convenient breakfast at **Grand Marais Tavern and Restaurant and** then hit the road for **Tahquamenon Falls State Park,** where you'll find what is hands down the most magnificent waterfall in the U.P.—and that's saying a lot! You can see the Upper Falls from the observation deck, which is only a short trail walk from the parking area. Four miles (6.4 km) downstream, the Lower Falls produce a similar spectacle. The awe-inspiring power of the falls is hard to overstate. As much as 50,000 gallons of water per second pour over Upper Tahquamenon, the second most powerful waterfall in the eastern United States, exceeded only by Niagara. Enjoy lunch at the **Tahquamenon Falls Brewery and Pub** before setting out for **Sault Ste. Marie.** Sail through the always fascinating **Soo Locks** with Soo Locks Boat Tours and marvel at how gargantuan ships can transit though the locks with just inches to spare. Cap off your adventure with a special dinner at **Lockview Restaurant.** Check in at the historic **Hotel Ojibway** for the night before departing for home the next morning.

Day 7

Enjoy one last breakfast before heading back to Mackinaw. Start planning your next trip on the drive home!

Main Street in Crystal Falls

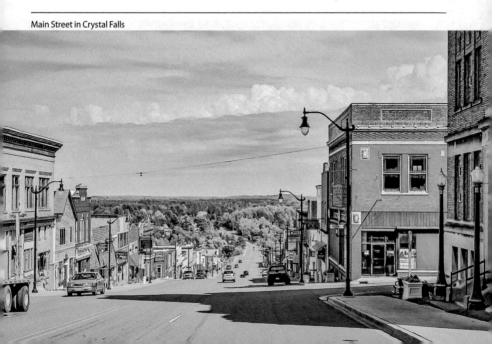

Best Hikes

PORCUPINE MOUNTAINS WILDERNESS STATE PARK

Escarpment Trail

8.8 miles (14.2 km) round-trip

This fairly short trail is a wonderfully scenic hike. The relatively high elevation offers a view of the Lake of the Clouds to the south, where summer greenery resembles a vast, lush carpet. Lake Superior is visible to the north (page 150).

PICTURED ROCKS NATIONAL LAKESHORE

Miners Falls Trail

1 mile (1.6 km) round-trip

A delightful option for those unable to undertake a longer trek, this trail is an easy, flat, and well-maintained walk through sparse maple forest. Its low density allows for excellent viewing of deer and an occasional moose. The big payoff, however, comes at the end—the roaring, majestic Miners Falls (page 247).

TAHQUAMENON FALLS STATE PARK

Tahquamenon River Trail

8 miles (12.9 km) round-trip

This great trail hugs the shore of the Tahquamenon River between the Upper and Lower Tahquamenon Falls—you're never more than about 20 feet (6 meters) from the roaring river. This is an especially nice walk in the springtime, when the current is strongest due to the melting of the winter snow and ice (page 269).

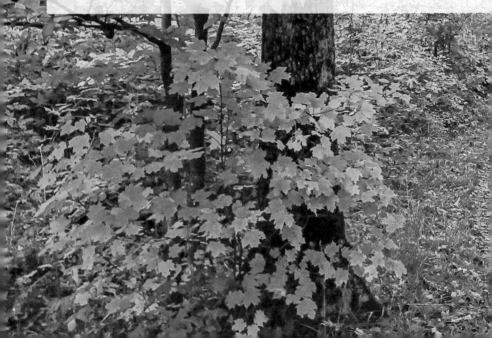

ISLE ROYALE NATIONAL PARK

Greenstone Ridge Trail

42.2 miles (67.9 km) one-way

Intended for the serious hiker/backpacker, this is perhaps the least ventured trail in the least visited park in the National Park System. Talk about experiencing nature in solitude! This four-day, three-night adventure will take you along the spine of the main island of the park. Seeing moose is not uncommon; if you're lucky, you may even see a gray wolf (page 199).

MARQUETTE

Sugarloaf Mountain

1.2 miles (1.9 km) round-trip

The path winds past old-growth trees and rock outcroppings. The real reward, though, awaits you at the summit. The spellbinding view of Marquette, Presque Isle, and Lake Superior will be truly unforgettable (page 214).

ST. IGNACE

Horseshoe Bay Hiking Trail

6 miles (9.7 km) round-trip

Despite being close to the city of St. Ignace, this trail offers a surprising level of seclusion. This easy route runs from the trailhead to the Lake Huron shore, passing through northern white cedars and punctuated with shallow ponds (page 67).

THE WILD WEST

Adventure awaits in the western half of Michigan's Upper Peninsula. Take your time to really examine the scenery—it's much more rustic than in the east, and nothing like what you'll find in the big city!

Day 1

Start your trip on the US 2 going west toward Iron River. Along the way you'll cross into the central time zone and begin to see some of the rough terrain the U.P. is known for. This area was the heart of iron country during the heyday of mining. To learn about this historic period, visit the **Iron Mountain Iron Mine** near Vulcan. Afterward, continue on US 2 and stop in **Iron Mountain** for lunch; try either **Bimbo's Wine Press** on East Main Street if you appreciate good Italian fare (owing to the area's Italian heritage), or **Famers** on Pine Mountain Road if you'd prefer a sports bar atmosphere. Continue west on US 2, taking a brief detour into a corner of Wisconsin on the way to **Crystal Falls.** You're entering the Superior Upland, the area of rough beauty also known as iron country. Stop in Crystal Falls just long enough to admire the spectacular view looking down Main Street and take a picture of the highlands in the distance. Continue west along US 2 until you come to Watersmeet. Book a room at the **Dancing Eagles Hotel at the Northern Waters Casino Resort** for a well-deserved rest. After dinner at the **Northern Waters Sports Bar,** make the short trek up US 45 to view the baffling **Paulding Mystery Light.**

Day 2

The most picturesque wilderness of the Upper Peninsula awaits you! After breakfast at the hotel, take US 45 north toward **Ontonagon,** where you'll find the eastern end of **Porcupine Mountains Wilderness State Park.** Pick up picnic supplies in town before taking M-107 up the large hill to **Lake of the Clouds Overlook.** Park your car and make the very short hike up to the top of the cliff to take in the breathtaking view. Follow M-107 through the park, being careful of the frequent turns in the road. After exiting the park near Union Bay you'll find a series of scenic turnouts along the Lake Superior shore. Most have tables, so stop here to enjoy your picnic lunch and chat with some of your fellow travelers. After lunch, head to **Ontonagon** to take in the **Ontonagon County Historical Museum,** which offers a fascinating look at the community's past, with an emphasis on the logging and mining industries. The historical society also offers tours of the **Ontonagon Lighthouse,** an 1853 structure gradually being restored. Grab dinner at **Syl's Café** and get a cabin for the night at the **Mountain View Lodges** on M-64, featuring a waterfront view and a sandy beach.

Day 3

Today you'll be heading into the **Keweenaw Peninsula,** as north as you can go while still being in mainland Michigan. From Ontonagon, take US 45 to M-26 and head north. As you progress, you'll see more pine and spruce trees mixed in with maples and elms. When you come to **Houghton,** a college town that's home to Michigan Technological University, stop and take a leisurely break, possibly at **Cyberia Café.** Stop to view the unusual "lift bridge" linking the city to Hancock across the Keweenaw Waterway. Continue north on US 41 until you come to **Calumet,** considered by some to be the capital of the once-dominant copper industry. Take some time to look around at the magnificent if somewhat neglected architecture flanked by abandoned mines. Continue until you get to **Copper Harbor** and the end of US 41. Book a room at the **Keweenaw Mountain Lodge.**

Day 4

Shift into nautical mode and board the *Isle Royale Queen IV* for the three-hour trip to **Isle Royale National Park,** one of the least-visited properties in the National Park System. Although the park is very rugged and most visitors choose

---

1: Lake of the Clouds in Porcupine Mountains Wilderness State Park 2: Rock Harbor on Isle Royale

Winter Wonderland

Although the allure of summer is what attracts most visitors to the Upper Peninsula, the cold-weather months reveal a different—and equally diverse—set of recreational opportunities. Thanks to an abundance of snow (over 200 inches/500 centimeters annually), the region's rugged topography, and temperatures that, while cold, seldom descend to subzero levels, the Upper Peninsula is tailor-made for almost any winter pastime.

SKIING

Downhill skiing can only be enjoyed at destination resorts. Here are a few of the best:

- Pine Mountain Resort, Iron Mountain (page 127)

- Big Powderhorn Mountain, Bessemer (page 144)

- Blackjack Ski Resort, Bessemer (page 145)

- Porcupine Mountains Ski Area, Porcupine Mountains Wilderness State Park (page 153)

CROSS-COUNTRY SKIING

Cross-country skiers are welcome on any of the dozens of designated trails throughout the Upper Peninsula. Try one of the following:

- Swedetown Trails, Calumet (page 174)

- Copper Harbor Pathway, Copper Harbor (page 187)

- Blueberry Ridge Ski Trails, Escanaba River State Forest (page 216)

- Big Bay Pathway, Huron Mountains (page 228)

SNOWSHOEING

Certain trails throughout the U.P. are dedicated exclusively to snowshoeing. Here are a few:

- Fumee Lake Natural Area, Dickinson (page 127)

- Active Backwoods Retreat trails, Ironwood (page 145)

- Michigan Tech trails, Houghton (page 174)

- Estivant Pines Nature Sanctuary, Keweenaw Peninsula (page 187)

SNOWMOBILING

Snowmobiling trails are plentiful in the entire Upper Peninsula. Visit www.michigan.gov/dnr and search for "Snowmobile Trail Maps" to find downloadable maps of trails that run throughout the state. Always be careful to respect private property rights and avoid trespassing. Also remember that all snowmobiles are required to be registered and have a state trail permit, available through the Michigan DNR and at snowmobile shops throughout the state.

Here are some especially choice locations for snowmobiling adventure:

- Fumee Lake and Trail 5, Iron Mountain region (page 127)

- Keweenaw, Stevens, and Bill Nichols Trails, Keweenaw Peninsula (page 172)

- Trails 8 and 417, Marquette area (page 216)

ICE FISHING

Anglers well versed in summer fishing may want to try the different art of winter ice fishing. Venturing out onto a thoroughly frozen lake, setting up a shanty, and lowering a line through a small hole can be a challenging way to spend an afternoon.

- Manistique Lakes, Curtis (page 92)

- Grand Island (page 235)

- Anna River and Munising Bay, Munising (page 239)

FESTIVALS AND EVENTS

A major festival is the annual **Winter Carnival** at Michigan Technological University, Houghton. Held in early February, the event includes snow statues, ice sculptures, a queen contest, and nighttime fireworks.

to camp, indoor accommodations are available at the **Rock Harbor Lodge** at Rock Harbor at the far eastern tip. Either way, you'll have virtually unlimited opportunities to commune with nature.

Hiking, fishing, observing wildlife, and kayaking are some of the activities you can enjoy. Spend two to three days exploring Isle Royale—a truly unforgettable experience.

Days 5-6
Take a few **day hikes** along some of the shorter trails into the island—**Scoville Point** and **Lookout Louise** are good choices, and the view from **Ojibway Tower** is phenomenal. Look into a National Park Service boat tour or rent a sea kayak and explore the shoreline yourself. Pack lunches and take them with you, but note that dinners at the Rock Harbor Lodge are satisfying.

Backwoods campers and hikers will have 165 miles (266 km) of trails to explore. There's no way to hike it all in a few days, but a well-planned trip will have you walking from campsite to campsite while you keep a lookout for moose.

Day 7
Make sure you're back at the ferry dock in time for the ride back to **Copper Harbor.** Aim to get into town a little before 6pm, just in time for dinner at the **Harbor Haus.** Make your way back home in the morning.

MACKINAC ISLAND GETAWAY

If you're looking for a long, romantic weekend away with your partner, look no further than Mackinac Island. You'll find plenty of Victorian charm, picturesque views, and recreational opportunities to enjoy with your significant other.

Day 1
After a long day of driving, take Shepler's ferry from St. Ignace to **Mackinac Island** for a relaxing evening. If you're splurging, spend the night at the **Grand Hotel.** If you're on a budget, try the **Inn at Stonecliffe.**

Day 2
Start your day leisurely with breakfast at the hotel and a **carriage tour** to get the lay of the land. Stops include the Butterfly House, Fort Mackinac, and Arch Rock. Be sure to also visit the Governor's Residence and stop for some fudge at Murdick's. If you're more athletically inclined, skip the carriage tour and rent **bicycles** from Ryba's Bicycle Rentals. Ride along **M-185** (Lake Shore Drive), which rings the island's perimeter. Pack a picnic to enjoy in between visiting the island's highlights. Regardless of how you spend your day, end it by watching the sunset before heading to **Woods Restaurant** (an off-site Grand Hotel property) for a decadent dinner.

Day 3
In the morning, return to St. Ignace for your last day of adventure. Take I-75 north to M-123, continuing for about an hour to reach **Tahquamenon Falls State Park,** home to one of the most beautiful waterfalls in North America. Plan on experiencing the falls up close—either by **hiking** the nearby trails or **canoeing** the Tahquamenon River. It's an experience you won't soon forget. From the park, check into the **Paradise Inn,** located in its namesake town. Spend an afternoon unwinding, and have a delightful meal at the **Tahquamenon Falls Brewery and Pub** before retiring. Return home in the morning.

More Ideas
- Take a sunset cruise at Pictured Rocks National Lakeshore.
- Go wine-tasting along the northern shore of Lake Michigan, from Manistique to Menominee.
- Rent a rustic cabin in the Porcupine Mountains Wilderness State Park for some privacy.

Chasing the Northern Lights

The northern lights, or aurora borealis, are a fascinating astronomical phenomenon. The majestic palette of pink, yellow, blue, and other shades occurs when charged particles emanate from the sun (a process known as solar wind) and interact with gas particles in the earth's upper atmosphere.

Northern latitudes are best positioned for viewing this spectacle, as they are the closest to the auroral dome, the area between 66 and 69 degrees north—far past Michigan. However, in northern areas of the continental United States, it is possible to observe the northern lights in the correct conditions.

Here are some things to keep in mind:

- The primary requirement is being in an area of near total darkness, away from any sources of light pollution and tall trees. This might include an isolated spot on the **Lake Superior shore.** Any other location that's at a high elevation (to optimize your range of visibility) and away from sources of artificial light will also work. The very best location in Michigan is the **Headlands International Dark Sky Park** near Mackinaw City, which is designated as such by the International Dark Sky Association.

- Seeing the lights on a given night depends largely on chance, as the lights can appear suddenly and unexpectedly. However, periods of the **solar maximum,** the peak of an approximately 11-year cycle of solar activity, are generally best.

- But don't be deterred if the calendar is not favorable. The most likely times of year to see the lights are during the **vernal and autumnal (spring and fall) equinoxes,** when the solar wind places the greatest pressure on the earth's magnetic field. Headlands has a page on its website (see below) devoted to planning a trip to see the lights.

- Choose a night with minimal (or no) cloud cover, and as little moonlight as possible.

- Waiting to see the northern lights (or any astronomical phenomenon) requires patience and often involves staying up until very late hours—often one or two in the morning. Even during the summer, this can mean chilly temperatures, so dress appropriately.

RESOURCES:

- **Headlands International Dark Sky Park** (www.midarkskypark.org/stargazing/northern-lights)

- **Aurora Borealis Forecaster** (www.softservenews.com)

- **SpaceWeatherNow** (www.swpc.noaa.gov/SWN)

Best Camping Spots

For those with an outdoors spirit, the Upper Peninsula is a truly quintessential camping destination. Campers usually arrive at their site of choice, set up camp, and venture off on day hikes or fishing adventures.

- **Tahquamenon Falls State Park** (page 264): From the Mackinac Bridge, take I-75 to M-123 and head north to Tahquamenon Falls State Park. Choose either the modern campground or its rustic counterpart, both located near the Lower Falls.

- **Mead Creek Campground** (page 258): Located off M-77 near the town of Germfask and right on the edge of the Seney National Wildlife Refuge, this campground is a true paradise for wildlife photographers and nature lovers. From the National Wildlife Refuge Visitors Center near the entrance road, choose from several nature trails, where you can see and hear loons, nesting bald eagles, beavers, river otters, and perhaps an occasional bear or moose—all of which thrive in this protected habitat.

- **Indian Lake State Park** (page 86): Just a short drive down US 2 from Manistique, you can experience a classic U.P. camping experience. Fish, swim, or rent a boat to venture out on crystal-clear Indian Lake. While you're in the area, don't forget to check out Kitch-Iti-Kipi, the fascinating natural spring in nearby Palms Book State Park.

- **Porcupine Mountains Wilderness State Park** (page 147): This is where you'll get the quintessential U.P. camping experience. The park offers backcountry camping, hiking trails of various distances, and stunning views of the majestic landscape. You'll also find over 35,000 acres of old-growth hardwood forest.

- **Straits State Park** (page 69): For those interested in a less primitive camping experience, Straits offers a spectacular view of the Mackinac Bridge as well as fully or partially serviced sites. There's also a 1-mile (1.6-km) nature trail.

Wildlife Watching

Observing wildlife is an immensely rewarding activity, especially in a fauna-rich region like Michigan's Upper Peninsula. Watching the activities of other species helps you relate to nature in ways both inspiring and intimate. But viewing animals in their natural habitat requires knowledge, determination, and an abundance of patience.

In many cases, the species listed are widespread in their particular habitat throughout the region. The locations given for each species are the ones that will give you the best chance of seeing that species.

- **Bears:** Lake Superior Nature Sanctuary, Craig Lake State Park, Oswald's Bear Ranch

- **Bobcats:** Drummond Island and the higher, rocky areas of the Superior Upland

- **Coyotes:** Ironwood and Ontonagon areas, plus the Lake Superior Nature Sanctuary

- **Deer:** Lake Superior Nature Sanctuary, Craig Lake State Park

- **Foxes:** Harbor Island National Wildlife Refuge, Isle Royale

- **Moose:** Isle Royale, McCormick Wilderness, Van Riper State Park

- **Snowshoe hares:** Harbor Island National Wildlife Refuge

- **Wolves:** Drummond Island, Seney National Wildlife Refuge

- **Eagles:** Seney National Wildlife Refuge, Sturgeon River Sloughs Natural Area, Whitefish Point

- **Hawks:** Keweenaw Peninsula, Whitefish Point

- **Herons:** Sturgeon River Sloughs Natural Area, Horseshoe Bay Hiking Trail in Hiawatha National Forest

- **Loons:** Drummond Island, Seney National Wildlife Refuge, Isle Royale, Whitefish Point

- **Ospreys:** Sturgeon River Sloughs Natural Area

- **Owls:** Whitefish Point, Sugar Island

- **Trumpeter swans:** Seney National Wildlife Refuge

VIEWING TIPS

For viewing and photographing species of migratory birds, early fall is the optimal time of year. For land animals, your chances are best during the species' mating season. For moose and elk, it's September and October; for wolves, look between January and February. Deer and foxes are likely to be seen between April and November and tend to be more active near dusk.

PHOTOGRAPHING WILDLIFE

If you're traveling the Upper Peninsula at a more leisurely pace and have an interest in photography, you may want to dedicate a day or more to testing your skills in the field—and possibly be rewarded with a few compelling wildlife images.

What you'll need: Obtaining a quality image requires two essentials: the proper gear and a good deal of patience. Since wildlife shots are normally taken from a considerable distance, a good DSLR camera equipped with a telephoto lens of at least 300 millimeters is a must. To avoid blurred images from camera shake, a tripod or some object on which to steady the camera and lens is also necessary.

What to do: Arrive at your intended viewing destination at an early hour—at daybreak if possible—and choose a spot close to where your intended subject is most likely to appear (near tall trees for birds of prey, alongside an inland lake or pond for moose or waterfowl). When setting up your equipment, set your aperture, shutter speed, ISO, and white balance in advance. To clearly capture an image of a bird in flight, a fast shutter speed (around 1/200th of a second) is important. Be aware that to compensate for this, a higher ISO will probably be necessary. Take frequent meter readings to guard against images that are either blown out or too dark. Finally, do your absolute best to remain quiet and alert. Good luck!

The Straits of Mackinac

The Straits of Mackinac have long separated the

"Yoopers" from the "Trolls." Yoopers get their nickname from the U.P., as in, "U.P.-ers," while "Trolls" is their good-natured name for Michiganders who live to the south, "under the bridge."

A particular curiosity is the locale's variant spellings. The city on the south side of the straits is Mackinaw City, but the bridge, resort island, and the straits themselves are all identified as Mackinac. Fortunately, the pronunciation is universal, with both pronounced "MACK-i-*naw*," and never "MACK-i-*nack*."

Five miles (8 km) wide at their narrowest point, the straits are largely responsible for the Upper Peninsula's profound isolation. Before the completion of the Mackinac Bridge in 1957, northbound traffic to the

Highlights

Look for ★ to find recommended sights, activities, dining, and lodging.

★ **Mackinac Island Butterfly House:** See a wide array of geraniums while being entertained by hundreds of butterflies (page 46).

★ **Grand Hotel:** This 1887 hotel lives up to its name with 385 rooms, the world's longest front porch, and a history of Hollywood glamour (page 47).

★ **Fort Mackinac:** British and American troops fought here during the War of 1812. Today, costumed interpreters bring its glory days to life (page 48).

★ **Lilac Festival:** This 10-day festival in early June showcases Mackinac Island at its best, with music, food, horses, and a parade (page 53).

★ **Mackinac Bridge:** Drive across the 5-mile-long (8-km) "Mighty Mac" or stop at Mackinac Bridge View Park to take pictures of this amazing feat of engineering (page 60).

★ **Headlands International Dark Sky Park:** This park is the perfect place to absorb the wonders of the night sky, a truly breathtaking experience (page 71).

★ **Colonial Michilimackinac State Park:** The site of the original fort, built in 1715, is the location of an archaeological dig, summertime reenactments, and a big wooden replica fort (page 72).

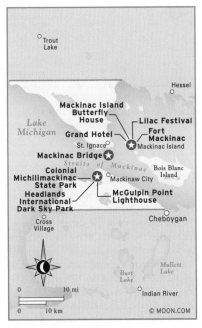

★ **McGulpin Point Lighthouse:** This late-19th-century lighthouse has been excellently restored. Climb the stairs to get a panoramic view of the Straits (page 74).

The Straits of Mackinac

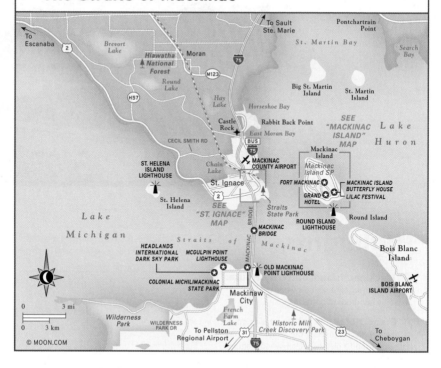

Upper Peninsula had to wait in seemingly endless lines for a spot on one of the cross-channel ferries.

Thanks to the bridge, the only ferries today are the passenger variety headed for Mackinac Island, one of the nation's incomparable travel destinations. Resting strategically between Lake Michigan and Lake Huron, and between the Upper and Lower Peninsulas, the island's 19th-century charm has welcomed visitors since 1875, when it became Mackinac National Park—the nation's second national park after Yellowstone. The State of Michigan has since assumed control of the park, which occupies about 80 percent of the island.

On Mackinac Island, you'll instantly notice the absence of automobiles, which have been banned since the 1920s. As a result, Mackinac Island really does seem frozen *Somewhere in Time,* which happens to be the name of a 1980 movie filmed on the island, starring Christopher Reeve and Jane Seymour. The Victorian architecture and atmosphere draws families, romantics, history buffs, and those simply looking for a good old-fashioned horse-and-buggy ride.

Try not to be offended if locals refer to you as a "Fudgie," which is usually said in good humor. While fudge wasn't invented on Mackinac, the island has become somewhat famous for it. Odds are you'll be buying at least a sliver of it while you're here, which is why residents have dubbed you and the

---

Previous: the Straits of Mackinac; Mackinac Bridge; Fort Mackinac.

millions of other visitors with the nickname. You might say it comes with the territory.

Mackinaw City in the Lower Peninsula and St. Ignace in the Upper Peninsula bookend the Mackinac Bridge. Each place possesses a distinct personality. Stop in Mackinaw City or Mackinac Island for the fudge, in St. Ignace for the auto shows, and in both for the history. Museums in each city retell the region's past from the original inhabitants through today. A noteworthy difference is the all-too-noticeable cultural divide. Despite being small, Mackinaw City has a slightly urban, if still northerly, atmosphere. St. Ignace, however, feels much more rustic.

If you're looking for a good base for day trips to other U.P. locations, you can take advantage of the area's plentiful lodgings and restaurants.

PLANNING YOUR TIME

If you're entering the U.P. from the south by crossing the bridge, you'll be passing through both Mackinaw City and St. Ignace. You may be on the way to Copper Harbor for some kayaking or driving west for Ironwood's downhill skiing, but in any event it's worth your time to get off the highway and spend some time in the straits, one of the most picturesque locations in Michigan.

Although two days will be enough time to see the best of the region, the straits' natural beauty and Mackinac Island's unique atmosphere often entice people to stay longer. It's best to plan on spending a full day on the island. Island lodgings tend to be more expensive (particularly the palatial Grand Hotel), but if you don't mind spending a little more, a stay on Mackinac Island is certainly worth it. Mackinaw City and St. Ignace can both be seen in a single day.

Summers are the busiest (and the best) season for visiting, with Mackinac Island drawing the largest crowds. St. Ignace tends to be best for outdoor activities. If you're interested in the area's history, you'll want to make an afternoon of Mackinaw City's numerous historical sites.

Accommodation Price Key

$	Less than $100 per night
$ $	$100-200 per night
$ $ $	More than $200 per night

HISTORY

Native Americans knew of the straits' abundant hunting and fishing long before the French or British arrived. Originally called Michilimackinac (Land of the Great Turtle), the island was considered sacred by the Anishinaabe-Ojibwa, who believed it was populated by the first people and home of the Great Spirit Gitchie Manitou. In addition to using the island as a gathering place, the Ojibwa, Ottawa, and other nations hunted on Mackinac Island and neighboring Bois Blanc Island. Their success allowed them to trade some of their catch to nations farther south in exchange for vegetables and grain.

Europeans arrived in the 17th century. The first were French Jesuits who arrived in the 1670s both to take advantage of the fur trade and to convert the Ojibwa to Christianity. Jacques Marquette, a priest and an explorer, founded a town and a mission at St. Ignace in 1671, naming it after the founder of the Society of Jesus, Saint Ignatius of Loyola. It was quickly followed by a trading post and later by Fort Michilimackinac on the site of present-day Mackinaw City.

During the 18th century, the British and French skirmished over the land, with the fort periodically changing hands. The 1763 Treaty of Paris, signed at the conclusion of the French and Indian War, gave all French land east of the Mississippi to the British. Seven years later, the British commander abandoned the fort for a more easily defendable position on Mackinac Island, where the British would overstay their welcome even after the land was given to the United States following the American Revolution.

American soldiers took possession of Fort Mackinac in 1796 and held it for almost 20 years. During the War of 1812, the British retook the fort by invading the island under cover of night and surprising the Americans, who surrendered without a fight. The British ran the fortification for two years, despite repeated American assaults aimed at retaking it. In 1814 the Treaty of Ghent ended the war and returned the island to the United States.

Throughout it all, the fur trade formed the foundation of the area's economy. Europeans traded canoe-loads of goods for pelts from beavers and other animals that had been trapped by the Ojibwa. Mackinac Island became one of the country's most valuable trading posts during the 1820s, making way for the country's first millionaire, John Jacob Astor. His American Fur Company was the leader in Mackinac's thriving fur trade. After overhunting ended the industry, it was replaced by commercial fishing.

After the era of military conflicts, Mackinac Island began to earn a reputation as one of the nation's most popular and fashionable resorts of the Victorian era, drawing travelers from the Midwest and beyond. By the second half of the 19th century, lumber barons, railroad magnates, and other wealthy Americans began building large, sumptuous cottages on the island, many of which still stand today and can be viewed on one of the Mackinac Island Carriage Tours.

When cars first arrived on the island, their presence proved highly controversial. These "mechanical monsters," as they came to be known, were loathed for their noise and emissions and also because they frightened the horses. Many communities around the country decided at first to ban automobiles, but eventually virtually all succumbed to the inevitable. Mackinac Island remains perhaps the last vestige of this era, where cars (and most other forms of motorized transit) have been prohibited since 1898. Some 600 horses serve visitors during the summer months—a number that dwindles to just a few dozen in the winter. The horses, carriages, and well-kept Victorian homes and hotels combine to give Mackinac its timeless charm, while maintaining its status as one of the Midwest's most popular vacation destinations.

Mackinac Island

During its peak tourism season, Mackinac Island draws some 15,000 people each day. This little island sports a rich history: Native Americans, French fur traders, and British soldiers eventually gave way to Victorian resorts. By design, the island today displays little evidence of the contemporary world.

Despite this fidelity to history, much of the downtown can feel somewhat touristy, especially when packed with visitors. But there are plenty of treasures here for those willing to look. Most of the island—80 percent of it—is undeveloped state land, some of which adjoins the downtown area by just a block or two. Fortunately, getting away from the showy commercialism is easy.

SIGHTS
Downtown
After disembarking from the ferry, you may decide to linger awhile so you can get a glimpse of the necessary "heavy lifting" that keeps Mackinac Island running. Workers unload cartons of vegetables from ferries and reload them by hand onto drays (horse-drawn wagons) for delivery to local restaurants. Another horse-drawn wagon pulls huge bales of hay to feed the island's numerous equines. Even the USPS and UPS carriers do their routes on bicycle, pulling carts loaded with letters and packages.

After spending a little time at the four blocks of shops and restaurants on **Main Street,** make the most of your visit by getting off the main drag. For an overview of what the island has to offer, take a carriage tour with **Mackinac Island Carriage Tours** (906/847-3307, www.mict.com, $39 adults, $16 ages 5-12, free under age 5, hours vary,

Mackinac Island

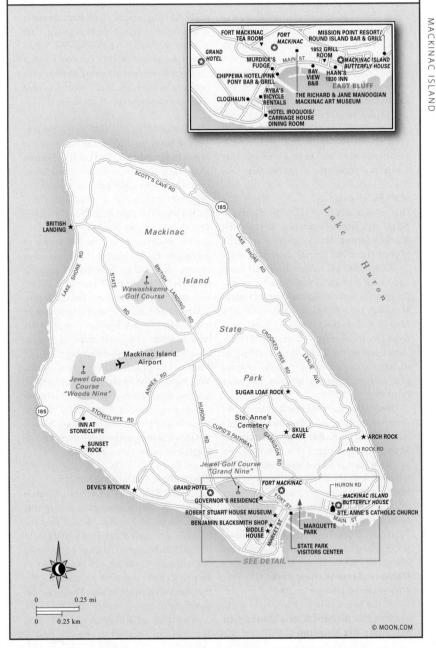

FORT MACKINAC
TEA ROOM
FORT MACKINAC
MISSION POINT RESORT/
ROUND ISLAND BAR & GRILL
GRAND HOTEL
MURDICK'S FUDGE
MAIN ST
1852 GRILL ROOM
MACKINAC ISLAND BUTTERFLY HOUSE
CHIPPEWA HOTEL/PINK PONY BAR & GRILL
BAY VIEW B&B
HAAN'S 1830 INN
EAST BLUFF
RYBA'S BICYCLE RENTALS
CLOGHAUN
THE RICHARD & JANE MANOOGIAN MACKINAC ART MUSEUM
HOTEL IROQUOIS/ CARRIAGE HOUSE DINING ROOM

SCOTT'S CAVE RD
185
BRITISH LANDING
Mackinac
Lake
Huron
LAKE SHORE RD
LAKE SHORE RD
STATE RD
BRITISH LANDING RD
Island
Wawashkamo Golf Course
State
CROOKED TREE RD
Mackinac Island Airport
Jewel Golf Course "Woods Nine"
ANNEX RD
Park
LESLIE AVE
185
STONECLIFFE RD
SUGAR LOAF ROCK
INN AT STONECLIFFE
HURON RD
Ste. Anne's Cemetery
SKULL CAVE
ARCH ROCK
SUNSET ROCK
CUPID'S PATHWAY
GARRISON RD
ARCH ROCK RD
Jewel Golf Course "Grand Nine"
DEVIL'S KITCHEN
GRAND HOTEL
FORT MACKINAC
HURON RD
GOVERNOR'S RESIDENCE
FORT ST
MACKINAC ISLAND BUTTERFLY HOUSE
ROBERT STUART HOUSE MUSEUM
STE. ANNE'S CATHOLIC CHURCH
BENJAMIN BLACKSMITH SHOP
MARKET ST
MAIN ST
BIDDLE HOUSE
MARQUETTE PARK
STATE PARK VISITORS CENTER
SEE DETAIL

0   0.25 mi
0   0.25 km

© MOON.COM

early-May-late Oct.), located across from Shepler's ferry dock next to the chamber of commerce. The pleasant, narrated tour takes about 1 hour and 45 minutes, rambling along at a relaxing pace past the Grand Hotel, Arch Rock, Skull Cave, Fort Mackinac, and most of the island's other key sites. This locally owned business is the world's largest horse-and-buggy livery, with more than 300 horses, mostly crosses of beefy Percherons, Belgians, and Clydesdales. Seasonal peak hours (mid-June through Labor Day) are 9am-5pm (weather permitting), with slightly shorter hours from early May to mid-June and after Labor Day through the end of October.

Market Street

One block inland from Main Street, some of Mackinac's original residences line up along **Market Street.** Much quieter than Main, Market Street has several interesting stops for visitors. At 7342 Market Street, the headquarters of John Jacob Astor's American Fur Company is now the **Robert Stuart House Museum** (906/847-8141, 10am-4pm daily May-Oct., donation). The 1817 building is named for the man who was once Astor's resident agent on the island. It retains many of its original furnishings, including fur company ledgers, fur weighing scales, and other artifacts.

One block west, knowledgeable interpreters demonstrate spinning at **Biddle House** and ironsmithing at the **Benjamin Blacksmith Shop.** These and other historic buildings are part of Mackinac Island State Park, and are included with the admission ticket to Fort Mackinac, although they have shorter hours than the fort: 11am-6pm daily, $13.50 adults, $8 ages 5-12. A discount is offered for online ticket purchases. For current information, stop by the park visitors center across from Marquette Park on Huron Street, or contact **Mackinac State Historic Parks** (231/436-4100, www.mackinacparks.com).

On the other side of Marquette Park, you'll find the **Richard & Jane Manoogian Mackinac Art Museum** (7070 Main St.,

906/847-3328, www.mackinacparks.com, 10am-6pm daily Memorial Day-Labor Day, 10am-4:30pm daily Labor Day-Oct. 8, $10 adults, $6.50 ages 5-12). The museum presents arts in various media that reflect a wide swath of regional history—hand-beaded Native American garments, 18th century maps of the Great Lakes, and stunning photographic prints from the early 20th century. Guided tours and rotating exhibits are offered.

★ Mackinac Island Butterfly House

Tucked away on McGulpin Street is the **Mackinac Island Butterfly House** (906/847-3972, www.originalbutterflyhouse.com, 10am-7pm daily summer, 10am-6pm daily May 1-Memorial Day and Labor Day-third week of Oct., $8 adults, $5 ages 5-11, free under age 5). Owner Doug Beardsley used to use his greenhouses to grow thousands of geraniums for the Grand Hotel and other clients. He relied on biodynamic growing methods, releasing beneficial insects to care for his plants instead of using chemical sprays. When economics made his small greenhouse less viable, he stuck with his insects. After hearing about a butterfly house in Europe, Beardsley added some different plants and began ordering pupae from around the world. Now hundreds of butterflies flutter freely in his greenhouse atrium, some nearly 6 inches (15 cm) long. You can observe them up close on walls and plants, or sit still long enough and they'll land on your knee—an experience that is both unusual and delightful.

Ste. Anne's Catholic Church

You'll find **Ste. Anne's Catholic Church** (906/847-3507, www.steanneschurch.org), the oldest church on Mackinac Island, near the butterfly house. It's worth even a brief visit to take in its architecture and history. Ste. Anne's is a testimony to the island's long history of Roman Catholicism, with Jesuits being the first nonnatives to arrive here. The parish has served the island community since the 1740s.

In addition to frequent masses (10:30am Sun., 11am Tues.-Fri.), you'll find a community square dance on the spacious front porch once a week. The basement hosts a small **museum** (10am-4pm Mon.-Fri., 10am-5:30pm Sat., 9am-3pm Sun., free) that preserves and interprets the religious history of Mackinac Island. A number of religious articles and church documents (baptismal, marriage, and burial records) date as far back as 1695.

Ste. Anne's gift shop has souvenirs and collectibles, plus standard religious items. If you're interested in old cemeteries, you'll want to check out Ste. Anne's Cemetery, up the hill behind Fort Mackinac on the way to Fort Holmes.

★ Grand Hotel

The iconic **Grand Hotel** (286 Grand Ave., 800/334-7263, www.grandhotel.com), a gracious edifice built on a scale appropriate to its name, has become practically synonymous with Mackinac Island. It is one of the largest summer resorts in the world, operating each year from early April through late October. Its famous 660-foot-long (200-meter) covered front porch gets decked out each spring with 2,500 geraniums planted in seven tons of potting soil. Its 12 restaurants and bars serve as many as 4,000 meals a day. The resort's impeccable grounds offer guests every amenity, from saddle horses to designer golf to bocce ball to swimming in the outdoor pool made famous by 1940s actress Esther Williams, who filmed *This Time for Keeps* here.

Opulence and refinement were the goals of the railroad and steamship companies when they formed a consortium to build the Grand Hotel in 1887, located on a hill with a commanding view of the straits. The wealthiest Mackinac Island visitors have stayed and continue to stay at the Grand Hotel.

Unlike other resorts from the Gilded Age that burned to the ground or faded, the Grand Hotel has managed to maintain its grace and dignity. It still hosts all manner of celebrities and politicians—five U.S. presidents to date— and still offers a sip of a truly bygone era with afternoon tea in the parlor each day and demitasse served after dinner each evening. Room rates still include a five-course dinner in the soaring main dining room. For men, the evening (6:30pm) dress code calls for jackets and ties, and for women, skirts, dresses, or formal pantsuits.

The Grand Hotel's time-capsule setting prompted director Jeannot Szwarc to choose it as the location for the 1980 film *Somewhere in Time,* starring Christopher Reeve, Jane Seymour, and Christopher Plummer. For whatever reason, the movie has developed a huge following; its fan club reunites at the hotel each year in late October.

While room rates can get outright absurd, they include breakfast, lunch, and dinner, and perhaps can be considered a worthwhile splurge if you'd like to experience a level of hospitality reminiscent of the Gilded Age. Each of the 385 rooms is decorated differently, and the entire hotel is air-conditioned. A more affordable option is to stay just one night for the experience and then book less expensive lodging on or off the island for the rest of your visit.

Enjoy this moment in time—take tea, loll in the recently updated pool, or dance to the swing orchestra in the Terrace Room. Nonguests can sneak a peek at the hotel's public areas and grounds for a mildly unreasonable fee ($10 adults, $5 ages 6-9, free under age 6). The charge is intended to reduce the number of sightseers. Highly recommended are a stroll through the grounds, which are filled with Victorian gardens blooming with 25,000 tulips in spring, and a visit to the snazzy Cupola Bar.

Governor's Residence

From Marquette Park, follow Fort Street up the hill to the **Governor's Residence** at the corner of Fort Street and East Bluff Road. The state purchased the "cottage" (the fact that it lacks central heat qualifies it as such) in 1945. The home is the official summer residence of Michigan's governor. The house is open for free tours of the main floor (9:30am-11:30am Wed., June-Aug.), except when the governor is

Somewhere in Time

the Grand Hotel

Beyond fantasy. Beyond obsession. Beyond time itself . . . he will find her.

Somewhere in Time

Your reaction to the tagline for *Somewhere in Time,* a 1980 movie starring Christopher Reeve and Jane Seymour that was filmed at the Grand Hotel, is a pretty good indication of whether you'll love or hate the movie. If you find it hopelessly romantic, a bit old-fashioned, and somewhat endearing—go rent the movie now. But if you thought it was too sweet and you shuddered a little, you might want to make another choice.

The film (which is based on the 1975 novel *Bid Time Return,* by Richard Matheson) tells the story of Richard Collier, a playwright, who one day has a strange encounter with an old woman who says to him, "Come back to me." While staying at the Grand Hotel, Richard tries to figure out who the old woman is. He soon learns she was an early-20th-century actress named Elise McKenna and quickly becomes enamored of her. Through self-hypnosis, Richard travels back in time, where he meets Elise and the two fall in love. But will Richard be able to stay in 1912?

Mackinac Island's Victorian setting, and in particular the Grand Hotel, made it a natural location for the film. Unfortunately, when the movie was released it was much maligned by film critics, and its only Oscar nod was for Best Costume Design. Still, it has found a passionate following among people who are enthralled by its story of timeless love and old-fashioned values. In fact, the *Somewhere in Time* fan club has met at the Grand Hotel for a weekend each October since 1991.

It really is a good, if affected, movie that's perfect for Valentine's Day or a first date, and it's a great way to relive your Grand Hotel stay or just to peek inside.

in residence. Photography is not permitted inside the house. For more information, contact **Mackinac State Historic Parks** (231/436-4100, www.mackinacparks.com).

★ Fort Mackinac

Located at the crest of the bluff, whitewashed **Fort Mackinac** (Huron Rd., 231/436-4100,

www.mackinacparks.com, 9am-5pm daily early May-early June, 9:30am-7pm daily early June-early Sept., 9:30am-5pm daily early Sept.-early Oct., 11am-4pm early Oct.-late

1: costumed interpreters at Fort Mackinac **2:** Mackinac Island Butterfly House **3:** the Governor's Residence **4:** Ste. Anne's Catholic Church

1

2

3

4

SAINTE ANNE
CHURCH
In 1670, Jesuit Father Charles
Dablon founded a birchbark
mission chapel on Mackinac
Island. The following year,
Father Jacques Marquette
relocated the mission at
Saint Ignace. Abandoned in
1706 and reestablished at
Fort Michilimackinac around
1715, the new church was
named Sainte Anne de
Michilimackinac. During the
winter of 1780-1781, British
troops relocated to the
island and moved the church
building across the ice. The
parish is the nation's oldest
dedicated to Saint Anne and

Oct., $15.50 adults, $9.25 ages 5-12) is worth a visit for the views alone, presiding over—as forts often do—the downtown, the marina, and Lake Huron. But there's also plenty to see at this military outpost, which the British and Americans fought over for nearly 40 years.

Along with peering over the parapets, you can wander in and out of 14 buildings that make up the fort. The barracks, officers' quarters, post hospital, and other buildings are filled with interpretive displays and feature period decor. Costumed guides lead reenactments, including musket firing and cannon salutes. A short audiovisual presentation, *The Heritage of Mackinac,* explains the fort's basic history.

Admission to the fort also includes admission to the Benjamin Blacksmith House, the Biddle House, and the Richard & Jane Manoogian Mackinac Art Museum. If you're planning to visit the sister parks on the mainland—Colonial Michilimackinac, Old Mackinac Point Lighthouse, or Historic Mill Creek Discovery Park—the Mainland Combination ticket ($31.75 adults, $22.25 ages 5-12), which is valid for seven days after purchase, is the best deal. For information, stop by the park visitors center across from Marquette Park on Huron Street.

East Bluff

Some of the island's more impressive cottages line up along East Bluff. Wander east from the governor's mansion to see some of these Victorian marvels. Happily, most survived the Depression era—when they could be purchased for pennies on the dollar. Today, these well-tended homes are often valued at over $2 million.

Work your way down one of the sets of public steps to the lakefront, where Main Street becomes Huron Street. Continue your walk east, passing smaller but no less appealing cottages and homes. Many are skirted with geraniums and lilacs, the island's signature flowers, and boast stunning views of the straits.

Mackinac Island State Park

Too often overshadowed by cultural attractions and touristy diversions, Mackinac Island's natural history has drawn scientific interest for over 200 years. In the early 19th century, botanists discovered several species new to science, including the dwarf lake iris, still found only in the Straits of Mackinac region.

The island's landscape comprises fields, meadows, marshes, coastline, swamps, bogs, and a boreal forest. Early scientists marveled at the island's unusual topography, especially the brecciate limestone that has been sculpted by millennia of wind and waves. The result is some dramatic rock formations, like the giant inland slab of limestone called **Sugar Loaf Rock,** the lakeside caves of **Devil's Kitchen,** and impressive **Arch Rock,** which rises nearly 150 feet (46 meters) above the eastern shore and spans some 50 feet (15 meters).

In recognition of the park's distinctive "natural curiosities" and growing tourism, the federal government created Mackinac National Park in 1875—following Yellowstone as the nation's second national park. Twenty years later it was returned to Michigan and became Mackinac Island State Park, Michigan's very first state park. Today the park is managed by an entity known as **Michigan State Historic Parks,** which includes Fort Mackinac, Old Mackinac Point Lighthouse, Colonial Michilimackinac, and the Historic Mill Creek Discovery Park. Admission fees vary considerably, so it's best to visit www.mackinacparks.com/explore-mackinac/admission for full information. Keep in mind that "package and family deals" are available if you're planning on visiting more than one park or if you're traveling as a family.

Walk, run, ride, or bike, but make sure you get out of the center to really see Mackinac Island. You'll be surprised how quickly you can leave the crowds behind as you set out on Lake Shore Drive, the paved 8-mile (12.9-km) path (which has a state highway designation, M-185) that circles the island. The road never wanders far from the pleasant shoreline and passes many of the island's natural features, which are well marked. Traveling clockwise, the first you'll reach is Devil's Kitchen; heading in the opposite direction, you'll arrive first at Arch Rock, the most dramatic of Mackinac's limestone oddities.

About halfway around, on the island's northwestern side, is **British Landing,** where British soldiers infiltrated the island during the War of 1812. They hiked across Mackinac's interior, surprising the American garrison at the fort—who were apparently looking the other way—and recaptured the island. There's a small **nature center** here, staffed in summer by a helpful naturalist. Hike the short (0.2-mile/0.3-km) **nature trail,** which has several interpretive signs as it weaves up a bluff.

After passing British Landing, you'll come to **Sunset Rock,** which is perhaps the most photo-worthy spot on the island. Located just behind the Inn at Stonecliffe and marked by a pleasant stone grotto, the location offers an unparalleled view to the west across the straits, prominently featuring the Mackinac Bridge.

British Landing is also a good spot from which to head inland and explore the island's interior. British Landing Road bisects the island and links up with Garrison Road near **Skull Cave,** leading to the fort. It's a hilly 3-mile (4.8-km) trip from shore to shore. British Landing Road is considered a major thoroughfare by Mackinac standards, meaning it accommodates horses, carriages, and bikes.

SHOPPING
Fudge

Sooner or later you'll succumb to Mackinac Island's famous fudge. A visitor treat since Victorian times, the confection can be found in shops lining Main Street. Two of the oldest, **Murdick's Fudge** (7363 Main St., 906/847-3530, www.murdicksfudgemackinacisland.com, 9am-10pm daily) and **Ryba's** (7314 Main St., 906/847-3347, www.ryba.com, 9am-10pm daily) have multiple island locations, while Murdick's also has a shop in Mackinaw City. Ryba's also has two Chicago locations and another in the Detroit suburb of Fraser. You can buy a sizable slab to take or mail home, or just a small sliver to nibble. Both stores also accept phone orders and will ship virtually anywhere. A little goes a long way—it's very rich stuff.

Another great source of the island's best known confection is the **Murray Hotel Fudge Company** (7260 Main St., 906/847-3360, www.mymurrayhotel.com/fudge-co, 8am-8pm daily), located inside the Murray Hotel. Situated right in the vintage hotel's lobby, the fudge shop offers some unusual flavors, including Bailey's Irish Cream, Lemon Meringue, and Grasshopper (mint, Oreo, and chocolate). Sound good?

Gifts and Souvenirs

The **Balsam Shop** (7427 Main St., Surrey Hill, 906/847-3591, https://balsamshop.com, 9am-5pm daily Apr.-Nov., by appointment Dec.-Mar., online shopping available year-round) is an upscale store featuring quality Mackinac Island-themed merchandise—drinkware, ornaments, and stationery plus a variety of candles and pottery.

ENTERTAINMENT

For the best of the island's **live music,** you'll want to check out the **Grand Hotel,** which offers plenty of live entertainment nightly. Catch live music at the Jockey Club at the Grand Strand, listen to the Grand Hotel Orchestra in the Terrace Room, or hear live bands at the Gate House. You can also find live entertainment at the Cupola Bar and at Woods Restaurant. All venues are under the aegis of the Grand Hotel, although the Gate House, Jockey Club, and Woods Restaurant are located nearby and are off-site. You'll find acoustic music at **Mission Point Resort**'s **Round Island Bar and Grill** downtown. It also features a number of HDTVs, providing a sports-bar atmosphere.

It's easy to understand why designated **pub crawls** are so popular on the island—it's

Tackling Mackinac by Bike

biking along M-185

For most visitors, their exposure to Mackinac Island is limited to the few blocks near the boat docks, Fort Mackinac, and maybe the Governor's Residence and the veranda of the Grand Hotel. But convenient alternatives are available to accommodate the more adventurous.

For a different perspective, rent a bicycle from any of the rental shops along Main Street and set off on a ride along **M-185,** better known as **Lake Shore Drive.** This idyllic route hugs the shoreline along the entire circumference of Mackinac Island and offers a bevy of scenic views—and a few challenging hills.

Despite the absence of motor vehicles, M-185 is an official Michigan state trunk line highway and is maintained by the Michigan Department of Transportation. Other than the noticeably narrower lanes, the road otherwise resembles any other highway: two lanes of paved asphalt complete with mileposts and directional signs.

The total length of the route is approximately 8 miles (12.9 km). If you choose to start out at Mission Street and pedal east, you'll find the first few miles the toughest, with most of the stretch running uphill.

But you'll be rewarded with some notable points of interest—Arch Rock, the British Landing site, plus Devil's Kitchen. Bring along your camera, as you'll find some very photo-worthy spots. When you get to British Landing (about two-thirds of the way if you ride counterclockwise) you'll find a pleasant rest stop with a concession stand and benches.

Most people take 1.5 to 2 hours to complete the ride. After finishing, head to one of the Main Street pubs and toast your adventure!

hard to get an impaired driving infraction when there are no cars. Local retailers join in the game, selling T-shirts commemorating the experience (you might not remember it otherwise). Try not to overdo it; finish your crawl over the course of a few nights.

A few quality destinations are the **Yankee Rebel Tavern** (1493 Astor St., 906/847-6249, www.yankeerebeltavern.com), **Millie's on Main** (7294 Main St., 906/847-9901, https://milliesonmain.com), and **Horn's Bar** (7300 Main St., 906/847-6154, www.hornsbar.com).

FESTIVALS AND EVENTS
★ Lilac Festival

For 10 days in early June, Mackinac Island celebrates the **Lilac Festival** (800/454-4227, www.mackinacisland.org), during which visitors can enjoy live music; A Taste of Mackinac, which showcases the talents of local chefs; and the Feast of Epona, the Celtic goddess of horses. Events culminate with the Grand Parade, one of North America's few all-hitch horse parades. Other events include a dog and pony show, an art print competition, and a 10K run. Each year the parade has a unique theme. The crowd is smaller than for the Labor Day Bridge Walk but still busy. Celebrations on this order represent Mackinac at its best. The event commemorates the lilac, which is Mackinac Island's unofficial flower.

Other Festivals

Early in August, the **Mackinac Island Horse Show** (www.mackinachorses.org) celebrates the island's love of all things equestrian, with events like showmanship and grooming, English and Western equestrian, and barrel racing. During the **Mackinac Island Fudge Festival** in late August, the Fudgies get their due as the entire island turns out to celebrate the estimated 10,000 pounds of fudge made each season.

RECREATION
Carriage Rides and Horseback Riding

With more than 600 horses calling the island their summertime home, you won't be able to turn a corner without bumping noses with these beautiful animals. But to be honest, who would want it otherwise? It isn't every day you get the chance to ride a carriage down Main Street or take a buggy on an island circuit. Just be certain to exercise appropriate courtesy. Do not pet or touch a horse until first asking permission from its rider, and do not step immediately behind a horse, as they can kick if they feel threatened.

Take a carriage tour with the island's largest livery, **Mackinac Island Carriage Tours** (7396 Market St., 906/847-3307, www.mict.com), operating since 1869, or **Gough Carriages** (corner of Main and Fort Streets, adjacent to Marquette Park, 906/847-1053, www.goughcarriages.com), both offering personalized tours of the island in relatively small carriages. The guides are knowledgeable, and hourly rates run $180-270, depending on the total number of guests, but if the tour includes two or more families, they can split the fee among them, allowing for a cost-efficient hour. Both companies begin their tours on Market Street near the Father Marquette statue.

You'll be able to take the reins during a drive-it-yourself buggy tour from **Jack's Livery Stable** (7754 Mahoney Ave. at Grand Ave., 906/847-3391, www.jacksliverystable.com, May-Oct., $100 per hour for 2 passengers, $120 for 4, $140 for 6). After gauging your skill with horses, one of the livery's professionals will give you driving instructions before setting you loose on the town with a free map. At their sister company, **Cindy's Riding Stable** (7447 Market St., 906/847-3572, www.cindysridingstable.com, May-Oct., $60 per hour), you can take one of the 30-plus saddle horses out on your own; located on Market Street across from the Biddle House, Cindy's Riding Stable rents horses only—no carriages.

Trails

Mackinac Island State Park has more than 2,250 acres with over 70 miles (113 km) of trails and footpaths suitable for exploration on a bicycle or on foot. Pick up a free Mackinac Island Map, available all over town, and venture off. The map marks the location of old cemeteries, rock formations, and other points of interest, but it's even more appealing just to explore the more obscure trails on your own and discover the pristine and tranquil side of Mackinac Island. Everything is well marked, and getting lost is difficult since you're on a relatively small island.

Runners can participate in the **Lilac**

Festival 10K in early June, the **Mackinac Island Eight Mile** in mid-September, or late October's **Great Turtle Half Marathon.** Visit **Run Mackinac** (810/487-0954, www.runmackinac.com) for more information.

There are plenty of shops that offer hourly **bicycle rentals** for single-speed bikes, mountain bikes, bikes for children, tagalongs, buggies, or tandems for the romantic. Most rentals run about $9 per hour or $65 per day, but rates vary depending on the equipment. **Ryba's Bicycle Rentals** (7245 Main St., 906/847-3208, www.rybabikes.com) is a great resource and also offers baby carts, strollers, tagalongs, and electric wheelchairs for disabled people. Another reputable source is the **Mackinac Island Bike Shop** (7425 Main St., just east of Shepler's dock, 906/847-6337, www.bikemackinac.com), where no deposit is required and the price you pay is prorated to the quarter hour.

If you plan to do a lot of cycling, you may want to bring your own bike, since you can transport it on the ferry for about $13 round-trip. A hybrid or mountain bike is best for negotiating the island's myriad trails.

In order to accommodate visitors with disabilities, Mackinac Island has relaxed its ban on motorized transportation, albeit slightly. For those in need, motorized scooters or wheelchairs can now be rented from vendors on Market Street, right near the ferry embarkation point. This makes it possible for people with physical challenges to enjoy Mackinac Island. Be aware, however, that most electric scooters are not powerful enough to climb the steeper inclines, such as the ramp up to Fort Mackinac.

On the Water

One way to enjoy the straits is on a **Sip 'n Sail** cruise (off Main Street between the Seabiscuit café and the taxi office, 844/906-9006, www.puremichiganboatcruises.com). There are eight cruise options, including the Sunset

Cruise with entertainment and libations; Easy Like Sunday Morning, a leisurely trip around the island's most noteworthy points, including Arch Rock, British Landing, and the Grand Hotel; and the Bloody Marys and Mimosa Tour under the Mackinac Bridge. All cruises are $53 per person. Children are welcome on board but must pay the full fare. Private charters are also available. All cruises are approximately 1.5 hours.

Mackinac Island's beautiful coastline is perfect for relaxation and picnicking, and often tempting for those looking to take a dip, especially children. The east side of the island is best for the little ones, but be warned: the rocky shores require swimming shoes or sandals, and there are no lifeguards, so swim at your own risk. The waters of the straits can also be rather chilly, even late in the season.

Of course, you can always bring a rod and reel and fish off the rocks on Mackinac Island's shore, but the lure of the Great Lakes makes deepwater **fishing** one of the island's most popular summer activities. There are no fishing charter services based on the island, but, as with **parasailing,** a few private boats dock here.

Golf

In addition to a pleasant afternoon on the links, golfing Mackinac brings with it a unique thrill: golf carts are among the very few powered vehicles allowed on the island. So while other visitors are struggling to rein in an unruly horse or hoofing it across the island, you'll be driving something that's actually motorized.

Mackinac is the proud home of the oldest continuously played golf course in Michigan, **Wawashkamo** (906/847-3871, www.wawashkamo.com, $95 for 18 holes with cart, $70 without, 9 holes $60 with cart, $45 without). Vacationers have been golfing the course's nine holes since 1898, and the second set of tee placements makes it possible to play a full 18 holes on rough natural terrain, which includes traditionally Scottish thistle and heather. Wawashkamo means "walk a

1: bikes on Mackinac Island 2: Mackinac Island State Park 3: trail on Mackinac Island

Winter on Mackinac Island

Mackinac Island is a bit trickier to get to once the straits freeze over, but for those willing to make the extra effort, a winter paradise awaits, along with considerably smaller crowds and a calming solace.

SKI AND SNOWSHOE TRAILS

The 70-plus miles (113-plus km) of trails that bring out the hikers, bikers, and runners in summertime are transformed into cross-country ski and snowshoe trails for winter. Volunteers of the Mackinac Island Ski Club team up with the state park to maintain a series of groomed winter trails.

Cross-country skiing and snowshoeing trails on Mackinac Island are concentrated on the eastern half of the island, bounded between M-185 on the east and British Landing Road on the west. One example is the **Crooked Tree Trail,** which begins just east of Mackinac Island Airport and continues for about 0.5 miles (0.8 km) before ending at Soldier's Garden. A more lengthy option (about 1.2 miles/1.9 km) is the **Tranquil Trail,** which branches off of the British Landing Nature Trail and continues north before curving gradually south and terminating at Eagle Point Cave.

Although some hotels have ski and snowshoe equipment they'll loan to guests, there are no outfitters on the island to rent equipment. A source to stop at en route to the island is **Bahnhof Sport** (1300 Bay View Rd., Petoskey, 231/347-2112, https://bahnhof.com). As a courtesy, flights transporting guests in the winter will allow ski equipment on the plane.

ACCOMMODATIONS

Since most of the island shuts down well before the snows come, winter lodging is limited. Check out **Bogan Lane Inn** (1420 Bogan Lane, 906/847-3439, www.boganlaneinn.com, $$), **Pontiac Lodge** (across Main St. from Shepler's dock, 906/847-3364, www.pontiaclodge.com, $$), or **Harbor Place Studio Suites** (7439 Main St., 800/626-6304, https://harbor-place-studio-suites-mackinac-island.booked.net, $$$).

GETTING THERE AND AROUND

Due to the thick ice that coats the straits each winter, ferry service is severely limited. The lone option is the Mackinac Island Ferry Company, which operates the **Star Line** (www.mackinacferry.com). Their fleet includes the *Huron,* which is equipped with a reinforced steel hull that can cut through ice. The Star Line offers three daily departures from St. Ignace for as long as possible during the winter season.

Once the ice becomes prohibitively thick, however, flying to the island is the only option. **Fresh Air Aviation** (www.freshairaviation.net) offers on-demand flights daily to **Mackinac Island Airport** (MCD) from St. Ignace (one-way $46.50 adults, $32.50 under age 12, with a two-fare minimum; round-trip rates are double).

Horse-drawn taxis are available from **Mackinac Island Carriage Tours** (906/847-3323, www.mict.com) with advance reservations. Be sure to bundle up!

crooked trail," and it is built on a former battlefield from the War of 1812, adding to its historical appeal. Lower rates are available for twilight golf (4pm-7pm) and during the spring and fall months.

The Grand Hotel's 18 holes, known as **The Jewel** (906/847-3331, guests $185 for 18 holes, $100 for 9 holes, nonguests $200 for 18 holes, $110 for 9 holes; all rates include cart), consists of two nine-hole courses—the original Grand Nine, across the street from the hotel, and the Woods Nine, in the island's interior. The Grand was built in 1901 and was redesigned in 1987 by noted golf course architect Jerry Matthews, who also designed the Woods course, added in 1994. Horse-drawn transportation is provided between the two courses.

Mission Point Resort hosts **The Greens at Mackinac** (906/847-3007, www.missionpoint. com, 18 holes $20 adults, $9 under age 13), the executive putting greens where even the most experienced putters can hone their skills or try out the merchandise from the pro shop selection of putters.

FOOD

One of the finest dining options on the island is the **Fort Mackinac Tea Room** (906/847-6327, www.grandhotel.com, 11am-3pm daily mid-May-mid-Oct., $12-17), located in the lower level of the Officer's Stone Quarters within the fort. Surrounded by thick masonry walls, the tearoom serves up both a great atmosphere and great food, such as soups, salads, and sandwiches, prepared by Grand Hotel chefs. Ask for a spot on the terrace—the high setting offers a dramatic panorama.

Everyone should hit the ★ **Pink Pony Bar & Grill** (7221 Main St., 906/847-3341, www. pinkponymackinac.com, 8am-2am daily, $30-40) at least sometime during a Mackinac visit. Located in the Chippewa Hotel, overlooking the marina, this is *the* party place following the famed Port Huron to Mackinac yacht race. The food's great too, with burgers, whitefish sandwiches, and such on the lunch menu and steaks, seafood, and ribs for dinner. Appetizers are especially popular in the dining room, where you'll find pan-fried calamari and honey apple brie flatbread—choices not often found on Mackinac Island. Outdoor patio dining is available in season.

The **Round Island Bar and Grill** (6633 Main St., 906/847-3312, www.missionpoint. com, 7am-midnight daily, only light snacks after 9pm, entrées and lunch menu $17-33, post-Labor Day menu $26-59) at Mission Point Resort has sandwiches and salads in a casual setting overlooking the straits and neighboring Round Island. The more robust "autumn menu" after Labor Day offers hearty options such as pan-seared duck breast and lamb osso bucco. Wednesday is Crab Legs Night ($39). Sample some of Michigan's best regional beers and wines here, too.

The island's best fine dining is at the high-end hotels and resorts. Try the **1852 Grill Room** (6966 Main St., 906/847-3347, www. theislandhouse.com, 5:30pm-9pm daily, $39-55) at the Island House Hotel, where offerings include seafood linguini and wild-caught Dover sole. Entrées at the Hotel Iroquois's **Carriage House Dining Room** (7485 Main St., 906/847-3321, www.iroquoishotel. com, lunch 11:30am-2:30pm daily Memorial Day-mid-Sept., dinner 5pm-9pm daily May 15-mid-Oct., $28-65) emphasize seafood choices, such as pan-seared diver scallops and seafood Mediterranean pasta. Lunch selections include a wide variety of salads and sandwiches ($14-25).

For the treat of a lifetime, choose the **Main Dining Room** (286 Grand Ave., 906/847-3331, www.grandhotel.com, 6:30pm-8:45pm daily, 5-course prix-fixe $121 adults, $63 ages 5-17, free under age 5) at the Grand Hotel. An exquisite five-course meal features choices from three rotating menus; you will not be disappointed. There's a special standard menu for kids. After 6:30pm, evening attire is required in all public areas of the Grand Hotel. For women, this means a dress, skirt, and blouse or a pantsuit; for men, a jacket, necktie, and dress slacks are required. Children 12 and above are expected to follow the same dress code.

The Grand Hotel's **Woods Restaurant** (8655 Cudahy Cir., 906/847-3699, www. grandhotel.com, lunch 11am-2pm Fri.-Sun., dinner 5:30pm-9pm Sun.-Thurs., 5:30pm-9:30pm Fri.-Sat., $36-68) offers a more casual dining atmosphere than the hotel's Main Dining Room. Dinner selections include chermoula-spiced whitefish and a dry-aged prime strip steak.

ACCOMMODATIONS

The **Grand Hotel** (286 Grand Ave., 906/847-333, www.grandhotel.com, $$$) has become practically synonymous with Mackinac Island, a gracious edifice built on a truly grand scale. It is the largest summer resort in the world, operating early May-late October.

Its famous 660-foot (200-meter) covered front porch is adorned each spring with 2,000 geraniums planted in seven tons of potting soil. While room rates at the Grand Hotel are astronomical, they can be a worthwhile splurge if you enjoy taking high tea, relaxing in the beautifully landscaped pool, or dancing to the swing orchestra in the Terrace Room.

Along with the Grand Hotel, there are many other places to stay on Mackinac Island that still manage to offer the true Mackinac Victorian experience. Rates can be high, and prices can vary considerably even within one property, with water views commanding a considerable premium. But don't dismiss staying on Mackinac Island; you can find reasonable rates at smaller B&Bs and apartments, and the latter often have good deals for weeklong stays. The options here tip both ends of the scale. For information on more island accommodations, including rates and photos, visit www.mackinacisland.org. Unfortunately, there is no camping on Mackinac Island.

Mission Point Resort

★ **Mission Point Resort** (6633 Main St., 906/847-3312, www.missionpoint.com, $$$) may have the island's absolute best location, spread across 18 acres at the island's southeastern tip. Though not of the Victorian era—it was built in the 1950s by the Moral Rearmament movement, a post-World War II patriotic group—the sprawling bright-white resort is attractive and well kept, offering beautiful lawns lined with Adirondack chairs. Amenities include an outdoor pool, tennis and volleyball courts, and loads of kids' activities.

In addition to the professional putting green, bicycle rentals, lawn bowling, croquet, tennis, and professional spa, Mission Point Resort offers hayrides around the island. The Tower Museum, eight stories up, provides a breathtaking panorama of the island and the straits. Interpretive displays on each floor present fascinating looks at topics such as maritime shipping history, Ojibwa heritage, and the construction of the Mackinac Bridge.

There are four restaurants, and the Lakeside Marketplace can provide you with a picnic lunch on your way out to explore the island; the Epicurean is the place for elegant dining and an impressive selection of wines. Rates are highest during the height of summer. With all it has to offer, Mission Point is a quintessential self-contained summer resort.

Hotels and Motels

The **Chippewa Hotel** (7221 Main St., 800/241-3341, www.chippewahotel.com, May-Oct., $$) is a venerable old Mackinac hotel that had a $3 million renovation in 1995. The result is a classy and comfortable place to stay, with a location at the heart of the island on Main Street, overlooking the marina. The 24-person lakeside hot tub alone may be worth the stay. If you enjoy being pampered, check out the relaxing Lilac Tree Spa (www.lilactree.com/spa).

Two separate buildings—Cudahy Manor and the Summer House—make up the **Inn at Stonecliffe** (8593 Cudah Circle, 906/847-3355, www.theinnatstonecliffe.com, May-Oct., $$$). More than 100 years old, the inn has undergone an extensive renovation. The Cudahy Manor is more B&B than hotel, a turn-of-the-20th-century Tudor manor with 16 rooms, the more expensive of which have views of the straits and the bridge. The Summer House has 33 studio suites. Note that most rooms do not have air-conditioning.

One of the island's most striking buildings, the **Hotel Iroquois** (7485 Main St., 906/847-3321, www.iroquoishotel.com, $$) was built in 1900 as a home for the island blacksmith. It has since been converted into a 46-room hotel with a fine-dining restaurant ($28-60) and a private sunbathing deck. Hotel Iroquois is a *Condé Nast Traveler* Gold List hotel and earned a perfect score for its stunning location. Suites are available for a higher price but are on par with the Grand Hotel's luxury rooms, so you'll be better off sticking with Hotel Iroquois's competitively priced rooms.

Bed-and-Breakfasts

Cloghaun (7504 Market St., 906/847-3885, www.cloghaun.com, May-Oct., $$$) was built in 1884 by Thomas and Bridgette Donnelly, who left Ireland during the potato famine and followed a relative to Mackinac Island. Today, this grand Victorian (pronounced CLAH-han) with large grounds is still owned and operated by their descendants. It's located on Market Street, next to some of the island's historic attractions and just one block from Main Street. Eight rooms have private baths; two others share a bath.

Below East Bluff near Ste. Anne's Church, **Haan's 1830 Inn** (6806 Huron St., 906/847-6244, www.1830inn.com, mid-May-mid-Oct., $$$) is a Greek Revival built by Colonel Preston, one of the last officers to preside over Fort Mackinac, generally recognized as the island's first mayor. Just try to drag yourself out of the wicker chairs on the big front porch. Four of the seven rooms have private baths.

Only a few minutes' walk from the ferry docks, **Bay View Bed & Breakfast** (6947 Main St., 906/847-3295, www.mackinacbayview.com, May-Oct., $$$) has rooms ranging from standards to suites facing the water. If you spend a little extra cash for a room with a view, you'll find yourself overlooking the yacht harbor. Breakfast is served on the veranda; make sure you try the custom Bay View Blend Coffee. There are homemade cookies each afternoon and delicious desserts offered each evening.

INFORMATION

For help with accommodations and other information ahead of time, contact the **Mackinac Island Chamber of Commerce & Tourism Bureau** (7274 Main St., 877/847-0086, www.mackinacisland.org). You can also get a visitors guide with maps of the state park at the **Mackinac Island State Park Visitors Center** (231/436-4100, early May-mid-Oct.), located on Main Street across from the island's Marquette Park.

GETTING THERE AND AROUND

Virtually all motorized vehicles are banned on Mackinac Island. The only exceptions are golf carts, scooters for the disabled, and a few public-service vehicles.

Boat

Two ferry lines offer service to Mackinac Island: **Shepler's Mackinac Island Ferry** (231/436-5023, www.sheplersferry.

Mission Point Resort

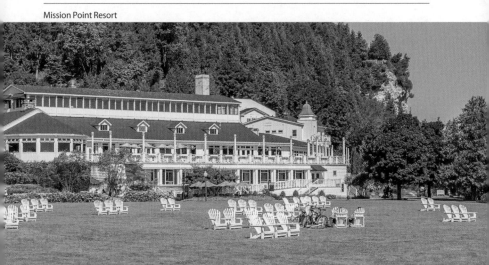

com, round-trip $30 adults, $19 ages 5-12) and the **Star Line** (800/638-9892, www.mackinawferry.com, $28 adults, $18 ages 5-12, discounts on the website). Both have departures from Mackinaw City and St. Ignace. Ferries run, in general, from Mackinaw City between May and October, and from St. Ignace from April through November. Free parking is available for day-trippers; overnight travelers are charged $20 per night.

If you're sailing your own boat, you can contact the **Mackinac Island State Harbor** (906/847-3561, www.michigan.gov/dnr) for reservations up to six months in advance of your stay. The marina's 76 slips are available late May to mid-September. You can contact the marina on radio channel 9. It's located at 45°50.40 N, 84°36.42 W.

Air

Mackinac Island Airport (MCD) is the only way to get to the island in the winter, and it's always an option in the summer too. Year-round flights are available from St. Ignace (one way $46.50 adults, $32.50 under age 12, two-fare minimum) through **Fresh Air Aviation** (www.freshairaviation.net). Horse-drawn taxi service is available from the airport to your hotel; contact **Mackinac Island**

Carriage Tours (906/847-3323, www.mict.com).

Getting Around

While on the island, horses are certainly the most unique means of getting around. Taxis can be hired at **Mackinac Island Carriage Tours** (7278 Main St., 906/847-3323, www.mict.com).

If you enjoy walking and hiking, you can get around Mackinac Island on foot; the island is about 8 miles (12.9 km) in circumference. Mackinac is a wonderful place for casual strolls and all-day hikes.

The island is also a great place to cycle. **Mackinac Island Bike Shop** (7425 Main St. next to Shepler's dock, 906/847-6337, www.mackinacislandbikes.com) at the Lake View Hotel has a wide array of choices, including mountain bikes for kids and adults, plus tag-alongs and Burley trailers for babies. They also offer equipment for disabled people to use, including electric wheelchairs and motorized scooters. At **Ryba's Bicycle Rentals** (7245 Main St., 906/847-3208, www.rybabikes.com), you'll find a similar selection. There are a number of other bicycle rental shops on the island, or you can bring your own across on the ferry for about $13.

St. Ignace

St. Ignace is directly at the north end of the Mackinac Bridge, and is noteworthy for both its history and its less expensive off-island lodging. It has made a reputation of its own: with an annual auto show and an abundance of attractions, this city, the first off the bridge, offers an introduction to the Upper Peninsula, where one instantly notices the more rustic feeling the U.P. is so known for. As such, St. Ignace doesn't have the glamour of Mackinac Island's resorts and lacks the touristy feel of Mackinaw City. Outdoors enthusiasts of all stripes will appreciate the access to the eastern branch of the Hiawatha National Forest.

SIGHTS
★ Mackinac Bridge

You can't miss it: it's that massive bridge, total length 26,372 feet (8,038 meters). At mid-span, the roadway is 200 feet (60 meters) above the water. It has 42,000 miles (67,600 km) of wire in the main cables, and its size and grandeur stand as a testimony to 20th-century engineering and the determination of the ironworkers who built it.

Known as "Mighty Mac" or simply "The Bridge," it stands out as Michigan's pride and joy. Stretching across nearly 5 miles (8 km) of open water, the Mighty Mac has one of the longest suspensions of any bridge in the world. There are other ways of measuring the length of a suspension bridge, such as the total length, the distance between towers, etc. Some of these methods put the bridge farther down on the list, but try telling that to a Michigander—of either peninsula.

There are several quality photo spots at either end of the bridge; just find St. Ignace's southern shore and you can't miss it. You can also try Straits State Park or Mackinac Bridge View Park just west of the toll plaza. Driving the bridge is different from looking at it, and if you can manage the approximately 10-minute-long and oddly exciting drive, you should do it. If you can't bring yourself to stay behind the wheel—and many can't—bridge personnel will drive your car across for $10, plus the appropriate toll. Pedestrians, bicyclists, and snowmobilers are prohibited on the bridge, but transportation is offered for them: $5 for pedestrians, $15 for a bike, and $20 for a snowmobile and driver. Snowmobile transport is only available 8am-8pm daily.

Father Marquette National Memorial

High above the open Straits of Mackinac, the largely open-air **Father Marquette**

National Memorial commemorates French explorer and Jesuit missionary Jacques Marquette. In the 1660s and 1670s Marquette paddled through the Great Lakes, establishing dozens of cities along the way, including Sault Ste. Marie and St. Ignace. Marquette then linked up with Louis Jolliet and paddled another several thousand miles to become the first European explorer of the Mississippi River.

Walking trails feature interpretive signs that discuss Marquette's Great Lakes travels and the impact the area's geography had on settlement. Scant emphasis is given to the effect Marquette's missionary work had on Native Americans, thousands of whom Marquette converted to Christianity. A small museum on the site burned down several years ago, but it's still worth a visit for the memorial, the outdoor trail, and the panoramic view of the Mackinac Bridge.

The memorial is on the grounds of **Straits State Park** (west of I-75 and south of US 2, 906/643-8620, daily Memorial Day-mid-Sept.). A State of Michigan Recreation Passport is required for entry.

Downtown St. Ignace

In contrast to the Father Marquette

Mackinac Bridge

St. Ignace

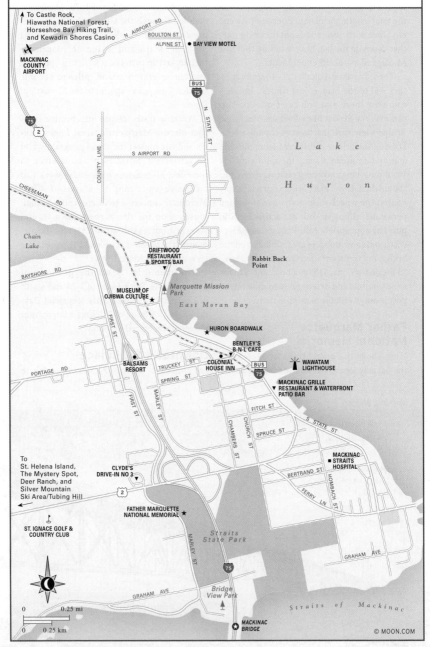

To Castle Rock,
Hiawatha National Forest,
Horseshoe Bay Hiking Trail,
and Kewadin Shores Casino

N AIRPORT RD
BOULTON ST
ALPINE ST
● BAY VIEW MOTEL

MACKINAC
COUNTY
AIRPORT

N STATE ST

BUS 75

I-75
US 2

S AIRPORT RD

COUNTY LINE RD

L a k e

H u r o n

CHEESEMAN RD

Chain
Lake

BAYSHORE RD

DRIFTWOOD
RESTAURANT
& SPORTS BAR ▼

Rabbit Back
Point

Marquette Mission
Park

MUSEUM OF
OJIBWA CULTURE ★

East Moran Bay

FIRST ST

HURON BOARDWALK ★

BENTLEY'S
B-N-L CAFÉ ●

PORTAGE RD

BALSAMS
RESORT ●

TRUCKEY ST

COLONIAL
HOUSE INN ●

SPRING ST

BUS 75

WAWATAM
LIGHTHOUSE

MACKINAC GRILLE
▼ RESTAURANT & WATERFRONT
PATIO BAR

FIRST ST

MARLEY ST

FITCH ST

CHAMBERS ST

CHURCH ST

SPRUCE ST

S STATE ST

To
St. Helena Island,
The Mystery Spot,
Deer Ranch, and
Silver Mountain
Ski Area/Tubing Hill

CLYDE'S
DRIVE-IN NO 3 ●

US 2

MACKINAC
■ STRAITS
HOSPITAL

BERTRAND ST

HOMBACH ST

FERRY LN

FATHER MARQUETTE
NATIONAL MEMORIAL ★

ST. IGNACE GOLF &
COUNTRY CLUB

MARLEY ST

Straits
State Park

GRAHAM AVE

I-75

GRAHAM AVE

Bridge
View Park

Straits of Mackinac

0   0.25 mi
0   0.25 km

MACKINAC
✪ BRIDGE

© MOON.COM

Building the Bridge

It had been a dream since 1884, when a story in the *Grand Traverse Herald* reported that ferry service had failed as a means of traversing the straits. The only way, it said, was a tunnel or a bridge.

For as long as Michigan has been a state, it has been cut in two by the Straits of Mackinac, with the northern third of the state isolated from the other two-thirds below. As early as 1897 and as late as the 1970s, there was serious talk of the Upper Peninsula seceding from Michigan and forming its own state called Superior. The physical separation of the land seemed to have led to an ideological divide, with (even today) many U.P. residents (or "Yoopers") considering themselves Yoopers first and Michiganders second.

For travelers, the separation also meant the time-consuming obstacle of waiting in lines that stretched for miles to board a ferry and cross the straits. After years of planning and lobbying to get financial backing, construction of the Mackinac Bridge officially began in 1954. It was the largest bridge construction fleet ever assembled at that time, and when the project was finished in 1957, designer David B. Steinman wrote that "The people of Michigan built the world's greatest bridge. They built it in the face of discouragement, of faintheartedness on the part of many of their leaders, of warnings that the rocks in the straits were too soft, the ice too thick, the winds too strong, the rates of interest on the bonds too high, and the whole concept too big." While the concept wasn't too big, it also wasn't easy. It took $99 million, three years of construction, and the lives of five men: Albert Abbot, Jack C. Baker, Robert Koppen, James R. LeSarge, and Frank Pepper. It was a steep cost for one of the world's finest engineering marvels.

"Mighty Mac" is 5 miles (8 km) long, with a center span between the main towers of 3,800 feet (1,158 meters). The main towers stand 552 feet (168 meters) above the water; the roadway is 200 feet (60 meters) up. It weighs 1,024,500 tons, has 4,851,700 steel rivets and 1,016,600 steel bolts, and can withstand winds up to an astounding 600 miles per hour (965 kph). The roadway is capable of moving as much as 35 feet (11 meters) east to west in high winds, but the Mackinac Bridge Authority shuts down traffic long before the swaying reaches that point.

The cost of operating and maintaining the bridge is covered by tolls. The labor needed to properly maintain the span is a staggering and unending job. But it's worth the cost and labor, for though it can be frightening for some to drive across the bridge (it visibly bows in the wind, and you're 200 feet (60 meters) up), it boasts an outstanding safety record.

And Michiganders are proud of their bridge, as they should be. It's beautiful and convenient, and without it, travelers from the south would be waiting in an hours-long line for ferries. With it, accessing the entire Upper Peninsula is as easy as keeping your eyes on the road and your hands on the wheel.

memorial, the **Marquette Mission Park and Museum of Ojibwa Culture** (500 N. State St., 906/643-9161, http://museum ofojibwaculture.net, 9am-5pm daily Memorial Day-June, 9am-8pm daily late June-Labor Day, 10am-5pm daily Labor Day-early Oct., donation) tells the story of the Ojibwa and the effect the European explorers had on their culture. The museum is also the presumed site of Jacques Marquette's grave and the site of his Jesuit mission.

Displays housed in a former Roman Catholic church include artifacts (some dating to 6000 BCE, from archaeological digs on

the grounds), explanations of how the Ojibwa adapted and survived in the area's often harsh climate, and a discussion of how they allied with the French fur traders despite how it greatly diminished their traditional way of life. Don't miss the museum's adjacent gift shop, featuring authentic locally made crafts such as ash baskets, quill jewelry, and more. It also offers an excellent selection of books on both Native American and French history in the area of the straits.

The **Huron Boardwalk** follows the shoreline for 1 mile (1.6 km), with interpretive signs explaining the role of the bay in the area's settlement. Outdoor displays explore the Straits of Mackinac history and include a rudder from a wooden steamer sunk in 1894 and the windlass from an 1891 shipwreck.

Castle Rock

Three miles (4.8 km) north of St. Ignace is one of those tourist spots that is hopelessly, almost embarrassingly, irresistible. **Castle Rock** (Castle Rock Rd., 906/643-8268, www.castlerockmi.com, daily early May-mid-Oct., $1) is a vertical tower that rises nearly 200 feet (60 meters) and provides unparalleled views of Mackinac Island, the straits, and Lake Huron. The oversize Paul Bunyan with Babe, his blue ox, is an exciting photo opportunity for children or adults with a certain sense of humor. Most visitors just head up the 170-step climb without looking twice. Nearby is a very touristy gift shop.

The Mystery Spot

The Mystery Spot (150 Martin Lake Rd., 906/643-8322, http://mysteryspotstignace.com, 9am-8pm daily mid-May-mid-June, 8am-9pm daily mid-June-Labor Day, 9am-7pm daily Labor Day-mid-Oct., $9 adults, $7 ages 5-11) would hardly bear mentioning if it weren't for the billboards you've seen around town and were no doubt wondering about. In the early 1950s, some surveyors apparently stumbled across an area where their equipment stopped working correctly. The laws of physics don't seem to apply here: tall people seem smaller, chairs balance with two legs in the air, and you'll be able to walk up a wall without falling. The experience can be fun. Whatever truth in the story of the Mystery Spot is enhanced by the strange angles at which the buildings are built, creating optical illusions that will no doubt make for some interesting photos.

Be sure not to miss the zip line ($20). Riders are propelled by gravity for 1,000 feet (305 meters) along a cable about 20 feet (6 meters) in the air. Don't do it on a full stomach. Discounts are offered to those wanting to take in both attractions.

The Deer Ranch

It's not uncommon to see wild white-tailed deer in the Upper Peninsula, but wouldn't it be great to get close enough to actually pet one? At the **Deer Ranch** (1540 W. US 2, 4 miles/6.4 km west of I-75, www.deerranch.com, 9am-5pm daily mid-May-mid-June and early Sept.-mid-Oct., 9am-8pm daily mid-June-Labor Day, $6 over age 5) you can do this and more. You'll find six large enclosures with a variety of deer habitats—from an open field to dense woods. Visitors can walk the perimeters and see 30 adult deer and about 15 fawns. Many of the deer are quite friendly, and they often stick their noses through the fence looking for a bit of affection. Coin-operated food dispensers allow visitors to hand-feed the deer.

Lighthouses

You can get a decent view of **St. Helena Island Lighthouse** from a US 2 turnout in Gros Cap, 6 miles (9.7 km) west of St. Ignace. Near the St. Ignace marina is **Wawatam Lighthouse,** which is deceptively new. Originally built in 1998 as a Michigan Welcome Center for visitors arriving from Ohio on I-75, in 2006 it was dismantled and shipped north. Today the 52-foot (16-meter) tower serves as an aid to navigation and is accessible to the public by appointment. Contact the **St. Ignace Visitors Bureau** (906/643-6950, https://stignace.com) for more information.

Hiawatha National Forest

Named after "The Song of Hiawatha," a poem by Henry Wadsworth Longfellow that tells the story of the 16th-century Iroquois chief, the **Hiawatha National Forest** is a swath of protected land stretching all the way from St. Ignace north to the Lake Superior shore. Many of the forest's 860,000 acres are found in the central U.P., but the separate eastern district is where you'll find many of St. Ignace's recreation opportunities. Information is available from the **St. Ignace Ranger District office** (1900 W. US 2, 906/643-7900, 8am-4:30pm Mon.-Fri.).

ENTERTAINMENT
Kewadin Shores Casino

The Upper Peninsula isn't much for metropolitan entertainment—nightclubs and lounges are almost nonexistent—but it does manage to get gaming right, although the local casinos tend to lack the Las Vegas-style flash and glitter. **Kewadin Shores Casino** (3105 Mackinac Trail, 906/643-7071, www.kewadin.com, year-round), more commonly called The Shores, has 25,000 square feet of space for games such as blackjack, poker, and roulette and more than 900 slot machines. From 4pm to 8pm Friday, each Kewadin location hosts its Friday Social, which includes bar specials, random draws for Kewadin Credits, match play, and double and triple points. The Northern Pines Lounge features live entertainment Friday and Saturday nights.

Eighty-one rooms are available at the casino's **hotel** ($80-95), on the shores of Lake Huron. Visitors can also enjoy the pool, fitness center, and game room. Dining options include **Horseshoe Bay Restaurant** (2pm-9pm Wed.-Sun., $9-12), which offers classic American fare, including Italian selections, battered whitefish, and a 10-ounce New York strip. Another dining option is the **Campfire Deli** (7am-11pm Mon.-Tues., 7am-midnight Wed.-Sun., $8-12), which offers a comprehensive menu including a variety of burgers, sandwiches, pizza, soups, and salads, in addition to breakfast offerings.

FESTIVALS AND EVENTS
Powwows

A great way to learn about the Upper Peninsula's original inhabitants is to attend a powwow. Powwows celebrate Indigenous heritage through colorful dancing, feasting, ancient stories, and ceremonies. Many are open to the public and can be wonderful learning experiences. Know that powwows and many other cultural events have a spiritual element to them. For this reason, halter tops and bare chests are considered inappropriate. Drinking, smoking, and other potentially objectionable behaviors should also be avoided. Take note of how others are dressed, or ask questions of the community's representatives. For a calendar of powwows, visit **Crazy Crow** (www.crazycrow.com/site/pow-wows-in-michigan). A powwow is held in Sault Ste. Marie (the specific location varies from year to year; contact the Sault Tribe Language and Culture Division at 906/635-6050 for current information) in early July by the **Sault Tribe of Chippewa Indians** (www.saulttribe.com). The three-day event includes a sunrise ceremony and spiritual gathering the first day; dance, drum, and singing competitions; and a chance to sample Indigenous food. The event is free, with vendors offering food.

Annual Mackinac Bridge Walk

On Labor Day, the Mackinac Bridge Authority dispenses with its no-pedestrian policy for the **Annual Mackinac Bridge Walk.** The walk runs in both directions, beginning at 7am in both Mackinaw City and St. Ignace, with the governor of Michigan traditionally leading the crowd from the St. Ignace side. To accommodate walkers, the bridge is closed to vehicles. Pedestrians are not allowed to start the walk after 11:30am, so make sure you arrive on time—or earlier, if possible. It takes about two hours to make the 5-mile (8-km) walk. Note that there are no restrooms on the bridge. Transportation back to your point of origin is your responsibility.

Auto Shows

Perhaps St. Ignace's biggest claim to fame is its several summer and fall auto shows, which include the **Annual Antiques on the Bay** event, held the third week of June; the **St. Ignace Car Show Weekend,** the last weekend of June; and the **Richard Crane Memorial Truck Show** in mid-September. For details, visit http://stignace.com.

SUMMER RECREATION
Trails

Thirty-five miles (56 km) of the **North**

Country National Scenic Trail lie in the eastern district of the **Hiawatha National Forest.** The trail stretches from Vermont to North Dakota. Off-limits to horses and motorized vehicles, the trail is perfect for hikers and leads through stands of cedar, aspen, pine, and northern hardwood. The flat to rolling trail is fully marked, but not all sections have been brought up to trail standards. The website www.nps.gov/noco has a full map of the trail. The trail is not yet complete.

The **Horseshoe Bay Hiking Trail** is a 6-mile (9.7-km) round-trip trail that leads from Foley Creek Campground to a secluded, sandy Lake Huron beach and back. Only 3 miles (4.8 km) from St. Ignace, the trail leads through northern white cedar lowlands, where you're likely to spot ducks and great blue herons in the numerous ponds. More information on the trail, including a complete map, is available from the **Michigan Department of Natural Resources** (www.michigan.gov/dnr).

The **Hiawatha National Forest** has more than 2,000 miles (3,200 km) of forest road available for motor vehicle use, plenty of which is within easy reach of St. Ignace. Detailed maps of **ATV/ORV trails** are available from the Hiawatha National Forest's **St. Ignace Ranger District office** (1900 W. US 2, 906/643-7900, www.fs.usda.gov/hiawatha, 8am-4:30pm Mon.-Fri.), along with trail maps and information on other recreation opportunities. Rules are strictly enforced, so make sure you're thoroughly familiar with them before setting out.

Fishing

If you're into deepwater fishing, it's hard to beat the Great Lakes, where you'll find salmon, perch, walleye, whitefish, herring, pike, and more. Visit **E.U.P. Fishing Charters** (724 Cheeseman Rd., 906/630-1665, catchfish1@att.net) for charters into the straits.

1: Father Marquette National Memorial 2: Castle Rock 3: North Country National Scenic Trail 4: Wawatam Lighthouse

Inland fishing is abundant in the area. Inland lakes, rivers, and streams provide famously good fishing from April right up to December's freeze. You'll need a valid Michigan fishing license. Visitors from outside Michigan must have a temporary non-resident license. Both are available online at www.mdnr-elicense.com and through most fishing charter services.

Other Water Recreation

Like the rest of the U.P., St. Ignace can be a summertime paradise. Visitors have come to love the sandy **beaches,** and the relatively warm waters of the straits can offer plenty of relaxation. You'll find ideal swimming spots at **Straits State Park** (720 Church St., 906/643-8620, www.michigan.gov/dnr) or at any number of smaller beaches along the Lake Huron and Lake Michigan shores.

If you thought the straits were beautiful at eye level, imagine seeing them from a harness attached to a parachute and a 600-foot (185-meter) cable. Parasailing excursions are available from **Mackinaw Parasailing** (866/436-7144 or 231/436-7144, www.mackinawparasailing.com, $85 single, $150 double, $225 triple), which docks at the Star Line Railroad Dock in St. Ignace. Mackinaw Parasailing has been giving visitors a new perspective for years from a custom boat that allows for easy flight-deck takeoffs and landings. You can also catch a ride from Mackinac Island and Mackinaw City. Parasailing is an exhilarating activity, but clearly not for the faint of heart.

Golf

For some stunning scenery, the **St. Ignace Golf and Country Club** (223 US 2, 906/643-8071, www.stignacegolf.com, $14 for 9 holes, $23 for 18 holes; $10 for cart per 9 holes) offers a beautifully tended course with stunning views of the Mackinac Bridge, Lake Huron, and the Straits of Mackinac. Rental clubs are available for $10, and powered carts can be had for just $10. The golf course is located off

US 2, a short distance west of I-75, next to the Big Boy restaurant.

WINTER RECREATION
Ski and Snowshoe Trails

The miles of hiking trails in St. Ignace don't disappear in winter, they just get covered in snow, perfect for **cross-country skiing** and **snowshoeing.** The North Country National Scenic Trail's 35 miles (56 km) in St. Ignace are popular with skiers. The **North Country National Scenic Trail** (https://northcountrytrail.org) is a multi-state hiking trail that stretches from Vermont to North Dakota, passing through eight states along the way. There's a warming cabin at the trailhead to **Sand Dunes Ski Trail,** located off US 2 about 5 miles (8 km) west of I-75. There are seven groomed trails suitable for every skill level. Trails range 1.5-7.6 miles (2.4-12.2 km). While on Loop A, look for marks left by black bears climbing the trees in the fall (bears hibernate during the winter). For more information, contact Hiawatha National Forest's **St. Ignace Ranger District office** (1900 W. US 2, 906/643-7900, www.fs.usda.gov/hiawatha, 8am-4:30pm Mon.-Fri.). Both the North Country Trail and the Sand Dunes Ski Trail are within the east unit of the Hiawatha National Forest.

Downhill Skiing

Believe it or not, you can actually find downhill skiing west of town, at **Silver Mountain Ski Area/Tubing Hill** (Cheeseman Rd. and US 2 W., 906/643-6083, gondola 8:15am-5pm, chairlift 9am-3:30pm daily, tubing sessions 9am-11am, 11am-1pm, 1pm-3pm Sat. only). While skiing is included and there are a few runs for beginner and intermediate skiers and snowboarders, Silver Mountain is very much an "all around," meaning it's a family-oriented winter resort that offers snow tubing with a rope tow, paddle towing, and groomed runs. Silver Mountain is an entertaining diversion, but serious skiers should head west to the Iron Mountain area for some of the U.P.'s best

downhill skiing. Hours may vary, so check the website before visiting.

Snowmobiling

About 3,000 miles (4,800 km) of snowmobile trails spread across Michigan's Upper Peninsula, and a few of the trailheads are right in St. Ignace. Bundle up and hit the trails to pristine winter wilderness or popular destinations like Tahquamenon Falls. The local snowmobile club maintains many of the trails, and snowmobiles can be rented from the **Quality Inn** (561 Boulevard Dr., 906/643-9700). If you're bringing your own, be aware that snowmobile crossings are not allowed on the Mackinac Bridge; transportation is provided by the **Mackinac Bridge Authority** (906/643-7600) for $20 per sled.

Remember that snowmobiling in the Upper Peninsula can be very dangerous, especially for newcomers. Every year there are several snowmobile-related deaths as reckless enthusiasts combine alcohol with driving and meet unfortunate consequences, such as plunging through the ice. Stay on marked trails and off of icy rivers and lakes. Abstain from alcohol for at least two hours before driving or riding a snowmobile. Also, keep a close eye out for pedestrians, especially young children, who can be difficult to see. Before setting out, talk to locals who know what's going on, and check trail conditions with the **Straits Area Snowmobile Club** (www.straitsareasnowmobileclub.com).

FOOD

To get a complete U.P. experience, sink your teeth into the crust of at least one pasty (pronounced PASS-tee). Stop by **Lehto's Pasties** (626 S. State St., 906/643-8542, www.lehtospasties.com, 10am-8pm Mon.-Sat., 10am-5pm Sun. Apr.-Oct., $6.50-11) for the traditional Yooper nosh, a potpie creation of beef or chicken, potatoes, onions, rutabagas, and other vegetables.

Clyde's Drive-In No. 3 (US 2, just west of the bridge, 906/643-8303, 9am-8pm Sun., Mon., and Thurs., 11am-7pm Tues.-Wed.,

9am-9pm Fri.-Sat. Apr.-Nov., $6.50-12) is another perennial St. Ignace favorite. Known throughout the U.P. as home of the best burgers on either side of the bridge, Clyde's Drive-In is not only an authentic curbside restaurant, it's also the best place for a meal on the cheaper side. You can choose to eat in if you prefer, but it gets pretty cramped. Clyde's menu includes fried shrimp, chicken, and perch; light breakfasts; old-fashioned malts and shakes; and the famous three-quarter-pound C Burger.

You'll find more old-fashioned dining at **Bentley's B-n-L Café** (62 N. State St., 906/643-7910, hours vary, $2-10), a fourth-generation diner that has a vintage soda fountain look. Try the whitefish salad or the nachos deluxe.

Some of the town's best pizza, as well as steak, seafood, and sandwiches, can be found at **Driftwood Restaurant & Sports Bar** (590 N. State St., 906/643-7744, www.thedriftwoodonline.com, 10am-1am daily), a family restaurant and sports bar. The restaurant offers great lunch choices ($9); while dinner entrées can climb as high as $27, a little steep for family dining, more moderately priced plates can be had for around $14.

For the best of St. Ignace's fine-dining scene—which manages to stay stubbornly unpretentious—grab a table the **Mackinac Grille Restaurant & Waterfront Patio Bar** (251 S. State St., 906/643-7482, www.mackinacgrill.com, 11am-10pm Mon.-Sat., 10am-10pm Sun. summer, 11am-9pm Mon.-Sat., 9am-2pm Sun. off-season, $8-27), which specializes in locally caught whitefish. Located on the marina, the restaurant offers a pleasant view of the straits, Mackinac Island, and the Star Line ferry dock.

ACCOMMODATIONS

St. Ignace is jam-packed with lodging options, which draw travelers who want to visit Mackinac Island without paying the high island prices. Unfortunately, many of St. Ignace's accommodations are rather run-of-the-mill and utilitarian. Don't expect to find the glitz of high-end lodging or expensive resorts like the island's Grand Hotel—but that doesn't mean you have to settle for a substandard room.

Hotels and Motels

Considering the stunning views of Lake Huron and waterfront access to a private beach and boardwalk, the **Bay View Motel** (1133 N. State St., 906/643-9444, mid-May-Oct., $) is surprisingly inexpensive and pet-friendly. Don't expect much from the Spartan rooms, of course, but what this motel lacks in decor it makes up for in its thrifty appeal and scenic location. Expect rates to jump during holidays and festivals.

An affordable and comfortable option is the **Budget Host Inn** (700 N. State St., 906/643-9666, $$). Here you'll find clean, basic accommodations with amenities including an indoor heated pool, fitness center, free Wi-Fi, and a complimentary breakfast. A great place to recharge your batteries.

Bed-and-Breakfasts

Although it also has seven motel rooms, the ★ **Colonial House Inn** (90 N. State St., 906/643-6900, www.colonial-house-inn.com, $$) is first and foremost a bed-and-breakfast, and St. Ignace's only one at that. The Victorian-style home overlooks the Straits of Mackinac and features a wraparound veranda and second-floor balcony. The daily breakfast includes fruit cups or yogurt, French toast or pancakes, or some variation of eggs. Each of the B&B's seven rooms is distinctively and individually decorated and has a double or a queen bed and a private bath. Occupancy is limited to two people per room, so families will need to stay in the adjacent motel, which offers rooms at a lower price. Pets are not allowed.

Camping

Of St. Ignace's many campgrounds, the most popular is **Straits State Park** (720 Church St., 906/643-8620, www.michigan.gov/dnr, $25-37). With 275 campsites, many with electricity and all with access to modern restrooms, the park's popularity is driven by a number of can't-say-no perks, including Lake Huron waterfront access, stunning views of the bridge, and the Father Marquette memorial and interpretive trail. Close to town, the campground is close to the center of activity, with easy access to Mackinac Island ferries and other attractions. It's almost worth putting up with the summertime crowds. Of the four modern campgrounds, aim for East Loop or West Loop, which have nicely wooded sites right on the straits.

Smaller crowds can be found at **Brevoort Lake Campground** (www.fs.usda.gov, from $30) in the Hiawatha National Forest, 20 miles (32 km) west of St. Ignace. The 4,233-acre lake has about 70 large forested campsites with tables and fire rings. Campers have access to the lake for boating, fishing, and swimming, and three hiking trails explore the surrounding forest. You'll find boat and canoe rentals, as well as groceries and other necessities, at a small store adjacent to the campground. You might also want to try one of the 54 sites at **Foley Creek Campground** (www.fs.usda.gov, from $16). Although still in Hiawatha National Forest, Foley Creek is only 6 miles (9.7 km) outside town. Smaller and more secluded than Straits State Park, this campground is close enough to the St. Ignace scene to use as a home base. Private campsites are set among large shade trees; Lake Huron beach access is a 1-mile (1.6 km) hike up Horseshoe Bay Trail. Contact Hiawatha National Forest's **St. Ignace Ranger District office** (1900 W. US 2, 906/643-7900, 8am-4:30pm Mon.-Fri.) for information about both campgrounds.

Other Lodging

The **Balsams Resort** offers cabins and a motel (1458 W. US 2, 906/643-9121 June-Labor Day, 313/791-8026 Labor Day-June, www.balsamsresort.com, $, weekly rates available for cabins). The cabins are cozy, fully furnished homes away from home. Balsams Resort can put you up in a one- or two-bedroom log cabin where you can prepare your own meals in the kitchen, relax in front of the fireplace, or wander over the streams and through the 40-acre woods. You won't be able to see Lake Michigan from every cabin, but the motel, which isn't quite as quaint, affords a decent view, and guests have access to a private beach.

Airbnb (www.airbnb.com) and **Vrbo** (www.vrbo.com) offer **cabins and cottages** for rent on a nightly or weekly basis, which is an attractive option for families or vacationers looking for a comfortable extended stay. With a wide range of rooms, locations, and availability, prices can be as low as $100 per night and can easily surpass $1,000 for week-long rentals. Pets are welcome, but often with significant restrictions.

INFORMATION

For visitor information, contact the **St. Ignace Visitors Bureau** (6 Spring St., Suite 100, 800/338-6660, www.stignace.com) or the **St. Ignace Chamber of Commerce** (560 N. State St., 800/970-8717, www.stignace.org). More particulars on the trails, camping, and recreation available in Hiawatha National Forest are available from the **St. Ignace Ranger District office** (1900 W. US 2, 906/643-7900, 8am-4:30pm Mon.-Fri.).

For medical emergencies, 24-hour emergency care is available at **Mackinac Straits Hospital** (1140 S. State St., St. Ignace, 906/643-8585).

GETTING THERE AND AROUND
Car

Traveling from the south, follow I-75 north across the bridge to St. Ignace. From the north, I-75 drops into St. Ignace from Sault Ste. Marie, while travelers coming east from Wisconsin can take US 2 into the city. If you're crossing the Mackinac Bridge from the Lower Peninsula, the 2023 passenger vehicle toll is $4, with an additional $2 for each axle if you're pulling a trailer. Trucks are $5 per axle. No toll increases are currently planned, but this is subject to change. Visit www.mackinacbridge.org for the latest.

Air

The two closest airports with scheduled passenger flights are **Pellston Regional Airport** (PLN, www.pellstonairport.com), south of Mackinaw City in the Lower Peninsula, and **Chippewa County International Airport** (CIU, www.airciu.com), in Sault Ste. Marie; both have rental-car providers.

Transit between St. Ignace and Mackinac Island is available on **Fresh Air Aviation** (www.freshairaviation.net) from the **Mackinac County Airport** (1220 State St., St. Ignace, 906/643-7327). Consult the Fresh Air Aviation site for fares and schedules.

Boat

Boaters can make reservations at one of the 120 slips at **St. Ignace Marina** (906/643-8131, https://stignacemarina.com). The harbormaster is on duty from mid-May through late September; you can reach the marina on radio channel 9. The location is 45°51.58 N, 84°43.06 W.

Ferry to Mackinac Island

Since you're in St. Ignace, you'll likely want to visit Mackinac Island. You can catch a ride on a ferry at **Shepler's Mackinac Island Ferry** (231/436-5023, www.sheplersferry.com, round-trip $30 adults, $19 ages 5-12) or the **Star Line** (800/638-9892, www.mackinawferry.com, $28 adults, $18 ages 5-12).

Bus and Train

Greyhound (800/231-2222, www.greyhound.com) has a bus terminal just across from the ferry docks, providing service to St. Ignace from points across the country. **Amtrak** (800/872-7245, www.amtrak.com) has partnered with Greyhound to provide transportation to St. Ignace from several major cities in southwest Michigan. **Indian Trails** (800/292-3831, www.indiantrails.com) offers bus service to St. Ignace from Chicago and a number of Michigan cities.

Mackinaw City

Mackinaw City, located at the very tip of the Lower Peninsula, serves as a gateway for travelers bound for Mackinac Island and has several historical attractions of its own. Despite the high density of strip malls and souvenir shops, downtown Mackinaw City also offers some "serious" retail, including bookstores, antiques shops, and clothing stores that don't specialize in T-shirts. Mackinaw City shares a special trait with its island cousin—beautiful Great Lakes views. You'll also find excellent food and lodging.

SIGHTS
★ Headlands International Dark Sky Park

While few of us are amateur astronomers, virtually anyone is amazed at the grandeur of a star-studded night sky. Yet in today's highly urbanized and industrialized world, the number of locations offering the right conditions to observe the heavens is vanishingly small. Responding to this reality, the International Dark Sky Association (IDSA) has certified a number of locations worldwide where stargazers can observe the night sky in near ideal conditions. The process the IDSA uses to evaluate potential new sites is rigorous. Local communities are required to demonstrate strong local support for establishing and maintaining a dark sky protection. Currently, there are only about 115 accredited dark sky parks worldwide.

Fortunately, one such park is located near Mackinaw City: **Headlands International Dark Sky Park** (15675 Headlands Rd.,

231/427-1001, https://midarkskypark.org, 24 hours daily). To get there, begin in downtown Mackinaw City and head west on Front Street. When you reach Wilderness Park Drive, turn left and continue for about 2 miles (3.2 km). The entrance will appear on your left. Once inside the grounds, follow the signs for the Headlands Waterfront Event Center.

Mackinac Historic State Parks

With a history as long and rich as Mackinac's, it isn't surprising to find a collection of sites that, together with Mackinac Island's Fort Mackinac and historic downtown, present nearly 300 years of Michigan history. If you're planning on visiting Colonial Michilimackinac, Old Mackinac Point Lighthouse, or the Historic Mill Creek Discovery Park, the Mainland Combo ticket ($31.75 adults, $22.25 ages 5-12) is the best deal. It is valid for seven days after purchase and provides admission to all these sites. Families might want to take advantage of the Mackinac Family Heritage Membership ($85) for season-long unlimited entry to all of the sites for up to two adults and all dependent children or grandchildren ages 17 or younger.

Historic Mill Creek Discovery Park

Historic Mill Creek Discovery Park (9001 S. US 23, 231/436-4100, www.mackinacparks. com, 9am-5pm daily early May-mid-Oct., 9am-6pm early June-late Aug., $10.50 adults, $8 ages 5-12) is an exceptionally pretty glen and rushing stream that creates a pleasant oasis for visitors, but it was once an innovative industrial site. When the British made plans to move from Fort Michilimackinac to Mackinac Island, Scotsman Robert Campbell recognized the obvious need for lumber. He purchased 640 acres of land surrounding the only waterway in the area with enough flow to power a sawmill. He built the mill in 1790 and later added a blacksmith shop and a gristmill.

The site was no longer profitable when the fort ceased operation, so it was abandoned in the mid-1800s. Archaeologists and historians have worked together since the 1970s to recreate the water-powered sawmill on its original site. Today, visitors can see the splashing waterwheel in action and visit the Orientation Center, which has an audiovisual presentation and displays on other artifacts uncovered during the dig. Make sure to walk the park's 3.5 miles (5.6 km) of trails, which wind through three kinds of forest or along the creek and mill pond, rising up to scenic overlooks with views of the straits and Mackinac Island.

Old Mackinac Point Lighthouse

Old Mackinac Point Lighthouse (550 N. Huron Ave., 231/436-4100, www. mackinacparks.com, 9am-5:30pm daily, last admission 5pm, $9.75 adults, $7 ages 5-12) is Mackinaw City's third historic state park. Located on a point just east of the Mackinac Bridge, this 1892 cream-brick light guided ships through the busy Straits of Mackinac for nearly 70 years. When the Mackinac Bridge was completed in 1957, it became obsolete, since vessels could navigate by the bridge's necklace lights instead of this diminutive 50-foot (15-meter) tower. Today, this charming lighthouse, topped with a cherry-red roof, houses a maritime museum complete with hands-on exhibits, a tour to the top of the tower led by a costumed interpreter, and historical images. The lighthouse grounds serve as their own delightful little park, with impressive views of the Mackinac Bridge, a beach, and picnic tables scattered across the tidy lawn.

★ Colonial Michilimackinac State Park

Believed to be the nation's longest-running archaeological dig, the site of **Colonial Michilimackinac State Park** (102 Straits Ave., 231/436-4100, www.mackinacparks. com, 9am-5pm daily early May-early June and late Aug.-early Oct., 9am-7pm early June-late Aug., $14.50 adults, $8.75 ages 5-12) has provided archaeologists with treasures since 1959. The 18th-century military outpost and fur-trading village is the finest of the Mackinac

The Joy of Charter Fishing

Traveling with an expert guide is always memorable. Embarking on a charter fishing expedition is a special treat, and northern Michigan offers them in spades along the Lake Superior and Lake Michigan shorelines. The proprietors—a.k.a. the ships' captains—take pride in providing hospitality and expert guidance to both amateur and experienced anglers. Highly knowledgeable of the local waters, your skipper can offer the latest information on how the fish are biting and the precise locations with the best chances for a big catch.

Many charter operators also use their vessels to offer sunset cruises or lighthouse tours. While it's always enjoyable just to see the Great Lakes, being out on the water is something truly special.

To assure safety, the charter boat industry is highly regulated and ship captains are required to be licensed by the U.S. Coast Guard. Ships that can carry seven or more passengers are inspected by the Coast Guard, while vessels that can ferry six or fewer are inspected by the State of Michigan. Remember that fishing anywhere in Michigan waters requires a valid state fishing license. For more information, visit the website for the Michigan Charter Boat Association (www. michigancharterboats.com).

Here are a few of the best in the U.P.:

- **E.U.P. Fishing Charters** (724 Cheeseman Rd., St. Ignace, 251/504-1046, catchfish1@att. net) offers half-day trips from St. Ignace and Mackinaw City.

- **Kimar's Charters** (E3216 State Rd. M-28, Shelter Bay, 906/892-8277, https://kimarscharters. com) offers serious sport trips of various lengths on Lake Superior between Au Train and Munising.

- **Lucky Line Fishing** (9052 26.6 Rd., Rapid River, 906/399-0760, https:// luckylinefishingcharters.com) is situated in Gladstone on the Lake Michigan shore and offers charters geared to catching either salmon or walleye. There are also trips offered to Wisconsin shores.

Historic State Parks. The site was long a well-traveled Ojibwa American hunting and trading ground; the French built a post here in 1715. The French exploited the Ojibwa, bribing them with gifts and alcohol as an incentive to assist them in the fur trade. Though this unfortunate relationship led many Ojibwa to abandon their traditional ways of life, the two groups rarely fought. Instead, the French feuded with the British, who sought to expand their landholding in the region. For the next 65 years, the fort along the straits alternately fell under French and British control.

The fort's most violent episode occurred while it was under British rule. In 1763, Pontiac, the Ottawa war chief, ordered an attack on British posts all over Michigan, an attempt to drive the growing British population out of Ottawa land. While Pontiac laid siege to Detroit, local Ojibwa stormed the fort, killing all but 13 soldiers. In the end, though, it was the feisty French colonists who sent the British fleeing from Fort Michilimackinac. They dismantled what they could and burned the rest to the ground in 1780, opting for a new, more defendable post on nearby Mackinac Island. In fact, much of the masonry from the original fort was used to build its successor on the island.

Today, Colonial Michilimackinac State Park portrays the lives of both the Native Americans and the European settlers, with costumed interpreters reenacting daily life at a Native American encampment and a stockade fort, a modern duplicate of the original. Displays include many of the artifacts excavated by archaeologists. Interpreters demonstrate various crafts and skills, from cooking and weaving to cleaning weapons. They're quite knowledgeable and able to answer most visitors' questions. Don't miss the underground archaeological tunnel exhibit

Treasures from the Sand. Other exhibits include *France at Mackinac 1670-1760, Redcoats on the Frontier,* and *Firearms on the Frontier,* which describes the remaining underground ruins of the original fort.

Mackinac Bridge Museum

It's nothing fancy, but the small **Mackinac Bridge Museum** (231 E. Central Ave., above Mama Mia's Pizza, 231/436-5534, www.mightymac.org/bridgemuseum.htm, 8am-midnight daily May-Oct., free) is a treasure trove of fascinating information and artifacts on the construction of the $100 million Mackinac Bridge. A very well-done video documents the bridge's design and construction.

Icebreaker *Mackinaw* Maritime Museum

When the U.S.C.G.C. *Mackinaw* was retired in 2006, ending 62 winters of clearing shipping lanes through the Great Lakes shipping channel, it was transferred to the Mackinaw Maritime Museum and docked in Mackinaw City. When it was built in the early 1940s to facilitate the transportation of war materials, the ship was the most cutting-edge icebreaker in the world. Located at the old railroad dock, the **Icebreaker *Mackinaw* Maritime Museum** (131 S. Huron Ave., 231/436-9825, www.themackinaw.org, 9am-5pm daily mid-May-mid-June, 9am-7pm daily mid-June-early Sept., 10am-5pm daily Sept., $12 adults, $6.50 ages 6-17, free under age 6, $38 family pass for 2 adults and all youth 17 and under) is open for tours.

Downtown Mackinaw City

Mackinaw City's downtown is partly a tourist trap but has some traditional businesses, including some worthwhile dining establishments. You will no doubt want to visit one or two of the city's innumerable **fudge shops** as well as **Mackinaw Crossings** (248 S. Huron Ave., 231/436-5030, www.mackinawcrossings.com), an outdoor mall with some good restaurants and shops.

The **Mackinaw Trolley Company**

(410 S. Huron Ave., 231/436-7812, www.mackinactrolley.com, May-Oct.) offers a local historical tour of Mackinaw City ($19.95 pp) as well as a historical tour that crosses the bridge to St. Ignace ($19.95 pp). The company can also be chartered for private tours or weddings.

Lighthouses

Mackinaw City is a place where lighthouse lovers will feel at home. The **Old Mackinac Point Lighthouse** stands guard in the shadow of the Mackinac Bridge. Visitors can tour the lighthouse and climb to the top, all while listening to a uniformed interpreter share secrets of the building's past. **McGulpin Point Lighthouse,** a few miles west, was a private home for most of the 20th century. There are plenty of other historic light stations nearby—enough to make the fascinating **lighthouse cruises** offered by Shepler's Ferry one of the city's more popular attractions.

★ McGulpin Point Lighthouse

In 2009 Emmet County purchased **McGulpin Point Lighthouse** (500 Headlands Rd., 231/436-5860, www.mcgulpinpoint.org, 10am-6pm daily June-Sept., limited hours May and Oct., $3, children under 5 free), decommissioned in 1906, and is gradually restoring it to its early-20th-century appearance. The residence is now a museum, displaying household items common during the late 19th century. Built in 1868, this is one of the oldest lighthouses in the area, and it is well preserved today due at least in part to its all-brick construction. The structure is nestled in a heavily wooded area just outside Mackinaw City. The lantern room and light at the top of the tower have been replaced, and visitors today can ascend the stairs to get a panoramic view of the straits. Bringing the structure back to life has been a labor of love for the Emmet County Historical Commission, an

1: Mackinaw City 2: McGulpin Point Lighthouse
3: Icebreaker *Mackinaw* 4: Mackinaw Crossings mall

Mackinac or Mackinaw?

First-time visitors to the straits often notice the variant spellings of their name and become curious as to the reason. The inconsistency can be traced to the area's multilayered history.

The original name given to the area by the Ojibwa was Michilimackinac. Although scholarly opinion is mixed, the consensus is the term meant "great turtle," the giver of life, since the shape of Mackinac Island resembles a turtle. When the French constructed Fort Michilimackinac in 1715, they took the name and attempted to spell it in their language (a process known as transliteration). The last syllable is universally pronounced "naw," and they ended the word with "nac," in keeping with the typical French spelling for this particular sound. Shortly after the name was shortened to Mackinac, the fort was moved to Mackinac Island for strategic reasons. Eventually the new name became associated with the straits themselves, which probably explains why the French spelling was chosen for the name of the bridge.

When the British established the city on the tip of the Lower Peninsula in 1857, they took the name and spelled it with standard English pronunciation: "naw." So while the city's name is distinguished by its spelling, the pronunciation is the same.

Today, the different spellings of place-names in this beautiful region remain a curious footnote in Michigan history.

accomplishment for which they are rightly proud.

St. Helena Island Lighthouse

Built in 1873, the 71-foot (22-meter) tower and attached keeper's quarters of the **St. Helena Island Lighthouse** (www.lighthousefriends.com) fell into disrepair after the lighthouse was automated in the 1920s, but it has since seen some restoration. Currently, day tours are available by contacting the Great Lakes Lighthouse Keepers Association (313/436-5580, www.gllka.org). St. Helena Island is a few miles northwest of the city in the Straits of Mackinac and can be seen on the Westbound Lighthouse Cruise offered by Shepler's Ferry.

Round Island Lighthouse

The **Round Island Light,** also known as the Old Round Island Point Lighthouse, was built in 1895 to guide ships among the shoals and channels between Mackinac Island and uninhabited Round Island, where it was built. Though unstaffed, the Round Island light still guides ships through the straits today. Your best bet to see it is the Eastbound Lighthouse Cruise offered in Mackinaw City by Shepler's Mackinac Island Ferry.

Lighthouse Cruises

The lighthouse cruises offered by **Shepler's Mackinac Island Ferry** (556 E. Central Ave., 231/436-5023, www.sheplersferry.com, early June 9-mid-Sept., $75 adults, $44 ages 5-12), which the company offers in addition to their standard ferry service, are very popular and for good reason. Choose between the Eastbound Lighthouse Cruise or Westbound Lighthouse Cruise; either way, you'll pass below the Mackinac Bridge for a glimpse of its underside and get close enough to at least four historic lights to snap some photos. The trips last about three hours and are narrated by members of the Great Lakes Lighthouse Keepers Association. Historic lights include Mackinac Island's Round Island Light Station and Round Island Passage Light; St. Helena Island Light, west of St. Ignace; and the White Shoal and Waugoshance lighthouses. For the diehard lighthouse enthusiast, extended east and west cruises are offered. The Extended Eastbound Lighthouse Cruise ($99.50 adults, $60 ages 5-12) includes the difficult-to-access Spectacle Reef Lighthouse, while the Extended Westbound Lighthouse Cruise ($105 adults, $61.50 ages 5-12) adds the Skillagalee Lighthouse to its itinerary. Cruises are subject to cancellation due to weather conditions, so be sure to call ahead. The ship sails continuously throughout the tours. Passengers only disembark at the conclusion of the cruise. All cruises begin and end at Mackinaw City.

The **Star Line** (801 S. Huron Ave., 231/436-5045 or 800/638-9892, www.mackinacferry.com, $75 adults, $65 ages 5-12) offers an exciting sunset cruise aboard a tall ship. Departures are at 8:30pm Thursday July-August from Mackinaw City, and 8:30pm Monday July-August from their St. Ignace dock. The cruise passes Round Island Lighthouse, Mackinac Island, Old Mackinaw Point Lighthouse, and Colonial Michilimackinac, and provides a running narration.

Another fun nautical event provides the opportunity to view the Mackinac Bridge from below. **Ugly Anne Boat Cruises** (229 S. Huron Ave., 231/436-5094, www.mackinawtour.com, $28 adults, $14 ages 3-12) offers a trip to the bridge each day at 5pm and 6:30pm in summer. Along the way, the captain will share information on local nautical lore and Ojibwa customs. Ugly Anne also offers sightseeing charters within the great Mackinac area.

SHOPPING
Fudge
Fudge shops are fairly ubiquitous in Mackinaw City. Noteworthy examples include **Joann's Fudge** (303 E. Central Ave., 231/436-5611, www.joannsfudge.com, 8:30am-8pm Sun.-Thurs., 8:30am-9pm Fri.-Sat. early May-late Oct.), **Marshall's Fudge Shop** (308 E. Central Ave., 800/343-8343, www.marshallsfudge.com, 8:30am-8pm Sun.-Thurs., 8:30am-9pm Fri.-Sat. June-Sept., 9am-5pm daily Oct.-May), and **Kilwin's** (176 S. Huron Ave., Mackinaw Crossings, 231/436-4067, www.kilwins.com, 10am-10pm June-Aug., reduced hours rest of the year), a national chain with a great number of Michigan locations.

Other Shopping
Mackinaw Crossings (248 S. Huron Ave., 231/436-5030, www.mackinawcrossings.com) is an outdoor mall that offers some interesting shops. One that's especially noteworthy is **Enchanted Knights** (231/436-4059, www.shop.enchantedknights.com), the perfect place to get outfitted for a Renaissance fair, but which also appeals to more modern people. You'll find clothing, gifts, jewelry, and, yes, swords, all of which may make you feel like you've just been deputized by the Sheriff of Nottingham. **True North Books and Gifts** (180 S. Huron Ave., 231/436-4000) is a wonderful source of all things Michigan. They offer fiction and nonfiction books, plus an assortment of themed wall clocks, art, clothing, and drinkware.

Another noteworthy destination and a great source for truly usual gifts is **Twisted Crystal** (301 E. Central Ave., 231/436-7020, www.twistedcrystal.com), where you'll find creative wire-wrapped jewelry utilizing rocks native to Michigan, including Petoskey stones, Leland bluestones, and greenstones, the official gemstone of Michigan.

Mackinaw Art Marketplace (120 S. Huron St., 231/703-9791) is the local go-to spot for quality contemporary paintings, plus custom framing and matting.

ENTERTAINMENT
Mackinaw Trail Winery
Mackinaw Trail Winery (180 S. Huron St., 231/436-6111, 10am-10pm Mon.-Sat., noon-10pm Sun. May-Oct.) is a tasting room for the Petoskey-based winery. Enjoy classic varietals, such as a dry Riesling, and regional exclusives, such as Marquette Nouveau or East Park Blanc.

FESTIVALS AND EVENTS
Hundreds of actors participate in Memorial Day weekend's **Colonial Michilimackinac Pageant,** which recreates historical events from the 1700s, including the famous 1763 attack. Perhaps taking a cue from St. Ignace's auto shows, Corvette enthusiasts gather at the **Corvette Crossroads Auto Show** in late August.

Mackinaw City's biggest event is Labor Day's **Annual Mackinac Bridge Walk,** which runs in two directions, originating in both Mackinaw City and St. Ignace. A few days later, in early September, thousands of people turn out for **Hopps of Fun,** the city's annual beer and wine festival, featuring more than 50 microbrews and 60 Michigan wines. Winter events include an annual **Winterfest** in early January. Information on all these events can be found at www. visitmackinawcitymichigan.com.

RECREATION
On the Water

One of the more popular fishing spots is the **Mackinaw City Fishing Pier.** Built specifically for fishing, this is where you may have some luck with perch, bass, salmon, or trout. You'll find the pier on the east side of town, near Railroad and Huron Avenues. **Cheboygan State Park** (4490 Beach Rd., 231/627-2811, www.michigan.gov/dnr), some 20 miles (32 km) east of the city, is also a favorite among anglers.

For excursions, St. Ignace's **E.U.P. Fishing Charters** (724 Cheeseman Rd., 251/504-1046, www.finandfield.com/organizations/ e-u-p-fishing-charters-st-ignace) docks in Mackinaw City for offshore fishing trips with views of Mackinac Island and the bridge. If you have nerves of steel, you may want to try parasailing over the straits. Contact **Mackinaw Parasailing** (209 S. Huron Ave., 866/436-7144, www.mackinawparasailing. com, $85 single, $150 double, $225 triple).

Beaches

Miles of shoreline surround Mackinaw City, and much of it is pristine sandy beach. About 4 miles (6.4 km) west of the city, on Wilderness Park Road, Lake Michigan curves into **Cecil Bay,** with sandy shores and shallow water. Public restrooms are available.

Golf

South of the city, the 18 holes and driving range of the **Mackinaw Club** (11891 N. Mackinaw Hwy., Carp Lake, 231/537-4955, http:// mackinawclub.com, daily mid-May-Oct., $25-35 for 9 holes, $40-45 for 18 holes) were built on the site of an emergency World War II landing strip for B-25 bombers.

FOOD

The **Historic Depot Restaurant** (248 S. Huron Ave., 231/436-7060, www. mackinawcrossings.com, 11am-10pm daily, $11-24) in Mackinaw Crossings is a casual restaurant with nightly entertainment, a full bar, and usually a pretty long wait for a table. As its name implies, the restaurant channels the bygone days of train travel. The outdoor seating is pet friendly.

The two-story ★ **Dixie Saloon** (401 E. Central Ave., 231/436-5449, www.dixiesaloon. com, 10:30am-11pm daily, bar until 2am, $14-28) was a Mackinaw City mainstay in the 1890s. The renovated cedar building is wide open on the inside and the menu features good all-American steaks, ribs, chicken, and burgers. Stop by the Dixie Saloon on weekends for year-round live entertainment; the restaurant also features a full bar and weekly karaoke. Attached to the Dixie is **O'Reilly's Irish Pub** (www.oreillysmackinawpub.com), a casual yet elegant bar and grill. Despite the Irish decor, however, the menu is pretty much standard American bar fare. Prices and hours are identical to the Dixie Saloon.

An excellent choice for quality family dining is **Darrow's Family Restaurant** (301 Louvigney St., 231/436-5514, www. darrowsrestaurant.com, 8am-8pm Sun.-Thurs., 8am-8:30pm Fri.-Sat., $10-23). A family-run establishment, Darrow's has evolved from a simple hot dog stand in the 1950s to a drive-in to today's incarnation as a sit-down restaurant. The eclectic menu includes soups, salads, sandwiches, and entrées, including Mackinaw-style smothered chicken breast, pot roast, and a bevy of Great Lakes fish offerings, including several versions of fresh whitefish.

ACCOMMODATIONS

With the straits as a major tourism draw, Mackinaw City alone has more than 3,000 guest rooms. There's nothing quite as extravagant as the island's Grand Hotel or Mission Point Resort, but the city has plenty of lodging at affordable rates.

Hotels and Motels

Families will probably find the prospect of staying at the **Fairview Beachfront Inn and Waterpark** (907 S. Huron Ave., 231/436-8831 or 800/822-8314, www.mackinaw-city.com, $$) irresistible. The 5,000-square-foot water park has plenty of room for the kids to splash and play with water cannons, waterfalls, buckets, and other toys that douse them with more than 1,700 gallons of water each minute. There's also plenty of private Lake Huron beach. The four floors of guest rooms and two- or three-bedroom suites, available at a higher price, can accommodate families of almost any size. That said, if you don't have kids, you may want to find rooms elsewhere.

If you're a bit less choosy, there are plenty of no-frills motels offering basic rooms. The following options are midrange ($$), but you can often find rooms for less during off-peak seasons: **Sunrise Beach Motel** (1067 S. Huron, 231/436-5461, www.mackinawcitymotels.com), **Bell's Melody Motel** (11460 W. US 23, 231/436-5463, www.mackinawcitymotels.com), and **Northwinds Motel** (11472 W. US 23, 231/436-7434, www.mackinawcitymotels.com). Like most Mackinaw City lodgings, these are fairly bare-bones.

Bed-and-Breakfasts

Located in one of Mackinaw City's oldest homes, the **Deer Head Inn** (109 Henry St., 231/436-3337, www.deerhead.com, $$) was built in 1913. The five rooms each try to capture the rustic northern Michigan spirit, with names like Hemingway, Wilderness, and Hiawatha, and decorations that include bearskins, caribou and fox pelts, and mission-style furniture. Don't worry—the B&B doesn't compromise elegance to achieve its woodsy charm. Deer Head Inn is open year-round, and room rates vary seasonally.

The ★ **Brigadoon Bed & Breakfast** (207 Langlade St., 231/436-8882, www.mackinawbrigadoon.com, May-early Nov., $$) is located across the street from Huron Avenue, the Lake Huron shore, and the ferry docks. Its 10 rooms mix modern appointments with a taste of the Old World. If you stay in the elegant butter-yellow building you'll find king or queen four-poster beds, heated marble floors in the private baths, and signature breakfasts on the veranda.

Camping

Mackinaw Mill Creek Camping (9730 US 23, 231/436-5584, www.campmackinaw.com, May-Oct., $16-57) has more than 600 sites, including full hookups for RVs, tenting sites, cabins, and a mile of shoreline. The amenity-rich campground (free Wi-Fi!) is great for families. Rates vary depending on the site's view and the level of electrical service, while cabin rates vary wildly according to seasonal and holiday demand.

The nearest state campground is 12 miles (19.3 km) west at wonderful **Wilderness State Park** (898 Wilderness Park Dr., 231/436-5381, www.michigan.gov/dnr, Apr.-Dec., campsites around $30), located at the end of a point. It offers 250 modern campsites, rustic cabins, and bunkhouses. The park has two campgrounds, one on the lakeshore and another tucked away in a grove of mature pines.

Twenty miles (32 km) east of Mackinaw City, **Cheboygan State Park** (4490 Beach Rd., 231/627-2811, www.michigan.gov/dnr, campsites around $26) has modern sites near Lake Huron's Duncan Bay, although none are directly on the water. Reservations are available from late March through early December.

Other Lodging

Private cottages are the draw at **The Beach House** (11490 W. US 23, 800/262-5353, www.mackinawcitybeachhouse.com, mid-May-mid-Oct., $$). The rooms are clean and well kept, but relatively Spartan. You'll want to stay here for the 250 feet (76 meters) of beach, the view of the bridge only a mile away, and the cottage-like feel. The rooms sleep one to five people and are pet-friendly. Kitchenettes are available. The cottages book quickly, so reserve far in advance.

INFORMATION

The **Mackinaw Area Visitors Bureau** (10800 W. US 23, 231/436-5664, www.mackinawcity.com) can provide visitor information, adventure guides, and brochures. The **Mackinaw City Chamber of Commerce** (216 E. Central Ave., 231/436-5574, www.mackinaw-city.com) offers plenty of visitor information, a comprehensive calendar of events, and community information.

GETTING THERE AND AROUND

Car

Mackinaw City is accessed by I-75 north from Lansing or south from Sault Ste. Marie. If you're driving east from Wisconsin, take US 2 to St. Ignace and join I-75 south across the bridge. If you're crossing the bridge from St. Ignace, the 2023 passenger vehicle toll is $4, with an additional $2 for each axle if you're pulling a trailer. Trucks are $5 per axle. No toll increases are currently planned, but this is subject to change; see www.mackinacbridge.org for the latest information.

Air

Delta Airlines currently has several scheduled flights daily to **Pellston Regional Airport** (PLN, www.pellstonairport.com), about 15 miles (24 km) south of Mackinaw City. Shuttle transportation is available from **Wolverine Stages** (800/825-1450, www.go-michigan.com/Wolverine-Stages-Shuttle, reservations preferred) and **Mackinaw Shuttle** (231/539-7005, www.mackinawshuttle.com). Make sure you call ahead for reservations and current rates. **Top of the Hill Taxi** (231/330-0575) provides taxi service, or you can rent a car through **Avis** (231/539-8302, www.avis.com) or **Hertz** (231/539-8404, www.hertz.com).

Boat

The **Mackinaw City Municipal Marina** (231/436-5269, www.michigan.gov/dnr) has a total of 104 slips and can be reached on radio channels 9 and 16. The harbormaster is on duty May 1-October 10, 7am-9pm. The marina is located at 45°46.55 N, 84°43.12 W.

Ferry to Mackinac Island

To book a spot on one of the two **ferries** with service from Mackinaw City to Mackinac Island, contact **Shepler's Mackinac Island Ferry** (231/436-5023, www.sheplersferry.com) or the **Star Line** (800/638-9892, www.mackinawferry.com).

Bus and Train

There is no Greyhound service, public transportation, or car-rental outlet in the city, so having your own vehicle is a must. **Amtrak** (800/872-7245, www.amtrak.com) has partnered with Greyhound to provide bus service from some cities in southeast Michigan.

Escanaba and the Lake Michigan Shore

US 2, the main road west from St. Ignace that

hugs the Lake Michigan shoreline, has a succession of places to pull over, breathe in the fresh air, and admire the lake. Stop at one or two to stretch your legs on the 90-mile (145-km) two-hour drive from St. Ignace to Manistique. The beaches here are sandier than Lake Superior's, and by late summer the water becomes warm enough for swimming.

Like most U.P. towns, Manistique isn't quite the booming place it once was. Since its heyday as a lumber port in the early 1900s, Manistique has shrunk to about 3,000 people. Its small size may well be the reason for its quaint atmosphere. The Manistique River flows through the center of town into Lake Michigan, and the scenic

Highlights

Look for ★ to find recommended sights, activities, dining, and lodging.

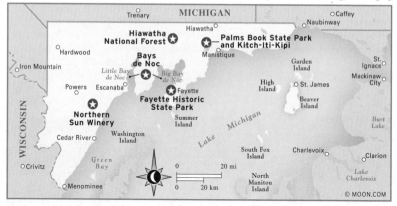

★ **Palms Book State Park and Kitch-Iti-Kipi:** Look down to the bottom of this crystal-clear lake and you'll see bubbles emerging from the earth (page 86).

★ **Fayette Historic State Park:** This historic townsite is one of the U.P.'s most famous ghost towns (page 94).

★ **Bays de Noc:** These bays have more than 200 miles (320 km) of shoreline, 120,000 acres of water, and irresistible walleye fishing (page 96).

★ **Hiawatha National Forest:** Experience true wilderness by hiking, paddling, or camping in the eastern part of this national forest, which spreads north from US 2 to Lake Superior (page 102).

★ **Northern Sun Winery:** Sample some uniquely northern Michigan varietals in an idyllic vineyard setting (page 102).

boardwalk makes for a pleasant stroll. Just west of Manistique, the Garden Peninsula drops south into Lake Michigan, framing the northern reaches of Green Bay.

You'll pass through Garden, the largest community on the peninsula, on your way to Fayette, the Upper Peninsula's most famous ghost town and a fascinating reminder of the area's industrial past. If you're curious, spend a morning or afternoon exploring the once bustling production town where pig iron was smelted during the Civil War.

The Green Bay shoreline, west of the Garden Peninsula, is known for its moderate climate, producing relatively mild (by Upper Peninsula standards) winters. The year-round temperate conditions make this corner of the Lake Michigan shoreline, nicknamed "the banana belt," a favorite destination for outdoors enthusiasts. Escanaba and Menominee (the U.P.'s third and fourth largest cities, respectively) make this region better than most for dining and lodging choices.

PLANNING YOUR TIME

There's plenty of scenic driving along the lakeshore and a few worthwhile stops along the way. You'll find more activity in Escanaba, Menominee, and Manistique than in the peninsula's smaller towns, but the biggest summertime draw is the fishing. Winter visitors will find miles of snowmobile trails packed into this small region. Pitching a tent at one of the forest campgrounds will encourage you to spend a whole week, but a visit to one of the larger towns should take only a day or two.

Accommodation Price Key

$	Less than $100 per night
$ $	$100-200 per night
$ $ $	More than $200 per night

HISTORY

The cities along the Lake Michigan shoreline share a common history with many other Upper Peninsula towns: Indigenous communities gave way to the mining and logging industries, which in turn collapsed as the natural resources became depleted. Manistique was a thriving port city central to the timber industry, while Escanaba flourished as a route for iron ore shipping. The Fayette historic townsite—a preserved ghost town—is an example of what happened to some of these once-bustling communities. Today Escanaba, Manistique, and Menominee are vibrant communities with economies supported largely by the U.P.'s appeal as a tourism destination.

St. Ignace to Manistique

SIGHTS
Driving US 2

US 2 is the main east-west thoroughfare in the southern portion of the Upper Peninsula and one of the most scenic drives around. The 88-mile (142-km) route from St. Ignace to Manistique is lined with scenic turnouts, beaches, and other detours but offers few entertainment or lodging options. You'll want to stop at one or two for a stunning view of Lake Michigan, but there's no need to stop at them all—even the most beautiful spots become repetitive.

Heading west along US 2, you'll pass through Brevort, Epoufette, and Naubinway. You won't need to look far to find a short hiking trail or two, a sandy beach, or a restaurant to experience off-the-beaten-path dining and a bit of local culture. A trip north on M-33 will bring you to the town of Curtis, nestled

Previous: Kitch-Iti-Kipi at Palms Book State Park; Snail Shell Harbor from Fayette Historic State Park; Hiawatha National Forest.

Escanaba and the Lake Michigan Shore

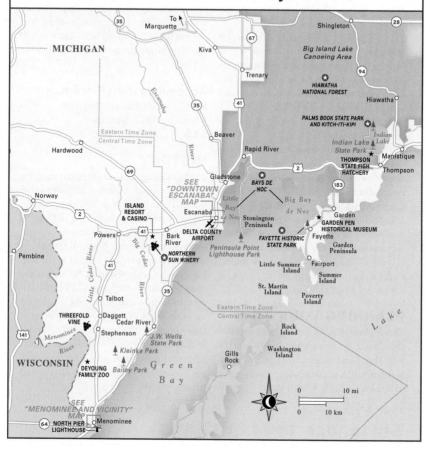

between **Big Manistique Lake** and **South Manistique Lake** and home to plenty of outdoor activities. Take a small southern detour along County Road 432 for a glimpse of Seul Choix Point Light, a spot that affords a better view than a typical lighthouse. On a clear day you can catch a glimpse of Beaver, Garden, and High Islands, not to mention a few passing freighters. The road reconnects to US 2 after passing between **McDonald** and **Gulliver Lakes.**

Siphon Bridge and Water Tower

Although it isn't nearly as big or impressive as the Mighty Mac, Manistique's **Siphon Bridge,** which crosses the Manistique River, may very well be the Upper Peninsula's second most interesting bridge. An innovative engineering feat, the 1919 structure is partially supported by the water underneath it, as the roadway lies 4 feet (1.2 meters) below water level. Its construction was prompted by

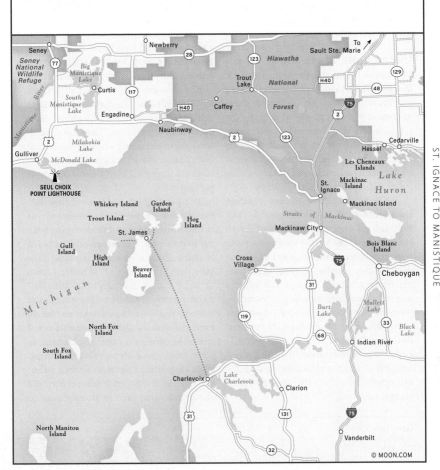

a paper mill upstream that needed to dam the river for its water needs, thus raising the level of the river.

Stop at the historic **Water Tower** (River St.) for a taste of regional history. Built in 1922, the 200-foot (60-meter) brick tower is located on the site of the Schoolcraft County Historical Park.

Thompson State Fish Hatchery

In Thompson, just a few miles west of Manistique, you'll find the working **Thompson State Fish Hatchery** (944 S. M-149, 906/341-5587, 7:30am-3:30pm daily, free), which produces several different fish species for the Great Lakes and inland lakes, including steelhead and brown trout, chinook salmon, and walleye. It isn't the prettiest stop on a tour of the U.P., but an interpretive center provides plenty of information about the importance of hatcheries and fisheries, small tributaries to the Great Lakes, and how watersheds work. The hatchery offers self-guided tours with informative signs that explain what you're seeing, and you can watch staff working with the fish in the ponds.

Indian Lake State Park

The Upper Peninsula's fourth-largest lake, **Indian Lake** is well known among anglers and RV campers (but be warned: Jet Skiers have discovered it, too). The anglers come for the perch, walleye, and muskie that thrive in the lake's warm, shallow waters. The RV campers come for the convenient location—just north of US 2 and the Garden Peninsula, which includes plenty of campsites and sandy beaches.

The best-known campsites are at **Indian Lake State Park** (8970 W. County Rd. 442, 906/341-2355, www.michigan.gov/dnr), which has two units, one on the south shore and another 3 miles (4.8 km) away on the west shore. Highly popular, the park offers fishing, boating, beaches, and picnicking. The lake is the focus here, so hiking is limited. To reach the park from Manistique, take US 2 to Thompson, then go north on M-149 and east on County Road 442; it's about a 7-mile (11.3-km) drive from Manistique. To reach the west unit, stay on M-149 and look for the signs. It's a distance of about 10 miles (16.1 km) from Manistique.

★ Palms Book State Park and Kitch-Iti-Kipi

Located on Indian Lake's western shore about 13 miles (21 km) from Manistique, **Palms Book State Park** (M-149, 906/341-2355, www.michigan.gov/dnr) guards one of the U.P.'s most remarkable natural attractions. **Kitch-Iti-Kipi,** or "Big Spring," looks like a deep, dark pool tucked away in a grove of cedars—until you get close. Then you discover it's an enormous spring, where gin-clear water (with a noticeable aqua tint) bubbles out of the earth at a staggering 10,000 to 16,000 gallons per minute.

The park maintains a convenient raft that allows you to propel yourself across the 200-foot-wide (60-meter) spring with the help of a hand-powered cable tethered to either shore. It's an amazing view. Take your time to peer 45 feet (14 meters) down (it doesn't seem that deep) into the clear, slightly emerald waters and erupting sand bottom. You'll see brown, lake, and brook trout glide among the skeletons of downed trees. The spring is a popular attraction, so come during the early morning or evening, when the surrounding trees cast their reflections on the still water. You'll need to hike about 100 yards/meters along the gated

Indian Lake State Park

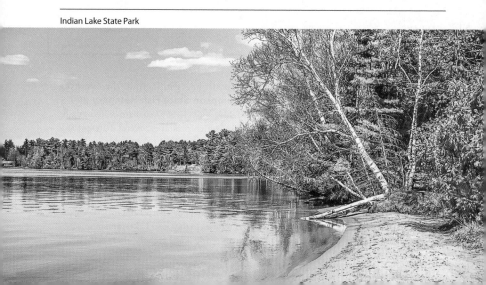

entrance trail, but Kitch-Iti-Kipi is such a magical place, you won't mind. Winter is a great time to visit too, as the spring never freezes over.

Lighthouses

Ten miles (16.1 km) south of Blaney Park at Gulliver, 14 miles (23 km) east of Manistique, a road leads down a point to the 1895 **Seul Choix Point Light** (Seul Choix Rd., 906/283-3860, www.greatlakelighthouse. com, 10am-6pm daily Memorial Day–mid-Oct., $5 adults, $3 children, $12 families), a worthwhile detour. Pronounced "sul-SHWA"—French for "only choice"—it sits at the end of a finger of land that offers boaters the only choice for hiding from storms along this stretch of the Lake Michigan shoreline. The township of Gulliver has done a splendid job restoring the light and creating a maritime museum in the fog signal building, complete with a third-order Fresnel lens. It includes an admirable scale model of the lighthouse, made by hand with thousands of miniature bricks. Climb the tower for great views of much of northern Lake Michigan. You'll have a good chance of seeing ship traffic, since Port Inland, just to the east, is an important commercial port. From US 2 at Gulliver, go southeast on County Road 431 (a gravel road) and travel another 4 miles (6.4 km) to the light. Hours are subject to the availability of volunteer guides, so call ahead.

The **Manistique East Breakwater Lighthouse** (906/341-5010) is located on the east side of Manistique, at the end of the east breakwater arm. The concrete breakwaters were built in the early 1900s as a means of creating safe harbor for large ships. You'll be able to see the red lighthouse, which dates from 1916, from throughout Lakeview Park; access to the pier and lighthouse can be found on the west side of the park. Visitors are not allowed inside, but you can get close enough for a good view. If weather permits, you can walk out to the lighthouse along the pier, but exercise caution.

SHOPPING
Books

Despite the growing popularity of e-readers and the Internet, many people still like to sit down with a good book—especially if planning to spend time on an Upper Peninsula beach. If that describes you, take a detour off US 2 to **The First Edition, Too Bookstore** (W4487 Worth Rd., Brevort, 906/292-5513, see the Facebook page for more information). To get there, take School House Road north, off of US 2 in Brevort. Continue for about a mile (1.6 km), then turn right on Worth Road, where you'll continue for about another quarter mile (0.4 km) until you see the shop on your right, located adjacent to the owner's home in an old five-room cabin, which feels more like an old library than a bookstore. Owner Mary Carney takes pride in offering quality new and used titles, mostly on the history of Michigan and the Great Lakes region but also including modern fiction, crafts, and gardening. The artfully humorous sign out front reads, "Open by chance or appointment," although those chances occur only between May and October. If you don't see Mary in the shop, you can head to her house next door—she's happy to open the shop when a prospective shopper arrives.

Antiques

A little-known secret is the cluster of antiques shops that can be found in Manistique and the surrounding towns of Gulliver, Thompson, and Garden Corners—all conveniently located along US 2. If you have a passion for antiques, be sure to stop by any of these frequently overlooked gems. A few examples are **Heirlooms Past and Present** (5590 US 2, Manistique, 906/341-7357) and **Christopher's Antiques & Collectibles** (211 Oak St., Manistique, 906/341-2570).

ENTERTAINMENT
Kewadin Manistique Casino

At **Kewadin Manistique** (5630W US 2, Manistique, 906/341-5510, www.kewadin. com), one of Kewadin's five Upper Peninsula

1

2

3

casinos, gamers can try the slots or hit the tables for blackjack, Let It Ride stud poker, and three-card poker. At the end of each work week, the **Team Spirits Bar** hosts its popular Fantastic Friday Social, which features drawings for casino credits and a monthly cash grand prize. Live local entertainment is offered the last Saturday of each month. Other nights, catch a game on the bar's big screens. If the bar menu isn't enough, visit Mariner's Cove, Kewadin Manistique's 60-seat restaurant, for breakfast, lunch, or dinner at surprisingly good prices. The casino is conspicuously located on the north side of US 2 in Manistique.

Mackinaw Trail Winery

The small, simply decorated **Manistique on the Harbor Tasting Room** (103 W. Lakeshore Dr., 906/341-2303, www.mackinawtrailwinery.com) is a testimony to Michigan's growing wine industry. Hours of operation vary considerably, with spring hours 10am-8pm Monday-Saturday, noon-6pm Sunday. After Memorial Day and running through the tourist season, hours often extend well into the evening. With more than 14,000 acres of vineyards, Michigan is one of the most prolific grape-growing states, producing more than 375,000 cases of red, white, and fruit wines each year. Mackinaw Trail Winery uses grapes harvested from across the state to make their award-winning wines. The tasting room in Manistique is one of three such facilities operated by the winery, in addition to the production facility in Petoskey. The company is so named because its tasting rooms are located along various northern Michigan locations, with Mackinaw City as its central point.

FESTIVALS AND EVENTS
Annual Manistique Folkfest

A special event on the Manistique calendar is

the **Annual Manistique Folkfest** (906/341-2290, www.cityofmanistique.org), held each year on the second Friday and Saturday in July. Arts and crafts vendors display their unique creations along Main Street, while an array of international foods is offered. For adults, there's the Paul Bunyan Beer Garden, while the kids can hang out at a children's play area.

SUMMER RECREATION
Hiking and Biking

Directly south of US 2 and about halfway between Naubinway and Manistique, a lovely trail hugs the Lake Michigan shoreline. Take Gould City Road south from Gould City until you hit **Gould City Township Park,** in the middle of the pathway. Head east along a moderately difficult off-trail route that extends about 3.5 miles (5.6 km) before doubling back to your car; you can keep going west for another 2.5 miles (4 km) or so. The trail is a little difficult to find, and the footing can be difficult at times, but the solitude and the views of the lake make it worthwhile.

With only 2 miles (3.2 km) of hiking trails, Indian Lake State Park won't top any lists of hiking destinations. However, the **Indian Lake Pathway** has 8.5 miles (13.7 km) of trails that are perfect for hikers and bikers. The three loops provide flat to rolling terrain and lengths of 1-4.5 miles (1.6-7.2 km). Don't confuse Indian Lake Pathway with the state park of the same name. The pathway is located west of the park; the easiest way to reach the trailhead is to take M-149 about 12 miles (19.3 km) north of Thompson.

There's also a much easier 3-mile (4.8-km) trail at **Camp Seven Lake Recreation Area,** 24 miles (39 km) north of Manistique in the Hiawatha National Forest, which can be completed in about two hours. The recreation area offers picnic grounds and a swimming area. **Rainey Wildlife Area,** on the north side of Indian Lake, has a hiking trail and boardwalks that lead to a wildlife observation platform, where there is a decent chance of seeing bald eagles in spring and

---

1: the emerald waters of Kitch-Iti-Kipi
2: Manistique's historic Water Tower **3:** Manistique East Breakwater Lighthouse

Following the U.P. Wine Trail

Long overshadowed by the winemakers of California, Michigan's vineyards and tasting rooms have in recent years found their way onto the connoisseur's map. Most, however, are located along the western coast of the Lower Peninsula, with the highest concentration in the Grand Traverse Bay area. An even more recent development has been the emergence of wineries on the northern side of the Mackinac Bridge.

Northern Sun Winery

The region of the Upper Peninsula stretching from Menominee up toward Escanaba has been identified by vintners as the "banana belt," an area that enjoys relatively mild winters as it is sheltered from the most severe cold coming off Lake Superior by the Porcupine Mountains to the northwest. In addition, the comparatively warm waters of nearby Green Bay further moderate winter temperatures.

Research done at the University of Minnesota has produced hardier grapes capable of flourishing at more northerly latitudes—locales include Marquette, St. Pepin, Brianna, and Frontenac. The result is a variety of cabernets, chardonnays, and pinot grigios capable of pleasing even the most discriminating palate.

Make a day of it and visit four of the best wineries north of the bridge. It takes about three hours to drive to each of these wineries, not including the stops. Be sure to go with a designated driver. Cheers!

- **Threefold Vine Winery** (S232 Menominee St., Stephenson, 906/753-6000, www.exploringthenorth.com/threefold/vine.html, 11am-5pm Mon.-Sat. May-Dec., 11am- 4pm Fri.-Sat. Jan.-Apr.): Located in a historic bank building in Stephenson, Threefold is currently selling wines from grapes grown on a vineyard on the Garden Peninsula. A new farm in Menominee County is currently in development to produce a greater variety of grapes. At present, their offerings are sold at their tasting room and at many Upper Peninsula retailers.

- **Northern Sun Winery** (983 10th Rd., Bark River, 906/399-9212, www.northernsunwinery.com, 1pm-6pm Wed.-Mon. Apr.-Oct.; 1pm-6pm Fri.-Sun. Nov.-March; 1pm-6pm Fri.-Sun., other days by appointment Apr.-Oct.): Known as an estate winery, Northern Sun, with over five picturesque acres, is an attraction itself as a setting for weddings and concerts. Carefully chosen grapes yield outstanding varieties of reds and whites. Try Marquette, a deep-red table wine that's a great complement to red meat and poultry.

- **Leigh's Garden Winery** (904 Ludington St., Escanaba, 906/553-7799, www.leighsgarden.com, noon-4pm Sun., noon-7pm Tues.-Thurs., noon- 8pm Fri.-Sat. May-Dec.; noon-7pm Thurs. and Sat., noon-8pm Fri. Jan.-March): Offering an extensive list of white, red, rosé, and seasonal varieties, Leigh's can ship your selections anywhere in Michigan.

- **Mackinaw Trail Winery** (103 W. Lakeshore Dr., Manistique, 906/341-2303, www.mackinawtrailwinery.com, noon-7pm Mon.-Thurs., noon-8pm Fri.-Sat., noon-6pm Sun.): The vineyard is in the northern Lower Peninsula, but Mackinaw Trail operates a cozy little tasting room off US 2 near where the Manistique River empties into Lake Michigan. Here you'll find some unusual varieties, including Cranberry, White Ibis, and Traminette, a dry wine that's very compatible with fish.

Best of the Lakes

- **Prettiest beach:** Twelve Mile Beach, Pictured Rocks National Lakeshore

- **Best area for swimming:** Mackinaw City

- **Best place to catch a sunset:** Little Girl's Point

- **Best fishing spot:** Stannard Rock in Lake Superior

- **Best place to sail:** Straits of Mackinac

early summer. Head north from Manistique on M-94 for about 5 miles (8 km), then take a left on Dawson Road. After 1.5 miles (2.4 km), take the access road north to the parking lot. It's definitely worth the detour.

Canoeing and Kayaking

You'll find some of the area's best canoeing in and around Curtis. You can paddle Big Manistique Lake, South Manistique Lake, and the smaller North Manistique Lake, but one of the area's most popular trips will take you down the **Manistique River,** which begins at the west end of Big Manistique Lake and empties into Lake Michigan some 70 miles (113 km) downstream, wending its way through the Seney National Wildlife Refuge. The river constantly twists and turns and promises to be anything but boring. There are a few access points just west of Big Manistique Lake and then a long 27-mile (43-km) stretch between easy take-outs at Mead Creek and Merwin Creek campgrounds. From the other direction, put in to the **Indian River** a good distance north, near Steuben, or farther west, where the river passes beneath Forest Road 13. From here, take the river about 30 miles (48 km) east and south to Indian Lake.

Fishing

The abundant rivers, streams, and large lakes in the area provide this stretch of the Upper Peninsula a bevy of fishing options.

For starters, you can cast a line at Walsh Creek and the Ditch, Creighton, Driggs, and Manistique Rivers, as well as a number of fishing pools. The more than 20,000 acres of the **Manistique Lakes** are generally less than 30 feet (9 meters) deep. Fish found here include muskie, northern pike, walleye, large- and smallmouth bass, perch, and bluegill. You'll also find perch, walleye, and muskie in the warm, shallow waters of **Indian Lake.** Be warned: The Manistique Lakes and Indian Lake are accessible to Jet Skis and water skiers. As an alternative, try the smaller **Camp Seven Lake** (906/341-5666) in Hiawatha National Forest. For more information on popular fishing spots, contact the **Manistique Tourism Council** (800/342-4282, www.visitmanistique. com), the **U.S. Forest Service** (2727 N. Lincoln Rd., Escanaba, 906/786-4062, www. fs.fed.us), or the **Michigan Department of Natural Resources** (906/452-6227, www. michigan.gov/dnr).

Open-water fishing trips can be chartered through **Delta Dawn Charters** (906/396-4001, www.deltadawnchartersup.com), which docks at Manistique for salmon fishing. Morning, afternoon, and evening charters are available. Half-day charters are $450 for up to four people, $50 each for each additional person, up to six total. Full-day charters cost $700 for up to four people, $50 for each additional person, up to five total.

Golf

If you've come to the U.P. to golf, you can find 18 holes at **Indian Lake Golf and Country Course** (1305N Birch St., Manistique, 906/341-5600, www.indianlakegolfcourse. com, $40 for 9 holes with cart, $65 for 18 holes with cart), on the northeast shore of Indian Lake. The course has a pro shop, cart and club rentals, a full bar and restaurant, and bentgrass greens and fairways. There were only nine holes here for more than 70 years, but the club added an additional nine in 2000 and did a thorough renovation of the entire course in 2017. Travel north on M-94 from downtown Manistique for 2.5 miles (4 km), turn left at the school, and travel 1 mile (1.6 km) to the golf course.

Stony Point Golf Course (8102 W. US 2, Manistique, 906/341-3419, www.visitmanistique.com/golf.shtml, mid-Apr.-mid-Nov., $10-28) is a nine-hole course just 2 miles (3.2 km) west of Manistique. The par-35 family-owned course has bent-grass greens and fairways and is nestled in the Upper Peninsula's renowned scenery.

Off-Road Vehicles

Unlike Michigan's Lower Peninsula, the Upper Peninsula allows off-road vehicles to operate on any state forest road, as long as it isn't specifically posted as prohibited. Although much of the U.P. is accessible via these roads, a designated trail system is also set aside specifically for ORV use. Plenty of multiuse trails thread through the U.P. along and north of US 2. Try the 36-mile (58-km) **Sandtown Trail,** just east of the Manistique Lakes. Take M-117 north to Sandtown Road and turn right on Hayes Road to the parking area. The **Brevort-Trout Lake Trail** starts north of Brevort Lake, a short distance from St. Ignace; from here, connect to the Newberry-Rexton Trail and a system of trails that makes its way west. Additionally, all Schoolcraft County roads are open to ORVs, provided you keep to the shoulder at a speed below 25 mph (40 kph). Detailed off-road vehicle maps are available from Michigan Department of Natural Resources (DNR) Service Centers; the closest ones are in Newberry and Marquette. You can also contact the **Manistique Tourism Council** (800/342-4282, www.visitmanistique.com).

WINTER RECREATION
Ski and Snowshoe Trails

The **Indian Lake Pathway** provides some of the area's finest groomed ski trails, with 8.5 miles (13.7 km) of flat to rolling terrain.

Snowmobiling

The area near US 2 and north of Lake Michigan can be traversed by snowmobile on **Trail 2,** which starts in St. Ignace and makes its way west to Escanaba and beyond. Smaller trails, too numerous to list, branch off and provide access to much of the U.P., including state and national forests and the Manistique Lakes. Nearing Manistique, Trail 2 skirts the Seney National Wildlife Refuge before dropping south into town. Take **Trail 41** or **Trail 7** northwest into the Hiawatha National Forest.

Ice Fishing

Fishing on a frozen lake is becoming a popular winter pastime, and if you'd like to try it, the **Manistique Lakes** near Curtis are a great choice. The ice tends to form in early December, providing some of the U.P.'s best seasonal fishing for northern pike, walleye, and perch.

FOOD

If you didn't stop at Clyde's Drive-In No. 3 outside St. Ignace, make a point of going to ★ **Clyde's Drive-In No. 2** (201 Chippewa Ave., 906/341-6021, 11am-8pm Sun.-Thurs., 11am-9pm Fri.-Sat., $11-15) in Manistique. You'll find the same old-school service, malts, and Big C burgers as at Clyde's other well-known U.P. drive-ins. You'll swear they're among the most delicious burgers you've ever tasted.

ACCOMMODATIONS

Several **chain motels** are represented along US 2, especially near Manistique, but there are also several independent motels. Let's hope places like **Star Motel** (1142 E. Lakeshore Dr., 906/341-5363, $) continue to thrive. Located about 2 miles (3.2 km) east of Manistique on US 2, this tidy, 1950s motel has large, clean rooms, attentive owners, and a tranquil setting on the lake. It allows well-behaved dogs.

Camping

Sherman's Resort & Campground (W18155 Nezor Point Rd., Curtis, 906/586-6761, www.shermansresort.com, campsites $30) offers both cabin rentals and campsites right on beautiful South Manistique Lake. With 800 feet (245 meters) of pristine beach and numerous modern campsites, complete with a bathhouse and fire pits, it's truly an idyllic lodging choice. The resort also offers a variety of comfortable two- and three-bedroom cabins and chalets. Rates vary depending on the season and length of stay.

The **Log Cabin Resort and Campground** (W18042 County Rd. H-42, Curtis, 906/586-9732 or 888/879-6448, www.uplogcabin.com, campsites $30-45, weekly rates available) has 600 feet (185 meters) of Big Manistique Lake frontage on more than 23 acres. You'll find boat slips, a games room, a sandy beach, and 50 campsites, 34 of which are full-service RV sites. There are also 10 cabins ($$, weekly rates available) of various sizes, sleeping anywhere from 4 to 13 people.

Highly popular **Indian Lake State Park** (8970 W. County Rd. 442, 906/341-2355, www.michigan.gov/dnr, $20-26) has two units, one on the lake's south shore and another 3 miles (4.8 km) away on the west shore. Both have modern campgrounds with boat launches. The western unit campsites, not on the water, tend to be less busy. If you're looking for a waterfront site in the southern unit, plan to arrive midweek or during the off-season, and keep your fingers crossed. To reach the park from Manistique, take US 2 to Thompson, then go north on M-149 and east on County Road 442. To reach the west unit, stay on M-149.

About 20 miles (32 km) north of Manistique, just off M-94, the **Indian River Campground** (Hiawatha National Forest, 906/341-5666, single site $22, double $44) operates from May 15 to September 7, and sits on a bluff overlooking the Indian River. The 10 private wooded sites provide plenty of seclusion and a feeling of solitude despite the camp's close proximity to the highway. This is an excellent stop for paddlers making their way down the Indian River Canoe Trail, offering clean drinking water, picnic tables, and grills.

The larger **Camp Seven Lake Campground** (906/341-5666, $22-52 depending on amenities), in the Hiawatha National Forest, operates from May 15 to September 30 and has 41 campsites, each with a table and a fire ring. Camp Seven Lake is perfect for boating, fishing, swimming, and hiking along a 3-mile (4.8-km) trail. Take County Road 442 8 miles (12.9 km) east of Forest Road 13, about 24 miles (39 km) northwest of Manistique.

INFORMATION AND SERVICES

The **Manistique Tourist Council** (800/342-4282, www.visitmanistique.com) is the source for visitor information in Manistique. You can also contact the **Schoolcraft County Chamber of Commerce** (1000 W. Lakeshore Dr., Manistique, 906/341-5010) and the **Michigan DNR** (906/228-6561, www.michigan.gov/dnr).

Schoolcraft Memorial Hospital (500 Main St., Manistique, 906/341-3200, www.scmh.org) is 0.25 miles (4 km) east of M-94. For banking and an ATM, stop at **State Savings Bank** (101 S. Cedar St., 906/341-4600) or one of Manistique's several other banks.

GETTING THERE AND AROUND
Car

US 2 winds from St. Ignace, just north of the bridge, for about 90 miles (145 km) before it runs into Manistique. It continues to Escanaba and on toward Wisconsin, but the long, easy stretch between St. Ignace and Manistique parallels the lakeshore for much of the drive. You'll want to detour on highways north and south of US 2 along the way. Coming from Wisconsin, take US 41 north from Green Bay, cross into Michigan at the twin cities of Marinette, Wisconsin, and Menominee, Michigan, then take M-35 north to US 2 and Manistique. From Munising on the Lake Superior shore, drive south on M-94.

Boat

The **Manistique Marina** (906/341-6841, www.

michigan.gov/dnr), located where the river flows into Lake Michigan, offers a small selection of seasonal and transient slips. There's a harbormaster on duty mid-June to September 1 who can be reached on channel 9 or 68. Marina coordinates are 45°57.08 N, 86°14.08 W.

Bus
Regular bus service is provided to Manistique as well as several small towns along US 2 by **Indian Trails** (800/292-3831, www.indiantrails.com), originating from St. Ignace, Escanaba, and Milwaukee.

Garden Peninsula

The Garden Peninsula, just a short 20-mile (32-km) drive past Manistique, is a quiet, peaceful point of land, filled with little-used asphalt roads perfect for cycling and a handful of sleepy farms and orchards. **Garden,** the largest city on the peninsula, is a pleasant stop on the way to Fayette, the Upper Peninsula's most famous ghost town. The moderate climate and scenic beauty make the peninsula one of the U.P.'s more attractive destinations.

SIGHTS
Garden Peninsula Historical Museum
If you're curious about the town of Garden and its history, stop at the **Garden Peninsula Historical Museum** (State St./M-183, 906/644-2165, 11am-3pm Wed.-Thurs., 1pm-3pm Sun. Memorial Day-Labor Day, donation). A quaint museum, it's located in a former one-room schoolhouse and has exhibits about the community's history, such as the logging and fishing industries. Those interested in the genealogy of the area should check out the research library.

★ Fayette Historic State Park
By far the Garden Peninsula's most notable attraction is **Fayette Historic State Park** (4785 II Rd., 906/644-2603, www.michigan.gov/dnr). If you make time for just one stop in this region of the U.P., make it this outstanding state park, once the site of a large smelting operation. Fayette's limestone furnaces converted raw iron ore from U.P. mines into pig iron that was loaded onto barges bound for Escanaba. In the 1880s, this gritty

industrial town claimed a population of 500, and its loud, hot blast furnaces worked seven days a week. By 1891, the nearby forests that provided the furnaces with fuel were all but depleted, while more efficient steelmaking methods were coming into use. The furnaces shut down, leading to the town's demise.

Nearly a century later, Fayette was reborn as a wonderfully restored historic site and state park. Today, Fayette is one of the nation's most scenic ghost towns, its dozen limestone buildings tucked alongside the sheer white bluffs and deep clear waters of Snail Shell Harbor. Start at the visitors center, which gives a good historical overview and features a helpful scale model of the village. You can wander in and out of the hotel, opera house, homes, and other buildings, some intact, some more decayed. Horse-drawn carriage rides and boat tours are available from Memorial Day to Labor Day. The town can be explored at any time, and a very early morning or off-season visit can add to the ghostly appeal of the place, a big plus when one considers the obvious irony of a crowded ghost town.

While the historic townsite is certainly the biggest draw, don't overlook the rest of the 750-acre park. It includes a semi-modern campground (offering electricity but no modern restrooms or showers) and several miles of hiking trails, including one that swings north along the bluffs above Snail Shell Harbor.

Fairport
If commercial fishing interests you, continue south on County Road 483 to Fairport, near

- The toll for an automobile crossing the Mackinac Bridge today is $4. When the bridge opened in 1957, it was $3.75—equivalent to $39.06 today.

- In 1923, Harvey Firestone, Thomas Edison, and Henry Ford embarked on a camping trip to the Upper Peninsula. Their favorable impression of the area motivated them to make considerable investments here, including the Thunder Bay Inn.

- Isle Royale National Park, an archipelago in Lake Superior, is Michigan's only national park, and the fourth least visited property in the National Park System. In a typical year, it receives only 16,000 visitors.

- The word "Yooper" as a vernacular for a resident of the Upper Peninsula only dates to the 1970s.

- The northwestern portion of the Upper Peninsula, including the Keweenaw, is the only place in the United States where Finnish Americans are a majority.

- Ironwood, the westernmost city in the U.P., is 600 miles (970 km) from Detroit—approximately the same distance from Detroit to New York City.

the tip of the peninsula, where a commercial fleet still operates. There's little else in this small town, but it's fun to watch the comings and goings of the fishing boats, especially in midafternoon, when they usually return with the day's catch.

FESTIVALS AND EVENTS
Fayette Heritage Day

Fayette Historic State Park comes to life during the annual **Fayette Heritage Day** festival (www.michigan.gov/dnr), celebrating the town's history. The second Saturday in August brings visitors to the state park for period music, food, and displays that channel the ghost town's once busy iron-smelting days.

SUMMER RECREATION
Hiking and Biking

There's more to **Fayette Historic State Park** (4785 II Rd., 906/644-2603, www.michigan.gov/dnr) than the historic townsite. A 5-mile (8-km) footpath affords views of the ghost town from the area's limestone bluffs, and some 17 miles (27 km) of trails wind through the forests surrounding the town. **Portage Bay State Forest Campground** (906/452-6227, www.michigan.gov/dnr) has just over 2 miles (3.2 km) of nice

trails on the Ninga Aki Pathway. Take M-183 (which becomes County Road 483) south from Garden for 10 miles (16.1 km).

Canoeing and Kayaking

If you're into kayaking—and sea kayaking in particular—you won't want to miss the opportunity to put in to Lake Michigan at **Fayette Historic State Park.** From here, head north to Snake Island and Garden Bay or south to Sac Bay. The waters close to shore are suitable for all but the least experienced kayakers, offering views of towering limestone cliffs and sandy beaches. Experienced kayakers can head south from the southern point to nose around the offshore islands, but there's plenty of open water involved, so caution is advised.

Fishing

Although the most adventurous fishing in the area can be found in the Bays de Noc, you'll be able to find some fishing at **Fayette Historic State Park** and the campground at **Portage Bay State Forest** (906/452-6227, www.michigan.gov/dnr). Both sites offer fishing from the shore—from a pier at Fayette or directly from the shoreline at Portage Bay. Both sites are known for lake trout, steelhead, and coho salmon. A good source for equipment,

☆ The Bays de Noc

With the possible exception of Green Bay, Lake Michigan's best-known inlets are the Bays de Noc. The Big and Little Bays are positioned at the northwest end of the lake and are known primarily for their world-class walleye fishing. Equally popular is the water itself—there are more than 120,000 acres of water between the two bays, making them one of the U.P.'s top summer destinations for fishing, boating, paddling, and swimming.

Both bays are defined by the area's two peninsulas. The Garden Peninsula serves as the eastern shore for Big Bay de Noc and separates it from Lake Michigan. The Stonington Peninsula forms the buffer of land that separates Big Bay de Noc from its smaller cousin, Little Bay de Noc.

The name of the bays refers to the Noquet (or Noc) people, Native Americans thought to be related to the Menominee. While Big and Little Bays de Noc have similarities (they share the title of Walleye Capital of the Midwest), there are differences. Little Bay de Noc is more developed along its shores, playing host to both Escanaba and Gladstone. The water is deeper than in its counterpart to the east, which allowed for ships carrying pig iron from Fayette to arrive and for lumber from area sawmills to be exported. Big Bay de Noc, on the other hand, is more rural, representative of the recreational character of the entire Upper Peninsula.

GET ON THE WATER

- **Fishing:** The bays are known for fishing, particularly for walleye during the fall. Many of the fishing charters and outfitters in the area are based out of Gladstone and nearby Rapid River (page 105).

- **Boating:** With 90,000 acres of water, Big Bay de Noc has some of the area's best boating. Landings can be found at Fayette Historic State Park and Garden Bay (page 96).

- **Kayaking:** Experienced open-water kayakers can paddle Little Bay de Noc. Rentals are available in Escanaba (page 104).

bait, and advice is **EFF'N OutFitters** (W7440 G 18 Rd., Daggett, 906/630-1492, www. effnoutfitters.guide).

Boating

With 90,000 acres of water, the larger of Delta County's two bays, **Big Bay de Noc,** fills the gap between the Garden Peninsula and Stonington Peninsula to the west, providing some of the area's best boating. There are boat landings at Fayette Historic State Park and Garden Bay, as well as at Little Fishdam River (to the north) and Nahma (a few miles south of US 2 on County Road 497). Fayette Historic State Park's Snail Shell Harbor has 300 feet (90 meters) of dock available for overnight or day use, and the waters are deep enough for larger craft. Boaters in search of larger marinas will need to dock at Gladstone or Escanaba on Little Bay de Noc

or at Manistique to the east, on the opposite side of the Garden Peninsula.

Beaches

Sac Bay Beach (906/786-4902 or 906/786-1020, www.deltacountyparks.com), located on Lake Michigan's **Big Bay de Noc,** is a 65-acre county park and beach. The beach is no-frills, offering a sandy lakeshore, a small play area, and a few picnic tables. It makes a nice rest stop while traveling the Garden Peninsula. **Fayette Historic State Park** also has a small swimming beach just south of the town.

Golf

While especially serious golfers may want to head west to the Bays de Noc golf trail near Escanaba, there is one golf course in the Garden Peninsula. **The Nahma Golf Club** (8588 LL Rd., 906/644-2648, http://

nahmagolfclub.com, $14 for 9 holes, $20 for 18 holes) consists of nine holes on fairly flat terrain, while offering unbeatable scenery. Cart rentals are available at additional cost ($12 for 9 holes, $20 for 18 holes). Take County Road 494 (or LI Road) south of US 2.

WINTER RECREATION
Ski and Snowshoe Trails
The same Garden Peninsula trails that make for popular summertime hiking become pathways through the Upper Peninsula's winter wonderland. The 5 miles (8 km) of trails that overlook the **Fayette Historic State Park** (4785 II Rd., 906/644-2603, www.michigan.gov/dnr) are regularly groomed for skiing each winter. Although the path is suitable for beginners, more advanced skiers will enjoy the views of Big Bay de Noc and the town, even if they do miss the challenge of a more difficult trail. Strap on some snowshoes for a trek through the townsite itself—although it can be brutally cold, you'll bypass the summer tourist crowds.

Snowmobiling
Connect to the U.P. snowmobile trail system via **Trail 415** (the only designated snowmobile trail in the Garden Peninsula), which starts in the city of Garden and makes its way north to Trail 2. From there, the U.P. is yours.

FOOD
As its name implies, **Sherry's Port Bar** (4424 Old 483, 906/644-2545, noon-10pm Sun.-Thurs., noon-midnight Fri., noon-2am Sat.), south of Garden, is primarily a drinking establishment, but it has managed to become a catch-all family restaurant with reasonably priced food and a hearty breakfast. Burgers and steaks are $12 and $30, respectively. Its proximity to Fayette Historic State Park makes it a popular stop.

ACCOMMODATIONS
On the north end of Big Bay de Noc and the Garden Peninsula, where US 2 and M-183 meet, **Moose Manor Resort & Motel** (16086 US 2, Cooks, 906/644-2318, www.

mooseresort.com, mid-Apr.-Nov., $$) has 12 modestly priced rooms, two with kitchenettes. The resort offers lake access, beach views, and, best of all, a diner-style restaurant next door.

Camping
Camping is readily available at dozens of rustic campgrounds within Hiawatha National Forest, and a particularly nice one is the very secluded—and difficult to reach—**Portage Bay State Forest Campground** (906/644-2603, from $15) on the Garden Peninsula's eastern shore. It's southeast of Garden, at the end of Portage Bay Road. For modern campsites, the best bets are often state parks (reservations 800/447-2757, www.michigan.gov/dnr) like **Indian Lake State Park** or **Fayette Historic State Park.**

INFORMATION AND SERVICES
For visitor information and assistance for the Garden Peninsula, contact **Visit Escanaba** (1001 N. Lincoln Rd., Escanaba, 906/789-7862, www.visitescanaba.com) or the **Delta County Chamber of Commerce** (1001 N. Lincoln Rd., Escanaba, 906/786-2192 or 888/335-8264, www.deltami.org).

Bank choices are limited in Garden, but you can do some banking at **First Bank Upper Michigan** (6322 State St., Garden, 906/644-3535, www.first-bank.com, 10am-4pm Mon.-Fri.). An ATM is offered.

Your best option for medical attention will be to head to Manistique to the **Schoolcraft Memorial Hospital** (7870W US 2, Manistique, 906/341-3200, www.scmh.org).

GETTING THERE AND AROUND
Having your own vehicle is really your only viable option for getting to and around the Garden Peninsula. There's no public transportation and no airport south of US 2, and although there are boat landings and docks at Fayette Historic State Park, Garden Bay, and Portage Bay, there are no large marinas such as those in Escanaba, St. Ignace, or Manistique.

Escanaba and Vicinity

A large city by U.P. standards, Escanaba and neighboring Gladstone (just a few miles north) are home to some 20,000 people, serving as the industrial and commercial center for the south-central Upper Peninsula. The natural deepwater port gave Escanaba its start during the Civil War, when a hastily built rail line linked the iron mines in Negaunee with the port, bringing needed raw materials to support the Union war effort. Today iron ore is still shipped out of Escanaba's modern port facilities in the form of iron-clay taconite pellets, bound for steelmakers in the Lower Peninsula, Indiana, and Ohio. Best of all, if you started your day near the Garden Peninsula, Escanaba is less than 50 miles (80 km) away, a drive of 80 minutes.

Unlike M-35 north of Gladstone, the stretch of highway from Gladstone to Menominee runs close to the coast, and it has been designated the **U.P. Hidden Coast Recreation Heritage Route.** You can follow it south from Gladstone to the Wisconsin border.

SIGHTS
Downtown Escanaba

Downtown Escanaba focuses on Ludington Street, an east-west route that runs from M-35 to the waterfront. Here's where you'll find most of the town's restaurants, shops, and a growing local arts community. If you're interested in astronomy, check out Walk of the Planets, a network of sidewalk kiosks scattered around downtown, each of which focuses on a particular planet of the solar system.

At the foot of Ludington Street, lovely **Ludington Park** offers paved pathways along the water and to a small island (in-line skates permitted), interpretive signs explaining local history, a band shell that hosts concerts

1: Fayette Historic State Park 2: whitecaps on Little Bay de Noc

on Wednesday and Sunday evenings in summer, a playground, a beach, tennis courts, and a boat launch.

Escanaba's art scene can perhaps best be witnessed during a visit to the **William Bonifas Art Center** (700 1st Ave. S., 906/786-3833, www.bonifasarts.org, 10am-5:30pm Tues.-Fri., 10am-3pm Sat.), a community arts facility housed in a 1938 building that was originally a gymnasium and auditorium. Today, the center hosts changing free gallery exhibits, theatrical productions, and classes. The **East Ludington Gallery** (1007 Ludington St., 906/786-0300, www.eastludingtongallery.com, 10am-4pm Wed.-Fri., 10am-3pm Sat.) displays and sells works by more than 35 regional artists.

Delta County Historical Society

Just east of the intersection of Ludington Street and Lake Shore Drive is the **Delta County Historical Museum** (16 Beaumier Way, 906/786-6790, www.deltahistorical.org/museum.htm, 11am-4pm daily Memorial Day-Labor Day, $3 adults, $1 children, $5 family), which has interesting and informative displays on local logging, Native American cultures, military history, and maritime history. The four-room museum has been collecting historical documents and artifacts for more than 50 years, and the result is an important documentation of regional heritage.

Lighthouses

One of Ludington Park's most popular attractions is the **Sand Point Lighthouse** (end of Ludington St., 906/786-6790, 9am-5pm daily Memorial Day-Aug., 1pm-4pm daily Sept., donation), an 1868 brick light that was restored and reopened in 1990 by the Delta County Historical Society. It was a big job: In the 1940s, the Coast Guard remodeled the obsolete light for staff housing, removing the

Escanaba

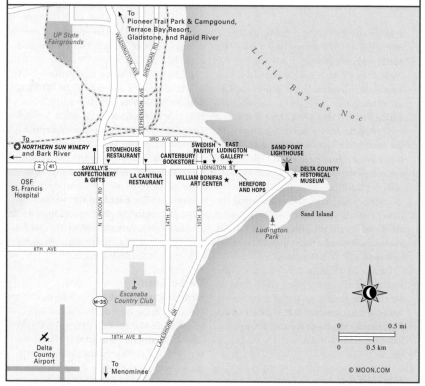

To
Pioneer Trail Park & Campground,
Terrace Bay Resort,
Gladstone, and Rapid River

UP State Fairgrounds

WASHINGTON AVE
SHERIDAN RD
STEPHENSON AVE

Little Bay de Noc

3RD AVE N

To
NORTHERN SUN WINERY
and Bark River

2 41

STONEHOUSE
RESTAURANT

SAYKLLY'S
CONFECTIONERY
& GIFTS

OSF
St. Francis
Hospital

N LINCOLN RD

LA CANTINA
RESTAURANT

CANTERBURY
BOOKSTORE

SWEDISH
PANTRY

LUDINGTON ST

WILLIAM BONIFAS
ART CENTER

14TH ST

10TH ST

EAST
LUDINGTON
GALLERY

HEREFORD
AND HOPS

SAND POINT
LIGHTHOUSE

DELTA COUNTY
HISTORICAL
MUSEUM

Sand Island

Ludington
Park

8TH AVE

M-35

Escanaba
Country Club

LAKESHORE DR

18TH AVE S

Delta
County
Airport

To
Menominee

0   0.5 mi
0   0.5 km

© MOON.COM

lantern room and the top 10 feet (3 meters) of the tower. You can climb the tower and take a look at the restored keeper's house. The light's first custodian, by the way, was Mary Terry, one of the nation's earliest female lightkeepers. The Delta County Historical Museum is nearby.

At the tip of the Stonington Peninsula, across Little Bay de Noc from Escanaba, **Peninsula Point Lighthouse Park** (9am-5pm Mon.-Fri. Memorial Day-Labor Day, 1pm-4pm Tues.-Wed. Sept., free) is the perfect place to sprawl out on a sunny day: an open meadow, a grassy picnic area, a great shoreline for beachcombing, and—the main attraction—an 1865 lighthouse. Climb the spiral stairway for one of the most expansive views around: a 270-degree survey of Green

Bay, and in clear weather even Wisconsin's Door County. The lighthouse was abandoned in the 1930s and replaced by a more effective shoal light several miles offshore. Local volunteers restored and reopened the old light, but it was subsequently ravaged by fire in 1959. The keeper's home was destroyed, but the tower survived the blaze. The lighthouse is operated by the Hiawatha National Forest. To get to the landmark, follow US 41 north from Escanaba, which will become US 2 at Rapid River. Continue on US 2 to County Road 513 T. Turn left and continue the entire length of the Stonington Peninsula. The road will end at the lighthouse, which lies at the southern tip of the peninsula.

1: Canterbury Book Store **2:** Sand Point Lighthouse

★ Hiawatha National Forest

The 860,000-acre **Hiawatha National Forest** spans much of the central U.P., with its western unit stretching from the Lake Michigan shoreline of the Stonington Peninsula to the Lake Superior shore near Munising. For information on hiking trails, campgrounds, canoe routes, and other attractions, stop at the **Visitor Information Station** (8181 US 2, just east of Rapid River, 906/474-6442, 8am-4:30pm Mon.-Fri.). You can talk with rangers and pick up a wide selection of maps and handouts. The station also includes interpretive displays and a small bookshop.

SHOPPING

Among the interesting shops in downtown Escanaba is **Canterbury Book Store** (908 Ludington St., 906/786-0751, https://canterburybookstore.com, 10am-5:30pm Mon.-Fri., 11am-4pm Sat.), a longtime community bookstore with a well-curated selection of both new and used titles. Owners Rebecca Bender and Jesse Traub are true bibliophiles. They'll happily order you any book not represented in their stock.

Sayklly's Confectionery & Gifts (1304 Ludington St., 906/786-1524, www.saykllys.com, 10am-5pm Mon.-Fri., 10am-3pm Sat.) is one of those unexpected special places you find that make a vacation more memorable. A community institution since 1906, Sayklly's has been producing and selling delicious treats including assorted chocolates, peanut brittle, and saltwater taffy to generations of visitors and locals alike. They even ship anywhere in the world. Their U.P. notoriety earned them national attention when the company was featured on the Food Network's *Unwrapped* in 2011. The store also features unique gift items from manufacturers such as Lladro, Waterford, Swarovski, and Dept. 56.

ENTERTAINMENT
Island Resort and Casino
Harris, a small town some 13 miles (21 km) west of Escanaba, has one of the U.P.'s finest gaming resorts. **Island Resort and Casino** (W399 US 2/41, 906/466-2941 or 800/682-6040, www.chipincasino.com) is a 24/7 casino with more than 1,400 slot machines and plenty of table games, such as craps, blackjack, roulette, poker, and Texas hold 'em. When you get hungry, stop at the Firekeeper's Restaurant for a cheap breakfast and lunch or daily all-you-can-eat dinner specials. Other on-site dining can be found at the 5 Bridges Steak & Seafood House, Coral Reef Grille, and T. McC's Sports Bar. The Island Showroom seats more than 1,300 for headliner shows; for local acts, visit Club Four One for weekly live bands and comedy nights every Sunday. A golf course, a 113-room hotel with an indoor pool, a salon, and an RV park cement Island Resort's reputation as one of the Midwest's premier resort destinations.

★ Northern Sun Winery
In Bark River, just a short drive west of Escanaba, you'll find another addition to the growing list of Upper Peninsula wineries. Visiting the **Northern Sun Winery** (983 10th Rd., 906/399-9212, www.northernsunwinery.com, 1pm-6pm Wed.-Mon. Apr.-Oct., 1pm-6pm Thurs.-Sun. and by appointment only Mon.-Wed. Nov.-Mar.) will make you feel like you've been transported to the French countryside. The vintners have perfected the art of growing high-quality grapes in a region that was often thought to be inhospitable. Northern Sun produces a variety of wines ranging from the Marquette, a deep red, medium-bodied wine, to the Léon Millot, a fruity wine with subtle notes of raspberry, cherry, and chocolate. From Escanaba, take US 2 west for 10 miles (16.1 km) before turning onto D Road. Continue on D Road for 2 miles (3.2 km) until you come to 10th Road, and make a right. Go one more mile (1.6 km) on 10th Road and you'll see the winery on your left. Please note that the hours of operation are posted in eastern time—an important consideration since the winery is very close to the time zone border.

FESTIVALS AND EVENTS

Upper Peninsula State Fair

On M-35 between Escanaba and Gladstone, you'll pass the U.P. State Fair Grounds. For decades Michigan had the rare distinction of hosting two state fairs, an event in Detroit as well as its Upper Peninsula counterpart. However, the tumultuous economy of the early 21st century caused the State of Michigan to end many traditions, and the fairs unfortunately were among them. Since 2010 the U.P. edition has been operated by the Upper Peninsula State Fair Authority, a quasi-public body governed by a board consisting of representatives from all 15 Upper Peninsula counties. (In 2013 a private nonprofit revived Detroit's edition of the fair in suburban Novi.) The **Upper Peninsula State Fair** (906/786-4011, www.upstatefair.net) continues to be held during the third week of August. For additional information, contact the **Delta County Chamber of Commerce** (1001 N. Lincoln Rd., Escanaba, 906/786-2192 or 888/335-8264, www.deltami.org).

Balloons on the Bay and Pioneer Days

The combination is interesting, to say the least—hot air balloons and pioneer heritage. Every year in late June, the U.P. State Fair Grounds become the staging area for hot air balloons that fill the sky above Lake Michigan. Jump in the basket for a tethered balloon ride or experience a bit of the old days while watching lumberjack exhibitions, old-fashioned craft demonstrations, and a barbecue cook-off. For more information, contact the **Delta County Chamber of Commerce** (1001 N. Lincoln Rd., Escanaba, 906/786-2192 or 888/335-8264, www.deltami.org).

Monarch Migration

There really isn't anything official about the annual monarch butterfly migration, aside from volunteers, organized by the U.S. Forest Service, who count the populations and help tag the insects for tracking. But when it comes to monarch viewing, you can join the throng of enthusiasts who make the trek to the **Stonington Peninsula** each August. The peninsula, which extends south into Lake Michigan between the Bays de Noc, is an annual gathering point in the butterflies' great migration south to Mexico; they stop in and around Peninsula Point Lighthouse Park before the long flight across Green Bay and the open waters of the lake. The brilliant orange and black monarchs are best seen in August, although the migration continues into September, often overlapping with the autumn colors Michigan is known for, and combining to form a stunning display of color.

SUMMER RECREATION

Hiking and Biking

Bay de Noc/Grand Island Trail

Hiawatha National Forest's 40-mile (64-km) **Bay de Noc/Grand Island Trail** follows an old Ojibwa portage route, used to carry canoes and supplies between Lakes Michigan and Superior. Today it ends just short of both lakes, beginning just northeast of Rapid River and ending 10 miles (16.1 km) shy of Lake Superior at Ackerman Lake. The trail parallels the Whitefish River, about 0.5-2 miles (0.8-3.2 km) away, tracing its eastern bluff and offering high, sweeping views of the forested river valley. Along the way, it hopscotches over several streams and passes a number of inland lakes. The high density of hardwoods makes the route especially beautiful during the fall color season.

Horses and mountain bikes are allowed on the Bay de Noc/Grand Island Trail, but not motorized vehicles. Primitive camping is permitted throughout the national forest, and no permit is required. To find the trailhead, follow US 2 east from Rapid River for 2 miles (3.2 km), then turn left on County Road 509 and drive another 1.5 miles (2.4 km). You'll see a parking area on the west side of the road.

Pine Marten Run

A few miles east of the Hiawatha National Forest Visitor Information Station, turn north off US 2 onto County Road H-13 to reach the great hiking and mountain biking trails of **Pine Marten Run.** The trail network lies between the Indian River to the north, County Road 440 to the south, Forest Road 2258 to the west, and County Road 437 to the east. This newly signed area includes 26 miles (42 km) of rolling single-track and overgrown double-track. Various loops wind through groves of huge hemlocks and white pines, a dozen lakes, and the stunning Indian River. From County Road H-13, turn right on County Road 440, and watch for the Forest Service sign directing you to Iron Jaw Lake. Alternatively, head north from County Road 440 on Forest Road 2258, where you'll find another trailhead just before the road crosses the Indian River. Maps and more information are available from the Hiawatha National Forest Visitor Information Station (US 2, just east of Rapid River, 906/474-6442).

Days River Pathway

Just 3 miles (4.8 km) north of Gladstone, the Escanaba River State Forest maintains the **Days River Pathway,** a fine 9-mile (14.5-km) hiking trail that loops through forest and along the scenic Days River, which cuts a deep gorge near the trailhead. This is a good stream for brook trout, so be sure to bring a fly rod. A camera and a set of binoculars are useful too since the area is thick with warblers and other songbirds. To reach the trailhead, follow US 2 east of Gladstone 3 miles (4.8 km), then turn left onto Days River Road. For more information, contact the **Escanaba Forest Area Office** (906/293-3293, www.michigan.gov/dnr).

Stonington Peninsula

On the opposite side of Little Bay de Noc, the **Stonington Peninsula** is largely bypassed by travelers, as it lacks accessible sandy beaches and significant commercial attractions. It's a soft and peaceful place, with smooth slabs of bedrock shoreline and sunny meadows that have reclaimed abandoned farmland. The Hiawatha National Forest manages a nice

stretch of shoreline along the peninsula's west side, including a few campgrounds and hiking trails. Look for the Forest Service signs south of Garth Point. The peninsula preserves several stands of old-growth hemlock, hardwood, and pine. One of the most notable examples is now protected as the **Squaw Creek Old Growth Area,** a part of the Hiawatha National Forest. Though these woods are not virgin timber, 19th-century loggers practiced selective cutting, quite unusual in those days, and left behind several large trees that have grown to be enormous. Trails are few—you'll find just a couple of abandoned logging roads open only to foot traffic. Walking is easy, however, since the high shade canopy created by the trees crowds out the underbrush usually found in the woods. Be sure to take a compass, or use the compass app on your smartphone.

The southern part of the 65-acre tract is particularly scenic, with the clear tea-colored waters of Squaw Creek sloshing between the massive trunks. You'll find the largest hemlocks south of the creek and huge hardwoods just to the north. Squaw Creek is not marked by a sign and shows up on only a few maps. To find it, drive south 9 miles (14.5 km) on County Road 513; just before and after the road crosses the creek, you'll see turnouts on the east side of the road and old roads leading inland.

Canoeing and Kayaking

In the Hiawatha National Forest, the **Indian River Canoe and Kayak Trail** offers some of the most scenic paddling in the entire Upper Peninsula. Beginning at Doe Lake (easily accessible by County Road H-44), the river meanders for 51 miles (82 km), making it ideal for a two-day trip. The river progresses in a southeastern direction before reaching its terminus at Indian Lake. The route passes by northern hardwoods, mixed conifers, gentle rolling hills, and marshlands. The Forest Service recommends waiting until mid-June. Prior to that, the water can be particularly high and fast.

Just north of Pine Marten Run and the

Indian River, the **Big Island Lake Canoeing Area** offers paddlers a quiet chain of nine lakes. Since there are few launches for power-boats, the lakes usually remain quite peaceful even in the height of summer. Again, be sure to obtain information and maps from the Hiawatha National Forest Visitor Information Station (US 2, just east of Rapid River, 906/474-6442); they will be a great asset during your adventure.

You'll find good paddling on the **Escanaba River.** Put in northwest of Gladstone and take the river all the way to Green Bay. There are more than 40 miles (64 km) of good paddling between Gwinn and Gladstone, with periodic access points; most of the river is suitable for those with moderate experience, though some sections are more challenging.

You can paddle a few miles along the **Ford River,** southwest of Gladstone. Beginners can take the river between County Road 414 and US 2, but there's some white water as you get closer to Green Bay. There's an access point at US 2 if you're nervous about continuing. Experienced open-water kayakers can paddle **Little Bay de Noc** and **Green Bay.** Rent a canoe, kayak, or other boat from **Richards Boatworks and Splash Rentals** (4528 E. M-35, Escanaba, 906/789-1009, 9am-6pm Mon.-Fri., 10am-2pm Sat.).

Fishing

Although it's the smaller of the two bays, **Little Bay de Noc,** with more than 30,000 acres of water, is still a sight to behold. **Delta Dawn Charters** (1328 Lake Shore Dr., Gladstone, 906/396-4001, www.deltadawnchartersup.com, full day $550 for 1-2 people, half day $450 for 1-2 people) is a great way to fish Little Bay de Noc and its environs. Captain Bill Myers is a seasoned pro who will lead you to the best spots for trout, salmon, smallmouth bass, and walleye. Rapid River's **Bay de Noc Charters** (7989 US 2, Rapid River, 906/474-9334, www.baydenoccharters.net, 6 hours $350 for 2 people, $375 for 3 people), on the northern tip of the bay, can take you on a fishing trip in

Little Bay de Noc, and charters into Big Bay de Noc are available as well. Gladstone is home to a bevy of fishing charters; contact **Visit Escanaba** (1001 N. Lincoln Rd., Escanaba, 800/533-4386, www.visitescanaba.com) to see what's offered.

Local tackle shops and outfitters include **Bay View Bait and Tackle Shop** (7110 US 2, 41 M-35, Gladstone, 906/786-1488, 8am-5pm daily) and **Walleye's Choice** (10132 M-35, Gladstone, 906/428-1488 or 888/883-4741, www.walleyeschoice.com, hours vary). Walleye's Choice also offers full- or half-day fishing trips to either of the Bays de Noc.

If you decide to fish from the shore, cast a line into the **Whitefish River,** which flows into Little Bay de Noc at Rapid River, for trout and smallmouth bass.

Beaches

In Gladstone, visit **Van Cleve Park** (906/428-2916) on Lake Shore Drive. There's a sandy beach for swimming in the waters of Little Bay de Noc, and a number of other facilities make this one of the area's best beaches for family fun—a fitness course, sand volleyball courts, horseshoes, basketball courts, a softball diamond, a gazebo, a playground, and more. You'll find the beautiful Gladstone Harbor here as well.

Golf

Golfing in the Upper Peninsula is like most U.P. activities—casual and unpretentious, without the pomp found at more expensive destinations. One of the U.P.'s finest golf trails consists of four top-notch courses in Delta County, each within 20 minutes of the others. The **Escanaba Country Club** (1800 11th Ave. S., 906/786-4430, www.escanabacc.com, 9 holes $20 walking, $30 with cart, 18 holes $30 walking, $45 with cart) is the oldest country club in Delta County, founded in 1915. The 18-hole par-71 course has a PGA professional on staff and one of the hardest finishing holes around.

Nearby **Gladstone Golf Club** (6514 Days River Rd., 906/428-9646, www.gladstonegolf.

com, 9 holes $20 walking, $30 with cart, 18 holes $30 walking, $38 with cart) is surrounded by scores of acres of forest. The Days River runs through 5 of the 18 holes. Take US 2 about 3 miles (4.8 km) north of Gladstone, turn left on County Road 446, and proceed for 2 miles (3.2 km).

One of the best courses in the area, the 18-hole **Terrace Bluff Golf Club** (7146 P Rd., Gladstone, 906/428-2343, www.terracebluff. com, 9 holes $21, $33 with cart, 18 holes $32, $49 with cart) features views of the bay and is suitable for golfers of every skill level. The amenities of the Terrace Bay Resort and Convention Center are close at hand. Finally, 7 miles (11.3 km) west of Escanaba on US 2, the **Highland Golf Club** (US 2, Bark River, 906/466-2791, www.highlandgolfclub.net, 9 holes $20 walking, $30 with cart, 18 holes $30 walking, $40 with cart) was Delta County's first 18-hole course.

Off-Road Vehicles

The **Forest Islands Trail** begins about 10 miles (16.1 km) south of Escanaba, west of M-35. Take 4.25 Road to H Road and turn right, then turn left on F Road to the parking area. The 33-mile (53-km) trail ends in Cedar River and is broken into the Limpert Road Loop, the Seven Mile Marsh Loop, and the Westman Road Loop near Cedar River at the south end of the trail.

WINTER RECREATION
Downhill Skiing

The Escanaba area is only a short distance east of Iron Mountain and the Upper Peninsula's best-known skiing runs, but beginning and intermediate skiers can try **Gladstone Sports Park** (900 N. Bluff Dr., 906/428-9130, http://gladstonemi.org, hours vary, $12 skiing, $10 tubing), just east of the city. It's a relatively low-key resort, but its combination of easy hills and tubing runs makes it ideal for families who want to avoid the crowds and prices of the bigger resorts to the west. There are a few rope tows and a T-bar, three tube runs with the only return lifts in the U.P., and a snowboard terrain park that includes a half pipe for riders. Food and drink are sold in the Ski Chalet.

Ski and Snowshoe Trails

The 9 miles (14.5 km) of **Days Rivers Pathway** (906/786-2351, www.michigan. gov/dnr), 3 miles (4.8 km) south of Rapid River, are among the most popular groomed ski trails in the area. Choose among loops of

A dogsled team crosses Little Bay de Noc.

1-8 miles (1.6-12.9 km), suitable for beginners as well as experts. Six miles (9.7 km) north of Rapid River, the **Rapid River Ski Trails** (906/786-4062, www.fs.fed.us) provide an especially beautiful excursion through varied terrain. Pay attention to the signs, and stay off the 10-mile (16.1-km) loop unless you're an expert cross-country skier—the other loops are suitable if you're less experienced. Snowshoers can make tracks alongside both trails, and both trails have donation boxes to help support trail maintenance and upkeep. In Escanaba, snowshoes can be borrowed for free for 24 hours from the Escanaba Civic Center (225 21st St. N., 7:30am-4pm Mon.-Fri., 906/786-3551).

Snowmobiling

Gain access to the Michigan's seemingly endless 6,100 miles (9,800 km) of interconnected snowmobile trails via the **Nahma Grade Snowmobile Trail;** the trailhead is approximately 3 miles (4.8 km) east of Rapid River. After following a natural gas pipeline for 11 miles (17.7 km), the trail heads north before merging with Trail 7 at Elkhorn, a distance of about 32 miles (52 km). From Escanaba, **Trail 2** takes you west toward Iron Mountain. For the first 15 miles (24 km) it parallels US 2. When it gets to Perronville, it curves in a southwesterly direction before terminating near Norway, a distance of about 49 miles (79 km).

FOOD

You'll find your best dining options in downtown Escanaba. The hottest spot in town is **★ Hereford and Hops** (624 Ludington St., 906/789-1945, www.herefordandhops.com, 11am-9pm Mon.-Sat., longer hours in summer, $12-26), a cook-your-own-steak place and microbrewery in the 1914 Delta Hotel. You'll find excellent seafood choices too, such as grilled salmon and tilapia bruschetta. True to its name, original craft beers are prominently featured. Examples include

Redemption IPA, a wheat ale, and Blackbird Oatmeal Stout, a hearty stout with oats added to the mash.

While you can get American meals at the **★ Swedish Pantry** (819 Ludington St., 906/786-9606, www.swedishpantry.com, 8am-3pm daily, $11-17), you'll also find that, true to its name, this cute little restaurant serves up traditional food the way a Swedish grandmother used to make it. No one will stop you from ordering the meatloaf or roast beef, but you might want to try the Swedish meatballs, potato sausage, and rutabaga. After your meal, grab a massive freshly baked cookie from the bakery and browse the Scandinavian merchandise at the gift shop.

For good, solid American food, try the **Ludington Grill** (1110 Ludington St., 906/553-7778, www.ludingtongrill.com, 11am-9pm Mon.-Thurs., 11am-10pm Fri.-Sun., $10-22). The food is pretty much what you'd expect, but that's not a bad thing. Classic sandwiches, tavern pizza, a bevy of burger options, and a few nice fish entrees round out the menu. And there's a full bar.

Hungry for something from south of the border? Head over to **La Cantina Escanaba** (1636 Ludington St., 906/212-2281, www.lacantinaescanaba.com, 11am-9pm daily, $8-17). The moderate prices, full menu (complete with vegetarian dishes and a bevy of combination meals), and excellent service will make you an instant fan.

The **Stonehouse Restaurant** (2223 Ludington St., 906/786-5003, www.stonehouseescanaba.com, lunch 11am-2pm Mon.-Fri., dinner 5pm-9pm Mon.-Thurs., 5pm-9:30pm Fri.-Sat., $14-37) doesn't look like much on the outside, but it has some fine food and a casual atmosphere. Lunch runs around $14 for sandwiches, salads, and entrées (look for the daily plate special), but plan on spending $21-37 for a dinner entrée—steak, lobster, scallops, duck, and more. The Carport Lounge serves mixed drinks and a passable list of wines by the glass.

ACCOMMODATIONS

The town's most iconic landmark is the **House of Ludington** (223 Ludington St., 906/723-8585, www.houseofludington.us, $$), a grand old Queen Anne resort hotel built in 1865. After enjoying a second hey-day in the 1940s and 1950s, the old hotel has stuttered and stumbled with some shoddy interior remodeling and mismanagement, but it's currently welcoming guests to its storied halls. Today, the building's imposing facade continues to anchor the downtown. The bar and restaurant may be closed; verify prior to arrival.

The typical sprawl of chain motels runs along M-35 between Escanaba and Gladstone, but some nice family-owned operations are still holding their own along the waterfront, with rates in the moderate range. The ★ **Terrace Bay Resort** (7146 P Rd., 906/786-7554, www.terracebayhotel.com, $$), on Little Bay de Noc, has immaculate and up-to-date rooms featuring great views of the bay. The 200-acre resort complex includes an 18-hole golf course, indoor and outdoor pools, tennis courts, and a games room. To find Terrace Bay, watch for signs on US 41, south of Gladstone.

About 6 miles (9.7 km) south of Escanaba on M-35, **Fishery Pointe Beach Cottages** (E5043 M-35, 906/398-9724, www.fisherypointecottages.com, Memorial Day-Labor Day, $) and **Sandy Shores Cottages** (4717 M-35, 906/786-3625, www.sandyshorescottages.com, May-Oct., $, weekly rates also available) offer housekeeping cottages on a nice stretch of sandy beach. Fishery Pointe Beach Cottages rents by the week only.

A few miles south of Escanaba, travelers can find some of the remote peace and tranquility the U.P. is known for by visiting **St. Michael's in Cedar Dells** (2726 M-35, Bark River, 906/280-2165, $$), a resort tucked away in a cedar grove overlooking Lake Michigan. The rustic but clean one- to three-bedroom cottages are perfect for families. Two units allow pets for a $10 per night fee.

Camping

Haymeadow Creek Campground (Rapid River Ranger District, 499 E. Lake Shore Dr., Manistique, 906/474-6442, www.fs.fed.us, free) is about 10 miles (16.1 km) north of US 2 on County Road 509 in Hiawatha National Forest. Each of the 15 campsites has a fire ring and a picnic table, and drinking water is available on-site. You'll be able to connect to the Bay de Noc/Grand Island Trail from here.

Closer to town, you'll find both tent and RV camping at the **Pioneer Trail Park and Campground** (6822 M-35, Gladstone, 906/786-1020, www.deltacountyparks.com, $18-27 tents, $31-39 RVs), a county park a few miles north of Escanaba. Of the 75 sites, only 17 are for tenting, but these include fire pits and picnic tables. The rest of the campsites have electrical hookups for RVs, and most of them have water. Pioneer Trail is ideal for families. Amenities include a playground and a playing field, a picnic area, showers, and optional cable TV. The campground is on US 2/M-35 between Gladstone and Manistique. There are 25 additional campsites at the **O. B. Fuller Park and Campground** (850 M-35, Bark River, 906/786-1020, www.deltacountyparks.com, $29-38), another county park on Lake Michigan, 15 miles (24 km) south of Escanaba. The campground features more than 80 wooded acres, Lake Michigan shoreline, fishing on the Bark River, and electricity and water at each campsite. Follow M-35 south from Escanaba to the Bark River crossing to get here.

INFORMATION AND SERVICES

Visitor information for Escanaba and the surrounding area can be obtained from **Visit Escanaba** (1001 N. Lincoln Rd., 800/533-4386, www.visitescanaba.com) and the **Delta County Chamber of Commerce** (1001 N. Lincoln Rd., 906/786-2192, www.deltami.org). For recreation information, contact the **Michigan DNR** (6833 US 2, Gladstone, 906/786-2351, www.michigan.gov/dnr) or the U.S. Forest Service's office for the **Hiawatha**

National Forest (2727 N. Lincoln Rd., Escanaba, 906/786-4062, www.fs.fed.us).

Seek medical attention at **OSF St. Francis Hospital** (3401 Ludington St., Escanaba, 906/786-3311, www.osfstfrancis.org). There are plenty of banks and ATMs in downtown Escanaba and in Gladstone, including the **Upper Peninsula State Bank** (430 N. Lincoln Rd., 906/989-7000 www.upstatebank. net) as well as smaller local and regional banks.

GETTING THERE AND AROUND
Car

If you're coming from the Mackinac Bridge or south on I-75 from Sault Ste. Marie and Ontario, you really couldn't have an easier time driving to Escanaba—take US 2 east from St. Ignace until you hit the city. Since Escanaba is far closer to Wisconsin than to the Lower Peninsula, many drivers will want to drive along Green Bay (the bay) from Green Bay (the city) on US 41 to M-35, which runs to Escanaba from the south.

Boat

There are two quality marinas in the vicinity of Escanaba, one in Escanaba itself and the other in Gladstone, a few miles north. The **Escanaba Municipal Marina**

(906/786-9614, www.michigan.gov/dnr) has 37 transient and 128 seasonal slips. The marina is open early May to early October, and the harbormaster can be reached 7am-4pm daily on channel 9. The marina offers showers, gas and diesel fuel, day-use dockage, pump-out, launch, bicycle rentals, a dog run, and snacks, plus cable TV hookups and free Internet access. Its location is 45°44.34 N, 87°02.05 W.

The **Gladstone Marina** (906/428-2916, www.michigan.gov/dnr) is located at 45°50.15 N, 87°01.00 W, and the harbormaster is on duty from mid-May to Labor Day. Gladstone Marina monitors radio channels 9 and 68.

Air

Delta Airlines has flights to **Delta County Airport** (ESC, 3300 Airport Rd., 906/786-4902, www.flyesc.com), a small airport just southwest of Escanaba, from Detroit. You can rent a car from **Enterprise** (3300 Airport Rd., 906/786-0603, www.nationalcar.com); you really will need a car while you're here.

Bus

Regular bus service runs to Escanaba from Green Bay, Ironwood, Marquette, St. Ignace, Green Bay, Chicago, and Detroit by **Indian Trails** (800/292-3831, www.indiantrails.com).

Menominee and Vicinity

Spiking like a canine tooth between Wisconsin and the waters of Green Bay (and only about 55 miles/89 km from Escanaba), the triangle of land comprising Menominee County and southern Delta County has been dubbed the peninsula's "banana belt." It's a fitting name, as it does have the U.P.'s most temperate climate, thanks to the relatively warm waters of Green Bay, and the lightest snowfall in the Upper Peninsula—just 50 inches (127 cm) a year on average, a quarter of what typically falls on the rest of the peninsula.

Locals take advantage of this quirk of nature not by growing bananas but by raising dairy cattle and crops like corn and soybeans. Farms dot the countryside, many on land long ago clear-cut by loggers. The logging industry still echoes through the region, however, in the historic waterfront district of Menominee and the mammoth Verso paper mill near Escanaba—a key factor in the area's stable economy. Many visitors have a tough time getting past the big lake always looming on the eastern horizon—the lapping waters of Green Bay are infinitely enticing and easily accessible.

Remember that Menominee is located in the central time zone, an hour earlier than Escanaba and the majority of the Upper Peninsula.

SIGHTS

The Menominee River empties into Green Bay between the twin cities of Marinette, Wisconsin, and Menominee, Michigan, once the region's richest lumber ports. Menominee's bustling business district is centered on 1st Street, along the waterfront. Fortunately, most of the 19th-century brick and sandstone buildings have survived, and their restoration is an ongoing task. You can explore the **historic district** guided by a walking tour brochure available at **Spies Public Library** (940 1st St.). Its 1905 beaux arts facade is one of the tour's most beautiful buildings. A growing number of shops and restaurants along 1st Street are adding new life to this pleasant area.

Menominee County Heritage Museum

The Menominee County Historical Society maintains the **Menominee County Heritage Museum** (904 11th Ave., 906/863-9000, noon-4pm Mon., Wed., Fri., and Sat. Memorial Day-Labor Day, donation) in a former Catholic church. Like many of the Upper Peninsula's regional history museums, the very local focus may be of limited interest to visitors, but it does outline the county's history since its beginnings and has displays about logging, Native American artifacts, and other aspects of Menominee's heritage, making it worth the stop for local history buffs.

Bayside Parks

The waterfront district is home to bayside parks, easily accessible on foot. **Great Lakes Marina Park** stretches along Green Bay between 6th and 10th Avenues, flanked by a marina and a band shell that hosts summer concerts on Tuesday and Thursday evenings. For a longer walk or bike ride, head 1 mile

(1.6 km) south along the water to the **Tourist Park** swimming beach. Continue another 1.5 miles (2.4 km) south to Lighthouse Ann Arbor Park, which includes **North Pier Light,** marking the entrance to Menominee Harbor with a beacon at the end of a rocky breakwater. Although the light is attractive, it's not open to the public. The lighthouse is about 0.25 miles (0.4 km) offshore at the terminus of a concrete breakwater.

De Young Family Zoo

About 15 miles (24 km) north of Menominee is the **De Young Family Zoo** (N5406 County Rd. 577, Mellen, 906/788-4093, www.thedeyoungfamilyzoo.com, 10am-5pm daily summer, 10am-5pm Sat.-Sun. mid-late Sept., $16 adults, $15 seniors, $14 ages 4-16, free under age 3), a pleasant diversion at the end of a long day's drive. You'll find some of the animals you'd expect in big-city zoos, including big cats, bears, primates, wolves, and foxes. Special programs include animal shows and feeding demonstrations.

SHOPPING

Ready for a bit of retail therapy? Head over to 1st Street in downtown Menominee for a visit to **Trends & Traditions** (615 1st St., 906/864-1568, www.trendstraditions.com, 10am-5:30pm Mon.-Thurs., 10am-5pm Fri., 10am-4pm Sat., 11am-4pm Sun.), a gift store and boutique with a wide assortment of reasonably priced women's clothing and accessories, including purses, scarves, and jewelry, plus numerous giftware choices such as wine and bar accessories, candles, kitchen items, and home decor. Readers of the *EagleHerald* have voted the store the area's best gift shop numerous times.

ENTERTAINMENT
Threefold Vine Winery

Stephenson, about 20 miles (32 km) north of Menominee, houses the tasting room of the **Threefold Vine Winery** (S232 Menominee St., Stephenson, 906/753-6000, www.exploringthenorth.com/threefold/vine.html,

Menominee and Vicinity

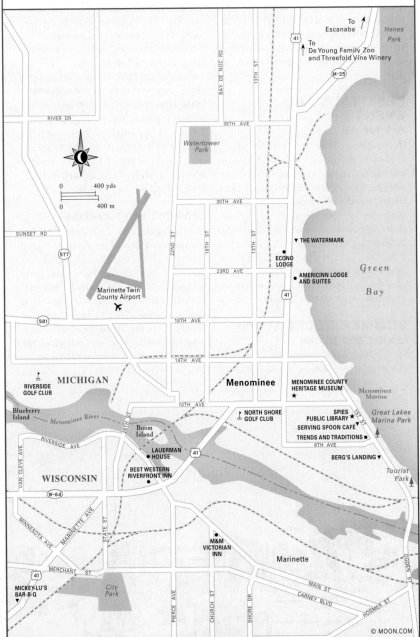

11am-5pm Mon.-Sat. May-Dec., 11am-4pm Fri.-Sat. Jan.-Apr.) in a former bank building. Take your time sampling any of 19 varieties of wines crafted by grapes grown in the Upper Peninsula, ranging from dry to sweet and to "dessert style." This is the perfect place to choose a bottle to complement a picnic on the beach.

FESTIVALS AND EVENTS
Art for All

If you happen to be in town on the last Sunday of June, be sure to visit **Art for All** (www. artforallinc.com) in Great Lakes Marina Park along 1st Street. The event is both a juried art fair and an exhibition featuring works in various media: paintings, drawings, photographs, pottery, glasswork, and sculpture. There's also live entertainment. All the work is for sale, so if you see a piece you like, remember that a fine painting or photograph will make a much nicer remembrance of your trip than a T-shirt. The event runs from 10am to 4pm.

SUMMER RECREATION
Hiking and Biking

Menominee's most popular park is a bit farther away, at the north end of town off M-35.

Henes Park (906/863-2656) occupies a 50-acre point that juts out into Green Bay. Designed by noted landscape architect Ossian Cole Simonds, this unusual park combines tracts of virgin hemlock and pine with traditional park amenities, walking trails, swimming beaches, and playgrounds.

At the Cedar River, 25 miles (40 km) north of Menominee on M-35, the **Escanaba River State Forest** (906/786-2351) offers a network of hiking and mountain biking trails, with four loops ranging 2-7 miles (3.2-11.3 km) over hilly terrain sculpted by ice age glaciers. The Cedar River Trail and Timber Trail in nearby **J. W. Wells State Park** (906/863-9747) both follow the Green Bay shoreline.

Canoeing and Kayaking

The 100-mile (160-km) stretch of the **Menominee River** from above Iron Mountain all the way through Menominee separates the Upper Peninsula from Wisconsin. The strong current offers paddlers an intense high-current ride. You'll have to portage around several dams and reservoirs, but the wildlife viewing and rugged scenery make the effort worthwhile. The upper reaches of the river are not for beginners, however—the Class IV and V white

Menominee marina

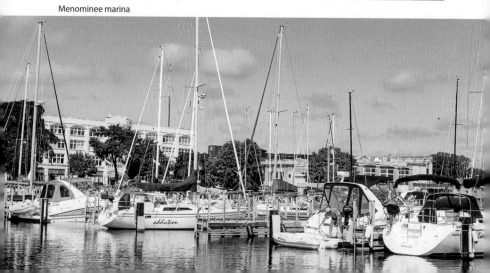

water is some of the U.P.'s fastest. If you're an inexperienced or timid paddler, put in at an access point closer to Menominee, where the flow is gentler and the slower rapids are more navigable.

Beaches

In the 55 miles (89 km) between Menominee and Escanaba, several parks and beaches lure you off the highway. About 13 miles (21 km) north of Menominee, **Bailey Park** is a favorite swimming beach for locals, with fine sand and low dunes on a point that stretches away from the highway. About 2 miles (3.2 km) north, **Kleinke Park** is more exposed to M-35 but offers campsites overlooking the bay as well as a sandy beach. There are small swimming beaches at **Tourist Park,** near the Menominee Harbor and the North Pier Light, and at **Henes Park,** on M-35 just north of town.

Fishing

There's some fishing available at **Cedar River,** north of Menominee, as well as at the Menominee River and several smaller local lakes and rivers—try **Hayward Lake** or **Walton River.** In town, anglers can cast a line off the **Menominee Municipal Pier**—the same pier that leads to the North Pier Light—but some of the best fishing is in **Green Bay** and **Lake Michigan.** Currently there are no fishing charter services operating from the Menominee area, although in nearby Peshtigo, Wisconsin, you'll find **Walleye Madness Guide Service** (5243 Morning Retreat Rd., Oconto, WI, 906/290-2939, www.walleyemadnessfishing.com, 7-hour day of fishing $545 for 1-3 people, $595 for 4). Captain Steve Paulsen will take patrons just about anywhere in Green Bay they wish, on either the Michigan or Wisconsin side. To get there, follow US 41 from Menominee south for 59 miles (95 km) to just past Oconto, exiting at McDonald Street, which soon becomes Airport Road. Follow Airport approximately 4 miles (6.4 km) before turning right onto Morning Retreat Road.

Boating

Green Bay, Little and Big Bays de Noc, and **northern Lake Michigan** are among the Midwest's most beautiful, temperate, and sailable waters. Along with sites in Escanaba and Gladstone to the north, boaters can put in at the **Menominee Marina** (906/863-8498, www.michigan.gov/dnr).

Golf

In Stephenson, about 20 miles (32 km) north of Menominee on US 41, golfers can enjoy a relaxing game at the rural **Indian Hills Golf Course** (N8881 Walnut Rd., Stephenson, 906/753-4781, www.indianhillsgolf.net, 9 holes $16, unlimited play $15, $12 for cart for 9 holes, club rental $5 per day). Perhaps due to its remote location, surrounded by fields of grain and corn, this nine-hole course holds a certain quaint attraction. Closer to Menominee, golfers can visit the **North Shore Golf Club** (2315 M-35, 906/863-3026, www.northshoregolfup.com, greens fees 9 holes $22 with cart, 18 holes $32 with cart) a few miles north of town on M-35. The club's 18 holes are well maintained, and—one of the most compelling reasons to swing a club here—a few holes provide dramatic views of Green Bay. You'll find many of the amenities you'd expect at a higher-level course: a PGA professional, a restaurant, a pro shop, and a driving range. Another option is **Riverside Golf Club** (3459 14th Ave., Menominee, 906/863-4837, http://riverside-up.com, 7:30am-dusk daily, $50 for 9 holes, $67 for 18 holes with cart). The oldest course in the U.P., Riverside is challenging for players of every caliber and provides all the amenities you'd expect from a quality golf facility, including a restaurant and pro shop.

WINTER RECREATION
Ski and Snowshoe Trails

One of the best places for ungroomed ski trails is **J. W. Wells State Park** (906/863-9747), on M-35 about 25 miles (40 km) north of Menominee. The park, open year-round, has almost 700 acres of land for public use crossed by 8 miles (12.9 km) of ski and snow-shoe trails, some of which lead skiers along the Green Bay shoreline. You'll find the groomed trails of **Cedar River Pathway** (906/786-2354, www.michigan.gov/dnr) about 3 miles (4.8 km) north of J. W. Wells State Park, where M-35 and County Road 551 meet. The pathway has several loops, ranging 2-9 miles (3.2-14.5 km), that are perfect for beginning skiers.

Snowmobiling

The expansive Michigan DNR snowmo-bile trail system doesn't extend south into Menominee County. The best bet for snow-mobiling is to head north on US 41 to Powers, where the trailhead for **Trail 331** connects to **Trail 2** a few miles north. Take Trail 2 west toward Iron Mountain or east to Escanaba.

Many of Menominee County's unpaved roads and the shoulders of paved roads are ac-cessible by snowmobile; double-check local ordinances for exceptions. Always use ex-treme caution when riding on public roads. More information about statewide snowmo-bile regulations is available from the website of the **Michigan DNR** (www.michigan.gov/dnr). Remember, safety first.

FOOD

Dining in Menominee offers mostly clas-sic American fare, with an emphasis on fish from the local waters. **Berg's Landing** (450 1st St., 906/863-8034, 5pm-8pm Tues.-Thurs., 5pm-8:30pm Fri.-Sat., $22-50) serves up terrific views of Green Bay along with good steaks, seafood, chicken, and veg-etarian dishes. Reservations are recom-mended. Locals will likely point you to **The Watermark** (2720 10th St., 906/863-7888, www.thewatermarkonthebay.com, 7:30am-8pm Fri.-Sat., 7:30am-3pm Sun.-Thurs., $11-18), on US 41, for daily-baked pies, generous sandwiches, and items that celebrate the area's heritage, like Swedish pancakes and Cornish pasties—all at very reasonable prices. You can enjoy a great view of Green Bay from The Watermark as well.

In addition to the traditional café

offerings—coffee, espresso, soups—the **Serving Spoon Café** (821 1st St., 906/863-7770, 6:30am-2:30pm daily, under $12) has earned a reputation for its Mediterranean-style pitas, light salads, vegetarian sand-wiches, and gluten-free options. Across the river on the Wisconsin side, **Mickey-Lu's Bar-B-Q** (1710 Marinette Ave., Marinette, WI, 715/735-7721, 9am-5pm daily) looks like a hole in the wall, but it's the place to go for *very* cheap food—authentic old-fashioned butter burgers, malts, and ice cream sundaes.

ACCOMMODATIONS

Lodging choices are limited to a few chain motels in Menominee and neighboring Marinette, Wisconsin. The best values are **AmericInn Lodge Suites** (2330 10th St., Menominee, 906/863-8699, $$), **Econo Lodge** (2516 10th St., Menominee, 906/863-4431, $$), which has rooms overlooking the bay, and **Best Western Riverfront Inn** (1821 Riverside Ave., Marinette, WI, 715/732-1000, $$) in Wisconsin, just west of US 41 at the river.

Cross the river into Wisconsin for com-fortable lodging at one of the area's nicest historic inns, the ★ **M&M Victorian Inn** (1393 Main St., Marinette, WI, 715/732-9531, www.mmvictorian.com, $$). The M&M is named after the twin cities of Marinette and Menominee, not the candy, and is a stunning restored 1893 Queen Anne-style home with elegant original woodwork, stained glass, and five guest rooms. Travelers can also stay at its sister facility, the **Lauerman House Inn** (1975 Riverside Ave., Marinette, WI, 715/732-7800, www.mmvictorian.com, $$).

Camping

J. W. Wells State Park (906/863-9747 or 800/447-2757, www.michigan.gov/dnr, $22), about 25 miles (40 km) north of Menominee on M-35, is the most extensive park along the highway. Flanking both sides of M-35, the

---

1: Green Bay as seen from a rocky shoreline at Henes Park **2:** cabin on Lake Michigan in J. W. Wells State Park

800-acre park is known for its 3-mile (4.8-km) stretch of rocky beach and large, modern campground. The campground doesn't offer much privacy, but all 178 sites are near the beach and 30 back up right to the water. All sites often fill on summer weekends. If you've planned well ahead, you might be able to claim one of the park's five rustic cabins ($62), stone and log buildings built as a Civilian Conservation Corps (CCC) project in the 1930s and tucked in secluded woods near the water. They sleep 8-16 people and feature barrel stoves for both warmth and cooking.

The **Cedar River North State Forest Campground** (906/863-9747, $17, no reservations) in Escanaba River State Forest is a quiet, rustic campground right on the banks of the river, just a few miles upstream from the mouth. The 18 sites are for tent and small trailer use, and 4 of them are walk-in tent-only sites. You'll find potable water from a rustic hand pump. From M-35 at the village of Cedar River, follow County Road 551 west for 8 miles (12.9 km).

Fox Park (M-35 at S. Fox Rd., Cedarville Twp., 906/753-4582, $20), 7 miles (11.3 km) north of Cedar River, has a 25-site primitive campground that rarely fills, along with a nice sandy beach. The more popular **O. B. Fuller Park** (850 M-35, Bark River, 906/786-1020, $16-30), 9 miles (14.5 km) north, has 25 modern sites, a sandy beach, a bathhouse, a boat launch, and access to the Bark River.

River Park Campground (502 5th Ave., 906/863-5101, www.cityofmenominee.org, $25-30) offers several amenities but has one significant drawback—it's located behind a retail strip center. Otherwise, the modern campground's 58 sites are clean, with paved parking pads and a playground. You'll also be within walking distance of a coin laundry. This is the exception rather than the norm; in Michigan's Upper Peninsula, most people come to find a campsite within walking distance of absolutely nothing at all.

INFORMATION AND SERVICES

Perhaps the most important piece of information (or at least the one plenty of travelers forget) is that Menominee County is in the central time zone, the same as Wisconsin. Most of the Upper Peninsula and the entire Lower Peninsula are in the eastern time zone. When traveling between Menominee and Escanaba, set your watch forward an hour when heading north to Escanaba, and back an hour when driving south. Most cell phones and GPS-enabled devices will reset automatically.

For visitor information, contact the **Marinette-Menominee Area Chamber of Commerce** (601 Marinette Ave., Marinette, 715/735-6681, www.mandmchamber.com).

Menominee banks include **Stephenson National Bank and Trust** (1111 10th St., 715/732-1732) and **First National Bank and Trust** (3805 10th St., 906/863-7861).

The closest hospital is Marinette's **Aurora Medical Center—Bay Area** (3003 University Dr., Marinette, WI, 715/735-4200 or 888/788-2070, www.bamc.org) in Wisconsin. Take US 41 south to Main Street and turn left, then go right on Shore Drive for 1.5 miles (2.4 km).

GETTING THERE AND AROUND
Car
Menominee is on the border of Michigan and Wisconsin, across the river from Marinette. Take US 41 from the north or south into town, or drive along the Green Bay coast south from Escanaba on M-35.

Boat
The **Menominee Marina** (906/863-8498, www.menomineemarina.com) has 20 transient slips and a whopping 243 seasonal slips. Open mid-May through mid-October, the marina has restrooms and showers, gasoline, laundry, and a picnic area with tables and

grills. Contact the harbormaster on channel 22 or 16. Menominee Marina is located at 45°06.21 N, 87°35.58 W.

Air

The airport that's most accessible to Menominee is the small **Delta County Airport** (ESC, 3300 Airport Rd., 906/786-4902, www.flyesc.com) near Escanaba, served by Delta Airlines from Detroit. You can rent a car from **Enterprise** (3300 Airport Rd., 906/786-0603, www.enterprise.com).

Bus

Bus service to Menominee is provided from Green Bay, Ironwood, Marquette, St. Ignace, Green Bay, Chicago, and Detroit by **Indian Trails** (800/292-3831, www.indiantrails.com).

The Superior Upland

The western interior is defined largely by its

austere, beautiful land. Known as the Superior Upland, this portion of the peninsula is filled with rocky crags, rugged landscape, and surviving old-growth forests. In short, it's the wildest portion of an already remote destination. Here the eastern U.P.'s flat, pastoral landscape gives way to the Porcupine Mountains, roaring streams, and pristine forests.

Gogebic County and the region surrounding Ironwood are known as the Big Snow Country, with the U.P.'s top destinations for downhill skiing. Though Michigan's Porcupine Mountains don't even reach 2,000 feet (610 meters), the resorts at Bessemer and Wakefield make for some of the best skiing between the Mississippi and the Alleghenies.

Highlights

Look for ★ to find recommended sights, activities, dining, and lodging.

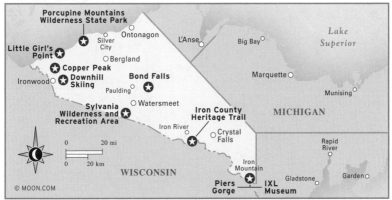

★ **IXL Museum:** This museum recreates the office environment of the Wisconsin Land & Lumber Co., a giant of the timber industry during the late 19th and early 20th centuries. It's probably the most realistic historic site you'll ever visit (page 122).

★ **Piers Gorge:** Here you'll find the ultimate wilderness river: rugged, tranquil, and picturesque, with rolling rapids to boot (page 124).

★ **Iron County Heritage Trail:** With the Iron County Historical Museum as its centerpiece, this fun string of attractions is a great destination for anyone interested in the area's iron mining past (page 130).

★ **Sylvania Wilderness and Recreation Area:** Over these 20,000 acres of land, you'll find 36 crystalline glacial lakes and endless opportunities for recreation (page 132).

★ **Bond Falls:** Don't miss one of the Upper Peninsula's most beautiful waterfalls (page 137).

★ **Little Girl's Point:** At this dramatic spot high on a bluff over Lake Superior, you'll find a spectacular view of both the lake and the mountains (page 140).

★ **Copper Peak:** Even if you're not here to ski off the highest artificial jump in the world, this is a great spot to enjoy spellbinding views (page 141).

★ **Downhill Skiing:** The immense snowfalls of the western Upper Peninsula make the Superior Upland the finest destination for downhill skiers between the Rockies and the Appalachians (page 144).

★ **Porcupine Mountains Wilderness State Park:** Virgin forest, Lake Superior shoreline, and miles of trails make the Porkies a rugged, secluded paradise that's perfect for getting away from the crowd (page 147).

The Superior Upland

© MOON.COM

Summertime visitors can enjoy the region's numerous waterfalls and hiking trails.

The Porcupine Mountains, or the Porkies, as they're affectionately known, are among the oldest highland ranges in the United States. The Ojibwa people had already named the peaks and crags along Lake Superior long before Europeans arrived and began harvesting the area's abundant resources. Logging had a drastic, often damaging impact on the landscape, and caused a threat to the mountains. In 1945, the State of Michigan established Porcupine Mountains State Park ("Wilderness" was added to its title in 1972), which helped save and preserve the mountains.

Today, the Porkies are home to one of the Great Lakes region's largest remaining old-growth forests, consisting of hardwoods and eastern hemlocks. To fully enjoy this spectacle of nature, be sure to bring your hiking boots. Much of the area—particularly the 85 miles (137 km) of trails in Porcupine Mountains Wilderness State Park—is only accessible on foot. It's a remarkably beautiful park, offering almost boundless recreational opportunities. If you're looking for old-growth hemlock, rustic cabins, and remote backpacking—plus fishing, canoeing, or camping—this is surely the place for you.

PLANNING YOUR TIME

The western U.P. is made for rugged isolation during the summers. In winter, it's where you'll find the best of Michigan's downhill skiing. Plan on two or three days to explore—and longer for ski trips or backcountry hiking. No matter the season, you'll want to set some time aside for the Porkies. Be mindful that the four Michigan counties (Gogebic, Iron, Dickinson, and Menominee) that border Wisconsin lie in the central time zone, one hour behind the rest of Michigan.

Accommodation Price Key

$	Less than $100 per night
$ $	$100-200 per night
$ $ $	More than $200 per night

HISTORY

This corner of the Upper Peninsula traces its heritage to iron, which is clearly reflected in the town names: Iron Mountain, Iron River, Ironwood, National Mine, and Mineral Hills. You'll see it in the faces of the residents, descendants of immigrant mine workers from Scandinavia, Italy, and Cornwall.

Federal surveyors first discovered iron ore in 1844 near present-day Iron River. As workers systematically surveyed this unfamiliar land recently acquired by Michigan, their compasses swung wildly near Negaunee, where iron ore was so plentiful it was visible on the surface, intertwined in the roots of a fallen tree. Today that tree appears on the city's official seal as homage to the community's mining heritage.

Apart from a handful of small mining operations, the potential wealth of the Upper Peninsula's iron deposits remained largely untapped for decades until the nation's ever-expanding web of railroad lines reached the area. In the 1870s, the arrival of the railroad prompted the development of the first major mines. World War II and its insatiable demand for iron forced area mines to maintain peak production, driving some to depletion. By the 1960s and 1970s, the western U.P. iron industry had grown quiet, after producing nearly two billion tons of ore. All underground iron mines in the U.P. were closed by 1978, casualties of foreign steelmaking and reduced demand, as newer manufacturing methods relied more on plastics.

Previous: Ottawa National Forest; the Lake of the Clouds; bridge over the Presque Isle River.

Iron Mountain and Vicinity

Iron Mountain sports a different kind of appeal, as it lacks the glamour of a typical tourist destination. The area's long heritage of logging and mining yields a trove of compelling historical sites, complementing the beauty of the surrounding forest.

Europeans began settling in Iron Mountain around 1880 when vast deposits of iron were discovered underfoot. The Chapin Mine, located on the north end of downtown near present-day US 2 and Kent Avenue, boosted the town's population to almost 8,000 by 1890. Italians were among the European immigrants working at the Chapin Mine. Today, Italian neighborhoods still thrive on Iron Mountain's north side, evidenced by the tempting array of Italian restaurants and corner markets.

The city's long-abandoned mines still serve an important role, however—as a magnet for brown bats. An estimated two million bats winter in the Millie Mine shaft, protected from predators while able to enter and exit freely due to the bat-friendly grates installed at the mine entrance. As the weather turns cool in the fall, the bats congregate all around Iron Mountain, creating an amazing sight, before returning to the mine.

While iron mining formed the backbone of the local economy, Henry Ford added some measure of diversification in the 1920s when he bought up huge tracts of nearby forest and built his first company sawmill on land southwest of town, which he named Kingsford in honor of Edward Kingsford, Iron Mountain's Ford dealer and Ford's cousin by marriage. Soon Ford's local empire included the main automotive plant that made floorboards for the Model T, residences for workers, a refinery, and even a chemical plant to make newfangled charcoal briquettes. The businesses were eventually closed or sold, including the briquette plant, which relocated to Oakland, California,

and was eventually acquired by the Clorox Corporation.

During World War II the facilities were devoted to the production of military hardware. The sawmill began building Waco CG-4A gliders for the U.S. Army Air Force, an indispensable tool during the Allied invasion of France.

Henry Ford's handprints can be found on a number of places. The local airport and main city park bear his name, and the nickname of the athletic teams at Kingsford High School is the "Flivvers," the name for an experimental aircraft once produced by Ford.

SIGHTS
Iron Mountain Iron Mine

The best way to become familiar with Iron Mountain and the Superior Upland is to visit the area's several interesting museums. The **Iron Mountain Iron Mine** (906/563-8077, www.ironmountainironmine.com, 9am-5pm daily Memorial Day-mid-Oct., $18 adults, $17 seniors 65 and up, $13 ages 6-12, free under age 6) is in Vulcan, 9 miles (14.5 km) east of Iron Mountain. Big John, a towering two-dimensional miner with a pickax in his hands, welcomes westbound motorists on US 2. The 40-minute tour takes visitors 400 feet (120 meters) below the surface on a 0.5-mile (0.8-km) journey. Outfitted in rain slickers and hard hats, visitors board an underground train to learn about the history and process of mining, including equipment demonstrations. You'll get set up for the tour in the gift shop, where you can also browse rock and mineral samples.

★ IXL Museum

A lot of museums bill themselves as a "step back in time," but you truly feel it at the **IXL Museum** (5551 River St. N., Hermansville, 906/236-5163, 12:30pm-4pm Thurs.-Sun. Memorial Day-Labor Day, donation) in

Iron Mountain

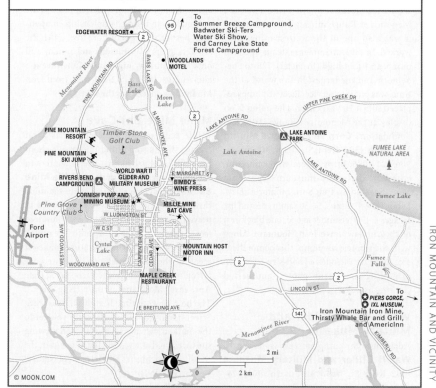

To
Summer Breeze Campground,
Badwater Ski-Ters
Water Ski Show,
and Carney Lake State
Forest Campground

EDGEWATER RESORT

WOODLANDS MOTEL

Menominee River

Bass Lake

Moon Lake

PINE MOUNTAIN RESORT

Timber Stone Golf Club

PINE MOUNTAIN SKI JUMP

RIVERS BEND CAMPGROUND

WORLD WAR II GLIDER AND MILITARY MUSEUM

CORNISH PUMP AND MINING MUSEUM

Pine Grove Country Club

Ford Airport

Crystal Lake

WESTWOOD AVE

WOODWARD AVE

MAPLE CREEK RESTAURANT

E BREITUNG AVE

BIMBO'S WINE PRESS

MILLIE MINE BAT CAVE

W LUDINGTON ST

W C ST

CARPENTER AVE

CEDAR AVE

MOUNTAIN HOST MOTOR INN

E MARGARET ST

LAKE ANTOINE RD

LAKE ANTOINE PARK

Lake Antoine

UPPER PINE CREEK DR

FUMEE LAKE NATURAL AREA

Fumee Lake

Fumee Falls

LINCOLN ST

Menominee River

KIMBERLY RD

To
Iron Mountain Iron Mine,
Thirsty Whale Bar and Grill,
and AmericInn

PIERS GORGE
IXL MUSEUM

0   2 mi

0   2 km

© MOON.COM

PINE MOUNTAIN RD

BASS LAKE RD

N MILWAUKEE AVE

downtown Hermansville, 28 miles (45 km) east of Iron Mountain. For more than a century, this wood-frame building served as the northern office of the Wisconsin Land & Lumber Company, which in the 1860s began building doors and window sashes in central Wisconsin. After the Great Chicago Fire of 1871, founder C. J. L. Meyer moved north to tap into the vast pine reserves of the Upper Peninsula. He built the Hermansville office and adjacent sawmill in 1881. IXL stands for "I excel" and was used as a logo on all the company's products.

Today, the preserved IXL building exists in a time warp and is one of the most fascinating museums in the Upper Peninsula; the Dictaphones, mimeograph machine, and payroll records are all still here, as if you'd stepped into the office on a weekend when everyone was off-duty. The second floor, which was originally apartments for Meyer and his family, now displays more historical documents and an assortment of machinery from the logging days. When Meyer expanded the business into Michigan, he came up with an ingenious invention: tongue-and-groove flooring, precision-milled in one operation. The Hermansville operation quickly became the largest flooring plant in the country, crafting the floors for notable clients that included the Mormon temple in Salt Lake City and Yellowstone National Park's main lodge. At its peak, it held 30 million board feet of lumber in its yards and operated three railroads to handle the ever-increasing shipments.

Cornish Pump and Mining Museum

Iron Mountain's Chapin Mine once led Menominee Range mining production, but it was also one of the wettest mines ever worked. In 1893, an immense steam-operated pump, a 54-foot-high (16-meter), 725-ton behemoth and the largest in the world at the time, was put into service. Electric pumps replaced it just 20 years later. The pump is on display at the Menominee Range Historical Foundation's **Cornish Pump and Mining Museum** (300 Kent St., Iron Mountain, 906/774-1086, https://menomineemuseum. com/cornish-pump-museum, 9am-5pm Mon.-Sat., noon-4pm Sun. Memorial Day-Labor Day, $7 adults, $6.50 seniors 65 and up, $4 ages 6-17, free under age 5), one block east of US 2 in downtown Iron Mountain. Along with the impressive pump, this comprehensive museum includes a good-size collection of mining equipment, photos, and period clothing as well as a small theater.

World War II Glider and Military Museum

Adjacent to the pump museum is the **World War II Glider and Military Museum** (302 Kent St., Iron Mountain, 906/774-1086, https://menomineemuseum.com/ glidermuseum, 9am-5pm Mon.-Sat., noon-4pm Sun. Memorial Day-Labor Day, $7 adults, $6.50 seniors, $4 ages 6-17, free under age 5), which shares the fascinating story of the Waco World War II glider. The museum also contains some small military planes and displays of uniforms and equipment. Combination tickets for the two adjacent museums are $12 adults, $11 seniors, $7 ages 6-17.

Badwater Ski-Ters Water Ski Show

Although it's located in Wisconsin, a trip to **Badwater Ski-Ters Water Ski Show** (www.exploringthenorth.com) at Vagabond Park is definitely worthwhile. Located on the Menominee River, just 5 miles (8 km) west of Iron Mountain, this world-class and nationally renowned water-ski team performs jumps, trick and barefoot skiing, and the pyramid. In 2015 the team took first place in the national jump team championship competition. Best of all, the shows are free. Catch the Ski-Ters at 6pm Wednesday and Sunday and on a few Saturday nights mid-June through late-August. Take US 2/141 west from Iron Mountain and look for the signs.

Millie Mine Bat Cave

While bats are often perceived as a bit creepy, there's something impressive about the million-plus bats that spend winters in the abandoned mine shaft of **Millie Mine Bat Cave.** Bats have free access to the mine through a grate, which was constructed to prevent people from falling several hundred feet to the floor of the mine shaft. The mine's constant 40°F (4°C) temperature makes it ideal for the bats, which can be viewed entering or leaving the mine each spring (late Apr.-early May) and autumn (Aug.-Sept.). The best viewing time is at dusk. Take Park Street north from US 2 east until you get to the marked viewing area. All seven viewing sites are listed at www.michigan.gov/dnr, the website of Michigan's Department of Natural Resources (DNR).

★ Piers Gorge

Where the U.P. isn't bordered by lakes, it's framed by rivers: The grand Menominee rambles from near Iron Mountain all the way to Lake Michigan's Green Bay, forming nearly half the Michigan-Wisconsin boundary. Just south of Norway, it narrows through **Piers Gorge,** a pretty run of frothing white water and waterfalls. In the mid-1800s, loggers relied on the Menominee to float logs to the river's mouth; they cursed this stretch of river for the logjams it caused, and they built a series of wooden piers in an attempt to slow the current and channel the flow—hence the name. To view the gorge, follow US 8 south from Norway and turn right on Piers Gorge Road just before you cross the river into Wisconsin. Follow the road about 0.5 miles (0.8 km) until it ends at a trail. Along the 1-mile (1.6-km) trail, you'll be treated to several views of the gorge that become progressively more dramatic, some as high as 70 feet (21 meters). There are several side trails of varying degrees of safety, some of which wind down to the river, but views of each of the falls can be enjoyed from the main trail. This is not a good choice for small children or those with physical limitations, since there are several narrow passes and steep drop-offs.

FESTIVALS AND EVENTS
Pine Mountain Music Festival
The **Pine Mountain Music Festival** (906/482-1542, www.pmmf.org), an annual summer event since 1991, has a lineup of opera, symphony, and chamber music performances that take place across the region at venues in Marquette, Houghton, Munising, and Iron Mountain. In 2017 folk singer-songwriter and native son Joshua Davis, a finalist on the NBC's *The Voice,* featured prominently in the schedule. The festival also features a special concert series called UPstarts, a platform for emerging musicians from the Upper Peninsula.

SUMMER RECREATION
Hiking and Biking
The trails that encircle the large lake at **Fumee Lake Natural Area** (http:// fumeelakes.weebly.com) give hikers the chance to see plenty of natural beauty, still untouched by motorized vehicles and development. There are 5 miles (8 km) of shoreline and more than 500 acres of water in both Fumee Lake and Little Fumee Lake. Choose among trail loops of 1, 2, or 7 miles (1.6, 3.2, or 11.3 km). Each offers different views of the lakes and wildlife. Bring your camera and a pair of binoculars. Fumee Lake Natural Area is located east of Iron Mountain, near Norway. Take Upper Pine Creek Road north of US 2.

Canoeing and Kayaking
Only experienced white-water kayakers who can handle Class III and IV rapids should consider running the **Menominee River.** The narrow canyon walls of Piers Gorge produce some of the Midwest's most thrilling and difficult white water. A great source for renting watercraft and obtaining other necessities is **Wind Rose North Outfitters** (427 10th Ave. Menominee, 906/424-0206, www.windrosenorth.com, 7am-5pm Mon.-Fri., 7am-3pm Sat.-Sun.).

Fishing
Even though Lakes Michigan and Superior don't border the Iron Mountain region, the abundant inland lakes offer plenty of great fishing. Try **Bass Lake** near the Wisconsin border, north of Iron Mountain and 2 miles (3.2 km) west of US 2, or larger **Lake Antoine,** 4 miles (6.4 km) north of Iron Mountain (take US 2 to Lake Antoine Rd.). **Carney Lake** is a little farther away, 16 miles (26 km) northeast of Iron Mountain on M-95 and Merriman Truck Trail, but it has over 100 acres and includes a boat launch and rustic campgrounds to make it worth the drive. Species of fish in both lakes include bass, northern pike, perch, and walleye. For more sites and advice on fishing the area's rivers, contact the **Dickinson County Tourism Association** (800/236-2447, www.ironmountain.org).

A great source for all sorts of fishing equipment and supplies is **Hardcore Outfitters** (1616 N. Stephenson Ave., Iron Mountain, 906/828-1034, www.hardcoreoutfitters.co, 10am-5pm Tues.-Fri., 9am-3pm Sat.).

Off-Road Vehicles
After the mining and logging industries petered out, they left behind a vast network of unpaved roads, making the backcountry around Iron Mountain perfect for off-roading. There are also nearly 30 miles (48 km) of ORV routes on the **Norway Trail.** Take County Road 573 east of Norway to Norway Truck Trail, then go north to the parking area, or take Foster City Road several miles north of US 2 in Waucedah.

Golf

The **Pine Grove Country Club** (1520 W. Hughitt St., Iron Mountain, 906/774-3493, http://pinegrovecc.org, $57 for 18 holes Mon. and Thurs., $64 for 18 holes Fri.-Sun., $19 cart) has been around for more than 100 years, but the semiprivate course has an elegant and updated clubhouse. Nonmembers are limited to specific tee times; they may tee off any time on Monday, before noon on Thursday and Friday, and after 11am on Saturday and Sunday.

You'll have a better choice of tee times at **Oak Crest Golf Course** (N1475 US 8, 906/563-5891, www.oakcrestgolf.com, Memorial Day-Labor Day, $25-27 for 9 holes plus $10 for cart, $37-39 for 18 holes plus $15 for cart) in Norway. The 18 holes are surrounded by oak trees, which gives the course its natural stately feel as well as its name.

You can also play at **Timber Stone Golf Club** (N3332 Pine Mountain Rd., 906/776-0111, www.pinemountainresort.com, $129 for 18 holes daily), part of Pine Mountain Resort. The course's 18 holes are set on 240 wooded acres. It's certified a five-star course by *Golf Digest* magazine; of 6,000 courses nationwide, only 24 are in this category. Playing can be pricey, but look for package deals that combine lodging and golf.

Waterfall

You'll find a couple of waterfalls in the area, although they aren't the Upper Peninsula's most dramatic. The pretty but small **Fumee Falls** has minimal water flow but is very easy to get to. A trail and a viewing platform just off US 2, just east of Iron Mountain, allow you to see the 20-foot (6-meter) cascade fairly easily.

WINTER RECREATION
Ski and Snowshoe Trails

Perhaps the most appealing feature about

Fumee Lake Natural Area is its year-round accessibility. The summer hiking trails transition nicely into cross-country ski and snowshoe pathways during the long and intense Upper Peninsula winters. There are loops of varying distance and difficulty, all wonderfully isolated from the nearby towns. An excellent example is the **Upper Pine Creek Road,** north of US 2, a few miles west of Norway and east of Iron Mountain. Also, the **Merriman East Pathway,** some 13 miles (21 km) northeast of Iron Mountain on M-95 at Merriman Road, has nearly 10 miles (16.1 km) of trails that make for pleasant cross-country skiing.

A local outfitter offering snowshoe rentals is **True North Outpost** (W5768 Old Piers Gorge Rd., Norway, 906/239-4971, www.truenorthoutpost.com, hours vary—call ahead). In addition to snowshoes, you'll also find necessities for water sports and fishing. They also offer guided day trips.

Downhill Skiing

Although Michigan's biggest and best ski resorts are farther west, the Iron Mountain region holds its own with two downhill ski resorts—plus a little something extra. **Pine Mountain Resort** (N3332 Pine Mountain Rd., 906/774-2747, www.pinemountainresort.com, $45-65 adults, $35-49 ages 9-17, age 8 and under free), in Iron Mountain, has multilevel skiing and lighted nighttime runs, two terrain parks, and a half pipe. But that pales in comparison to the **Pine Mountain Ski Jump** (N3330 Pine Mountain Rd., 906/779-1110, www.kiwanisskiclub.com), a towering 175-foot-tall (53-meter) scaffold with a run of 380 feet (116 meters). An international competition here draws 20,000 people each year to the world's largest artificial ski jump.

Snowmobiling

More than 120 miles (193 km) of snowmobile trails cross Dickinson County, connecting to trails throughout the U.P. and northern Wisconsin. Iron Mountain and Norway are connected by a trail that skirts **Fumee Lake**

1: Big John welcoming visitors to the Iron Mountain Iron Mine 2: Menominee River at Piers Gorge

(you can take it east toward Escanaba), while **Trail 5** will take you north toward Marquette and Lake Superior.

FOOD

Italian is the way to go if you're eating out in Iron Mountain. Homemade ravioli, slow-roasted pork, Italian sausage, Roma red sauce—you'll find it all in the town's unassuming Italian eateries. **Bimbo's Wine Press** (314 E. Main St., Iron Mountain, 906/774-8420, 11am-2am daily, $12) serves hearty Italian sandwiches like porketta and Italian hot beef for incredibly reasonable prices. Except for the thin-crust pizzas, **Famers** (N3332 Pine Mountain Rd., Iron Mountain, 906/774-2747, www.pinemountainresort.com, 8am-9pm Sun.-Thurs., 8am-10pm Fri.-Sat., $21-34) is the place to go when you're looking for something a bit less Italian. Part of Pine Mountain Resort, Famers is a sports bar complete with good appetizers, five TVs, cocktails, and big steaks, and is the perfect place to catch the big game.

For good hearty fare (try the half-pound burger), head to the ★ **Thirsty Whale Bar and Grill** (825 Murray Rd./US 2, Norway, 906/563-5466, 11am-2am daily, $11-15), west of town. Friday nights feature a tempting fish fry. A good choice for families is the **Maple Creek Restaurant** (1052 S. Stephenson Ave., Iron Mountain, 906/774-1777, 6am-4pm daily, breakfast $7-10, lunch $9-12), where you'll find satisfying family-style fare at moderate prices.

ACCOMMODATIONS

Look for standard chain motels in downtown Iron Mountain. The ★ **Pine Mountain Resort** (N3332 Pine Mountain Rd., Iron Mountain, 877/553-7463, www.pinemountainresort.com, $$) anchors a full-service ski and golf resort on the northwest side of town, complete with a dining room, indoor and outdoor pools, a sauna, tennis courts, and hiking and mountain biking trails. In addition to lodge rooms, higher-priced condos are also available to rent.

Just off US 2, the ★ **Edgewater Resort** (N4128 US 2, Iron Mountain, 800/236-6244, www.edgewaterresort.com, $$) makes the most of its fine setting overlooking the Menominee River, with 10 log cabins scattered across its grounds, along with a picnic area, a playground, a volleyball court, and canoes and fishing boats for rent. (A Michigan or Wisconsin license is valid for fishing on the Menominee.) There are one-, two-, and three-bedroom cabins with kitchens and pets are permitted. The resort offers wireless Internet and laundry facilities. Weekly rental rates are also available.

The **Mountain Host Motor Inn** (1451 S. Stephenson Ave., Iron Mountain, 906/776-0700, https://mhminn.com, $) is a very reasonably priced motor lodge that offers some unusual amenities. Each room is equipped with a fax modem in addition to wireless Internet, plus hair dryers and cable TV with movies. The motel offers an exercise room with a sauna and tanning bed, a copy service for the business traveler, and daily continental breakfast.

The **Woodlands Motel** (N3957 US 2, Iron Mountain, near M-25, 906/774-6106, www.exploringthenorth.com/wlandsim/wood.html, reservations 800/394-5505, $) is another classic independent operation. Each of the 19 clean and comfortable rooms has a kitchenette, queen beds, and wireless Internet access. There's a playground for kids, and as an extra bonus for winter vacationers, it's close to the area's snowmobile trails.

You'll love the comfort and serenity of the ★ **AmericInn** (2005 S. Stephenson Ave., Iron Mountain, 906/774-1900 or 800/634-3444, www.wyndhamhotels.com/americinn/iron-mountain-michigan, $$) at the end of a long day's drive. The welcoming atmosphere in the lobby and the soothing water of the hot tub will ease your tension and recharge your batteries for the next day. AmericInn offers complimentary continental breakfast and a pool with a hot tub. All rooms are nonsmoking.

Camping

Carney Lake State Forest Campground
(906/875-3324, www.michigan.gov/dnr, $16)
has 16 rustic sites suitable for tents and trailers. There are no showers or laundry, but you will find vaulted toilets and clean water from the campground's hand pump. The sites are first-come, first-served and fill quickly in summer high season. The fishing is excellent. To get here, take M-95 north of Iron Mountain and head east on Merriman Truck Trail.

Summer Breeze Campground
(W8576 Twin Falls Rd., 906/774-7701, www.summerbreezecampground.com, May-Oct., tents $20, hookups $34-39, weekly and seasonal rates available) represents "upscale" camping—amenity-rich, busy, and plenty of room for even the largest RVs. Beyond the hot showers and a camp store are a heated swimming pool, DVD rentals, Wi-Fi, and a book exchange. There are fire rings and tables at every site. The 70 campsites are grassy and shaded, 28 with full hookups and 42 with water and electricity. There is also a cabin with electricity but no running water that rents for $55 per night. Take M-95 north to Twin Falls Road and turn left to get to Summer Breeze Campground.

You can also find campsites at **Lake Antoine Park** (N3393 Lake Antoine Rd., 906/774-8875, $34) and **Rivers Bend Campground** (N3905 Pine Mountain Rd., 906/779-1171, $34). Both are modern campgrounds offering sites with or without electricity. Also available are flush toilets, showers, and potable water. Both operate from Memorial Day through Labor Day. For reservations, call the County Parks Office (906/774-8875).

INFORMATION AND SERVICES

For information on Iron Mountain and the surrounding area, contact the **Tourism Association of the Dickinson County Area** (600 S. Stephenson Ave., 800/236-2447, www.ironmountain.org). Also remember that Iron Mountain is in the central time zone, an hour earlier than most of the Upper Peninsula.

If medical attention is necessary, **Marshfield Medical Center—Dickinson** (1721 S. Stephenson Ave., Iron Mountain, 906/774-1313, www.dchs.org) is on US 2/141 heading southeast from town. In addition to a few local banks, **Upper Peninsula State Bank** (www.upstatebank.net) has a location in Iron Mountain (1890 S. Stephenson Ave., 906/779-2141). In Crystal Falls you'll find the **Northern Interstate Bank** (125 Superior Ave., 906/875-4505).

GETTING THERE AND AROUND

Car

Iron Mountain is located on Michigan's border with Wisconsin, at the intersection of two major highways. Driving into town from the east, take US 2, which is US 2 and US 141 when you come from the west. North from Wisconsin or south from other parts of the U.P., US 141 leads into town. Take US 2/141 north to Crystal Falls, US 2 east to Norway, and US 2 west to Iron River.

Air

There are a few nearby options for flying to Iron Mountain. **Ford Airport** (IMT, 500 Riverhills Rd., Kingsford, 906/774-4870, www.fordairport.org) in Kingsford has flights on Delta Airlines from Minneapolis and Detroit. Car rentals are offered by **Avis** (906/774-0411, www.avis.com). If you arrive by air, a car will be an absolute necessity during your stay.

Delta County Airport (ESC, 3300 Airport Rd., Escanaba, 906/786-4902, www.flyesc.com), a small airport just southwest of Escanaba, has flights from Detroit on Delta. You can rent a car from **Enterprise** (3300 Airport Rd., 906/786-4902, www.enterprise.com).

Sawyer International Airport (MQT, 125 G Ave., Gwinn, 906/346-3308, www.sawyerairport.com) has daily American flights to and from Chicago, while Delta offers daily flights to and from Detroit and

Minneapolis. You'll find major car rental agencies, including **Alamo** (906/346-6378), **Avis** (906/346-6398), **Budget** (906/346-6398), **Enterprise** (906/346-6378), and **National** (906/346-6378). Sawyer is just south of Marquette and about a two-hour drive from Iron Mountain, but with more regular flights, it can be the easier option.

Bus

Iron Mountain is served by the **Indian Trails** (800/292-3831, www.indiantrails.com) bus line.

Taxi

For taxi service, call **Tri-City Cab** (906/774-7878).

Iron River and the Ottawa National Forest

Iron County's population centers on **Iron River,** an iron mining center, and **Crystal Falls,** the picturesque county seat 15 miles (24 km) east. Both retain a rustic, almost rough-hewn charm. Like Iron Mountain, Iron River is a simple town to pass through while on your way to some great skiing or backwoods campsites. Still, it makes for a quaint visit and a convenient stop.

The real draw to the region is the **Ottawa National Forest.** Sprawling on nearly 100,000 acres, the Ottawa National Forest blankets much of the western peninsula from the Wisconsin border to US 141, which runs north from Iron River. The Ottawa National Forest lacks contiguous boundaries, but is rather a patchwork of protected lands surrounding tracts of private property, numerous small towns, and several state parks and forests.

Named for the Indigenous Ottawa people who lived and traded in this region (although they actually populated the eastern half of the U.P. in greater numbers), the Ottawa National Forest encompasses more than 400 lakes, seven major river systems, some of the U.P.'s most spectacular waterfalls, 27 campgrounds, and three wilderness areas: Sylvania, the Sturgeon River Gorge, and the McCormick Tract.

SIGHTS
★ Iron County Heritage Trail
There are 14 stops along the Iron County

Heritage Trail (www.iron.org/local-treasures/heritage-trail), a path of historic places scattered throughout the county. You won't find a lot of dramatic lighting and fancy display cases at the **Iron County Historical Museum** (100 Brady Ave., Caspian, 906/265-2617, www.ironcountyhistoricalmuseum.org, 10am-3pm Mon.-Fri., 10am-2pm Sat. July-Aug., $15 adults, $10 ages 6-18, free under age 6), 2 miles (3.2 km) south of US 2 off M-189 in Caspian. What you will find is an interesting, appealing, and eclectic blend of local history and culture at this rambling, funky, and homegrown museum. Located on the site of the once productive Caspian iron mine—the mine's rusting head frame still looms over the complex—it survives largely on the admission fees, donations, and plenty of volunteer labor. In the main building, displays cover Native American history, logging, mining, sporting equipment, and kitchenware from the early 1900s. The perennial favorite display is the mechanized iron mine and railroad model: for a nickel, a miniature ore skip hauls rocks to the surface and loads them on the railroad.

Other displays not to miss: the Mining Memorial, with a database of area mines and miners along with a video of life in the mines; a 3-D acrylic mine diagram that will enable you to appreciate the depths of the mine, precisely where the ore has been extracted, and where it remains. You'll also see a 50-foot-long

(15-meter) diorama of a logging camp, complete with hundreds of folk-art figures by local artist William Monogal; newspaper clippings on Iron River's 1920 "rum rebellion," when federal agents from Chicago stormed the home of a priest and discovered eight barrels of rum, only to be condemned by the county prosecutor. Topping it off is an exhibit depicting the history of the local labor movement, which helped boost miners' earnings from $365 per year in 1931 to $1,886 per year a decade later.

Outside, several relocated buildings occupy the grounds. One is a barn that houses the actual streetcar that once traveled between the mines in Caspian and Iron River.

Head to Crystal Falls for a look at the small-town life of miners at the turn of the 20th century. Tour the **Harbour House Museum** (17 N. 4th St., 906/875-4341, www. crystalfallsmuseum-harbourhouse.org, guided tours 11am-2pm Sat.-Sun. May-June and Oct.-Nov., 11am-2pm Fri.-Sun. June-Sept., $4 adults, $10 families), a restored Queen Anne colonial revival home that houses a two-story museum, complete with authentic furnishings and decorations and several exhibits displaying regional artifacts. The first floor contains a music room, library, and dining room, all preserved to look as they did in the early 1900s. Five exhibit rooms on the second floor celebrate the area's mining heritage.

The **Mile Post Zero and Treaty Tree** appears to be simply a mile marker and a tree, yet it holds historical significance. The site marks the precise location of the survey point that set the boundary between Michigan and Wisconsin in 1840. To get here, follow M-73 west of Iron River until you come to Ottawa Lake Road. Bear to the right when you come to the intersection with Hagerman Lake Road. Lake Ottawa Road will become West Brule Lake Road at this point. Follow the road until you arrive at the Stateline Picnic Grounds. Once there, trail signs will direct you to the marker; it's about a 0.5-mile (0.8-km) hike.

Other sites on the Iron County Heritage Trail include a museum, the county courthouse, and a pioneer church. Contact **Friends of the Heritage Trail** (906/875-6642, www. iron.org/local-treasures/heritage-trail) for maps and additional information.

Triangle Ranch

Much of the U.P. is dotted with ghost towns, but **Triangle Ranch** may be its only ghost farm. In the 1920s, a developer had grand plans for some of Iron County's clear-cut logging land. He purchased nearly 10,000 acres and built pens, corrals, barns, and a rancher's home with the intention of raising beef cattle. The idea went bust after just one year—it proved too costly to care for the animals over the long U.P. winter. Most of the land was sold back to a pulp-and-paper company and has since been reforested, but the skeletons of the beef operation remain. Triangle Ranch remains on the Michigan state map; from Crystal Falls, take US 141 north about 15 miles (24 km) to the marked Triangle Ranch Road, which is a few miles north of Amasa. Follow the road east about 1 mile (1.6 km) to the remains of the ranch.

Paulding Mystery Light

If inexplicable or supernatural happenings fascinate you, or if you don't believe in them but are simply curious, a fun evening pastime is visiting the **Paulding Mystery Light,** alternatively known as the Lights of the Paulding or the Dog Meadow Light, in Watersmeet. The small, mysterious light reportedly appears in the distance almost every night. According to the sign at the site, "Legend explains its presence as a railroad brakeman's ghost, destined to remain forever at the site of his untimely death. He continually waves his signal lantern as a warning to all who come to visit." To get there, take US 2 east of Iron River, then follow US 45 about 5 miles (8 km) north of Watersmeet to Robbins Pond Road—brown signs will help you find the way from there. Over the years there have been several attempts to explain the origin of the phenomenon. The most sophisticated occurred in 2010 when students from Michigan Technological University used a telescope to examine the light and concluded that it was car headlights from nearby US 45.

★ Sylvania Wilderness and Recreation Area

Sylvania protects its assets well—36 crystalline glacial lakes hidden among thick stands of massive old-growth trees. Sylvania can be a truly magical place for anglers who dream of landing that once-in-a-lifetime smallmouth bass, paddlers who yearn to glide across deep quiet waters and along untrammeled shoreline, and hikers who want to travel under a towering canopy of trees and hear nothing more than the haunting whistle of a loon. This is nature's solitude at its very finest.

One of three wilderness areas within Ottawa National Forest, the **Sylvania Wilderness** (www.fs.usda.gov/recarea/ottawa), near Watersmeet, stretches across 18,000 acres roughly bordered by US 2 to the north, US 45 to the east, and the Wisconsin border to the south. The adjacent **Sylvania Recreation Area** includes an additional 3,000 acres of lakes and woodlands. There are a few modern services, including a drive-in campground, a nice beach, flush toilets, and running water.

Once viewed as just another tract of good timber, Sylvania's fate turned in the late 1890s, when A. D. Johnston, a lumberman from Wisconsin, purchased 80 acres near the south end of Clark Lake, decided it was too lovely to cut, and instead kept it as his personal fishing retreat. Johnston invited his wealthy friends, some of whom were executives at U.S. Steel, who were also captivated by the land. Together, they purchased several thousand additional acres and formed the private Sylvania Club.

Like other upscale U.P. "great camps," the Sylvania Club soon had grand log lodges along its shores along with guards to keep trespassing anglers away from its bountiful lakes, and caretakers to squelch any forest fires as they cropped up. Ownership shifted over the

decades and eventually fell into the hands of Lawrence Fisher, one of the seven brothers of the famous auto body-maker, Fisher Body. When Fisher died, his heirs sold the property to the federal government for $5.7 million. It was operated as a recreation area from the late 1960s until 1987, when the bulk of it was converted to wilderness status.

We can partly thank old money for the condition of the land today. With most people previously barred from fishing here, Sylvania's lakes are now a paradise for anglers, especially those looking for smallmouth bass. Its land and waters remain pristine due to the lack of development and powerboat access. Sylvania lies on the watershed divide between Lake Superior and the Mississippi, so it isn't exposed to runoff from nearby lands. And whatever your thoughts on fire management, Sylvania's decades of fire protection mean that visitors today can marvel at a virgin forest of white pines, hemlocks, maples, and basswood trees more than 200 years old.

Begin a trip to Sylvania with a call or visit to the **Ottawa National Forest Visitors Center** (906/358-4724), at the intersection of US 2 and US 45. The staff can help you with maps, regulations, campsite reservations, and other information. Sylvania's rules can be quite idiosyncratic, especially the fishing regulations. Take time to ask questions and read through the materials rangers provide. To reach Sylvania, follow US 2 west about 4 miles (6.4 km) from the visitors center and turn south on Thousand Island Lake Road. Travel about 4 miles (6.4 km) and follow the signs to reach the entrance building. All visitors are required to register on arrival.

The entrance is in the recreation area, near the drive-in campground on Clark Lake. If you intend to travel into the wilderness area, plan on treating your own water; you'll find water pumps only in the recreation area. Cooking stoves are encouraged as well to lessen the number of feet tramping through the forest in search of deadwood. During summer months, make sure you also have ample insect repellent and a head net to combat mosquitoes and blackflies.

ENTERTAINMENT
Northern Waters Casino Resort

If you're looking for local U.P. gaming, you can find it at **Northern Waters Casino Resort** (N5384 US 45, Watersmeet, 906/358-4226 or 800/583-3599, www.lvdcasino.com) in Watersmeet, operated by the Lac Vieux Desert Band of the Lake Superior Chippewa tribe. It's a bit of a drive west on US 2 and then north on US 45, but it's worth the trip from Iron River. The 24/7 gaming room has more than 500 video and reel slots, roulette, blackjack, craps, bingo, a poker room, and plenty more gaming fun. Stop by the **Northern Waters Sports Bar** for food, drinks, and free live entertainment every night until 1am (2am Fri.-Sat.). There's a snack bar for light fare and a restaurant with several buffets in addition to a full menu.

FESTIVALS AND EVENTS
Annual End of Summer Blues Fest

During the fourth weekend of August, head over to the tiny community of Alpha for its **Annual End of Summer Blues Fest** (906/875-3913, https://ironcountylodging.com/blues-fest, $20), presented by the Iron County Chamber of Commerce. The event features a Veterans Freedom Memorial Ride for both motorcycles and cars, followed by an afternoon blues concert. Alpha is located along County Road 424 just 2 miles (3.2 km) off US 2 and just southwest of Crystal Falls. If you're heading out from Crystal Falls, take US 2/141 south about 3 miles (4.8 km) until you get to the County Road 424 turnoff. Make a right onto CR 424 and continue for about 2 miles (3.2 km).

Rodeo

One of the biggest events to hit Iron County is the annual **U.P. Championship Rodeo** (906/284-9680, www.upprorodeo.com), which has been hosting professional rodeo events since 1968. The rodeo is usually held during the third weekend of July. Popular events like steer wrestling, bull riding, and bareback riding, among others, continue to draw crowds for a good serving of Western-style fun. The venue is the Iron County Fairgrounds (720 Franklin St., Iron River).

SUMMER RECREATION
Biking and Hiking
Lake Ottawa Recreation Area

In the far south of the Ottawa National Forest, a few miles south of Iron River, the **Lake Ottawa Recreation Area** (Lake Ottawa Rd., 906/265-9259, www.fs.usda.gov/recarea/ottawa) has about 9 miles (14.5 km) of trails. One of the more popular is the primitive but nice Ge-Che Trail, which follows a 2.5-mile (4-km) loop from the boat landing area. Try the 2-mile (3.2-km) Brennan Lake Loop too. The Lake Ottawa Recreation Area is listed as part of the Iron County Heritage Route.

Sylvania Wilderness and Recreation Area

The **Sylvania Wilderness and Recreation Area** maintains 15 miles (24 km) of trails, including a 7-mile (11.3-km) trail, marked with blue blazes, around Clark Lake. It provides access to campsites and trails to other lakes. Most of Sylvania's trails are old roads from its fishing camp days. While not always well marked, the trails are quite easy to follow. These same roads become a great **cross-country ski** network in the winter months. Ottawa National Forest staff groom 15 miles (24 km) of trails within Sylvania.

Bewabic State Park

Hikers in search of a short, easy trail will find it at **Bewabic State Park** (1933 US 2 W., Crystal Falls, 906/875-3324, www.michigan.gov/dnr), located just off US 2 between Iron River and Crystal Mountain, closer to Crystal Mountain. The 2-mile (3.2-km) nature trail leads visitors from the campground to the day use area and back—expect to spend about an hour on the trail.

Pines and Mines

The marked and mapped **Pines and Mines** (https://lakegogebicarea.com) trail system gives a glimpse of the enticing opportunities for mountain biking in the western Upper Peninsula. A joint effort of local tourism and economic development groups, the Ottawa National Forest, and a local trail-access organization, Pines and Mines comprises some 200 miles (320 km) of trails in three networks. Routes range from tame gravel roads to single-track trails deep in the woods. Many of the trails reveal stunning waterfalls, remote lakes, and historical landmarks.

Near Marenisco in Gogebic County, the **Pomeroy-Henry Lake Network** offers 100 miles (160 km) of gentle biking on wide gravel roads around a national forest area peppered with small lakes. It's a good choice for families. The **Ehlco Network,** just south of Porcupine Mountains Wilderness State Park, includes more single-track deep in the forest on grass or dirt paths. This area can be wet, due to some lowlands and the work of local beavers, so it's best to avoid it after a rain. Perhaps the best of the three networks is the one located outside the national forest: the **Iron County (Wisconsin) System.** Trails radiating out of Hurley, Wisconsin, lead past waterfalls, large flowages, and old mining relics like the Plummer head frame near Pence, Wisconsin. Good interpretive signs help make sense of historic sites. Routes in this system range from gravel to single-track roads, though the map makes it difficult to distinguish between them. Single-track trails 6 and 13 are the best.

While the Pines and Mines trails are great, the map provided is mediocre. It's best to bring your own topographic map, and before you set out, obtain local advice from Ottawa National Forest rangers or local bike shops such as **Hobby Wheel** (1435 E. Cloverland Dr., 906/932-3332, https://hobbywheel.com) in Ironwood. Pick up a map at the Wisconsin

or Michigan state information centers; both are on US 2 near the border. You can also find maps at local bike shops or at the **Ottawa National Forest Headquarters** (E6248 US 2, Ironwood, 906/932-1330, www.fs.usda.gov/ottawa, 8am-4pm Mon.-Fri.) in Ironwood.

Canoeing and Kayaking

Seven major river systems flow within the Ottawa National Forest: a staggering total of 1,000 miles (1,610 km) of navigable waters. Congress has designated more than 300 of those miles as "wild and scenic" or "recreational" rivers, protecting their pristine condition. In general, rivers like the Ontonagon and Presque Isle offer quiet water in their southern reaches, winding through relatively flat woodlands. North of M-28, they begin a more rugged descent through hills and bluffs, requiring more advanced skills and boats appropriate for white water. For strong paddlers with good white-water skills, these rivers offer some of the finest paddling in the Midwest.

Remember, however, that rainfall and the time of year can affect conditions. Rivers that normally flow gently often become torrents in the spring. Always check with U.S. Forest Service officials before setting out. Also, the Forest Service distributes an extensive *River Digest,* a free publication that outlines navigable rivers, launch areas, and liveries, in addition to high and low flow times. Pick one up at a district ranger office.

The three branches of the mighty Ontonagon spread across the western U.P. like a spider web; at times it seems every road you travel crosses one branch or another. While many parts of the river system are worth exploring, one spot gets particular attention: the upper reaches of the middle branch of the Ontonagon, where **Bond Falls** cascades down a series of black boulders.

Paddling is the best way to explore the **Sylvania Wilderness.** Most of the lakes are

1: canoeing on Crooked Lake in the Sylvania Wilderness 2: Bond Falls

linked by water or by relatively easy portages, though there are a couple "grunt portages" of 2 miles (3.2 km) or more. Many campsites are accessible only by water. Motors and other mechanized equipment are forbidden, including sailboats. The one exception is Crooked Lake, which allows electric motors of 4 hp or less. From the entrance road, you can park your vehicle and put in at Clark Lake or Crooked Lake. According to rangers, Clark (the largest), Crooked, and Loon Lakes are the three busiest. Some of the smaller lakes see less traffic and are just a short portage away; these include Mountain and High, which are both accessible from Crooked Lake. One ranger recommends bringing snorkel gear: the crystal-clear waters provide great visibility for viewing several species of large fish. Canoes and kayaks can be rented from **Sylvania Outfitters** (23423 US 2, 906/358-4766, www.sylvaniaoutfitters.com) in Watersmeet. You can outfit your entire trip here, with boats, food, fishing gear, and maps. You can even arrange to have your equipment delivered and picked up at the water's edge.

Five miles (8 km) west of Crystal Falls is a small but pleasant chain of lakes, part of Bewabic State Park, called **Fortune Lakes** (1933 US 2, 906/875-3324, www.michigan.gov/dnr). Boaters can put in at the first of the lakes and make their way to Fourth Lake, which is an easy day's paddling. Though First Lake can be somewhat frenetic on summer weekends, the waters get quieter and downright pristine as you proceed down the chain. Paddlers can escape fishing boats by darting under the low US 2 bridge to Mud Lake. The park itself has a modern 144-site campground with good privacy, a small stretch of sandy beach, tennis courts, and other amenities. Camping reservations are generally not necessary, but they can be made via the state park reservation system (800/447-2757, www.michigan.gov/dnr).

Fishing

Bewabic State Park (1933 US 2, 906/875-3324, www.michigan.gov/dnr) has some fine fishing for perch and bass on First Lake (also known as Fortune Lake), the park's largest (192 acres) and deepest (72 feet/22 meters). There are more than 300 lakes here, and miles of rivers and streams for fishing. Iron County is home to five of the Upper Peninsula's 13 blue-ribbon trout streams, the highest certification awarded by the Michigan DNR. Try the 12-mile (19.3-km) stretch of **Iron River** extending upstream from the city, wade into **Brule River** between M-73 and M-189 south of town, or head to **Cooks Run,** south of US 2. For more information on fishing in Iron County, contact the **Economic Chamber Alliance** (50 E. Genesee St., Iron River, 906/265-3822, www.iron.org).

Golf

Iron County is also home to some of the most interesting golfing in the entire Upper Peninsula. You won't want to miss the 18 holes at the **George Young Recreational Complex** (159 Young's Ln., 906/265-3401, www.experienceyoungs.com, $65 with cart per day during peak season). Not only is it the area's only 18-hole venue, but as a professional course measuring 7,030 yards, it's also the U.P.'s longest. You can play the standard course at just shy of 5,400 yards if you prefer. The elegant complex is run by a nonprofit corporation dedicated to recreation and preservation. Its lands include miles of trails for biking, hiking, and cross-country skiing. The **Crystal View Golf Course** (602 Wagner St., 906/214-4727, https://crystalviewgolfcourse.com, $40 with cart for 18 holes) in Crystal Falls is a nine-hole course owned by the city, located on the banks of Paint River. Please note: Use of the course is limited to men on Wednesdays and women on Thursdays. Another nine-hole course, **Iron River Country Club** (110 Hiawatha Rd., 906/265-3161, www.ironrivergolf.com, $65 for 18 holes with cart Mon.-Fri., $70 Sat.-Sun.), is nearby in Iron River.

Off-Road Vehicles

Off-road enthusiasts can find a designated ORV route stretching 67 miles (108 km) from Iron River northwest to Marenisco. There are miles of additional trails that network throughout Ottawa National Forest, some of which are the beds of former railroad tracks. Be careful to stay on designated and marked roads and trails. Contact the **U.S. Forest Service** (E6248 US 2, Ironwood, 906/932-1330, www.fs.fed.us, 8am-4pm Mon.-Fri.) for maps and more information.

Waterfalls

Just off the Black River National Forest Scenic Byway, the Black River rolls and tumbles over seven magnificent waterfalls north of Bessemer before rushing into Lake Superior. The site is believed to be the largest concentration of waterfalls in the state. The first two, **Chippewa Falls** and **Algonquin Falls,** 9.5 and 9 miles (15.3 and 14.5 km) north of Bessemer, are a little tough to find without a topographic map, since they don't lie near well-marked trails. The next five are a different story. Ottawa National Forest has marked and mapped a good trail network, beginning from a parking lot off County Road 513, about 13 miles (21 km) north of Bessemer. From this lot you can hike, from south to north, to **Great Conglomerate, Potawatomi, Gorge, Sandstone,** and **Rainbow Falls.** Only strong hikers and serious waterfall enthusiasts should try to cover them all in one 10-mile (16-km) outing—it's a huge number of steps and several waterfalls.

Like babies and sunsets, each waterfall is beautiful in a different way, and it's impossible to name the best one. Potawatomi is the closest, just a few minutes' walk from the lot, and accessible by wheelchair. It is a lovely delicate fretwork of foam cascading over remnants of an ancient lava flow. The last falls, Rainbow, is the largest of the group, cascading 40 feet (12 meters). The resulting spray sometimes creates a rainbow effect—hence the name. The best view of Rainbow Falls is from the east side of the river, which you can access from a suspended footbridge near the river's mouth at **Black River Harbor.**

★ Bond Falls

Bond Falls is one of the most spectacular falls in the Upper Peninsula, despite being over-developed with walkways and viewing platforms. Bond Falls is located near Paulding off US 45 in Ontonagon County, 3 miles (4.8 km) east on Bond Falls Road, and is well-marked by signs. Though virtually surrounded by national forest land, the falls themselves sit on power company property, just below a dam that forms the adjacent Bond Falls Flowage, a popular area for fishing, swimming, and camping. To view the falls, follow the trail down the west side of the river. Ignore the spillway, cement retaining wall, and other power company additions. Once you begin descending the stairs, the falls come into view on the right, close enough to touch. Continue down the path to a footbridge that spans the base of the falls for an up-close view. Water gushes down a 50-foot (15-meter) face of chiseled rocks, so dramatic it almost looks artificial.

If you haven't gotten your fill of waterfalls, **Agate Falls** is another striking waterfall, just a few miles north of Bond Falls, and offers a bridge for easy viewing. To get there, take US 45 north from Watersmeet, then M-28 east from Bruce Crossing.

WINTER RECREATION
Downhill Skiing

Without the benefit of the Big Snow Country marketing muscle that serves the ski resorts of Gogebic County, **Ski Brule** (397 Brule Mountain Rd., Iron River, 906/265-9346 or 800/362-7853, www.skibrule.com, prices vary) is left to its own devices to sell this appealing ski area 6 miles (9.7 km) south of Iron River. Its gimmick is that it's "first to open, last to close," which translates to about six months of skiing. Brule is reliably open for downhill skiing by mid-November and continues through April. The terrain is nice, with 500 vertical feet (150 meters), eight chairs and T-bars, and a nice half pipe for snowboarders.

Ski and Snowshoe Trails

Ski Brule (397 Brule Mountain Rd., Iron River, 906/265-4957 or 800/362-7853, www.skibrule.com) is an ideal place for cross-country skiing. Skiers can check out 14.2 miles (22.9 km) of groomed and tracked trails ($12 pp), some of which wind along the Brule River. Because they aren't covered by the resort's snowmaking, the cross-country trails don't always open as soon as the downhill area. There are some 8.5 miles (13.7 km) of groomed trails at **The Listening Inn** (339 Clark Rd., Crystal Falls, 906/822-7738, trail use $8), a splendid log lodge and B&B 9 miles (14.5 km) north of Crystal Falls. Two beginner loops, separate snowshoe trails, and ski rentals make the inn an ideal ski destination. As with hiking, one of the finest trails for cross-country skiing in the **Lake Ottawa Recreation Area** (Lake Ottawa Rd., Iron River, 906/265-9259, www.fs.fed.us) is the groomed and marked Ge-Che Trail.

Ottawa National Forest grooms 15 miles (24 km) of trails within the **Sylvania Wilderness and Recreation Area,** which provides a great cross-country ski network in winter months.

A good local source for renting and purchasing skis and snowshoe equipment is **ABR Trails** (E5299 W. Pioneer Rd., Ironwood, 906/932-3502, www.abrski.com, opens at 9:30 am CST, but hours may vary). They also offer ski lessons.

Snowmobiling

As with ORV trails, a network of snowmobile trails leaves Iron River and winds through the Ottawa National Forest. **Trail 2** heads west into the forest, eventually reaching Ironwood, while plenty of routes branch off to the north and south into Wisconsin. Trails 2 and 16 head east for Escanaba.

FOOD

At ★ **Alice's Italian Supper Club** (402 W. Adams St., 906/265-4764, 4:30pm-9pm daily, $17-28) you'll find authentic Italian specialties brought over from the old country and passed down through generations, such as homemade ravioli and other pasta dishes, gnocchi, and soups, along with several meat options.

For picnics, pick up supplies at **Super One Foods** (833 Riverside Plaza, US 2 E., 906/265-5107, www.superonefoods.com, 7am-8pm daily). An ordinary-looking modern supermarket from the outside, inside it surprises with a superb bakery, produce department, and deli.

ACCOMMODATIONS

The **Lakeshore Motel** (1257 Lalley Rd., Iron River, 906/265-3611, www.lakeshoremotelicelake.com, $) sits on the edge of the spring-fed Ice Lake in Iron River, just east of downtown on US 2. It has tidy motel rooms (some with kitchenettes) and cabins. It's a great find complete with a sandy beach and a boat launch. Also on US 2, in Iron River just east of downtown, is ★ **AmericInn** (40 E. Adams St., Iron River, 906/265-9100, www.americinn.com, $$), with a nice indoor pool, a whirlpool, and a sauna; suites are available.

You'll find great lodging at ★ **Chicaugon Lake Inn** (1700 County Rd. 424, 906/265-9244, www.chicaugonlakeinn.com, $$), predictably located near Chicaugon Lake in Iron River. The year-round hotel has sparsely decorated but well-kept rooms, whirlpool suites, and free wireless Internet access. Check out their special rates for the fall color season. **Lac O' Seasons Resort** (176 Stanley Lake Dr., 906/265-4881 or 800/797-5226, $$$) rents 14 cabins and cottages on the shores of Stanley Lake. Each lodging features either three or four bedrooms, a gas stove, and a kitchen with a dishwasher. Some have decks and outdoor fire rings. In Crystal Falls, **Michi-Aho Resort** (2181 M-69, 906/875-3514, www.michi-aho.com, $) has rooms and cottages on the banks of the Michigamme River. These are no-frills accommodations, yet their knotty pine walls and mission-style furniture engender a real "up north" feeling.

If you like to play and stay at the same location, the **Dancing Eagles Hotel at Northern Waters Casino Resort** (N5384

US 45, Watersmeet, 906/358-4226 or 800/583-3599, www.lvdcasino.com, $$) in Watersmeet is a great choice. Operated by the Lac Vieux Desert Band of the Lake Superior Chippewa tribe, the 132-room hotel offers a bevy of amenities, including a heated indoor pool, sauna, and whirlpool, and fireplaces in some rooms.

Camping
The ★ **Ottawa National Forest** (www.fs.usda.gov) maintains 27 auto-accessible campgrounds, all with tent pads, fire grates, and some form of toilet facilities. Many are located along rivers and lakes. Most tend to be quite rustic and secluded, with the exception of Black River Harbor, Sylvania, and Bobcat Lake. A few, like Black River Harbor, require a fee and allow reservations through a central reservation system (800/280-2267 or 800/283-2267). Rates for these campgrounds are $16 per day, with a 14-day maximum stay. For more information on a specific campground, contact a district ranger station or the **Ottawa National Forest Headquarters** (E6248 US 2, Ironwood, 906/932-1330 or 800/562-1201, 8am-4pm Mon.-Fri.).

INFORMATION AND SERVICES
For more information on the Iron River area and Iron County, contact the **Economic Chamber Alliance** (50 E. Genesee St., Iron River, 906/265-3822, www.iron.org). All of Iron County is in the central time zone.

Aspirus Iron River Hospital (1400 W. Ice Lake Rd., Iron River, 906/265-6121, www.aspirus.org) can see to your medical needs. For financial needs, including ATMs and branch locations, try **Flagstar** (234 W. Genesee St., 906/265-5144, www.flagstar.com) or **Miners State Bank** (312 W. Genesee St., 906/265-5131, www.msbir.com).

To make sense of what the Ottawa National Forest has to offer, start with a map. You can pick up a small free brochure or large topographic map ($4) at the **Ottawa National Forest Headquarters** (E6248 US 2,

Ironwood, 906/932-1330, 8am-4pm Mon.-Fri.) in Ironwood or at the **Watersmeet Ranger District Office** (US 2 and US 45, Watersmeet, 906/358-4551). Other district offices, in Bessemer, Bergland, and Ontonagon, should have maps and brochures, although budget cuts have forced them to curtail other visitor services.

GETTING THERE AND AROUND
Car
Like many of the larger cities in the U.P.'s western reaches, Iron River is close to the state's border with Wisconsin. If you're coming from Wisconsin, take W-139 across the border; it becomes M-189 in Michigan. US 2 runs from Ironwood east to Iron Mountain. If you're traveling to or from the Keweenaw Peninsula, take US 141.

Air
Generally, the farther west you go in the Upper Peninsula, the farther you get from conveniently located airports. One of the drawbacks to the area's isolation is the considerable distance many destinations are from an airport. Thankfully, both **Delta County Airport** (ESC, 3300 Airport Rd., Escanaba, 906/786-4902, www.flyesc.com), near Escanaba, and **Sawyer International Airport** (MQT, 125 G Ave., Gwinn, 906/346-3308, www.sawyerairport.com), near Marquette, offer plenty of options for car rentals. Wisconsin's **Rhinelander-Oneida County Airport** (RHI, 3375 Airport Rd., Rhinelander, WI, 715/365-3416, www.flyrhinelander.com) is a bit closer and has daily flights to and from Minneapolis-St. Paul on Delta Airlines and vehicle rentals through Alamo, Avis, Budget, and Enterprise.

Bus
Getting to Iron River is easy on **Indian Trails** buses (800/292-3831, www.indiantrails.com), which run regular trips from Escanaba to Ironwood.

Ironwood

With mammoth Lake Superior providing the requisite moisture, the northwestern corner of the U.P. certainly deserves its moniker of Big Snow Country. Cool air moving across the warmer waters of Lake Superior creates lake-effect snow when it hits the land, generating an astounding 200 inches (508 cm) per year on average. Combined with the rugged hills, it's no surprise this area is home to many of the Midwest's largest downhill ski resorts. As a result, the western U.P., especially around Ironwood, is one of Michigan's most heavily marketed tourism areas, luring sizable crowds of skiers up US 51 every weekend from Detroit, Chicago, and eastern Wisconsin.

Ironwood hugs the Montreal River, which forms the border between Michigan and Wisconsin. On the other side of the river lies Ironwood's sister city of Hurley, Wisconsin. Together they were once the center of activity for the iron miners of the Gogebic Range. Ironwood had the stores and services; Hurley provided the bars and brothels. During the heyday of iron mining—from the early 1900s to about 1930—their combined population topped 15,000. As the mines became less productive over time, much of the prosperity left the region. But in the wake of the exodus, opulent mansions and other monuments of wealth were left behind, similar to what happened in Keweenaw copper country.

Ironwood today is a hardscrabble town that still hints at its prosperous past. The locals are friendly and would probably agree that the natural beauty of the land surrounding Ironwood is what attracts visitors, much more than the city itself.

SIGHTS
Downtown Ironwood

There are a few interesting diversions in Ironwood's downtown, one of which is the **Ironwood Memorial Building** (213 S. Marquette St.), a beautiful structure that serves as a memorial for area residents killed in combat. World War I scenes are portrayed in stained glass, a statue of a soldier stands guard in the lobby, and displays outline the history of the region. Stop by the **Old Depot Park Museum** (150 N. Lowell St., 906/932-0287, www.ironwoodchamber.org, 8am-2pm Mon.-Fri., free), once the train station and now an interesting museum devoted to the area's history. Another noteworthy site is the **Miners Memorial Mural** (E. McLeod Ave., just east of S. Suffolk St.). Painted on the side of a building, it shows the faces and names of several dozen miners who died on the job. You can also visit the **Historic Ironwood Theater** (113 E. Aurora St., 906/932-0618, www.ironwoodtheatre.net, office open noon-4:30pm Wed.-Fri.) to learn more about the town's heritage. Docent-led tours (Wed.-Fri. summer, donation) are usually offered in the late morning or early afternoon.

Hiawatha

After encountering Big John, the absurdly tall miner at the Iron Mountain Iron Mine, you'd be correct for thinking the Upper Peninsula has a thing for oversize historical figures. Case in point: **Hiawatha** (Suffolk St.), the 50-foot (15-meter) fiberglass rendering of a Native American that serves as a very touristy roadside attraction.

★ Little Girl's Point

Just minutes from the strip-mall world of US 2, a genuine U.P. experience awaits. Follow County Road 505 north from Ironwood to reach **Little Girl's Point,** an area favorite. Perched high on a bluff over Lake Superior, this tranquil county park features a sandy beach, a boat launch, picnic tables, grills, and fantastic views. Take time to absorb the stunning Porcupine Mountains to the east and the Apostle Islands to the west.

Black River National Forest Scenic Byway

Gogebic County tourism folks heavily promote this 15-mile (24-km) stretch of County Road 513 from Bessemer north to Lake Superior, and for good reason. The two-lane road itself is pleasant enough, a wooded drive that twists in tandem with the Black River, hidden away in the forest just off the road's eastern shoulder. But even better, it links together several noteworthy attractions.

The end of County Road 513, Black River Harbor, is a popular Ottawa National Forest campground on Lake Superior, with a large day-use area, sand beach, and boat launch. You can also pick up the North Country National Scenic Trail here. For campground reservations, call the U.S. Forest Service central reservation system (800/280-2267 or 800/283-2267).

★ Copper Peak

You'll see the peak long before you reach it. About 9 miles (14.5 km) north of Bessemer, the rocky outcrop of Copper Peak rises 364 feet (111 meters) above the surrounding countryside, crowned by the 421-foot (128 -meter) **Copper Peak Ski Flying Hill** (906/932-3500, www.copperpeak.org). Ski flying is similar to ski jumping but uses different equipment to achieve even longer distances. Copper Peak, built in 1970, is the only ski flying hill in the western hemisphere and the highest artificial jump in the world.

From Memorial Day to Labor Day and on weekends through mid-October, a chairlift, elevator, and steps run to the top for a heart-thumping skier's-eye view of the chute (9:30am-4:30pm, $25 adults, children 5-14 $10, children under 5 free). This is not a trip for the faint of heart. But if you can get over a little knee knocking, you'll be wowed by the panorama of the surrounding countryside, with views stretching across the undulating green of the national forest, the serpentine Black River, and the aqua blue horizon of Lake Superior. The Copper Peak complex also offers 12 miles (19.3 km) of mountain biking trails.

ENTERTAINMENT
Microbrewery

Cold Iron Brewery (104 S. Lowell St., Ironwood, 906/285-7020, https://coldironbrewing.com, noon-9pm Wed. and Sun., noon-11pm Thurs.-Sat.) is a tempting craft brewery/watering hole strategically located in downtown Ironwood just a few blocks from the Wisconsin border. Its cleverly named offerings include Michiconsin Honey Cream (an homage to its location), Ski Race Sweet Stout, and Grapefruit Shandy. Stop in for a pint between your outdoor activities.

FESTIVALS AND EVENTS
Festival Ironwood

A midsummer tradition, **Festival Ironwood** (906/932-1122, www.ironwoodchamber.org) celebrates this resilient town's culture and character on the third weekend of July. Held at Depot Park, near the museum, the event features food, music, games, plus other fun diversions. This event is a great way to meet and chat with local people, who are known for their friendliness.

SUMMER RECREATION
Hiking and Biking

The lengthy **North Country National Scenic Trail** (www.nps.gov/noco) has been mentioned before, but the footpath really is the area's best hiking. When it's completed, the North Country Trail's 4,600 miles (7,400 km) will make it the longest off-road hiking trail in the United States, more than double the length of the renowned Appalachian Trail. The section that passes through Ontonagon and Gogebic Counties cuts through the Ottawa National Forest and Porcupine Mountains Wilderness State Park and into Wisconsin near Ironwood. Although it's one of the nation's longest trails it's also one of the least traveled, providing plenty of solitude for long stretches along the path.

In a land filled with stunning views, you'll find one of the best on the **Gogebic Ridge Hiking Trail,** a spur from the North Country Trail about 40 miles (64 km) northeast of Ironwood. The trail is 8 miles (12.9 km) long and reaches its pinnacle at an overlook on one of the longest, tallest cliff faces in the state, complete with views of Lake Gogebic and the forested countryside. The south end of the trail skirts Weary Lake. Contact the **U.S. Forest Service** (906/884-2411) for additional information about both the North Country and Gogebic Ridge trails.

When the snow isn't on the ground, the extreme western U.P. is prime mountain biking territory. More than 100 miles (160 km) of the **Pines and Mines Mountain Bike Trail** cut through Gogebic County alone, while 9 miles (14.5 km) of trails form the **Wolverine Mountain Bike Trail.** One of the fat-tire highlights is **Copper Peak,** where cyclists can enjoy a ride up the hill that would be a ski lift in the wintertime, then tear through the woods on the way back down.

Canoeing and Kayaking

Some of the best paddling the U.P. can offer is in Ottawa National Forest's 2,000 miles (3,200 km) of streams and rivers. Paddlers in the Ironwood region will likely want to make the short trip east to the forest.

Fishing

Lake Superior, the largest, deepest, and coldest of the Great Lakes, offers spectacular opportunities for deep-water fishing. Operating from the Black River Harbor near Ironwood, an excellent partner is **Glacier Girl Charter Fishing** (E7651 Harding Rd., Bessemer, 715/892-4613, www.glaciergirlcharters.com) for full-day ($800) and half-day ($550) charters. Your best bet for stream, river, and inland lake fishing is to head east to Ottawa National Forest's 2,000 miles (3,200 km) of waterways and 500 lakes.

1: Little Girl's Point 2: bridge over the Black River in the Ottawa National Forest on the North Country National Scenic Trail

Golf

One of the western U.P.'s finest golf courses can be found in Ironwood itself. The **Gogebic Country Club** (200 Country Club Rd., 906/932-2515, www.gogebiccountryclub.com, $42 for 18 holes with cart, $30 for 9 holes with cart) has been a favorite Michigan golf spot since the early 1920s, when the attractive stone clubhouse was constructed. Its 18 holes measure around 6,000 yards. Take US 2 a few miles west of Ironwood and turn south on Country Club Road.

Off-Road Vehicles

The closest major off-road vehicle trail in Ottawa National Forest is the 67-mile (108-km) route that runs from Marenisco, 25 miles (40 km) east of Ironwood on US 2, to Iron River. There are, of course, smaller trails closer to Ironwood, but remember that ORVs are prohibited in the national forest except on designated, marked trails. Maps are available from the **U.S. Forest Service** (E6248 US 2, Ironwood, 906/932-1330, www.fs.fed.us, 8am-4pm Mon.-Fri.) and the **Michigan DNR** (427 US 41 N., Baraga, 906/353-6651, 8am-5pm Mon.-Fri.).

Waterfalls

From Little Girl's Point, north of Ironwood on County Road 505, continue west on County Road 505 to reach **Superior Falls.** The rushing Montreal River puts on its final spectacular show here, plummeting more than 40 feet (12 meters), then squeezing through a narrow gorge before spilling into Lake Superior a short distance away. You can also reach the falls by taking US 2 about 11 miles (17.7 km) west from Ironwood and turning north on W-122, which becomes County Road 505 when you cross back into Michigan. In about 4.8 miles (7.7 km), watch for a small brown sign that directs you west into a small parking area near a Northern States Power substation. From there, it's a short walk to the falls. You can also continue down the path past the falls to the shores of Lake Superior, an excellent place to watch the sunset. Be advised that the power company sometimes limits access to the falls, and the gate is occasionally locked.

Choosing a Ski Resort

When thinking of downhill skiing, famous destinations such as the Rocky Mountains or the Alps usually come to mind before the Great Lakes region. And while it would be misleading to say Ironwood has the same caliber of skiing as those famous places, it is fair to say that the abundant ski runs, resorts, and snowfalls of the western Upper Peninsula make it perhaps the finest destination for downhill skiing between the Rockies and the Appalachians.

There are numerous ski resorts within a short drive of Ironwood. Whether you like carving a half pipe or leaving the first tracks on a backcountry slope, you'll find enough variety and deep snow to keep you satisfied, often for a fraction of what you'd pay at one of the large Colorado resorts. Here is a handy list to help you choose:

- **Best for families and newbies:** Big Powderhorn Mountain
- **Best for ungroomed trails and snowboarders:** Blackjack Ski Resort
- **Cheapest choice:** Ski Brule
- **Most challenging slopes:** Indianhead Mountain Resort
- **Best terrain and views:** Porcupine Mountains Ski Area
- **Highest jumps:** Pine Mountain Ski Jump and Copper Peak Ski Flying Hill

As its name implies, **Interstate Falls** is located on the border of Michigan's Upper Peninsula and Wisconsin. Like Superior Falls, Interstate Falls is part of the Montreal River, but this waterfall is shorter, at 20 feet (6 meters), and wider, with a fairly impressive flow when the water level is high. You'll want to cross into Wisconsin to see it. Take US 2 west into Wisconsin to an unpaved road about 0.25 miles (0.4 km) past the border and follow the signs for **Peterson Falls,** which is a short walk upstream.

Heading north from Bessemer on the Black River National Forest Scenic Byway will take you to a beautiful and popular lineup of five waterfalls on the Black River, which run roughly parallel to the byway. In the last few miles before Lake Superior, you'll be able to see the **Great Conglomerate, Potawatomi, Gorge, Sandstone,** and **Rainbow Falls.**

WINTER RECREATION
★ Downhill Skiing

With the exception of the ski area in the Porcupine Mountains Wilderness State Park, the area's downhill ski resorts line up conveniently along a short stretch of US 2 just east of Ironwood. Each venue welcomes both downhill skiers and snowboarders. Lift ticket prices vary with the season; package rates that include lodging usually offer the best deals. Those who want to explore all the area's terrain should ask about the interchangeable lift ticket, which is available at each participating resort. It's good on weekdays only at the area's four major resorts: Powderhorn, Blackjack, Indianhead, and Whitecap Mountain, located just over the border in Wisconsin.

Heading east from Ironwood, the first resort you'll reach is **Big Powderhorn Mountain** (N11375 Powderhorn Rd., Bessemer, 906/932-4838 or 800/501-7669, www.bigpowderhorn.net, daily in season, day pass $89 adults, $72 ages 10-17 and over age 64, $42 ages 7-9) in Bessemer. Powderhorn radiates an early 1970s feel, and the giant fiberglass skier at the entrance—complete with red and blue vintage '70s skiwear—says it all. The resort's 25 downhill runs are on two faces, with 700 vertical feet (213 meters) and nine double chairlifts. Perhaps more than the others, Big Powderhorn Mountain caters to families, with affordable lift tickets, mostly tame runs, and plenty of ski-in, ski-out lodging bordering its slopes. In the main lodge at the base you'll find a cafeteria, ski rental and repair, a ski school, and a bar.

In 2014, **Indianhead Mountain Resort** and **Blackjack Ski Resort** merged under the management of a new company, **Big Snow Resort** (800/346-3426, www.bigsnow.com, $79 adults, $65 ages 6-15). Both resorts continue to operate under their legacy names, but Big Snow lift tickets are valid at both resorts. **Indianhead Mountain Resort** (500 Indianhead Rd., Wakefield, 9am-4pm Sun.-Fri., 9am-8pm Sat. and holidays) is the area's largest resort, with 638 vertical feet (194 meters), five chairlifts, two T-bars, and 22 runs. Indianhead offers some of the region's most challenging, although overly groomed, skiing and pleasant runs that wind for more than a mile through the woods. Indianhead's lodging and sales, rentals, and repair services are located at the top of the resort and offer more choices than area competitors. The day lodge even offers great views of the Ottawa National Forest spilling out across the valley and far beyond the slopes.

Blackjack Ski Resort (N11251 Black Jack Rd., Bessemer, 9am-4pm daily) makes the most of its terrain. Cameron Run and Spillway are often left ungroomed and offer good bump skiing, and Blackjack is arguably the best resort for snowboarders, with the area's best half pipe, served by its own rope tow, and a great terrain park on Broad Ax. Look to Blackjack for a variety of snowboard events, including camps and competitions. Blackjack offers 16 runs, four double chairlifts, and 465 vertical feet (142 meters). A day lodge at the base offers food service along with ski rental and repair. A limited number of condo accommodations line the slopes. The Loggers Lounge upstairs hosts the area's liveliest after-ski scene.

Mt. Zion Ski Hill (E4946 Jackson Rd., Ironwood, 906/932-3718, www.gogebic.edu, hours vary, $45 full day, $25 half day) is operated by the students at Gogebic Community College and is the perfect place for family winter recreation. In addition to skiing, snow tubing and equipment rental are also offered.

Ski and Snowshoe Trails

Milje Trails (2 miles/3.2 km south of Wakefield on County Road 519, 906/229-5267, donation), also called Miljevich Trail, is a groomed 9-mile (14-km) cross-country skinning trail. Amenities include a warming cabin and light refreshments.

Active Backwoods Retreat (E5299 W. Pioneer Rd., Ironwood, 906/932-3502, www. michiweb.com/abrski, $10-12), or **ABR** for short, grooms 25 miles (40 km) of trails for skiing and striding or snowshoeing on hundreds of acres of private land 3 miles (4.8 km) south of Ironwood. The trails are open daily as well as some nights for lighted skiing or moonlight skiing. A warming hut, lessons, and rentals are available.

Between Ironwood and Bessemer, take Section 12 Road north from US 2 to reach **Wolverine Nordic Trails** (www. wolverinenordic.com, donation). Situated on private land and maintained by volunteers, the 9.3 miles (15 km) of groomed trails wind through the hilly country south of the Big Powderhorn ski area. In fact, you can ride one of Powderhorn's chairlifts ($3) to access the network. Otherwise, begin at the lot with the warming hut on Sunset Road off Section 12 Road.

If solitude is more important to you than set trails, don't overlook the vast terrain available in the 982,895-acre Ottawa National Forest. The **U.S. Forest Service** office (E6248 US 2, Ironwood, 906/932-1330, www.fs.fed.gov, 8am-4pm Mon.-Fri.) has national forest maps and can suggest trails to try.

Snowmobiling

Of the western U.P.'s hundreds of miles of snowmobile trails, plenty are accessible from Ironwood. **Trail 2** heads east from Ironwood across the rest of the Upper Peninsula. Take **Trail 11** north to Porcupine Mountains State Park and Lake Superior. Heading the opposite direction, Trail 11 runs northwest to Lake Superior where Michigan and Wisconsin meet. Plenty of these trails drop south into

Wisconsin and connect with that state's network of snowmobile trails.

FOOD

It looks like a classic corner tavern, but **Don & GG's** (1300 E. Cloverland Dr., 906/932-2312, 4pm-8:30pm Mon.-Thurs., 4pm-9pm Fri.-Sat., under $13), on US 2 in Ironwood, might surprise you with its vegetarian dishes and smoked trout salad. Don't worry—you can still get burgers and chicken dinners. The **Hoop 'N' Holler Tavern** (115 Hoop 'N Holler Rd., Bergland, 906/575-5555, noon-midnight Sun.-Fri., noon-10pm Sat., under $10) is a tavern in the classic mold, complete with plenty of good cheer and some very good tavern food, including burgers, sandwiches, and pizza. Located on Lake Gogebic's northwest side, Hoop 'N' Holler has a beach available in the summertime. Bergland is in the eastern time zone, one hour ahead of Ironwood.

The ★ **Kimball Inn** (6622 US 2, Hurley, WI, 715/561-4095, 4pm-8pm Wed.-Sat., $8-20) is actually in Wisconsin, but it's worth the extra 4-mile (6.4-km) drive west on US 2 from the border to sample its smoked barbecue, charbroiled steaks, grinders (Italian sandwiches), and more.

ACCOMMODATIONS

You'll find a large selection of independent motels along US 2, many of which offer great deals and clean and comfortable, if simple, rooms. A couple of good choices are the **Classic Motor Inn** (1200 E. Cloverland Dr., Ironwood, 906/932-2000, www.westernup.com/classicmotorinn, $) and the **Cedars Motel** (777 W. Cloverland Dr., Ironwood, 906/932-4376, $) at the west end of US 2.

The larger ski resorts have slope-side or near-slope accommodations that range from dormitories to simple motel rooms to deluxe condominiums. Prices range widely for almost every budget, and good value can be had outside ski season. Try **Indianhead Reservations** (500 Indianhead Dr., Wakefield, 800/346-3426, www.bigsnow.com,

$$$) or **Big Powderhorn Mountain and Lodging** (N11375 Powderhorn Rd., Bessemer, 800/222-3131, www.bigpowderhorn.net, $$$) for plenty of choices. Ask about package deals with lift tickets if you're traveling in winter.

For something more intimate, you can't beat the **Bear Track Cabins** (N15325 Black River Rd., Ironwood, 906/932-2144, $). National forest land practically surrounds the inn's three log cabins, which have a great location 1 mile (1.6 km) from Lake Superior's Black River Harbor and are near scores of hiking, biking, and skiing trails. Each cabin has a full kitchen and use of the Finnish sauna. The **Regal Country Inn** (1602 E. US 2, Wakefield, 906/229-5122, $$) looks nothing like an old Victorian home from the outside, but if you're inside one of its Victorian or historic rooms you'll swear you're staying at a B&B. Antique beds and decorations, pictures of local historic figures, quilted bedspreads, and a gourmet breakfast (for an additional charge; continental breakfast is included) all add to this inn's charm. Free wireless Internet is an added plus.

Finally, chain motels cluster near the US 2/US 51 interchange, including the **Days Inn by Wyndham** (13355 US 51, Hurley, WI, 715/629-9731, $$), with an indoor pool. Some rooms include microwaves and refrigerators.

Camping

True to Michigan state park form, **Lake Gogebic State Park** (800/447-2757, www.michigan.gov/dnr, $19-22) offers a fine modern campground, with large, open sites on the western shore of Lake Gogebic. A boat launch, a small sandy beach, and a nice picnic area are nearby. Lake Gogebic is known for great walleye and perch fishing, so pack a rod even if you don't come with a boat. Reservations are accepted but generally not needed.

INFORMATION AND SERVICES

For visitor information, assistance, and planning, contact the **Ironwood Area Chamber of Commerce** (150 N. Lowell St.,

906/932-1122, www.ironwoodchamber.org) or the **Western Upper Peninsula Convention and Visitor Bureau** (906/932-4850 or 800/522-5657, www.explorewesternup.com).

Ironwood's hospital is the **Aspirus Ironwood Hospital** (10561 N. Grand View Ln., 906/932-2525, www.aspirus.org), just north of US 2 between Bessemer and Ironwood. There's no shortage of banks in Ironwood and Bessemer. You'll find offices of both local and regional banks.

GETTING THERE AND AROUND
Car

Ironwood is tucked just about as far into the U.P.'s western corner as you can get. In fact, Ironwood is as far from Detroit as Detroit is from New York City. US 2 runs through Ironwood from the east or the west. From the south, drive up W 77 or US 51. M-28 connects the north and east in the Upper Peninsula.

Air

Sawyer International Airport (MQT, 125 G Ave., Gwinn, 906/346-3308, www.sawyerairport.com), near Marquette, is the largest facility in the Upper Peninsula and has daily flights on **American Airlines** with nonstop service from Chicago O'Hare Airport and on **Delta Airlines** to Detroit.

Closer to the Ironwood area is **Houghton County Memorial Airport** (CMX, 23810 Airpark Blvd., Calumet, 906/482-3970, www.houghtoncounty.org), which has scheduled flights from Chicago on **United Airlines,** as well as vehicle rentals by **Alamo** and **National.** In Wisconsin, **The Rhinelander-Oneida County Airport** (RHI, 3375 Airport Rd., Rhinelander, WI, 715/365-3416, www.fly-rhi.org) has daily flights from Minneapolis-St. Paul on **Delta Airlines** and vehicle rentals by **Alamo, Avis, Budget, Enterprise,** and **National.**

Bus

Getting to Ironwood by bus is pretty easy, even if you're coming from Chicago, Detroit, or farther afield. A combination of **Greyhound** (800/231-2222, www.greyhound.com) and **Indian Trails** (800/292-3831, www.indiantrails.com) routes can get you there with relative ease. Ironwood is on Indian Trails' St. Ignace-Escanaba-Ironwood line.

Porcupine Mountains and Ontonagon

If the Superior Upland is known for its ruggedness, then the jagged, heavily wooded terrain of the Porcupine Mountains region can be virtually impregnable. Here you'll find the closest thing Michigan has to offer in the way of highlands, with steep trails descending into rocky valleys amid thick hardwood and evergreen forests. Cities seem to be little more than an afterthought. Many of the businesses exist to serve the hardy hikers, anglers, and campers who make treks here each summer. If you're looking to have your outdoors skills tested, you've come to the right place.

SIGHTS

TOP EXPERIENCE

★ Porcupine Mountains Wilderness State Park

Anchored along the Lake Superior shore in the northwest corner of the U.P., **Porcupine Mountains Wilderness State Park** (906/885-5275, www.michigan.gov/dnr) covers 60,000 acres, making it the largest property in Michigan's state park system. The Porcupine Mountains were a national park site in the 1940s but came under state control

Porcupine Mountains

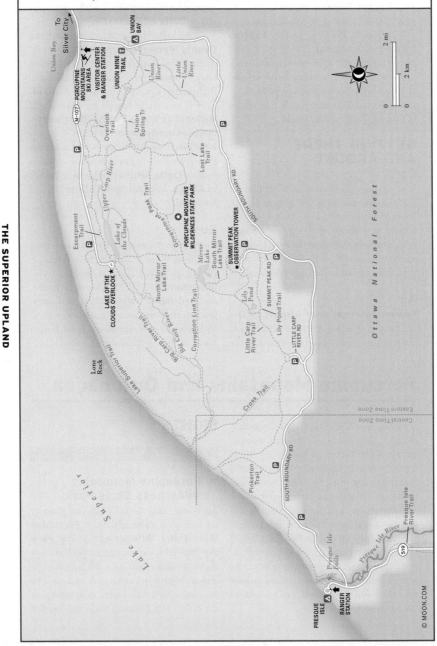

To Silver City

Union Bay

PORCUPINE MOUNTAINS SKI AREA

VISITOR CENTER & RANGER STATION

UNION BAY

UNION MINE TRAIL

M-107

Union River

Little Union River

Union Spring Tr

Overlook Trail

Escarpment Trail

Upper Carp River

Lost Lake Trail

SOUTH BOUNDARY RD

Escarpment Trail

Government Peak Trail

PORCUPINE MOUNTAINS WILDERNESS STATE PARK

Mirror Lake

South Mirror Lake Trail

SUMMIT PEAK OBSERVATION TOWER

LAKE OF THE CLOUDS OVERLOOK

Lake of the Clouds

North Mirror Lake Trail

Correction Line Trail

Big Carp River

Lily Pond

SUMMIT PEAK RD

Lily Pond Trail

Little Carp River Trail

Little Carp River Trail

Big Carp River Trail

LITTLE CARP RIVER RD

Lone Rock

Lake Superior Trail

Cross Trail

Lake Superior

Ottawa National Forest

Eastern Time Zone

Central Time Zone

Pinkerton Trail

SOUTH BOUNDARY RD

Presque Isle River

Presque Isle Falls

Presque Isle River Trail

519

PRESQUE ISLE

RANGER STATION

0   2 mi

0   2 km

© MOON.COM

in 1945 when loggers threatened the virgin timber resources before the state acted.

According to legend, someone once decided that this rumpled landscape of low mountains and tall pines resembled the silhouette of a porcupine. The name stuck, along with its affectionate nickname: "The Porkies." The area is a focal point for casual hikers and hardcore backpackers, with 90-plus miles (145 km) of well-marked and well-maintained trails—more than you'll find in many national parks, and certainly more than you'll find in most of the Great Lakes region.

In this case, bigger means better. The park preserves vast stands of virgin hemlock, pine, and the largest tract of virgin hardwoods between the Rockies and the Adirondacks. There are also secluded lakes, wild rivers, and some of the Midwest's highest peaks. Summit Peak tops out at 1,958 feet (597 meters). Unlike most state parks, Porcupine Mountains Wilderness is large enough to provide a true sense of serenity and isolation, offering a treasured escape from the civilized world.

Many visitors to the Porkies head immediately toward the justly famous **Lake of the Clouds Overlook.** From the parking lot at the western terminus of M-107, it's just a few steps to the overlook, where the placid lake slices a long sliver of blue through a thick blanket of jade forest hundreds of feet below. The exquisite view is arguably the most dramatic in Michigan. Photographs fail to do it justice—it really has to be seen to be appreciated.

Ontonagon County Historical Museum

The Ontonagon Boulder was pried from its namesake riverbank a few miles upstream from the Lake Superior shoreline community of Ontonagon. Today, the two-ton mass of native copper resides at the Smithsonian, and Ontonagon's mining heritage thrives only in museums, especially since the mine and smelter in nearby White Pine closed in 1995. White Pine now is little more than a forlorn ghost town of 1950s tract housing.

You can see Ontonagon's happier days presented at the very worthwhile **Ontonagon County Historical Museum** (422 River St., 906/884-6165, www.ontonagonmuseum.org, 10am-4pm Tues.-Sat., $5), a lavender building on US 41/M-38, downtown's main street. The historical society also offers self-guided tours of the nearby Ontonagon Lighthouse (11am-3pm daily, donation), which is time well spent.

Adventure Copper Mine

In Greenland, 12 miles (19.3 km) southeast of Ontonagon, the **Adventure Copper Mine** (200 Adventure Ave., Greenland, 906/883-3371, www.adventureminetours.com, 9am-6pm Mon.-Sat., 11am-6pm Sun. Memorial Day-mid-Oct., tours $32-145) operated for 70 years without turning a profit. Today, it's more successful as a tourism destination, offering surface and underground tours that range from 45 minutes to five hours. One of the tours recreates the experience of old-time miners by having visitors rappel down a mineshaft in total darkness, explore small areas, and get a little dirty. There are some tamer underground tours, too. To get here, take Adventure Road off M-38 in Greenland.

Old Victoria

Originally established by copper miners in the 1840s, the tiny town of **Rockland** was nearly destroyed by fire in 1890. It was rebuilt in the popular Victorian style of the day. Several Victorian facades still decorate this small community in the Ontonagon River valley, which is 14 miles (23 km) south of Ontonagon on US 45. From downtown Rockland, follow Victoria Dam Road southwest 2 miles (3.2 km) to **Old Victoria** (906/886-2617, www.ontonagon.net/oldvictoria, donation), a cluster of miners' log homes huddled around a once-lucrative copper mine shaft. Locals continue their strenuous efforts to save this historic site. Its new designation as a Keweenaw National Historical Park cooperating site may attract new attention and needed funds. The homes are open most summer afternoons when guides are available. Visitors are welcome to wander the grounds at any time; donations are accepted and appreciated. Continue past Old Victoria to the **Victoria Dam,** a hydroelectric facility and a surprisingly pretty spot popular with local anglers.

Ontonagon Lighthouse

The county historical society's current project is the restoration of the 1866 **Ontonagon Lighthouse,** which replaced the original built in 1853. Contact the **Ontonagon County Historical Society** (906/884-6165, www.ontonagonmuseum.org) for information on public tours and the ongoing restoration effort.

SUMMER RECREATION
Hiking and Biking Trails

Detailed maps for the following hikes and more can be found at online at **Michigan Trail Maps** (www.michigantrailmaps.com).

The **Lake of the Clouds Overlook** at **Porcupine Mountains Wilderness State Park** (906/885-5275, www.michigan.gov/dnr) serves as the trailhead for some of the park's most rugged and scenic routes. To fully appreciate the Lake of the Clouds view, hike the aptly named **Escarpment Trail,** which winds east and skims over Cloud Peak and Cuyahoga Peak, running parallel to M-107. Bordered by a sheer cliff, the 4.4-mile (7.1-km) trail (one-way) is considered by many to be the most beautiful in the park. It's also one of the more challenging hikes. Allow ample time to stop and enjoy the shimmering lake and valley floor spreading out around you.

At its eastern trailhead, the Escarpment Trail links up with the 7.5-mile (12-km) one-way **Government Peak Trail** at a point about 0.5 miles (0.8 km) south of M-107. This secluded route (also one of the more challenging) drops south over the Upper Carp River and past Trap Falls, then swings west and scales Government Peak. As quickly as it rises, the trail drops down to quiet Mirror Lake, a perfect spot to soak weary feet after a full day of hiking.

Beginning at the Lake of the Clouds

Overlook and continuing west, the **Big Carp River Trail** runs 16 miles (26 km) out and back to Lake Superior. This fine route begins at the unspoiled Lake of the Clouds (although it can be walked in either direction), with its dramatic peaks, and leads hikers along a shaded river valley of hemlocks and ferns, past the park's highest waterfall (the 25-foot/8-meter Shining Cloud Falls), and along a dry ridge top. This route is considered rather challenging.

Near the park's southern tier, visitors can enjoy a somewhat easier hike while taking in the highest view in the park from the **Summit Peak Observation Tower** at 1,958 feet (598 meters), which is made even taller with a 40-foot (12-meter) observation tower at its crest. It's an inspiring panorama, a vast landscape unscarred by humans. In fact, the only sign of civilization is a spindly ski jump 18 miles (29 km) away, rising above the tree line like a circus clown on stilts. On a clear day, scour the horizon for a glimpse of Lake Superior's Apostle Islands, nearly 40 miles (64 km) west. To access the trailhead, take the South Boundary Road south from Silver City for approximately 10 miles (16.1 km) until you arrive at Summit Peak Road. Turn right and continue for 1 additional mile (1.6 km) before arriving at the Summit Peak Scenic Area. From there it's a 0.75-mile (1.2-km) hike to the tower.

One of the park's most spectacular trails is probably its most accessible: the **East and West River Trail** parallels the wild and turbulent Presque Isle River. From the Presque Isle Campground at the park's west end, you can follow the river 1 mile (1.6 km) upstream and down the opposite bank as it corkscrews through narrow rock walls and tumbles into Lake Superior. Keep a tight hold on children and pets along this trail, and don't think about wading—the current is swift and dangerous. To dangle your toes or let your dog take a

1: Lake of the Clouds Overlook 2: Escarpment Trail 3: the Ontonagon Lighthouse 4: the Carp River valley in fall

swim, there's a wonderfully deep, clear, and placid backwater pool just east of the main channel right near Lake Superior. With relatively flat terrain and a fairly short length (2 miles/3.2 km out and back), this is a fairly easy hike.

Long before the Porcupine Mountains were preserved for their virgin forest and natural beauty, miners harvested the rich minerals buried in the bedrock. At the east end of the park, the **Union Mine Trail** provides a glimpse into life in the 1840s, when the Porkies were part of the area's copper rush. Marked with white mine shovels to indicate points of interest, this self-guided interpretive trail forms a 1-mile (1.6-km) loop along the spring-fed Union River and the site of an old copper mine, now largely reclaimed by nature. In the shadow of lofty hemlocks, you'll see how miners tunneled shafts into the riverbank and learn about their lives in the wilderness—still untamed today. This is a short and easy hike.

Fishing

Fishing is one of the many recreational benefits in this vast expanse of wilderness. The park's most striking location, Lake of the Clouds, is accessible to anglers, along with a number of other lakes and streams. Try Mirror Lake and the Carp River, Presque Isle River, and Union River. Contact the **DNR Park Headquarters and Visitors Center** (906/885-5275) for regulations and information.

Beaches

Porcupine Mountains Wilderness State Park is known for its beaches along more than 50 miles (80 km) of Lake Superior shoreline. The most popular is **Union Bay,** which is easily accessible by car at the east end of the park. It's a lovely place, but the water is rarely warm enough to allow for swimming.

Golf

Golfers can play the nine holes at **Ontonagon Golf Course** (19906 Firesteel Rd., Ontonagon,

906/884-4130, $15 for 9 holes, $30 for 18 holes). The clubhouse is fairly Spartan, but the par-35 course makes for a nice round, and the pro shop can provide you with everything you need for an afternoon on the links.

Off-Road Vehicles

The old Copper Range Railroad grade bisects Ontonagon County and the southern Keweenaw Peninsula from Mass City north to Houghton, a distance of more than 41 miles (66 km). Throughout the state, the DNR has purchased many of these old grades and removed the rails, maintaining them as multiuse trails. In the U.P., that usually means snowmobiles and ATVs. Near the intersection of M-26 and M-38 at Lake Mine, the trail spans the Firesteel River on three bridges, which range 65-85 feet (20-26 meters) high. Stop at the **Michigan DNR Office** (427 US 41 N., Baraga, 906/353-6651, 8am-5pm Mon.-Fri.) in Baraga for a map of the rail trail that shows access points. Where the trail crosses a road, look for a yellow-and-black snowmobile crossing sign on the highway or a DNR ATV wooden trail sign on the trail.

Waterfalls

The Porcupine Mountains' more than 60 waterfalls can seem a bit overwhelming, but despite the many choices, some stand out. Make the brief trek to **Presque Isle Falls** in the western portion of the park. Presque Isle Falls is actually a chain of three falls—Manabezho, Manido, and Nawadaha. The first two are accessible from the nearby parking areas. Manabezho has a fairly low drop, with rocky points punctuating the water. Manido occupies a wide spot on the river and resembles a stairway with a gentle, undulating flow. Nawadaha is the uppermost of the falls and requires a short but slightly rugged hike along the West River Trail. The swift current provides a power and roar seldom seen.

WINTER RECREATION
Downhill Skiing

Downhill skiers are often surprised to

find a state-run downhill ski area within **Porcupine Mountains Wilderness State Park,** and even more astonished to find it offers 42 beginner to advanced runs with 787 vertical feet (240 meters). The runs at **Porcupine Mountains Ski Area** (906/885-5209, www.porcupineup.com/pm-ski-area, 9am-5pm Fri.-Mon., $25-45), just west of the park headquarters on M-107, span a north-facing flank served by two chairlifts, one T-bar, and a tow rope. The ski area recently added more than 100 acres of backcountry terrain when it opened Everest, a 0.5-mile-wide (0.8-km) section of virgin forest with more than 17 runs and snow cat service. A day lodge at the base offers food service, rentals, and a small ski shop. The lifts may be old and a bit creaky, but the terrain is wonderful, the snow is reliable (the annual average tops 175 inches/445 cm), and the views of Lake Superior from the top are phenomenal. However, on days when a strong north wind is blowing, this may not be a good choice.

Ski and Snowshoe Trails

The chalet and base area of **Porcupine Mountains Ski Area** (906/885-5275, www.porcupineup.com/pm-ski-area, 9am-5pm Fri.-Mon.) also serve cross-country skiers, who can access a terrific network of trails. The park grooms and tracks 14.2 miles (22.9 km) of the park's hiking trails, which wind through the eastern end of the park. Some skirt the Lake Superior shoreline, where snow and ice sculptures form. Others scale the hilly terrain in the interior of the park and can be reached via one of the ski lifts. For day visitors, there is no admission cost. Lift tickets ($45 adults, $35 under age 18) can also be bought in a package that includes ski rentals. Check the website for complete pricing information.

Snowmobiling

In addition to the marked trails in Ottawa National Forest, you can take unplowed M-107 to Lake of the Clouds for a great groomed snowmobile trail in the Porkies that ends at a spectacularly beautiful location.

FOOD

Paul's Restaurant (120 Lincoln Ave., Silver City, 906/885-5311, noon-9pm daily, $12-28), in Silver City's AmericInn Porcupine Mountain Lodge, gets high marks for fish and other supper club fare. In Ontonagon, **Syl's Café** (713 River St., Ontonagon, 906/884-2522, 7am-9pm daily, $7-12) is a classic small-town café with some of the best pasties around. Fifteen minutes south of Ontonagon on US 45, **Henry's Never Inn** (74 National Ave., 906/886-9910, 10:30am-2am Mon.-Sat., 9:30am-2am Sun., $16) in Rockland draws crowds from far and wide with its enormous buffets with various fish dishes on Friday night and Italian delicacies on Saturday. Soups and sandwiches are great too, but it's really the spirited locals who add flavor to this old mining haunt. Henry's has a very colorful history, having served as a "blind pig" (speakeasy) during Prohibition.

If you're camping in the Porkies, your closest full-service grocery is in Ontonagon, 17 miles (27 km) east of the park. For last-minute supplies, try the **Silver City General Store** (210 Lincoln Ave., 906/885-5885). It has basic camping and fishing supplies as well as picnic staples like cheese and bread.

ACCOMMODATIONS

You'll find a string of motels along M-64 between Silver City (2 miles/3.2 km east of park headquarters) and Ontonagon. Many are plain, somewhat Spartan independent establishments, but they'll work just fine after a long day outdoors. One option to consider is **Mountain View Lodges** (34042 107th Engineers Memorial Hwy., Silver City, 906/885-5256, www.mountainviewlodges.com, $$$, minimum 2-night stay), which features two-bedroom cottages on Lake Superior with amenities like fireplaces and fully equipped kitchens that include dishwashers. And the **AmericInn Porcupine Mountain Lodge** (120 Lincoln Ave., Silver

154

City, 906/662-9111, www.wyndhamhotels.
com, $$) offers the full array of motel services,
including an indoor pool, a sauna, meeting
rooms, a dining room, and a bar. The cozy
lawn behind the lodge closely abuts the shore-
line and is ideal for taking in a dazzling Lake
Superior sunset. For other options, contact the
Ontonagon Chamber of Commerce (424
River St., 906/884-4735, http://ontonagonmi.
org, 9am-5pm daily).

Camping

Campers have their choice of two modern
campgrounds, both with a number of sites
overlooking Lake Superior: **Union Bay** ($28,
full hookups) at the east end of the park or
Presque Isle ($17, no hookups) near the
mouth of the Presque Isle River on the park's
western edge. Both offer flush toilets and
showers. In addition, there are three rustic
campgrounds ($17, called "outposts") with
3-11 sites each that are located off the South
Boundary Road, accessible by car; there are
no facilities here. They tend to offer more
privacy than the modern campgrounds.
Reservations (800/447-2757, www.michigan.
gov/dnr) are recommended for all campsites
in summer.

As another option, the park offers 16
hike-in rustic cabins (reservations 906/885-
5275, www.midnrreservations.com, $70).
These are great retreats after a day on the
trail. They come with 2-8 bunks, mattresses,
a woodstove, basic utensils, and protection
from the elements, but no electricity or run-
ning water. Bring your own stove for cooking.
Cabins situated on inland lakes even come
with a rowboat, so you can finish the day with
a lazy drift across the water. It's best to reserve
a cabin far in advance. In the Porkies, you'll
want to do so as much as a year in advance.

Two more options for backpackers: There
are three hike-in **Adirondack shelters** with
sleeping platforms, available only on a first-
come, first-served basis, as well as backcoun-
try camping. Trailside camping is permitted
throughout the backcountry, as long as you
stay 0.25 miles (0.4 km) or more from cabins,

shelters, scenic areas, and roads. All back-
packers must register ($6/day) at the visitors
center before setting out.

INFORMATION AND SERVICES

Visitor information can be had from the
**Porcupine Mountains Convention
and Visitor Bureau** (906/884-2047, www.
porcupineup.com) or the **Western Upper
Peninsula Convention and Visitor
Bureau** (906/932-4850 or 800/522-5657,
www.explorewesternup.com). For maps and
information about the state park, visit the
**Porcupine Mountains Wilderness State
Park Headquarters** (412 S. Boundary Rd.,
Ontonagon, 906/885-5275, www.michigan.
gov/dnr, 8am-6pm daily mid-May-mid-Oct.).

If you need a hospital, you'll find the
Aspirus Ontonagon Hospital (601 S.
7th St., 906/884-8000, www.aspirus.org) in
Ontonagon; take Greenland Road (M-38) to
7th Street and turn north. Banking services
can be found at **Citizens State Bank of
Ontonagon** (501 River St., 906/207-6800,
www.micsb.com).

GETTING THERE AND AROUND
Car

M-38, M-64, and US 45 all converge on
Ontonagon, located on the shores of Lake
Superior. From Ironwood, take US 2 to
M-28/64 before turning north on M-64.
From Ontonagon, take M-64 to M-107 to
get to Porcupine Mountains Wilderness
State Park—the headquarters are on South
Boundary Road, just south of 107th Engineers
Memorial Highway.

Boat

Ontonagon has a small marina that has
29 seasonal slips and 7 transient slips. The
Ontonagon Village Marina (906/884-
4225, www.michigan.gov/dnr) operates early
May to early October and can be reached on
radio channels 16 and 68. Coordinates are
46°52.57 N, 89°19.58 W.

Air

Ontonagon's county airport does not offer scheduled passenger flights, but you'll be able to fly into **Houghton County Memorial Airport** (CMX, 23810 Airpark Blvd., Calumet, 906/482-3970, www. houghtoncounty.org), which has scheduled flights from Chicago on United Airlines.

Alamo and National offer vehicle rentals, and taxi and limo service is available through **Copper Country Limo and Transport** (906/370-4761). Marquette's **Sawyer International Airport** (MQT, 125 G Ave., Gwinn, 906/346-3308, www.sawyerairport. com) is a more distant option, over two hours' drive from Ontonagon.

Keweenaw Peninsula and Isle Royale

If Lake Superior resembles the head of a wolf, then the Keweenaw Peninsula (KEE-wuh-naw) is seized firmly in its jaw. Parts of the land do look like they've been gnawed on: Vestiges of the 19th-century copper boom are still in evidence, earning this narrow strip of land the nickname "Copper Country."

Today, the Keweenaw's wealth is measured not in copper but in its boundless natural beauty. This narrow finger of land extending into Lake Superior is a mother lode of wild rivers, hidden waterfalls, and lonely beaches. While there's civilization too, the Keweenaw is thinly populated even by Upper Peninsula standards. Houghton is the largest city, with Hancock, just across the river, a close second. Together they have a combined population of around 11,000—although that

Highlights

Look for ★ to find recommended sights, activities, dining, and lodging.

★ **A. E. Seaman Mineral Museum:** Get a fascinating glimpse of "natural art"—a sampling of thousands of colorful minerals from Michigan and around the world (page 162).

★ **Quincy Mine:** This mine north of Hancock tops the list of Keweenaw historical sites. The full two-hour tour takes you deep into the mine (page 162).

★ **Downtown Calumet:** This diamond in the rough is a three-dimensional reminder of the once prosperous copper industry. Friendly townspeople make it all the more enjoyable (page 165).

★ **Downtown Laurium:** Take a self-guided walking tour of some of the grandest homes in Michigan (page 167).

★ **Fort Wilkins Historic State Park:** Learn about one of the few remaining wooden forts in the country. During the summer, costumed interpreters recreate military life (page 178).

★ **Western Shoreline Drive:** Take this route west out of Copper Harbor and your impressions of Michigan will never be the same. The stunning lakeshore view is the envy of nature lovers everywhere (page 179).

★ **Keweenaw Underwater Preserve:** Dive among interesting geologic formations and

shipwrecks in the crisp water of Lake Superior (page 185).

★ **Hiking Isle Royale:** It takes some work to get here, but once you do, you'll find 165 miles (265 km) of trails and some of the country's last true wilderness (page 197).

158

Keweenaw Peninsula and Isle Royale

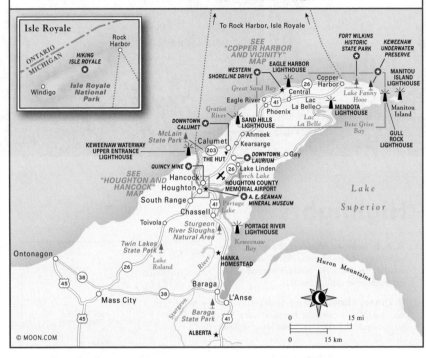

figure swells during the academic year due to the student population of two universities. Houghton and Hancock are separated by the Keweenaw Waterway, an extension of the Portage River and Portage Lake, which collectively split the peninsula in half.

Copper Harbor, on the shores of Lake Superior at Michigan's extreme north, is the literal end of the road. Just past town is the terminus of US 41, which originates in Miami. The surroundings are emblematic of the area's extreme northern latitude—which looks and feels different from almost any other place in Michigan. Copper Harbor enjoys a well burnished reputation as an outdoor destination for kayakers, bikers, and snowmobilers. It's

also a spot where rugged travelers bound for Isle Royale National Park begin their journey.

Also part of Michigan, Isle Royale National Park—some 48 miles (77 km) north of the peninsula—is a wild, craggy, roadless archipelago in Lake Superior with lakes and forests, moose, and hiking trails. This wonderfully remote location makes possible the park's status as one of the least visited properties in the National Park System.

The remote Keweenaw has never had the tourism appeal and associated amenities of a larger community like Marquette, but this is slowly changing. With the Keweenaw National Historical Park as a draw, more museums and other attractions are opening, and each year more people are discovering the

Previous: Hungarian Falls; downtown Calumet; vista of Copper Harbor and Lake Superior.

peninsula's unspoiled beauty. The backcountry is filled with amazing hiking and mountain biking trails that lead to waterfalls and other natural gems.

Yet for those who crave adventure and solitude, the Keweenaw Peninsula and Isle Royale offer it in spades. As it was for those early copper miners, the Keweenaw today remains a remarkable land of discovery.

PLANNING YOUR TIME

It's only about a two-hour drive from the base of the Keweenaw Peninsula to Copper Harbor, but with scenery this stunning and outdoor activities this isolated, you're going to want to plan on spending considerably more time here. Houghton and Hancock make a great base for outdoor excursions—you can get pretty much anywhere in the peninsula in slightly more than an hour at most. Depending on how many hours you're looking to spend on the trail or in the kayak, visitors often find that a weekend is plenty of time for a good recreation and sightseeing vacation. If you're planning on a visit to Isle Royale, you'll want to add several days. The island wilderness is vast, with over 165 miles (265 km) of trails, several inland lakes, and other natural curiosities.

Accommodation Price Key

$	Less than $100 per night
$ $	$100-200 per night
$ $ $	More than $200 per night

HISTORY

Like a ragged dorsal fin on the back of the Upper Peninsula, the Keweenaw Peninsula was quickly shunned by early European immigrants to the Michigan Territories as hopelessly remote and rugged: nearly surrounded by Lake Superior, laden deep in snow for half the year, and blanketed by impenetrable forests that grew from untillable rock and infertile sand. They dismissed it as nothing more than a wasteland, even more so than the rest of the Upper Peninsula.

But around 1840, state geologist Douglass Houghton confirmed the presence of copper—vast unclaimed deposits of pure native copper, much of it near the surface. The still young United States quickly developed an insatiable appetite for the metal, first for use in new industrial machinery and later for Civil War hardware, electrical wiring, and other innovations. The value of Houghton's discovery seemed incalculable.

The copper rush commenced almost immediately, beginning with prospectors and followed by large mining enterprises that flocked to the remote Keweenaw. It was the nation's first mineral rush. Copper employed thousands of immigrant laborers, built cities, made millionaires, and financed extravagant luxuries like opera houses and mansions for the copper barons. Before it was over, King Copper generated more than $9.6 billion in wealth, exceeding the value of the California gold rush tenfold.

But eventually the copper deposits were exhausted, turning boom to bust. Today, the aftermath looms large, taking the form of abandoned mines, ghost towns buried in the forest, and the peculiar sight of lavish buildings in almost forgotten towns. Unfortunately much of copper's legacy was demolished, thrown away, or crushed under the weight of winter snows. Yet a remarkable amount remains. Efforts by historical preservationists began in the 1970s, resulting in the 1992 establishment of the Keweenaw National Historical Park, an ongoing development. While chain restaurants across the United States decorate their walls with fake tools and other implements, here you'll find the real thing: scores of mining artifacts displayed in a variety of public venues.

Outside, a magazine dedicated to outdoor sporting life, once listed Houghton (HOE-ton) among the nation's 16 best places to live. *Outside* may indeed have been on to something. Houghton and the adjacent city of Hancock offer both sporting diversions while boasting a robust multicultural flair. Streets lined with beautifully preserved early-1900s buildings and the presence of a university add an atmosphere of culture and sophistication.

While the Keweenaw's cities provide a refreshing dose of urbanity, there are plenty of outlying towns and destinations that are also worthy of exploration. Houghton and Hancock's central location makes it a great place for hub-and-spoke traveling—find your lodging, spend the evenings in the city, and make your way out on engaging day trips throughout the Keweenaw.

SOUTH OF HOUGHTON AND HANCOCK

The Keweenaw Peninsula begins at Ontonagon on its western shore and at L'Anse on the east, an imaginary line traced roughly by M-38. Between this highway and the Keweenaw Waterway, the southern portion is quiet and sparsely populated—quite a change from the turn of the 20th century, when the Copper Range Company operated a network of successful mines. Like elsewhere in the Keweenaw, the tall skeletons of mining shaft houses, dying relics of the copper rush, frequently lurch skyward out of the pines.

At the foot of Keweenaw Bay, between Baraga (BARE-a-ga) and L'Anse (LAHNS), the enormous wooden statue *Shrine of the Snowshoe Priest* looms 35 feet (11 meters) above Red Rock Bluff. It commemorates the life of Bishop Frederic Baraga, a Roman Catholic missionary from Slovenia who gained recognition for his work with local Ojibwa people in the mid-1800s, traveling by snowshoe to reach distant communities. Unlike most missionaries in his day, Baraga is believed to have worked to support the Ojibwa's rights by helping them gain title to their land, a stance unpopular with the local European fur traders and government Indian agents. Baraga spoke the Ojibwa language fluently, and he later wrote an Ojibwa dictionary and grammar.

A few miles south of L'Anse, on US 41, a white clapboard lumber mill marks your arrival in **Alberta.** In 1935, Henry Ford built the mill and dammed the nearby Plumbago Creek for the mill's water supply. He also constructed housing for the mill's workers. It's a classic example of a company town, one that has changed little since operations shut down in the early 1950s. Today, the facility is operated by Michigan Technological University (www.mtu.edu/forest/fordcenter) as a forestry research center. The grounds are open to the public (9am-5pm Mon.-Fri.). The sawmill is currently closed, but guests are welcome to visit the museum and the adjacent Knothole Gift Shop.

Ford built many other facilities across the western U.P., mostly sawmills to harvest the nearby timber for automotive applications. The outpost in Alberta, however, is much smaller, and was constructed mostly for PR purposes.

Hanka Homestead

The Hanka family from Finland established this farmstead, hidden away in the creases of the landscape above Keweenaw Bay between Baraga and Houghton, in 1896. The buildings include a log house, a barn, a milk house over a spring for natural refrigeration, and a sauna, in keeping with Finnish tradition. The self-sufficient Hankas raised dairy cows and chickens, grew vegetables and grains, and tanned hides to eke out a living and

Houghton and Hancock

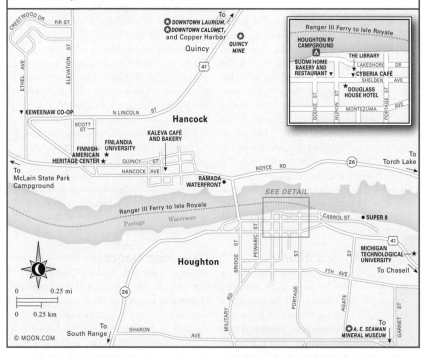

get through the harsh winters. What they didn't do much was modernize. Even though Jalmar Hanka, the last surviving family member, lived here until the mid-1960s, the **Hanka Homestead** (906/334-2575, www.hankahomesteadmuseum.org, noon-4pm Tues.-Thurs. and Sat.-Sun. Memorial Day-Labor Day, $4) remains as it was in about 1920, complete with the Hankas' belongings filling the home and its nine outbuildings. Guides offer comprehensive tours, and the homestead is a cooperating site of the Keweenaw National Historical Park. It's best to call ahead before making the trip. To find the homestead, head north about 10 miles (16.1 km) on US 41 from Baraga, turn west on Arnheim Road, and follow the small wooden signs, which may refer to it as the "Finnish Homestead Museum."

HOUGHTON AND HANCOCK

Houghton (pop. 7,000) and Hancock (pop. 4,000) face each other across the Keweenaw Waterway, with homes and churches tumbling down steep 500-foot (150-meter) bluffs reminiscent of San Francisco, especially on the Hancock side. The waterway effectively slices the Keweenaw in two, a 21-mile (34-km) passage that saves boaters the 100-mile (160-km) trip around the peninsula.

Native Americans used the route for centuries to cross the peninsula, traveling from Keweenaw Bay across Portage Lake and along the ancient Portage River, then crossing over land the rest of the way to the shores of Lake Superior. In the late 1800s a dredged canal eliminated the need for the west-end portage. Commercial traffic plied the waterway, largely to serve the smelters, stamping plants, and vibrant cities serving the burgeoning copper trade.

A unique **lift bridge** spans the waterway that links Houghton and Hancock. Functioning in a way similar to a drawbridge, its huge center section rises like an elevator to let ship traffic pass below. Today, the Keweenaw Waterway largely serves pleasure boats and the 125-foot (38-meter) *Ranger III,* a ferry operated by the National Park Service that transports hikers to Isle Royale. Houghton and Hancock are considered gateways to the Keweenaw and to Isle Royale, but visitors just passing through will miss an appealing slice of the region. The twin cities offer the studious atmosphere of college towns combined with pride in their Finnish heritage.

Downtown Houghton

You can conduct your own historical walking tour of Houghton by strolling down Shelden Avenue, the city's main street. Tall facades of redbrick and red sandstone line the street, including the **Douglass House Hotel** (517 Shelden Ave.), built in 1860 as a luxury hotel and dining establishment for travelers through the Keweenaw Waterway. An addition in 1899 made it the lavish building you see today. Inside, the Victorian interior of the **Douglass House Saloon** (906/482-2003) still reflects those genteel days, with original Tiffany chandeliers, leaded glass windows, and frilly curtains. The upper floors have been converted into apartments.

On the east end of town, the campus of **Michigan Technological University** (1400 Townsend Dr., 906/487-1885, www.mtu.edu) stretches out along the Keweenaw Waterway. Over 6,500 students attend Michigan Tech, the majority of whom study some type of engineering. Geology, mining, and industrial archaeology are some of the school's most notable fields. Students in the mining field get real-world experience here, learning hands-on mining practices deep inside the nearby Quincy Mine.

★ A. E. Seaman Mineral Museum

Michigan Tech is home to the highly regarded **A. E. Seaman Mineral Museum** (1404 E. Sharon Ave., 906/487-2572, www.museum.mtu.edu, 9am-5pm Mon.-Sat., $8 adults, $7 seniors, $4 students, $3 ages 9-17, free under age 9), the official mineralogical museum of the state of Michigan. The Keweenaw is considered one of the most geologically rich and fascinating regions in the world, and the Seaman Museum holds the premier collection of area minerals and gemstones, including crystallized copper, silver, datolites, greenstones, and agates. Don't miss the informative exhibit on an iron mine and glowing fluorescent minerals. The museum also houses an impressive collection of minerals from around the world numbering more than 30,000 specimens. Parking is plentiful and free.

Downtown Hancock

Michigan Tech isn't the only local university: Across the waterway is **Finlandia University,** which began in 1896 as a Finnish academy to serve the area's ever-growing number of immigrant miners' families. Today, enrollment is approximately 550. The institution's **Finnish-American Heritage Center** (435 Quincy St., 906/487-7302, www.finlandia.edu/fahc, 9am-4pm Mon.-Fri., free) maintains a gallery open to the public that highlights Finnish artists and the archives of the area's Finnish settlement.

★ Quincy Mine

Just north of Hancock, the mammoth shaft house of the **Quincy Mine** (906/482-3101, www.quincymine.com, daily May-mid-Oct.; hoist and mine tour $35 adults, $20 youth under 18, free under age 7; surface tour, which includes the smelter, $15 adults, $10 youth under 18, free under age 7) dominates the skyline. The Quincy ranked as one of the world's richest copper mines in the late 1800s, producing over a billion pounds of copper.

1: a lift bridge that links Houghton and Hancock **2:** Quincy Mine **3:** Hanka Homestead **4:** downtown Houghton

Today, a few of its buildings still stand, and the land beneath it remains riddled with the shafts (vertical tunnels) and adits (horizontal tunnels) of the mammoth mine, which stretch more than 1.5 miles (2.4 km) deep on 92 levels and 2 miles (3.2 km) wide.

The Quincy Mine is a key site in the Keweenaw National Historical Park, and it offers a fascinating tour that takes you through the historic buildings and deep into the mine itself. Many of the tour guides are mining students at nearby Michigan Tech, who can handle just about any mining or engineering question. The tour begins with a look at the gargantuan steam hoist, the world's largest. A giant spool of sorts, it powered the steel pulleys that hauled the miners and mine cars loaded with copper in and out of the mine. The machine's mammoth size—more than double the size of the average hoist—was necessitated by the extreme depth of the mine.

The building itself is as interesting as the hoist. In an era when miners made $1 a day, a good wage for the time, the Quincy Mining Company built its hoist house of poured concrete, then decorated it with tasteful arched windows, lined the walls with Italian tile, and topped it off with green tiles imported from Spain. Because it was so overengineered, the immense room remains in excellent shape today. It also houses numerous artifacts and photos, including bilingual safety instructions posted next to the machinery, due to the high number of immigrant Finnish miners.

From the hoist house, the tour continues with a rather dramatic ride in a glass enclosed tram down the side of a steep hill. Views of Houghton and Hancock are terrific as the tram descends to an entrance to the mine, an adit at Level 7. A tractor carries you about 2,000 feet (610 meters) into the mine, where guides demonstrate mining techniques and give you a feel for what it was like to work deep inside the earth—a drippy, damp environment with only hand tools and candles. Contact the **Quincy Mine Hoist Association** (49750 US 41, 906/482-3101, www.quincymine.com) for tour times and other information.

Lighthouses

Two of the lighthouses in the Houghton and Hancock area are the **Keweenaw Waterway Upper Entrance Lighthouse** and the **Portage River Light,** located on opposite sides of the Keweenaw Peninsula. The Keweenaw Light is at the end of the breakwater at McLain State Park. Built in 1950, the steel tower is one of the Keweenaw's newest lights, which takes nothing away from its beauty. Take M-203 about 10 miles (16.1 km) north of Hancock to McLain State Park. The lighthouse is about 0.5 miles (0.8 km) offshore, plainly visible but off-limits to the public.

The **Keweenaw Waterway Upper Entrance Lighthouse** is on the east side of the Keweenaw Peninsula at the Portage River in the town of Lake Linden, located offshore. This light was built 30 years before its companion on the opposite side of the river. A long walk along the breakwater pier will allow you to get close.

You'll also find the land-based **Portage River Light** (38741 Jacobs St., Lake Linden), a well-preserved 1869 structure that sits at the entrance to the Portage River. Today the property is a private residence, so please admire the building from a distance.

NORTH OF HOUGHTON AND HANCOCK

At the height of the Keweenaw's copper mining glory, the Calumet and Hecla Consolidated Copper Company, which operated largely in Calumet, proved the grandest operation of all. At the turn of the 20th century, C&H employed some 11,000 workers who extracted more than 1.5 billion tons of copper from a web of mines that tunneled under Calumet and adjacent Laurium. A surface plant in town, considered the most efficient in the nation, roared and whistled with the sound of 50 steam engines at work.

C&H ultimately generated more than $72 million in revenue. It built low-cost housing for its miners, consisting of some 1,000 dwellings lined up like chess pieces. Groups of homes formed towns and were named Swedetown or Limerick—American namesakes of miners' ancestral homes. Most significantly, C&H spawned the city of Calumet, then known as Red Jacket, making it a booming community of more than 60,000 residents. Striking red sandstone buildings with false fronts and cornices lined the 12-square-block business district. Downtown Calumet was filled with elegant shops, soaring churches, some 70 saloons, and even a lavish theater that attracted the nation's leading vaudeville stars. The city buzzed day and night, both above and below ground.

After the mining industry declined, Calumet's economy became stagnant and the city remained largely frozen in time. But Calumet continues to be a trove of early 1900s architecture, as the sturdy sandstone buildings have survived the decades beautifully. They became the pivotal reason for the community's national historical park status. "We are fortunate that this area has been little disturbed since those glory days," said a park supporter. "Few modern intrusions have marred the area's scale and the feeling of its mining heritage." Today, Calumet (pop. 621) anchors the new Keweenaw National Historical Park, one of the park's two key units and a designated historic district.

★ Downtown Calumet

Thanks to its federal status and renewed civic pride, downtown Calumet's historic character is more evident than ever. Ugly mid-century facades have been removed from the elegant sandstone and brick buildings, and new investment continues to promote historic restoration. To appreciate this architectural legacy, stop by the **Keweenaw Convention and Visitors Bureau** (56638 Calumet Ave., 906/337-4579 or 800/338-7982, www.keweenaw.info) and pick up a walking tour guide. A few stops of particular note: The **Union Building** (5th St. and Red Jacket Rd.) was home of one of the area's first banks in 1888 and remains in excellent shape, with a decorative metal cornice. **Shute's Bar** (322

6th St.) doesn't look special from the outside, but inside you can see the preserved ornate plaster ceilings and the magnificent back bar with a stained-glass canopy. Across the street, the **Red Jacket Fire Station** typifies the Romanesque style favored for public buildings and churches at the time. Examine the detail on the **Red Jacket Town Hall and Opera House,** now called the **Calumet Theatre** (340 6th St., 906/337-2610, www.calumettheatre.com). Free self-guided tours are possible during box office hours (noon-5pm Wed.-Fri.), and guided tours are available by appointment. Perhaps more than any other, this building was truly the pride of the community. The theater portion, added in 1898, was the first municipally owned theater in the country. It was a showy extravagance of plaster rococo in cream, crimson, green, and gilt, and even had electric lights, a rarity at the time. Referred to as "the greatest social event ever known in copperdom's metropolis" when it opened in 1900, the theater attracted a bevy of A-list celebrities, including John Philip Sousa, Harry Houdini, Douglas Fairbanks Jr., and Sarah Bernhardt. Today the theater hosts a variety of events—classic movies, concerts, and live productions.

Keweenaw National Historical Park

The **Keweenaw National Historical Park** (200 5th St., 906/337-3168, www.nps.gov/kewe) is not so much a place on a map but a place in time. One of the National Park Service's newest units, it was established in 1992 "to commemorate the heritage of copper mining on the Keweenaw Peninsula; its mines, its machinery, and its people."

Unlike a park with simply defined boundaries, the Keweenaw National Historical Park consists of historic attractions throughout the peninsula. Two units anchor the park, the Quincy Unit at the Quincy Mine in Hancock, and the Calumet Unit in historic downtown Calumet, although some of this land remains privately owned. Land owned outright by the National Park Service includes noteworthy

historic sites. In addition, the park has designated "cooperating sites" throughout the peninsula, including mine tours and museums that remain in private ownership but benefit from increased visibility and federal funding.

The park will continue to be under development for many years while continuing to restore buildings, create interpretive displays, and develop educational programs. The **park headquarters** (25970 Red Jacket Rd., Calumet, 906/337-3168) currently operates with just a skeleton administrative staff. For visitor information, contact the **Keweenaw Convention and Visitors Bureau** (56638 Calumet Ave., Calumet, 906/337-4579 or 800/338-7982, www.keweenaw.info).

C&H Industrial Core

One of Calumet and Hecla's mines was located right in town, in an area bisected by Red Jacket Road, just west of US 41. Beginning at the Coppertown USA museum, a self-guided industrial core walking tour takes you past a drill shop, a powder house, a machine shop, and several other mining buildings in various states of restoration. The National Park Service is adding interpretive signs to guide you along and share mining information, but you'll also want an information sheet that maps the route, available from the Keweenaw Tourism Council, the park headquarters, or the Coppertown USA museum.

Coppertown USA

The mine's pattern shop, where wooden patterns were made as molds for machine parts, now serves as the home of **Coppertown USA** (25815 Red Jacket Rd., 906/337-4354, www.uppermichigan.com/coppertown, 11am-5pm Mon.-Sat. June-mid-Oct., $4 adults, $3 with National Park Pass, $2 ages 6-15, under age 6 free), a privately run museum and national park cooperative site that traces the region's copper industry. It includes numerous artifacts, a display of area minerals, a replica of a mining captain's office, a diorama of Native

American mining, and more. Don't miss the pattern shop area, which still houses thousands of patterns, lined up on shelves as if they haven't been touched for 50 years (some have been relocated to the Smithsonian). Another interesting exhibit is a 1876 scale model that shows elaborate plans for Calumet, including a cultural center, a festival plaza, and a products exhibit center. The museum is located near the intersection of US 41 and Red Jacket Road.

★ Downtown Laurium

Just across US 41 from Calumet is Laurium. Largely a residential district for the area mines, the west end (closest to Calumet) has a few streets of plain company homes that now appear rather rough and dilapidated. But a few blocks east, around Pewabic and 3rd Streets, managers of the mining companies built a neighborhood of quiet and stately homes, an area well worth visiting today. Pick up a *Laurium Walking Tour* guide from the **Keweenaw Convention and Visitors Bureau** (56638 Calumet Ave., 906/337-4579 or 800/338-7982, www.keweenaw.info) in Calumet. It will direct you to impressive homes like the one at 305 Tamarack Street, where a wise mining investor made enough money to create this grand home with seven fireplaces, a third-floor ballroom, and a carriage house.

But the finest home belonged to Captain Thomas Hoatson, founder of the Calumet and Arizona Mining Company, who built his dream mansion in 1908. Today it operates as the **Laurium Manor Inn** (320 Tamarack St., 906/337-2549, www.laurium.info, tours noon-3pm daily Memorial Day-late Oct., $15 adults, $10 children under 18), which means the public can enjoy a glimpse of this remarkable place. Sprawling across 13,000 square feet, the 45-room mansion includes ceilings covered in silver leaf, elephant hide wall coverings, a triple staircase of hand-carved oak, and a turntable in the carriage house so carriages could be rotated to face forward. The inn is open year-round, with room rates of $129-219.

Copper Country

Copper Country, the nickname associated with the Keweenaw Peninsula, is a well-earned moniker. After the discovery of copper in the mid-1800s, mines near the tip of the Keweenaw were among the first to open. The copper business grew slowly for several years until just before the Civil War, and by 1860 Copper Country was producing some 12 million pounds of the metal per year. By 1890 the region was sending about 100 million pounds of copper annually on ships that traveled through the Great Lakes or on trains headed to Chicago and the rest of the nation. Over the course of 40 years, Michigan produced more copper than any other state, occasionally accounting for as much as 90 percent of the nation's total output.

As the boom took off, the Keweenaw region soon saw an influx of workers from all over North America, followed by immigrants from Cornwall. They were later joined by immigrants from Norway, Finland, Denmark, and Sweden who had come to the Upper Peninsula. They worked tirelessly in both the copper and iron mines to earn an honest living. The newcomers also brought with them their cultures, cuisine, and languages. Many of the old mining communities in Keweenaw and around the U.P. are still influenced by this heritage. Even today, the Finnish community is one of most prominent in the Upper Peninsula.

Copper Country mining camps and small towns grew seemingly overnight to become cities and industrial centers. In Hancock, the region's mining and immigrant heritage survives, exemplified by the Quincy Mine, a national historic landmark, and by Finlandia University, founded in 1896. Other towns born during the copper boom include Calumet, Laurium, and Lake Linden.

As the copper deposits became depleted, the industry began its long decline, culminating with the last mines closing by the 1970s.

The economic impact on the area was severe and long-lasting. In most U.P. communities, the hole left by the demise of mining has yet to be filled with another industry. Today, logging (conducted in a responsible and sustainable manner) and tourism hold the best hope for the area's economic future. These industries permit utilization—but not exploitation—of the Upper Peninsula's prized natural resources.

Football or cinema fans may want to view the decidedly less dramatic home at 432 Hecla Street. Laurium's most famous citizen was born here—**George Gipp,** the Notre Dame football star, immortalized in the movie *Knute Rockne, All American.* "The Gipper" was undoubtedly Ronald Reagan's most famous role until he was elected president. A George Gipp Memorial decorates the corner of Tamarack Street and M-26.

Ghost Towns

Ghost towns litter the Keweenaw, faded testament to the boom and bust days of copper. The ruins of old mines and stamping plants (facilities that separated copper from rock) line M-26 between Hancock and Calumet. The gray piles of residue are mine tailings or stamping plant leftovers called "stamp sand." Several bona fide ghost towns hide in the

woods too, especially between Calumet and Copper Harbor. At **Central** (watch for the small brown sign on US 41, about 11 miles/17.7 km north of Mohawk), an exceptionally rich mine produced nearly $10 million worth of copper by 1898 while the surrounding town grew to 1,200. Today, nature has all but reclaimed Central, with just a few clapboard houses creaking in the breeze. Turn right near the top of the hill for a look at the mine ruins and rows of house foundations. Be sure to watch your step while walking.

Just south of Copper Harbor on US 41, another sign announces your arrival in **Mandan,** directing you down a dirt road disappearing into birches. Follow it south for about 50 yards/meters and a row of ramshackle homes and small buildings erupts out of the woods. Welcome to Mandan, the last stop on a trolley line from Hancock. Mandan was the location of two copper mines. Neither was as productive as other area mines, and both were abandoned by 1910.

ENTERTAINMENT
Ojibwa Casino and Resort

The **Ojibwa Casino** (16449 Michigan Ave., Baraga, 906/353-6333 or 800/323-8045, www.ojibwacasino.com) in Baraga is tucked away in the southeast corner of the Keweenaw Peninsula, where the long land formation meets the rest of the Upper Peninsula. There's enough gaming here to satisfy all but the choosiest players, with more than 300 slot and video poker machines that take denominations as low as a penny and up to $5. If you prefer table games, the casino offers craps, roulette, blackjack, poker (including 3-5-7 and Texas hold 'em), and more. Get something to eat at the **PressBox Bar & Grill** (11am-1:30am daily), which serves up exactly the type of food you'd expect at a sports bar. You'll find other sports bar trappings here too, like happy hour specials and big-screen TVs. There are a few other things you might not expect, such as an eight-lane bowling alley and a dance floor. The PressBox hosts DJs or live bands on weekends. The lodging is good too. The Ojibwa Casino hotel has gone through a series of renovations to its 40 guest rooms, which include double rooms and whirlpool suites at remarkably modest rates ($95 d, $110 suites). To get there from Houghton and Hancock, take US 41 south to M-38, turn right, and go a little more than a mile. From Ontonagon, take M-38 east.

Microbrewery

Keweenaw Brewing Co. (408 Shelden Ave., Houghton, 906/482-5596, www.keweenawbrewing.com, 3pm-10pm Mon.-Wed., 11am-11pm Thurs.-Sat., noon-8pm Sun.) is a no-nonsense microbrewery where a patron can enjoy a pint in the taproom for just $3. Offerings range from wheat ales to stouts and include Early Autumn Ale, Galaxy IPA, Lift Bridge Brown Ale, and Widow Maker Black, a dark selection with a drop of molasses.

Calumet Theatre

Opening in 1900, the **Calumet Theatre** (340 6th St., Calumet, 906/337-2610, www.calumettheatre.com) has been Keweenaw's destination for live opera and other entertainment. In its early days, the theater enjoyed a good run, hosting greats such as John Philip Sousa, among others. But as the era of live theater declined, the theater's fortunes faded. Later, as copper mining waned and motion pictures grew in popularity, the Calumet was converted into a cinema. Summer stock took place a few times during the 1950s and the 1970s but didn't enjoy a permanent resurgence until the Calumet Theatre Company was incorporated in 1983, which brought year-round entertainment back to this glamorous hall. And glamorous it is: The auditorium, with its bowl-shaped proscenium, stunning paintings, and elegant woodwork, was restored in the 1970s, followed by exterior work during the late 1980s. Today, the theater is part of the Calumet Historic District, a national historic landmark district. The venue regularly hosts theater and opera performances as well as symphony concerts, dance, music, and classic movies. Some 30,000 people come through the doors each year. You can take a self-guided tour of the historic theater during box office hours (noon-5pm Wed.-Fri., donation), and guided tours are available by appointment. Take US 41 into town and turn north on 6th Street to get to the theater.

FESTIVALS AND EVENTS

Leave it to those engineering students at Michigan Tech to design and build elaborate snow sculptures at the university's **Winter Carnival** in January. Houghton also hosts the **Bridgefest and Seafood Fest** (www.bridgefestfun.com) the second weekend in June, with food and music in Ray Kestner Park. Chassell's **Strawberry Fest** (www.coppercountrystrawberryfestival.com) is the second week in July, just in time for the sweet and juicy harvest. Perhaps the most elaborate annual event is the **Heritage Days Celebration** (www.mainstreetcalumet.com) in Calumet. Running a full week during mid-August, the occasion celebrates the area's Finnish heritage and includes ethnic foods, a parade, and art and craft vendors.

SUMMER RECREATION
Hiking and Biking

Mountain bikers new to the area can hardly believe the wealth of trails in the Keweenaw, literally hundreds of miles of old mining and logging roads, overgrown double-track routes, and technical single-track. They loop through towering pines to backwoods waterfalls, otherwise inaccessible Lake Superior shorelines, and even past ghost towns now buried deep in the woods, but please note that many trails may dead-end suddenly.

Vast tracts of land in the Keweenaw are privately owned by large corporations, either mining firms or paper companies. In exchange for a break on state taxes, the companies allow public use of the land for recreation, including hiking, fishing, and mountain biking. Still, for liability reasons, some outfitters and bike shops are reluctant to hand out maps or endorse these lands for riding. If you ask, though, most bike shops tend to be quite helpful about suggesting trails, especially **Cross Country Sports** (507 Oak St., Calumet, 906/337-4520, www.crosscountrysports. com, 10am-6pm Mon.-Sat.). If you're going on your own, snowmobile maps make decent trail guides. Cross-reference them with a topographic map. Snowmobile trails often cross frozen lowlands that are impassable during summer months.

Always remember to use common sense. Don't venture out without a map and compass and the skill to use them. Stay away from active logging areas, which are usually marked by signs and the audible presence of buzzing logging equipment. If you hear a logging truck coming, don't just move to the side; get completely off the trail. Logging trucks are wide

and heavy, and they can blaze down roads at surprising speeds.

Jack Stevens Rail Trail

Many old railroad grades threading across the northern Keweenaw have been converted to public multiuse trails, intended for snowmobiles, ATVs, and perhaps to a lesser extent, mountain bikes. For cyclists not comfortable venturing deep into the woods, they're a nice way to get off the road. The **Jack Stevens Rail Trail** runs 14 miles (23 km) from Hancock north to Calumet on the former Soo Line grade.

Keweenaw Rail-Trail

Somewhat less appealing, because it parallels M-26 for a lengthy stretch, is the **Keweenaw Rail-Trail,** an 18-mile (29-km) route from Hancock along Torch Lake, also ending in Calumet. Trail surfaces can be a rough collection of rock, gravel, wood, and sand or whatever happened to be there when they removed the rails, so they're not appropriate for narrow-tire bikes. For more information and a map listing access points, contact the Keweenaw Tourism Council at 800/338-7982.

Swedetown Trails

For something a little less adventurous, pedal the **Swedetown Trails** (www. swedetowntrails.org), a cross-country trail network on the southwest edge of Calumet. From 6th Street near St. Ann's Church, pick up Oceola Road and follow it south. The trail network has about 15 miles (24 km) of trails over rolling hills and through woods, and all are great for biking except the northernmost loop (the Red Trail), which is usually too wet. From this small network, you can veer off onto what seems like an endless network of side trails. In winter, these trails offer great cross-country skiing, including a charming chalet with a snack bar and a warming stove (noon-5pm Mon.-Tues., noon-8pm Wed.-Fri., 10am-8pm Sat., 10am-5pm Sun.). For information, contact the **Keweenaw Convention and Visitors**

Bureau (906/337-4579 or 800/338-7982, www.keweenaw.info).

Canoeing and Kayaking

Rivers in the Keweenaw tend to be somewhat rocky, so white-water kayaking is limited, although river levels vary with each year's level of precipitation. Sea kayaking, on the other hand, is outstanding. It's the perfect way to access bluffs, caves, sea stacks, and rocky islands all along the Lake Superior shoreline. The **Keweenaw Water Trail,** still under development, guides small craft around the peninsula and through the Keweenaw Waterway. Canoeing is popular on inland lakes, but open boats are not recommended on Lake Superior.

The **Keweenaw Water Trail** provides a mapped passageway of more than 100 miles (160 km) through the Keweenaw Waterway and along the Lake Superior shore, indicating accommodations, campgrounds, launches, and more. For more information and to purchase a water trail map, contact the **Keweenaw Convention and Visitors Bureau** (906/337-4579 or 800/338-7982, www.keweenaw.info). For white-water boaters, **Down Wind Sports** (308 Shelden Ave., 906/482-2500, www.downwindsports.com) in Houghton is your best source for local information on river conditions.

Fishing

One of the finest fishing rivers in the Houghton and Hancock area is the **Salmon Trout River.** Flowing for about 12 miles (19.3 km) from tiny Perrault to Lake Superior, the river is an excellent spot to cast for steelhead and brook trout. Take M-26 a few miles south of Houghton to Old M-26/Erickson Drive in the village of Atlantic Mine. Turn right, then right again on County Road A-65, which continues as Obenhoff Road to an access point a few miles west.

Another popular site is **McLain State Park** (18350 M-203, 906/482-0278), 7 miles (11.3 km) north of Hancock on M-203. You can also try both **Portage Lake** and **Torch Lake** for walleye, bass, perch, and

northern pike. On the other side of town, try the **Hancock Recreation Area** for fishing in the Portage Waterway.

A good source for fishing and other types of outdoor gear is **Northwood's Sporting Goods** (120 Quincy St., Hancock, 906/482-5210, 9:30am-5:30pm Mon.-Fri., 9am-5pm Sat.).

Golf

The only choice for 18 holes in the Keweenaw Peninsula is **Portage Lake Golf Course** 46789 US 41, Houghton, 906/487-2641, www.mtu.edu, 7:30am-9pm daily May-mid-Oct., $40 for 18 holes, $25 for 9 holes), a fine course belonging to Michigan Technological University. Although it's located off the main drag as you enter Houghton, the well-kept greens are peaceful and the holes have the tree-lined horizons you'd expect from a U.P. golf course. The clubhouse has a pro shop and a bar and grill, the cleverly named Par and Grill. Players can get a beer at the grill or from one of the beverage carts. There's also a putting green and a driving range that closes at dusk.

About 15 miles (24 km) south of Houghton, in Toivola, the **Wyandotte Hills Golf Club and Resort** (5755 E. Poyhonen Rd., 906/288-3720, May-Oct., $23 for 18 holes, $18 for 9 holes) is a nine-hole course that does double duty as an overnight getaway, with four cabins that can be rented year-round. The wooded and watered course makes for good golfing, while the clubhouse serves an excellent lunch and dinner Monday to Friday and lunch only on Saturday. In Calumet, you'll find the **Calumet Golf Club** (54720 Golf Course Rd., 906/337-3911, http://calumetgolfclub.com, $30 for 18 holes, $20 for 9 holes), another nine-hole course with club rentals and a reasonably priced restaurant.

Bird-Watching

Bird watchers will find a variety of northern species in the Keweenaw, including red- and white-winged crossbills, Canada geese, hawks, peregrine falcons, and bald eagles. An estimated 20 species of warblers are frequently spotted throughout the peninsula.

Just north of the Hanka Homestead, the Sturgeon River bleeds across the lowlands before emptying into Portage Lake, forming sloughs that attract migrating waterfowl. For the best access, stop at the **Sturgeon River Sloughs Natural Area,** marked by an observation tower along US 41 near Chassell. The 1.5-mile (2.4-km) **De Vriendt Nature Trail** follows a series of dikes and boardwalks back into the slough, with interpretive signs describing herons, ospreys, eagles, kestrels, ducks, and dozens of other species that frequent the area.

Off-Road Vehicles

The Michigan DNR's ATV route, the **Hancock-Calumet Trail,** stretches all the way from Hancock to Calumet. Like other DNR trails, this one is kept lightly groomed. The rail trails and other old railroad grades that can cause headaches for mountain bikers are more suitable for ORV riders. Bear in mind that you'll likely be sharing the pathway with nonmotorized travelers.

Another good bet for off-roading is the state forest roads in **Copper Country State Forest.** All state forest roads are open to ORV use unless specifically marked otherwise. To get to the forest from Houghton, take M-26 south until you reach US 45. Turn left and continue for 8 miles (12.9 km) before arriving at the forest on your left.

Waterfalls

Far south of Houghton and just north of the imaginary line that forms the base of the Keweenaw Peninsula, the **Wyandotte Falls** drop 20 feet (6 meters) down multiple steps in a beautiful display. Take Wyandotte Hills Golf Course Road less than a mile west of M-26 to the parking area, then follow the trail to the falls. It's about 25 miles (40 km) and about 31 minutes from Houghton. The **Hungarian Falls,** north of Hancock, are better still. Take M-26 north to Hubbell, and then turn left on 6th Street. Take the left fork two blocks up and

turn left onto the second trail road. It's about a 9-mile (14.5-km) trip that takes roughly 15 minutes. Both forks lead to the falls. The right fork leads to the Upper Falls, while the left heads to the Lower Falls. At 25 feet (8 meters), the Upper Falls drop farther, but the Lower Falls are more beautiful, at a still impressive 15 feet (5 meters).

WINTER RECREATION
Snowmobiling

A giant **snow gauge** on US 41 south of Phoenix proudly marks the Keweenaw's record snowfall, a staggering 390.4 inches (991.6 cm) in the winter of 1977-1978. It wasn't an aberration; the surrounding waters of Lake Superior routinely produce colossal lake-effect snows, often exceeding 300 inches (760 cm) per year. That reliable level of snow, combined with the remarkable local terrain, makes the Keweenaw a haven for snowmobilers.

There are more than 2,000 miles (3,200 km) of snowmobile trails throughout the U.P., with more than 200 of them located in the Keweenaw. They stretch from south of Houghton all the way to the tip. Most are clearly identified, well groomed, and 10-16 feet (3-5 meters) wide. Most of the trails south of the bridge pick up in Houghton and connect to the 1,800-plus miles (2,900-plus km) of trails that blanket the interior of the Upper Peninsula. The **Keweenaw Trail** (Trail 3) is the main route into and out of Houghton and Hancock, and it connects to numerous other branches: The **North** and **South Freda Trails** lead toward Lake Superior, while **Stevens Trail** connects to Calumet.

Keweenaw Trail joins the 55-mile (89-km) **Bill Nichols Trail,** which ends farther south in Mass City, near Ontonagon. A popular multiuse trail during warmer weather, this converted rail line is one of the most popular scenic snowmobile routes in the Keweenaw. For a detailed map, including the locations

1: trail to Hungarian Falls 2: Hungarian Falls 3: Mont Ripley ski hill

of gas stations, contact the **Keweenaw Convention and Visitors Bureau** (56638 Calumet Ave., Calumet, 906/337-4579 or 800/338-7982, www.keweenaw.info).

Snowmobiles can be rented from **Copper Country Rentals** at the **Trailside Lodge** (57900 US 41, Calumet, 906/337-9905, www.thetrailsidelodge.com). Rental rates are from $250 to $350 per day. Helmets and other necessary safety equipment is provided. Children between the ages of 12 and 16 must successfully complete a Michigan-approved snowmobile safety course. For more information on safety courses, visit www.michigan.gov/dnr.

Ski and Snowshoe Trails

Thankfully, skiers and snowshoers will find there's more than enough wilderness to go around. Many towns have developed cross-country ski trail systems. For backcountry skiing and snowshoeing, pick up a snowmobile map and avoid the marked trails. Also note that some accommodations located on signed and groomed trails cater to snowmobilers, and the roar can get pretty deafening. Don't be afraid to ask about the presence of "sleds," as they're sometimes referred to, before booking lodging in winter months.

Snowshoers should stay off groomed ski trails, but **Michigan Tech** in Houghton has a series of marked snowshoeing trails. In Calumet, try the marked **Swedetown Trails** (www.swedetowntrails.org), 16 miles (26 km) of groomed cross-country ski trails. Three miles (4.8 km) are illuminated with trail lights until 8pm. There are also several backcountry loops. The trailhead (which includes a warming chalet) is on the west side of Osceola Road about a mile south of downtown Calumet.

Skis and snowshoes can be rented from **Down Wind Sports** (308 Shelden Ave., Houghton, 906/482-2500, www.shopdownwindsports.com). Cross-country ski rentals run $30 per day. Snowshoe rentals are $20 per day.

Downhill Skiing

If you're into serious skiing, head north to Mount Bohemia near Copper Harbor, but for novices or skiers who appreciate tamer terrain, **Mont Ripley** (49051 Ski Hill Ln., Hancock, 906/487-2340, www.mtu.edu/mont-ripley, full day $60), near Houghton and Hancock and owned and operated by Michigan Technological University, also offers some good downhill runs and is lit for night skiing. It's only about a mile from campus and offers a stunning view of the buildings from just across the waterway.

FOOD

Combine a college town with a large multicultural population and you come up with a good range of eating options in the Houghton and Hancock area.

★ **The Library** (62 N. Isle Royale St., Houghton, 906/481-2665, www.thelibraryhoughton.com, 11am-midnight Mon.-Sat., noon-midnight Sun., $14-38) ranks as the most popular place in town, drawing both students and locals. Offerings include steaks, seafood, salads, pizza, pastas, and a bevy of sandwich choices. The Library also offers a comprehensive list of craft beers through its brewing operation, Copper Country Brewery. Their diverse selections include Shafthouse (an Irish dry stout), Redbrick (rye beer), and Copper Town Ale (American pale ale).

Just north of Calumet in Kearsarge is an undiscovered gem. **The Hut** restaurant (58542 US 41, Kearsarge, 906/337-1133, www.hutinn.com, 11am-9pm Sun.-Thurs., 11am-10pm Fri.-Sat., $18-36) resides in a 1950s-era building that resembles a Frank Lloyd Wright structure and offers great food and warm hospitality. Steaks, seafood, and a great array of pasties make this place well worth the stop.

Along with basic eggs-and-hash-browns fare, **Suomi Home Bakery and Restaurant** (54 N. Huron St., Houghton, 906/482-3220, 7am-2pm daily except Wed., under $10) includes a few Finnish specialties on the menu. Try the *pannukakku,* billed as a Finnish pancake but more like deep-dish custard pie topped with raspberry sauce. Most breakfasts come with *nisu,* a Finnish yeast bread spiced with cardamom. The restaurant can be a bit hard to find. It's partially hidden under Houghton's covered walkway, a block down the hill from Shelden Street.

Cyberia Café (800 Sharon Ave., Houghton, 906/482-2233, www.cyberiacafe. com, 7am-11pm Mon.-Fri., 9am-11pm Sat.-Sun.) is an Internet café that offers terrific java and the best cinnamon rolls you've ever tasted.

Over on the Hancock side, the **Kaleva Café and Bakery** (234 Quincy St., Hancock, 906/482-6001, www.mykaleva.com, 8am-2pm Wed.-Sun., under $11) draws the locals for its baked goods, including its self-proclaimed "famous" whipped-cream cakes. Kaleva makes a good pasty, which is a potpie creation of beef, potatoes, onions, and rutabagas—just the kind of hearty self-contained meal that miners could take with them deep underground. You'll also find pasties at coffee shops and grocery store deli counters throughout the Upper Peninsula.

Though you'll find plenty of traditional grocery stores along M-26 south of town and US 41 north, a better choice just might be the **Keweenaw Co-Op** (1035 Ethel Ave., Hancock, 906/482-2030, www.keweenaw. coop, 9am-8pm daily). Friendly staff, excellent organic produce, and plenty of reasonably priced staples make this a great option for picnic supplies. As you head up the hill on US 41, veer left onto Ethel when the highway swings hard right. Watch for the colorful wooden sign. The co-op is a couple of blocks ahead on the right.

You can find homemade coffee-shop fare and Finnish bakery items like saffron bread, not to mention the classic pasty, at ★ **Toni's Country Kitchen** (79 3rd St., Laurium, 906/337-0611, 7am-5:30pm Tues.-Fri., 7am-5pm Sat.). The setting is unpretentious, but the food will keep you coming back. The scent of sweet treats like sticky buns, cookies, and tarts wafts through the air. The coffee is top-notch as well.

Despite its name, the **Lindell Chocolate Shoppe** (300 Calumet St., Lake Linden,

906/296-8083, 7am-1pm Mon., Wed., and Thurs., 7am-2pm Fri.-Sun., $16-20) is actually a full restaurant. Visitors come to marvel at the beauty of this untouched 1920s shop, gleaming with golden oak, stained glass, and marble. Locals, though, come for the food, especially the extensive breakfast offerings.

ACCOMMODATIONS

There are a few good options south of Houghton. **Carla's Lake Shore Motel** (14258 US 41, Baraga, 906/353-6256, www. carlasinn.com, $), on US 41 north of Baraga, has both clean, inexpensive motel rooms and a few cabins, all with a stunning view of Keweenaw Bay. Another attractive option in Baraga is the **Baraga Lakeside Inn** (900 S. US 41, 906/353-7123, www.baragalakesideinn. com, $$). Rooms are clean and spacious, and some are equipped with hot tubs. Breakfast, lunch, and dinner are available at the on-site Lakeside Restaurant and Lounge, which offers an attractive view of Keweenaw Bay.

Perhaps due to the presence of the university, Houghton accommodations can be on the pricey side for such a small place. But bargains are available. Tucked below downtown Houghton along the Keweenaw Waterway, **Super 8** (1200 E. Lakeshore Dr., Houghton, 906/482-2240, www.super8.com, $$) offers one of the best locations in town, right on the water and the bike path. Amenities include an indoor pool and continental breakfast.

In Hancock you can find clean rooms, moderate amenities, and a terrific location at the **Ramada Waterfront** (99 Navy St., Hancock, 906/482-8400, www. ramadahancock.com, $$). Enjoy a premade to-go breakfast and the indoor pool.

The ★ **AmericInn Motel and Suites** (5101 6th St., Calumet, 906/337-6463, www. americinn.com, $$), north of Hancock, is the only full-service motel in greater Calumet, with an indoor pool and other amenities. The lobby's comfortable lodge-like setting is a calming oasis at the end of a long travel day. For something more traditional, look into the opulent copper-baron mansion at the ★ **Laurium Manor Inn** (320 Tamarack St., Laurium, 906/337-2549, www.lauriummanorinn.com, $$) in Laurium. Across the street, the owners have also restored the 1906 brick **Victorian Hall** (906/337-2549, $$). All rooms have private baths.

Camping

For campsite reservations at any Michigan state park, contact **Michigan DNR Reservations** (800/447-2757, www.midnr reservations.com). To rent rustic cabins or walled tents, contact the individual parks directly.

At Toivola, head 6.2 miles (10 km) west on Misery Bay Road, then north and west on Agate Beach Road for 4 miles (6.4 km) to **Agate Beach Park** (906/482-8319), a rather unknown little spot on Lake Superior. There's electricity but no modern plumbing. You will find an idyllic and quiet sandy beach, Lake Superior sunsets, and a low $9 tenting fee ($13 for sites with electricity). **Baraga State Park** (1300 US 41 S., Baraga, 906/353-6558, www.michigan.gov/dnr, $22-34) is almost entirely campground. Most visitors come for its more than 100 modern sites, with electricity, showers, and a convenient location just off US 41, 1 mile (1.6 km) south of the town of Baraga. Reservations are usually not necessary. Across the highway, a day-use area offers a sand beach and a bathhouse.

The Bill Nichols Trail passes through **Twin Lakes State Park** (6204 E. Poyhonen Rd., Toivola, 906/288-3321, www.michigan.gov/dnr, $25-29) in the southern Keweenaw. There is also a former single-family home that is now a park lodge ($$). Formerly the park supervisor's residence, the three-bedroom lodge can accommodate up to eight people and can be rented by only one family or group at a time. Though situated along the highway, many of the park's modern sites sit on the shores of Lake Roland, which was once determined to be the warmest lake in the Upper Peninsula. Sunsets get top billing at **McLain State Park** (18350 M-203, 906/482-0278, www.michigan.

gov/dnr, $22-30), where the sky often glows peach and pink before the sun melts into Lake Superior. As at most Michigan state parks, the 98 campsites are more than adequate, and many come with waterfront views. Cabins are also available for a higher rate.

Continuing up M-203 7 miles (11.3 km) north of Hancock, the **City of Houghton** maintains an **RV-only campground** (1100 W. Lakeshore Dr., Houghton, 906/482-8745, www.cityofhoughton.com/rv-park, $50). Each site is located near the water; no pets are allowed. Tent campers will be more attracted to the **Hancock Recreation Area** (2000 Jasberg St./M-203, Hancock, 906/482-7413, www.cityofhancock.com, mid-May-mid-Oct., $15-25), which sits on the Keweenaw Waterway. Follow M-203 1 mile (1.6 km) from downtown to get there. The primitive sites are situated in a quieter area apart from the 50 RV sites that are so modern they even include cable TV. Showers and laundry are on the premises.

INFORMATION AND SERVICES

The twin towns of Houghton and Hancock represent the area's largest population center, where you'll find most of the area's essential services, including tourism information and medical care. The area also serves as the unofficial gateway to the upper Keweenaw. The **Keweenaw Convention and Visitors Bureau** (56638 Calumet Ave., Calumet, 906/337-4579 or 800/338-7982, www.keweenaw.info) serves as an excellent one-stop source for attractions and lodging information. If you're interested in Copper Country's interesting history, you won't want to miss the fascinating **Keweenaw National Historical Park** (200 5th St., Calumet, 906/337-3168, www.nps.gov/kewe, 9am-5pm Mon.-Fri.).

If you need medical attention while in Houghton and Hancock, **UP Health System—Portage** (500 Campus Dr., Hancock, 906/483-1000 or 800/573-5001, www.uphealthsystem.com/portage) is the place to go. The hospital is just west of US 41;

take US 41 north or south to Campus Drive, turn west, and follow the road for 0.5 miles (0.8 km) until you reach the UP Health System sign. Farther north, just outside Calumet, is **Aspirus Keweenaw Hospital** (205 Osceola St., Laurium, 906/337-6560, www.aspirus. org). Take US 41 into town to M-26/School Street and go east to 2nd Street. Turn right on 2nd Street and then left on Osceola to arrive at the hospital.

There are several banks on either side of the river. You can find national banks such as **Flagstar Bank** (1303 College Ave., Houghton, 906/299-6972, www.flagstar. com), Midwestern banks such as **Huntington Bank** (400 Quincy St., Hancock, 906/482-6002, www.huntington.com), and local banks such as **Superior National Bank and Trust** (235 Quincy St., Hancock, 906/482-0404; 56788 Station Dr., Calumet, 906/337-5983; 53115 M-26, Lake Linden, inside Louie's Fresh Market, 906/296-6611, www.snb-t.com).

GETTING THERE AND AROUND
Car
By car, US 41 west from Marquette and M-26 north from Mass City are the main routes to the peninsula, meeting and crossing in Houghton and Hancock and then merging again at Calumet. Many of the secondary roads in the Keweenaw are dirt or gravel. For old logging roads and other questionable routes, a 4WD vehicle is strongly recommended.

Air
Houghton County Memorial Airport (CMX, 23810 Airpark Blvd., Calumet, 906/482-3970, www.houghtoncounty.org) is located a short distance northwest of Hancock. **United Airlines** (800/864-8339) has scheduled flights twice daily to and from Chicago. Ground transportation is available

for both local and long-distance trips with **Copper Country Limo** (906/370-4761, https://coppercountrylimo.com). Houghton County Memorial Airport also offers car rentals through **Alamo** (906/482-6655) and **National** (906/482-6655).

In addition, **Isle Royale Seaplanes** (906/483-4991 or 877/359-4753, www.isleroyaleseaplanes.com) offers daily one-way ($250) or round-trip ($360) seaplane flights to Isle Royale National Park.

Boat
The **Houghton County Marina** (906/482-6010, www.houghtoncounty.net, May-Oct.) is located in Hancock, with 44 seasonal slips and 10 transient slips. The marina is amenity-rich and offers close-up views of the lift bridge. You can contact the harbormaster on channels 16 and 68. Entry into the Portage Waterway is at 47°14.08 N, 88°34.19 W from the east, or at 46°57.40 N, 88°26.00 W from the west, with the marina itself located at 47°07.30 N, 88°34.19 W. The **Markhams Marina** in Houghton does not rent slips to the public and is only a service and repair facility.

Bus
Bus service tends to be spotty in the U.P., especially in the Keweenaw. **Houghton Motor Public Transit** (906/482-6092, www.cityofhoughton.com, $2 adults, $1 seniors) runs a regularly scheduled Downtowner Route that loops around from the Michigan Tech campus and ends at the Copper Country Mall. It's convenient but doesn't go much farther than you could get walking or on a bicycle. It does offer on-demand service for locations inside ($5) and outside ($6) city limits, but its scope is limited to the immediate area. Likewise, **Hancock Public Transportation** (906/482-3450, www.cityofhancock.com, $5 adults, $3 students, $2.50 seniors) runs a door-to-door on-demand service within a limited area.

Copper Harbor and Vicinity

Wedged between Lake Superior to the north and tranquil **Lake Fanny Hooe** to the south, Copper Harbor has always been an outpost in the wilderness—for the copper prospectors who came in the mid-1880s, for the military who built a fort to keep the miners and the Native Americans at peace, and today for those who come for its water and woods.

Copper Harbor literally marks the end of the road in the Keweenaw Peninsula: US 41 ends here in a small, unceremonious loop 1,990 miles (3,200 km) from its other end in Miami, Florida. When visitors arrive, they discover one of the Upper Peninsula's most scenic natural areas and one of its most appealing little towns.

Tiny Copper Harbor, population 136, offers much more than you might expect from its size. In a town just a few blocks long, street addresses are generally used only by the postal service. And for such a small place, Copper Harbor offers some excellent shopping opportunities.

This serene tip of the Keweenaw is a favorite vacation spot for kayakers, canoers, and boaters. With its location in the far north of the U.P. and bounded on three sides by Lake Superior, Copper Harbor feels like the end of the earth, or, at very least, the end of Michigan.

SIGHTS
Downtown Copper Harbor and Around

The **Astor House Antique Doll and Indian Artifact Museum** at the **Minnetonka Resort** (562 Gratiot St., 906/289-4449, www.minnetonkaresort.com, 10am-5pm daily July-Sept., $2, free under age 12) offers an amazing array of artifacts within a small space. Here you'll find a collection of some 400 antique dolls from around the world, Great Lakes nautical memorabilia, and examples of tools used by miners during the era of big copper.

Downtown Copper Harbor and its environs are conducive to leisurely walks. From the parking lot of the municipal marina, west of the ferry dock, a 3.2-mile (5.2-km) round-trip trail winds through the woods to **Hunter's Point.** This small appendage of land forms the west end of the harbor. On the open Lake Superior side, **Agate Beach** is a good spot to look for the eponymous banded rocks.

Downtown, a sign will point you toward **Estivant Pines Nature Sanctuary** (www.michigannature.org), a 377-acre sanctuary of virgin white pines just a few miles south of town. As recently as the 1970s, local conservationists like the late Jim Rooks saved these magnificent trees from loggers. Some tower nearly 10 stories high and date back almost 1,000 years. At first, the pines will seem hidden by the maturing oaks and maples, but a quick glance up will offer a dazzling perspective. To get there, begin at the intersection of Gratiot (US 41) and Manganese Road in downtown. Take Manganese south until you come to Burma Road (also signed as Clark Mine Rd.). Make a sharp right turn and continue for 1 mile (1.6 km). You'll find a parking area for Estivant Pines on your left.

★ Fort Wilkins Historic State Park

The presence of **Fort Wilkins Historic State Park** (15223 US 41, 906/289-4215, www.michigan.gov/dnr, 8:30am-dusk daily mid-May-mid-Oct.) reveals a curious aspect of local history. With miners pouring north during the copper rush, the federal government feared fighting would surely erupt between the newcomers and the local Native Americans, so it ordered the construction of a garrisoned fort. In 1844, the government sent approximately 100 soldiers to build barracks, a mess hall, a hospital, and other buildings behind a tall stockade fence. But

Copper Harbor and Vicinity

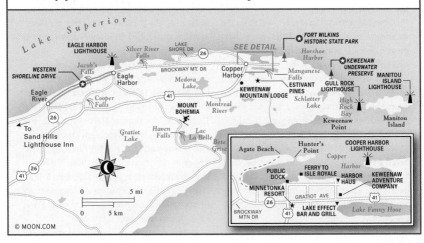

the anticipated fighting never occurred, and the winters proved long, cold, and desolate. Half the troops were pulled out in 1845 and sent south, where the country faced the threat of war with Mexico; by 1846 the rest of the troops were gone.

Today, Fort Wilkins stands as one of the few remaining wooden forts east of the Mississippi, with 16 whitewashed buildings meticulously restored and filled with exhibits of life on the northern frontier. From mid-June to late August, costumed interpreters recreate military life. Along with the fort, the state park includes rocky and scenic Lake Superior frontage, a few short hiking trails, the 1866 Copper Harbor Lighthouse (accessible only by private boat), plus an excellent **campground** (reservations 800/447-2757, www.midnrreservations.com) on Lake Fanny Hooe.

Brockway Mountain Drive

Dubbed "the most beautiful road in Michigan," this 9-mile (14.5-km) route traces the spine of a 735-foot-high (224-meter) ridge between Copper Harbor and Eagle Harbor and is the highest paved road between the Rockies and the Allegheny Mountains. The route starts from M-26 at Silver River Falls, just over 4 miles (6.4 km) east of Eagle Harbor, and rejoins the highway immediately west of Copper Harbor's downtown. A parking area midway allows you to stop and soak in the panorama of Lake Superior and the rolling forests of the Keweenaw. Watch for ravens, bald eagles, and peregrine falcons, which will sometimes soar below you. While you can drive this in either direction, traveling west to east offers an opportunity to get a postcard-quality shot of Copper Harbor, tucked between Lake Superior and Lake Fanny Hooe.

★ Western Shoreline Drive

Beginning at Copper Harbor, this route continues for a total of 97 miles (153 km) southwest to Silver City, the gateway to the Porcupine Mountains.

The stretch of M-26 between Copper Harbor and Eagle River lives up to its name: Lake Superior looms alongside the road, studded with rocky islands and swelling dunes. Unfortunately, you miss about 10 miles (16.1 km) of the route if you take **Brockway Mountain Drive.** A good strategy is to try both—Brockway is better when traveling east, while this drive is better heading west.

About 5 miles (8 km) south of Copper Harbor, **Hebard Park** is a good picnic, sunset, or agate-hunting spot. Where M-26 and Brockway Mountain Drive meet, watch for the small sign marking **Silver Falls.** It's a short downhill walk to this lovely little waterfall that splashes and pools in the forest.

West of Eagle Harbor, the road climbs above **Great Sand Bay** toward Eagle River. From this high vantage point, you can sometimes see huge 1,000-foot-long lake freighters out in the shipping lanes, which squeeze close to shore to round Keweenaw Point. Inland, beach peas, sand cherries, and wild roses cling to windswept, volatile mounds of sand. Like beach grasses, the plants' spreading root systems help trap the sand, stabilizing and building dunes.

The Keweenaw's tilted fault line is particularly pronounced in this part of the peninsula. To the south rises the exposed basalt face of the Cliff Range, while to the north, the fault line drops away so quickly that Great Sand Bay plummets to depths of more than 1,000 feet (305 meters). In between, deep ridges allow microclimates to thrive. Along the south side of the road, watch for faintly marked **Michigan Nature Association Trails** that dip into dark, deep forests, where lichen drapes from the pines and deep cushions of moss cover the rocky path. As the drive continues southwest, the route curves inland and passes through a series of thick woodlands, which carry special appeal during fall.

Lighthouses

Although it's located on the mainland, **Copper Harbor Lighthouse** is accessible only by boat since the adjacent property owners refuse to grant an easement. Until recently, a DNR-sanctioned business would ferry visitors from the Copper Harbor Marina for tours, but since the company went out of business, the only way to access this magnificent structure is by private boat. Originally built in 1849, the stone lighthouse is the oldest operating light on Lake Superior. Today an automated tower built during the 1930s allows ships to navigate. It was on this point where Douglass Houghton first spotted a thick green stripe in the rock indicating the presence of copper, a discovery that unleashed the Keweenaw's copper boom.

There are a few other lighthouses around Copper Harbor: **Gull Rock Lighthouse** and **Manitou Island Lighthouse,** the oldest spindle-shanked light tower on the Great Lakes. Like the Copper Harbor light, they're accessible only by private boat. One such service is **Hooked Up Charter Fishing** (12627 Superior St., Lac La Belle, 906/370-4450, www.hookedupcharter.com, $550 for a 5-hour cruise). While the business caters primarily to accommodating anglers, Captain Steve Erbisch also welcomes sightseers.

A few miles west of Eagle Harbor, the **Eagle River Lighthouse** is worth a brief look and makes for a nice picture, but today it's a private residence and not open to the public. The light went out of service in the early 1900s. On the other side of the peninsula, in Bete Grise, historic lighthouse aficionados will want to track down **Mendota Lighthouse** (sometimes called Bete Grise Lighthouse) for a picture, but it's also a private residence not open to the public. The owner maintains an excellent website (www.mendotalighthouse.com) that offers a virtual tour, plus an abundance of information on the history, evolution, and ongoing restoration of this historical gem.

South of Eagle Harbor, you'll find the **Sand Hills Lighthouse** (5-Mile Point Rd., Ahmeek). The 1917 lighthouse was made for three keepers and their families, and it operated as a bed-and-breakfast from 1995 to 2018. Currently the building is closed for restoration.

Eagle Harbor

One of the Keweenaw's most charming little towns, Eagle Harbor has a sleepy, comfortable feel to it, with a wonderfully protected natural harbor, a perfect crescent of beach, and even a historic lighthouse with an observation deck out on the rocky point. In short, it's a classic summer getaway.

The redbrick **Eagle Harbor Lighthouse** (670 Lighthouse Rd., Eagle Harbor, 906/289-4990, www.keweenawhistory.org, 10am-5pm Mon.-Sat., noon-5pm Sun. mid-June-early Oct., $8, children free), built in 1871, is one of the area's most attractive. Its outbuildings contain a small museum filled with information on shipwrecks, mining, and commercial fishing. In 2013 a new museum was opened, covering the lifesaving efforts of the Coast Guard over the years. The top of the lighthouse is off-limits to visitors, as the Coast Guard still operates the automated light.

The **one-room schoolhouse** (Center St., 2 blocks west of the harbor) was the birthplace of the Knights of Pythias, a secret fraternal society known for its elaborate rituals and fanciful costumes.

SHOPPING

The **Laughing Loon** (242 1st St., 906/289-4813, www.thelaughingloononline.com, 10am-5pm Mon.-Tues. and Thurs.-Sat.) is the quintessential destination for nontouristy gifts that reflect the true nature of the north. **Swede's Gift Shop** (Gratiot St./US 41 and 4th St., 906/289-4596) offers a good selection of local stones and minerals. **The Fisherman's Daughter** (5th St. at the waterfront, 906/289-4285, summer only) is another shop offering ceramic pottery, clothing, jewelry, and rare minerals.

The **Thunderbird Gift Center** at the **Minnetonka Resort** (562 Gratiot St., 906/289-4449, www.minnetonkaresort.com, hours vary) is a terrific source for books on mining, shipwrecks, and other historical subjects. The shop also has a lot of interesting artifacts for sale, such as lanterns and clay pipes discarded long ago by miners.

Jampot (6500 M-26, Eagle Harbor, 906/289-4388, www.poorrockabbey.com, 10am-5pm Tues.-Sat. mid-May-mid-Oct.) is a wonderful source for homemade preserves, baked goods, fruitcakes, and gourmet coffee. What is unusual about this shop is that it's run

by a group of Orthodox Christian monks from the Society of St. John, who live in a nearby monastery. The monks bring a great deal of personal commitment to their shop, which they operate as their means of support. Look for the shop on the east side of M-26 about halfway between Eagle Harbor and Eagle River. It's located at a bend in the road immediately north of Jacobs Falls.

ENTERTAINMENT
Microbrewery

A great place to toast your Copper Harbor adventure is at the **Brickside Brewery** (64 Gratiot Ave., at 1st St., 906/289-4772, www.bricksidebrewery.com, noon-9pm daily May-Oct. 3pm-9pm Tues.-Sun. Nov.-Apr.). The selections rotate but typically include beers like Fake Lake Blonde, Chocolate Milk Dark, and Jackpine Savage, an English special bitter.

FESTIVALS AND EVENTS

Copper Harbor hosts the peninsula's best **Fourth of July** fireworks show, and Sam Raymond, owner of Copper Harbor's Keweenaw Adventure Company, puts on a growing **Fat Tire Festival** the day before Labor Day. For more information on area festivals and celebrations, contact the **Keweenaw Convention and Visitors Bureau** (56638 Calumet Ave., Calumet, 906/337-4579 or 800/338-7982, www.keweenaw.info).

SUMMER RECREATION
Hiking and Biking

You'll need a map to reliably navigate this complex area. A snowmobile trail map (available through local shops and the Keweenaw Convention and Visitors Bureau) is adequate for major routes; the *DeLorme Atlas and Gazetteer* includes a few more, although a topographic map is best. However, no map yet shows even half the trails in the area. Sam Raymond, owner of the **Keweenaw Adventure Company** (155 Gratiot St., Copper Harbor, 906/289-4303, www.keweenawadventure.com, hours vary), has

mapped and signed dozens of miles of mountain biking routes, although the signs keep disappearing. He's also clearing and maintaining the trails with only the help of a few friends. It's a huge undertaking for minimal return, so show Sam your appreciation by giving him your business. Keweenaw Adventure Company rents and services mountain bikes and sells those ever helpful maps.

Red Trail

Not surprisingly, Keweenaw Adventure Company is also your best source for trail suggestions in the area. The **Red Trail** (1.7 miles/2.7 km) is the region's classic route, a single-track trail with plenty of technical twists and turns. It runs roughly from the gravel **Burma Road Trail** past the south end of the Keweenaw Mountain Lodge golf course and the north shore of Lake Manganese, where you can pick up **Paul's Plunge** back to Lake Fanny Hooe. Another good loop is the two-track **Surprise Valley Trail** (2.2 miles/3.5 km), which hooks up with the **Kamikaze Trail** that traces the southern side of Lake Fanny Hooe.

Clark Mine Trail

In the same general area, the **Clark Mine Trail** dips south away from Copper Harbor at the south end of Lake Fanny Hooe. Just outside town, brown-and-white signs will direct you to **Manganese Falls,** a pleasant walk down into a ferny oasis; **Manganese Lake,** a popular fishing and swimming hole; and the **Clark Mine,** where the old brick furnace chimney still stands against a backdrop of mine tailings. Where the Clark Mine Trail (5.5 miles/8.9 km) swings east, make your way south to meet up with the Montreal River if you're interested in a little trout fishing.

1: Copper Harbor marks the end of US 41.
2: Copper Harbor Lighthouse **3:** restored general store on display at Fort Wilkins State Park **4:** Eagle Harbor Lighthouse

Bare Bluff Trail

On the far southern shore of the Keweenaw is **Bare Bluff Trail,** a short (3.1 miles/5 km) but moderately challenging hike. The loop trail takes the hiker to an elevation of some 300 feet (90 meters) from the trailhead. The ascent can be fairly steep at points, but your effort will be rewarded when you arrive at the top of the namesake peak, affording a dramatic view of Bete Grise Bay. To get there, take Gay Lac La Belle Road off US 41 near Delaware. Continue for 3 miles (4.8 km) until you reach the hamlet of Lac La Belle. When you come to a fork in the road, bear to the left and continue on Bete Gris Road (in places this road is alternatively identified as Lac La Belle) until you come to Smith's Fishery Road. Turn left and continue for about 2 miles (3.2 km) until you reach the trailhead and a small parking area. The signage will say Russell and Miriam Grinnell Memorial Nature Sanctuary.

Tip of Keweenaw Peninsula

Copper Harbor is at the top of the Keweenaw Peninsula, but it's not at the end. The peninsula curves to the east and slightly south and continues about 10 miles (16.1 km) beyond town, which terminates at the Keweenaw's tip. This leaves about 60 square miles (155 sq km) east and south of Copper Harbor with no pavement, development, or attractions. In short, it's a nature lover's dream, where you can hike, mountain bike, fish, or just get out alone in the woods.

Probably more than 100 miles (160 km) of trails crisscross the tip of the peninsula; there is no accurate count. They range from deer trails to tight single-track to wide gravel and dirt roads used by logging trucks and snowmobiles. Aside from a few tracts held by the state and the Nature Conservancy, the vast majority of the land is owned by International Paper, which uses it for logging. The paper company has put the land in what is called a Commercial Forest Reserve (CFR). These lands, common throughout the U.P., provide tax breaks to companies that agree to keep the land open to the public for recreation. That means you are free to hike, bike, and otherwise explore this area. Avoid any active logging areas and follow the same guidelines you would anywhere: respect No Trespassing signs, take nothing but photographs, and leave nothing but footprints.

Canoeing and Kayaking

Paddling is at its finest in the Keweenaw, where there are plenty of islands, rock formations, and wilderness coastlines to explore. **Keweenaw Adventure Company** (155 Gratiot St., 906/289-4303, www.keweenawadventure.com, hours vary) rents kayaks and offers guided trips and lessons. Beginners should try the 2.5-hour Porter's Island Paddle, which includes novice dry land instruction and an enjoyable trip around the harbor and along the Lake Superior shoreline. Keweenaw Adventure Company also offers some daylong trips around the peninsula to Horseshoe Harbor, Agate Harbor, and the mouth of the Montreal River, as scheduling permits. Check the website or give them a call for more specifics.

If you have your own boat, don't overlook the peninsula's inland waters. Fanny Hooe, Medora, and other nearby lakes offer classic north woods peace and scenery, often with the company of bobbing loons or black bears on the shoreline.

Fishing

The **Gratiot River,** which crosses M-26/US 41 north of Amheek and Mohawk and continues west to Lake Superior, is a good place to cast a line for brook and rainbow trout, as well as the occasional steelhead. There's an access point on M-26/US 41. To find access where the Gratiot River crosses Cliff Drive, take the turnoff in the village of Amheek and follow Cliff Drive to the water. For another fishing spot, follow Five Mile Point Road from Amheek to Farmer's Road and turn left to the river and its Upper Falls.

You can cast a line at Gratiot River Country Park. To get here, take US 41 to Allouez and turn at the gas station onto Bumbetown Road;

continue onto Gratiot River Road for just over 4 miles (6.4 km).

Beaches
Horseshoe Harbor and High Rock Bay

In addition to the trails south of Copper Harbor, there are other destinations to consider. At the end of US 41 look for Mandan Road, a dirt and gravel road that continues eastward. Follow it for about a mile to the first main left branch (High Rock Bay Road), which winds north and east to the Lake Superior shore and **Horseshoe Harbor,** a fine place to spend an afternoon scrambling around the rock ledges and beaches. This picturesque sliver is owned by the Nature Conservancy, which prohibits mountain bikes on their property.

Backtracking to the Mandan Road, continue east about 3 miles (4.8 km) to another left (northeast) turnoff (also called High Rock Bay Road), which skirts Schlatter Lake and continues on to **High Rock Bay** at the tip of the peninsula. Like an oasis in the desert, the beauty of Hard Rock Bay feels like a reward after what can be a taxing journey. While scores of other points in the U.P. are tranquil and isolated, this place truly feels like the end of the world. The unparalleled view of Manitou Island and the crystalline waters of Lake Superior are the attractions here. Don't be surprised to see a couple of camps set up. *A word of warning:* The dirt roads described above are very rough in places. Only vehicles capable of off-road travel should be used.

Boat Trips and Tours

The Kilpela family, who run the Isle Royale ferry service, also offer 90-minute **sunset cruises** (906/289-4437, www.isleroyale.com, Wed. July 4-late Aug., $30 adults, $25 over age 59, $20 ages 5-14) on the *Isle Royale Queen IV.* Cruises depart on Wednesday at 8:30pm in July, at 8pm in August, from the foot of 5th Street near Brockway Avenue in Copper Harbor. Call for reservations and to double-check the schedule, which varies throughout the summer as the time of sunset changes. From mid-May through the end of September, the *Queen* also earns her keep by ferrying passengers from Copper Harbor to Isle Royale National Park, a 4.5-hour trip.

Private Boats

Sand Point Charters (22950 Airpark Blvd., Calumet, 906/370-2257, www.sandpointcharters.com) offers fishing (2 people full day $850, half day $500) and sightseeing charters (2 people for 3 hours $550), and even a fishing/sightseeing combination ($450-550). The sightseeing cruise passes by Mendota, Gull Rock, and Manitou Lighthouses. An alternative itinerary will take you to Stannard Rock, Huron Island, and Granite Rock Lighthouses.

TOP EXPERIENCE

Diving

The crisp water of Lake Superior offers outstanding visibility for divers. Although there's little in the way of plant and animal life—the cold water makes for a pretty sterile environment—there are interesting geologic formations and shipwrecks.

★ **Keweenaw Underwater Preserve**
Ships have been running aground for well over 100 years around the Keweenaw Peninsula, a major navigational hazard. Within the 103-square-mile (267-sq-km) **Keweenaw Underwater Preserve** (www.michiganpreserves.org/keweenaw.htm), divers can explore the *Tioga,* a freighter that ran aground near Eagle River in 1919, and the *City of St. Joseph,* which met its fate north of Eagle Harbor in 1942. Both ships are in less than 40 feet (12 meters) of water, with large sections of their hulls, deck machinery, and other artifacts clearly visible.

One of the Upper Peninsula's oldest shipwrecks, the *John Jacob Astor,* lies just offshore of Copper Harbor, near the Fort Wilkins State Park Lighthouse Overlook. An Underwater Trail marks the location of the rudder, anchor,

and other remnants of the *Astor,* which sank in 1844. Local lore explains that before the Keweenaw Underwater Preserve was established in 1989, townspeople learned of a small group of salvage divers who were planning to retrieve one of the anchors. Without the legal protection of an underwater preserve, the local divers took the matter into their own hands: They hauled up the anchor themselves and hid it in nearby Lake Fanny Hooe, where it remained until recently, when it was safely returned to its original wreck site. Today, disturbing or removing any underwater artifact is a felony under Michigan law.

The U.S. Coast Guard has to be more than a little embarrassed about the preserve's most popular dive site, the cutter *Mesquite.* In 1989, the 180-foot (55-meter) *Mesquite* ran aground on a reef off Keweenaw Point while tending to a navigational buoy. Efforts to free the ship failed, and winter winds battered it so badly that the Coast Guard decided to scuttle it and have it become a dive site rather than pay the costs of retrieving and repairing the aging vessel. Today the *Mesquite* sits in 110 feet (34 meters) of water in Keystone Bay with virtually all its equipment on deck. Experienced divers can explore the *Mesquite's* interior.

Currently there are no sources in the Keweenaw for diving equipment or instruction, so you'll need to be prepared before arriving in the area. The following charter services primarily cover eastern Lake Superior, but they also rent equipment to divers headed to other parts of the U.P.: **Abyss Dive Charters** (39800 Dursum Ave. NE, Ada, 616/295-6542, www.abyssdivecharters.com) in Mackinaw City services divers in northern lower Michigan and in Whitefish Bay. Although the company operates out of Mackinaw City, its physical location is in Ada in the Lower Peninsula. **Great Lakes Divers** (400 Cedar St., Alpena, 989/916-9990, www.greatlakesdivers.com) in Alpena offers charters to the Straits of Mackinac Shipwreck Preserve and to the Thunder Bay National Marine Sanctuary in Lake Huron. You'll want to dive in the warmer months with scuba gear

Golf in Northern Michigan

When thinking of Upper Peninsula recreation, hiking, fishing, and boating might first come to mind. But the great game of golf also ranks as a popular leisure pursuit—and the Upper Peninsula delivers in spades.

By far the biggest draw of U.P. courses is the relative lack of crowds, even during the peak summer months. In addition, U.P. courses blend harmoniously with their wooded surroundings, unlike some of their counterparts in more populated areas. Many stay open until just before the snow flies, treating fall duffers to an exquisite palette of red, gold, and amber. But despite hosting fewer patrons, most U.P. courses still have all the customary amenities, including pro shops, restaurants, and shower facilities.

Try one of the following major U.P. golf destinations:

- **Wild Bluff Golf Course** (page 281) near the Bay Mills Resort and Casino in Sault Ste. Marie offers both scenic fairways and a stunning view of Lake Superior.

- **The Rock** (page 291) on Drummond Island will make you feel like you're at a private club (which it once was). This is a rare find.

- The **Keweenaw Mountain Lodge** (page 186) near Copper Harbor is as close to wilderness as a golf course gets. You'll likely see deer, foxes, and sandhill cranes crossing the fairway as you line up your shot.

and a full wetsuit, as the waters can be cold, especially below the surface. For both companies, prices and schedules vary widely; call for details.

Golf

The nine holes of the **Keweenaw Mountain Lodge** (14252 US 41, Copper Harbor, 906/289-4403 or 888/685-6343, www. atthelodge.com, $35 for 9 holes, $45 for 18 holes, cart fees $25 for 9 holes, $35 for 18 holes) have a reputation for their beautiful scenery as well as for a good game of golf. It's one of the Keweenaw's best rounds. There's a pro shop and meals available at the lodge. If the weather's nice and the blackflies aren't circling, try dining on the porch. After a full day on the links, you'll appreciate the full bar, wine list, and great food.

Waterfalls

The Montreal River tumbles over some beautiful waterfalls before joining Lake Superior just to the southeast, but they're difficult to reach. The best way is to start at Bete Grise (bay-duh GREE), the arm of Lake Superior on the southern shore of the Keweenaw directly south of Copper Harbor. Just before you reach Bete Grise Bay, you'll see two dirt routes heading east into the woods. One is signed "This is *not* the road to Smith Fisheries." Take the unsigned road. It will lead you around Bear Bluff to an old commercial fishing enterprise, which is now private property. Continue on the smaller trail behind the fishery, a terrific path that traces the steep bluffs of the shore. It's about another 1.5 miles (2.4 km) to the mouth of the Montreal River and its stellar waterfalls. West of Bete Grise, the pleasant **Haven Falls** are located at a roadside park. Take Lac La Belle Road south for 4.5 miles (7.2 km), bear right at the fork, and continue on to the park.

In Copper Harbor, you won't want to miss the **Manganese Falls,** a thin but inspired flow that drops about 45 feet (14 meters) into a narrow gorge just outside town. To get there, turn south on Manganese Road for less than a mile; the falls are a short walk from the roadside. Eagle Harbor has a few shorter falls, each about 7 feet (2 meters) high. There are taller, more impressive falls in the Keweenaw

Peninsula, but these are pretty easy to get to. **Silver River Falls** is a short walk from M-26, a little more than 4 miles (6.4 km) east of Eagle Harbor. The falls are wide and reasonably picturesque, with a picnic area and roadside park nearby. **Copper Falls** is about 3 miles (4.8 km) south of Eagle Harbor, on the cutoff road between US 41 and town. As you pass Owl Creek on your way south, take the second trail road to the left and park. The falls are a very short walk straight off the end of the road.

Eagle River's falls are much more impressive than Eagle Harbor's and even more convenient to get to. Both **Eagle River Falls** and **Jacob's Falls** are more or less on the shoulder of M-26. There's a parking area and pedestrian bridge just off the highway as it enters Eagle River, providing great access to the 60-foot (18-meter) falls. You can see the smaller Jacob's Falls as you drive past on M-26, 3 miles (4.8 km) northeast of Eagle River, but you'll want to stop to admire the 40-foot (12-meter) drop.

WINTER RECREATION
Downhill Skiing

Downhill skiers can check out Michigan's most challenging terrain at **Mount Bohemia** (6532 Lac La Belle Rd., 906/360-7240 or 888/937-2411, www.mtbohemia.com, lift tickets $87), near Lac La Belle. Mount Bohemia offers one of the Midwest's highest vertical drops, at 900 feet (275 meters), with some steep pitches, rocky outcrops, and gladed terrain that may make you think you're somewhere in the Rockies.

Ski and Snowshoe Trails

A few trails stand out from the northern Keweenaw's many miles of cross-country skiing possibilities. First among these is the **Copper Harbor Pathway.** With regularly groomed loops and trails that range from beginner to expert, the miles in and around Copper Harbor provide pleasant skiing and include marked snowshoe trails. The **Fort Wilkins State Park Loop** is in the region between Copper Harbor and the north shore of Lake Fanny Hooe, while the long **Kamikaze Trail** (not for beginners) hugs the lake's southern shore for more than 2 miles (3.2 km). Snowshoers will want to make their way into **Estivant Pines Nature Sanctuary,** 350 acres of virgin pine and towering hardwoods south of town that are purported to be the oldest living trees in the state. You'll be able to choose among three loops ranging 1-2.5 miles (1.6-4 km), and the ancient woods are worth going out of your way for. Here you can walk in peace since snowmobiles and motorized vehicles are prohibited.

There are no outfitters of ski and snowshoe equipment in the Copper Harbor area. Your best bet is to stop at **Cross Country Sports** (507 Oak St., Calumet, 906/337-4520, www.crosscountrysports.com, 10am-6pm Mon.-Sat.) in Calumet on your way farther north.

Snowmobiling

The Copper Harbor region, like the rest of Keweenaw, has plenty of well-groomed snowmobile trails. The Keweenaw Trail curves north to east as it ascends from Hancock, eventually connecting with the Lac La Belle Trail (steer clear of the Mount Bohemia skiers), Eagle's Loop, Mandan Trail, Harlow Trail, and other snowmobile routes with trail numbers in the 130s. Take the Brockway Mountain or Powder House Trails into Copper Harbor, and for an end-of-the-road journey to the point of the Keweenaw, take the High Rock Trail to Lake Superior, east of the city. A good trail map is available from the **Keweenaw Convention and Visitors Bureau** (56638 Calumet Ave., Calumet, 906/337-4579 or 800/338-7982, www.keweenaw.info).

Snowmobiles can be rented from **Copper Country Rentals** at the **Trailside Lodge** (57900 US 41, Calumet, 906/337-9905, www.thetrailsidelodge.com).

FOOD

The ★ **Lake Effect Bar and Grill** (160 Gratiot St., 906/289-4010, Copper Harbor, https://copperharborpines.com, 6:30am-3pm daily, $8-17), a small café, is an unbeatably warm, inviting place complete with knotty pine, a stone fireplace, and good basic Yooper fare, such as burgers, hearty sandwiches, and a delicious turkey dinner on Sunday. Get a booth by a window and take in a true "up north" experience.

For something a bit more upscale, the ★ **Harbor Haus** (77 Brockway Ave., 906/289-4502, www.harborhaus.com, 4pm-8:30pm daily, $25-48) in Copper Harbor offers top-notch dining overlooking the harbor. Think entrées like sautéed pork tenderloin or butter poached lobster tails. When the *Isle Royale Queen IV* passes by, the staff drop what they're doing to rush outside and perform the cancan.

You'll find something for everyone at the **Mariner North** (255 Gratiot St., 906/289-4637, http://manorth.com, 11am-9pm daily, $8-14). Small-plate entrées include fresh Lake Superior smoked trout dip and bruschetta. There's also an array of sandwich offerings, including the Seafarer (beer-battered whitefish) and Sailor's Choice (shaved pit ham with melted Swiss cheese). This Copper Harbor institution lost some of its spirit when the original log building burned down in 1991, but the rebuilt lodge remains a popular gathering place.

Inside the Eagle River Inn, ★ **Fitzgerald's Restaurant** (5033 Front St., 906/337-0666, www.eagleriverinn.com, 3pm-8pm Mon.-Thurs., noon-8pm Fri.-Sun., $16-27) offers upscale dining overlooking Lake Superior. The menu features pan-seared salmon, Nashville hot chicken, hardwood-smoked barbecue, and an extensive variety of craft beers.

You won't find a full-service grocery store in Copper Harbor, so load up in Houghton or Calumet if you're planning a campout or cabin stay. However, the exceptionally friendly **Gas Lite General Store,** also affectionately known as The Genny (Gratiot St. near 1st St., 906/281-9281, www.atthegenny.com, 10am-5pm Mon.-Fri.) has all the basics. It also happens to be the spot to catch up on local news. For fresh or smoked fish, head to

the ferry dock for **Jamsen's Fish Market** (4 Waterfront Landing, Copper Harbor, 906/289-4000, www.jamsen.biz, 7am-3pm daily summer high season), run by the last commercial fishing family still working the local waters. The store also includes a bakery serving a variety of Finnish recipes.

ACCOMMODATIONS

Located high on a ridge above Copper Harbor, the log lodge and cabins of the **Keweenaw Mountain Lodge** (14252 US 41, 906/289-4403 or 888/685-6343, www.atthelodge.com, $$) were built as a WPA project in the 1930s. Reservations can be difficult to obtain, but the charming cabins offer an experience distinct from a typical motel room. Near the western tip of Lake Fanny Hooe, **Lake Fanny Hooe Resort and Campground** (505 2nd St., 906/289-4451, www.fannyhooe.com, $$) offers a lakefront motel and cottages. Each motel room includes queen beds, cable TV, a kitchenette, a full bath, and individual room heat. Canoes and boats can be rented to enjoy the peaceful lake.

The no-frills rooms at the **King Copper Motel** (447 E. Brockway Ave., Copper Harbor, 906/289-4214 or 800/833-2470, www.kingcoppermotel.com, $$) come with great views of the harbor and are just a few steps from the ferry dock—perfect for a warm shower and a real bed after a week on Isle Royale.

Between Copper Harbor and Eagle Harbor on M-26, **Eagle Lodge** (13051 Lakeshore Dr./M-26, Eagle Harbor, 906/289-4294 or 888/558-4441, $$) offers simple housekeeping cabins perched on Lake Superior's shore. In Eagle River, the **Eagle River Inn** (5033 Front St., Eagle River, 906/337-0666, www.eagleriverinn.com, $$) offers pleasant accommodations in a similarly idyllic setting, right at the water's edge and flanked by a long sand beach. All rooms come with lake views.

Camping
Fort Wilkins State Park (15223 US 41, 906/289-4215, www.michigan.gov/dnr,

$19-26) has 165 modern sites in two camp-grounds, both on Lake Fanny Hooe. Many sites back up to the water and offer decent pri-vacy. You can make a reservation (but not for a specific site) by contacting the Michigan state parks central reservations system (800/447-2757, www.midnrreservations.com). **Lake Fanny Hooe Resort and Campground** (505 2nd St., 906/289-4451 or 800/426-4451, www.fannyhooe.com, $40-65) offers uninter-esting sites in an open grassy area, but with a decent location near town and the south shore of Lake Fanny Hooe.

West of Ahmeek on Five Mile Point Road, **Sunset Bay Campground** (2701 Sunset Bay Beach Rd., 906/337-2494, www.sunset-bay.com, late May-early Oct., $35-50) indeed offers a fine view of the sunset from your tent flap. Several of its 12 primi-tive sites sit on Lake Superior. There are 18 RV sites available. Many locals simply head out into the woods on weekends and set up camp near a favorite stretch of beach or river. If you choose to do the same, respect the No Trespassing signs and observe all backcountry camping practices (bury waste, hang packs, stay 50 feet/15 meters from the water)—you'll be sharing the woods with plenty of black bears.

INFORMATION

For Copper Harbor visitor information, con-tact the **Copper Harbor Improvement Association** (906/289-4212, www.copperharbor.org) or stop by the **Visitors Center** (Grant Township Bldg., US 41 and 2nd St.). The booth is staffed during the summer months, but even if no one is work-ing, you can get brochures from the lobby at any time. The **Keweenaw Convention and Visitors Bureau** (56638 Calumet Ave., Calumet, 906/337-4579 or 800/338-7982, www.keweenaw.info) is also a great source for information and maps.

Medical emergencies will necessitate going south again, though not all the way to Hancock, to the **Aspirus Keweenaw Hospital** (205 Osceola St., Laurium, 906/337-6500, www.aspirus.org). Heading into Laurium from Copper Harbor or northern Keweenaw, take US 41 to M-26/School Street and turn left. Take School Street to 2nd Street, turn right on 2nd, then left on Osceola to the hospital.

You'll have to head south of Copper Harbor to find a bank. Keweenaw's regional bank, **Superior National** (56788 Station Dr., 906/337-5983, www.snb-t.com) in Calumet is the closet branch to Copper Harbor. You can

Keweenaw Mountain Lodge

find an ATM at the Gas Lite General Store on the corner of US 41 and 1st Street.

GETTING THERE AND AROUND
Car

The two main roads that lead north and east to Copper Harbor are the same highways from the base of the Keweenaw to Houghton and Hancock. US 41 and M-26 merge at Calumet until Phoenix, where they split again. US 41 doubles as the Copper Country Trail Scenic Byway, which starts in Hancock, and it really is a pleasant drive, striking more or less through the middle of the peninsula. The trail pairs Keweenaw's natural beauty, which is especially striking during the fall, with a smattering of history at old mines, museums, and other heritage sites. Drivers may want to consider M-26 for the journey between Phoenix and Copper Harbor. Not only does it pass through Eagle Harbor, a pleasant town in its own right, but it also hugs the Lake Superior shore the entire way. As pleasant as the Copper Country Trail is, you'll get a more scenic drive on the detour east. The best combination is to take Brockway Mountain Drive (US 41) east to Copper Harbor and the Scenic Lakeshore Drive (M-26) when traveling west toward Eagle Harbor.

Air

If you're flying in, the closest airport is the **Houghton County Memorial Airport**

(CMX, 23810 Airpark Blvd., Calumet, 906/482-3970, www.houghtoncounty.org), with daily flights on **United Airlines** to and from Chicago. For car rentals at the airport, contact either **Alamo** or **National** at 906/482-6655.

Boat

The northern part of the Keweenaw is small, but it has a great deal of shoreline and two marinas. The **Copper Harbor State Harbor** (906/289-4698, www.michigan.gov/dnr) is small, with only 10 transient slips available, but you'll find a rich array of amenities (gas, showers, pump-out, dog run, a boater's lounge, and restrooms), unlike Eagle Harbor. The harbormaster is on duty 9am-5pm daily and can be reached on radio channel 9. Copper Harbor's dock is located at 47°28.42 N, 87°51.50 W.

The **Eagle Harbor State Harbor** (906/289-4215, www.michigan.org), about 14 miles (23 km) west of Copper Harbor, has transient docking, showers, pump-out, gasoline, and electricity (20 amp). You can find the dock at 47°27.52 N, 88°09.33 W.

Public Transportation

There is no public transportation in the Copper Harbor area, save for limited taxi and shuttle service in Houghton and Hancock and at the airport, although this is a very costly option. There is no bus service to the area.

Isle Royale

Sequestered in the vast waters of Lake Superior, Isle Royale is perhaps the model of an ideal national park: wild, rugged, and remote. A 45-mile-long (72-km) archipelago, Isle Royale is one of the least visited properties in the National Park System, attracting just 18,000 visitors a year—fewer than Yosemite receives in just a single weekend. Here, wireless communications (which are spotty) represent the only link with the outside world.

Civilization on Isle Royale (pronounced ROY-al, as if there were no "e") is concentrated in two small developments at opposite ends of the island. **Windigo,** on the southwest end, includes a National Park Service information center, a camp store, and a marina. **Rock Harbor,** near the east end, offers the same, plus a simple lodge and restaurant across from the ferry dock and a handful of cabins overlooking Tobin Harbor. The rest of the island is backcountry, 210 pristine square miles (545 sq km) of forested foot trails, rocky bluffs, quiet lakes, and wilderness campsites.

Those who make the trek by either boat or seaplane come to hike Isle Royale's 165 miles (265 km) of trails, fish its 46 inland lakes, and paddle its sawtooth shoreline. Wildlife viewing is popular too, especially for moose, which originally swam across from Ontario several decades ago, and eastern timber wolves, which arrived on the island after following their prey across the winter ice. While the wolves are notoriously elusive, rest assured that your sightings of other wildlife will far outnumber your human contacts while on Isle Royale.

GEOGRAPHY

Backpackers will take note of Isle Royale's distinctive topography as they traverse the long, narrow island, which runs southwest to northeast and is less than 9 miles (14.5 km) across at its widest point. A series of ridges and valleys fall away from the park's high interior backbone, the Greenstone Ridge, creating a washboard of forest and rock. Mount Desor marks the highest point on the island, rising from the Greenstone Ridge to 1,394 feet (425 meters).

The Precambrian lava flows that formed the Keweenaw Peninsula more than a billion years ago were also responsible for the formation of Isle Royale. After each lava flow, wind and rain carried sand and other sediments into the area, producing slabs of soft rock sandwiched between hard layers of basalt and creating the island's characteristic ridge and trough pattern. Hikers crossing the width of the island will feel this in their quads, as the trail continually rises and falls with each ridge.

This geological feature becomes most apparent on the park's northeastern shore. The ridges become long rocky fingers, and the valleys become narrow slivers of water wedged between the rocky points. This formation occurred when Lake Superior's basin subsided and layers of rock on Isle Royale were thrust upward at an angle, giving the island

a northeast side of steep ridges and bluffs, along with a gradually sloping southwest shore with lowlands and bogs. The northern Keweenaw Peninsula is a near mirror image of Isle Royale, with a gradual northern shore and more steeply angled southern side.

The geography of Isle Royale is intimately related to the water that surrounds it. Along with its namesake island, the largest in Lake Superior, Isle Royale National Park actually consists of an archipelago of some 400 islands, all of them remnants of the same landmass. More than 80 percent of the park lies underwater, beneath shallow ponds, bogs, inland lakes, and the clear, cold water of Lake Superior. An interesting bit of trivia: Ryan Island, located on Isle Royale's Siskiwit Lake, is the largest island in the largest lake on the largest island in the largest lake in the world.

CLIMATE

Isle Royale is the perfect escape from a hot, sticky summer. With its water temperature rarely exceeding 45°F (7°C), Lake Superior does a fine job as North America's largest natural air conditioner. It has a significant moderating effect on the island: summers are generally cooler than on the mainland, with daytime temperatures from mid-May to mid-August ranging 65-75°F (18-24°C). Nights can be cool, often dipping into the 40s (4-9°C) and even the 30s (-1 to 4°C). Clouds obscure the sun more than half the time in summer, and fog can strike anytime. More than one disappointed backpacker has returned from Isle Royale without any memories of the island's lovely vistas.

The lake's moderating effect works in reverse during the cold months. Winters are slightly warmer than on the mainland, though here that can be little consolation. Once Lake Superior turns from cobalt blue to dark gray in late autumn, and its infamous winter storms begin churning, the island becomes shrouded in fog, whipped by wind, and buried under several feet of snow.

In addition to its isolated location, the

Isle Royale

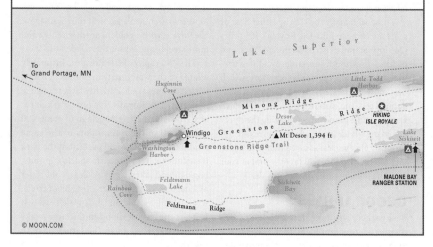

low number of annual visitors can be attributed also to the island closing down in mid-October, much like a summer resort—the only national park to do this. The ranger staff head for Houghton or take seasonal work in warmer climes. Only wildlife researchers continue their work, tracking free-roaming wolves and moose by air.

PLANTS AND ANIMALS

Isolated from the effects of civilization, Isle Royale acts as a living laboratory, a study of how plants and animals interrelate in the ebb and flow of nature's cycles. Owing to these unique natural qualities, the United Nations declared the park an International Biosphere Reserve in 1980.

Plants

Spruce, fir, and jack pine share the island with beech and maple forests, but numerous varieties of wildflowers take center stage in June and July. Forests can be dotted with yellow lady's slipper and American starflower; lowlands are brightened by wild irises, calla lilies, and yellow pond lilies. In July and August different species of berries make their appearance; look for blueberries, thimbleberries, and red raspberries, especially in the sunnier, rockier high areas.

Moose and Wolves

Naturalists believe **moose** first arrived at Isle Royale in the early 1900s, when several swam the 15 miles (24 km) from mainland Ontario. With ample vegetation for food and no natural predators, the moose multiplied rapidly, their numbers soaring to somewhere between 1,000 and 3,000 by the late 1920s. Soon after, their numbers depleted the available food sources. Starvation and a succession of harsh winters killed off hundreds of the huge mammals in the 1930s. A fire in 1936 prompted a regrowth of vegetation. With revived food sources, the moose population skyrocketed again, followed by another round of starvation.

The seesaw pattern might have continued for decades, but nature intervened in the form of the eastern **timber wolf** (also known as the gray wolf). During the exceptionally cold winter of 1948-1949, the lake iced over between Ontario and Isle Royale, and a small pack of wolves made its way to the island. The wolves found a bountiful food source in the local moose and multiplied, reaching a peak population of about 50 animals by 1970.

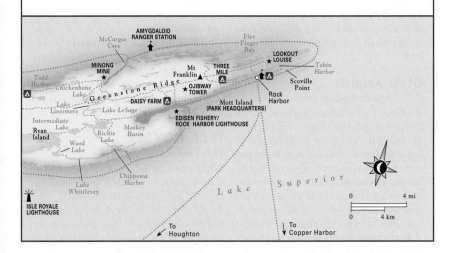

Since then the two species, fenced in by the waters of Lake Superior, have provided scientists with a fascinating study of the predator-prey relationship. In 2023 the island marked its 65th year of wolf-moose research and study. The study is a joint effort of the National Park Service and Michigan Technological University, and it has become the longest predator-prey study ever undertaken. In a large moose herd, wolves cull the sick, young, and old, preventing overpopulation. In fact, moose make up around 90 percent of the wolves' diet. But the resulting moose herd—stronger and healthier—makes hunting more difficult, which in turn reduces wolf breeding.

Populations of both animals have fluctuated dramatically over the decades. Today, the moose population is around 2,600, up considerably from previous decades. Not surprisingly, hikers have an excellent chance of spotting these 1,000-pound mammals, which often feed in ponds and lowlands or along inland lakeshores. Hidden Lake, across Tobin Harbor south of Lookout Louise, is an exceptionally good place to spot them, since the moose have a taste for its mineral licks. If you're lucky enough to come upon a moose,

give it a very wide berth. Although they look cartoonish and friendly, moose can be exceptionally dangerous if approached too closely. Cows safeguarding their calves and males behaving aggressively during the fall mating season are capable of inflicting lethal blows with their hooves.

Isle Royale's wolf population plummeted in the 1990s. Although biologists did not fully understand the reason behind this, they feared a lack of genetic diversity may have been a critical factor. By 1998, just 14 wolves roamed the island in three packs. After a brief rebound between 2000 and 2008, the decline resumed. In the winter of 2017, only 2 wolves were recorded, and this low figure is cited as the primary reason for the increasing moose population.

In 2018, the National Park Service began a relocation program to introduce additional wolves to Isle Royale. Twelve wolves were captured in Minnesota, Canada, and the mainland Upper Peninsula and relocated to Isle Royale. Some have produced pups, with the current wolf population standing at 28.

Backpackers rarely spot the shy and stealthy wolves, and the "wolf howls" often heard at night are most likely the haunting calls of loons. But the notion that even a very few wolves are out there, somewhere, and perhaps even watching from deep in the forest, is compelling enough for most, especially those lucky enough to spot a paw print along the trail.

Other Animals

Other large mammals common to the northern Great Lakes region are notably absent from the island. Black bears never migrated to Isle Royale, and white-tailed deer introduced for hunting vanished early in the 20th century. Caribou and lynx, present in the 19th century, also disappeared. Instead, hikers may spot red foxes (which love to scavenge around campsites, so hang your pack), beavers, muskrats, hares, red squirrels, otters, and mink.

Bird watchers will enjoy scanning the water's surface for the common loon, which is indeed common here, along with Canada geese and ducks including buffleheads, black ducks, mergansers, and mallards. Smaller birds frequenting the island include warblers, chickadees, thrushes, woodpeckers, and kingfishers.

None of Isle Royale's inland lakes can be reached by car or motorized boat, and many require serious effort to reach on foot. This combination makes for great **fishing.** Sport fishing boats ply the Lake Superior waters around Isle Royale for lake trout. But nearly all of the island's inland waters offer the ultimate fishing experience. Northern pike is considered a prime fish for its fighting spirit, and can be found in almost any of the local lakes. Hungry hikers will be pleased to know that walleye, perch, and trout are also quite plentiful. Bring along a pack rod to fish from shore. Many lakes, like Feldtmann, Desor, Siskiwit, Richie, and Chickenbone, have trails leading directly to them. Other more remote lakes are open to fishing but require good backcountry skills to reach. No license is needed to fish Isle Royale's inland lakes, although Michigan regulations still apply. If you plan to drop a line in Lake Superior, however, you'll need a Michigan license, which are available at the island's two camp stores.

A discussion of Isle Royale's animal life is not complete without mention of the island's insects. Like much of the Upper Peninsula and many other wilderness areas, Isle Royale provides a fine home for **mosquitoes** and **blackflies,** especially in low-lying areas. From mid-June to mid-August, keep insect repellent with DEET close at hand. In general, insects are less of a problem on higher trails, which often catch a lake breeze.

ISLE ROYALE NATIONAL PARK

While many national parks struggle with their fates of being islands of wilderness surrounded by a more developed world, Isle Royale is immune to this challenge. Its location on an actual island has the advantage of a large buffer zone protecting it from outside encroachment and influence. As a result, it's one of the most proactively managed holdings in the National Park System and possesses some unique conservation advantages. Isle Royale is one of the few parks that regulate the number of visitors who pass through its gates. Though logistics have done a good job of keeping numbers down thus far, the National Park Service could easily reduce the number further by cutting back on ferry service or on the number of campsites.

Limited access also allows the National Park Service to enforce rules more effectively. Dogs, for example, are not allowed on the island for fear they might bring rabies and other diseases to the island's wolf pack. The National Park Service also takes great pains to preserve the island's backcountry solitude, with a park brochure reminding hikers to "refrain from loud conversation," "avoid songfests," and "select equipment of subtle natural tones rather than conspicuous colorful gear."

Boat Tours

The **National Park Service** (906/482-0984, www.nps.gov/isro) shuttles visitors to various island attractions on its 25-passenger **MV Sandy.** On Tuesdays, Thursdays, and Saturdays the *Sandy* makes the short trip across the mouth of Moskey Basin to **Edisen Fishery.** The historic fishery of Peter and Laura Edisen has been restored to show what life was like when commercial fisheries once thrived on the island. From Edisen Fishery, it's a 0.25-mile (0.4-km) walk to the stout and simple **Rock Harbor Lighthouse,** a white edifice built in 1855 to guide ships to Isle Royale's then-busy copper ports.

On Tuesday, Wednesday, and Friday evenings, the *Sandy* embarks on a sunset cruise to **Raspberry Island,** on the far eastern tip of the archipelago. The tour includes time to stroll along a boardwalk through a spruce bog, as well as a loop around Scoville and Blake Points, a picturesque view of the Canadian shore, and a dramatic Lake Superior sunset. On Mondays, Wednesdays, and Fridays, the *Sandy* makes the trip to **Passage Island.** The trip includes a 2-mile (3.2-km) self-guided hike to visit the **Passage Island Lighthouse.**

Food and Accommodations

Those just looking for a quiet island stay and some pleasant day hikes can set up a base in comfort at the **Rock Harbor Lodge** (906/337-4993 or 866/644-2003, www.rockharborlodge.com, $$$). Lodge rooms are basic motel-style, but they are right at the water's edge with glorious views of the nearby islands and the open water of Lake Superior. This is probably why this slice of civilization in the wilderness comes at a steep price. The lodge also offers housekeeping cottages nearby, at a similar price, that come with a small kitchen, a double bed, and a bunk bed. Reservations are a must. Guests have use of an adjacent day lodge with a comfortable wood-burning fireplace.

The Rock Harbor Lodge **dining room** is open to the public daily for breakfast, lunch, and dinner. Dinner offerings often include fresh lake trout from the restored Edisen Fishery. For those fresh off the trails, its meals will taste like a gourmet feast. The **Marina Store** in Rock Harbor also carries a good supply of food, as well as camping supplies, fuel, and other essentials. Amenities include showers and laundry facilities.

Rock Harbor Lodge also offers two rustic **camper cabins** ($) in Windigo, about 45 miles (72 km) from the lodge. They lack electricity and indoor plumbing, but they do offer basic shelter. A well-equipped camp store, similar to the one in Rock Harbor, also has showers and laundry facilities.

If you want to see more of the island, **camping** is the only way to do it. Rustic campsites are located throughout the island, with three types of sites available: individual tent sites for 1-3 tents, group sites for 7-10 people, and three-sided shelters that hold up to 6 people. You must first obtain a camping permit outlining your itinerary from the ranger station. Groups of 6 or fewer must obtain a small-party backcountry camping permit (free) and may use individual sites on a first-come, first-served basis. Groups of 7-10 must obtain a group camping permit ($25). Groups of this size must make reservations in advance and are required to use specially designated group campsites.

Should you reach a site at the end of the day and find it full—this can happen, especially in August, and especially at sites that are a day's hike from Rock Harbor—the unwritten rule is that you double up. No one expects you to hike off into the dwindling light to the next campsite.

Come prepared. The camp stores, though well supplied, are not the places to outfit your trip. Carry a stove and fuel, since many sites do not permit fires and dead wood is limited. Unless you plan to boil your water, also bring a filter. Potable water is only available in Rock Harbor and Windigo, and chemical purifiers like halazone tablets will not kill the hydatid tapeworm found in Isle Royale waters.

Information

For general information on the park, camping, transportation options, and more, contact **Isle Royale National Park** (906/482-0984, www.nps.gov/isro). The summer headquarters for the park is on Mott Island, a barrier island on the south side of Rock Harbor Channel.

Isle Royale was one of the first national parks to charge a park user fee, currently $7 per person per day. If you're traveling to the island by ferry or seaplane, the concessionaire will collect your fee. If you're traveling by private boat, you can pay at the ranger station at Windigo, Rock Harbor, Malone Bay, or Amygdaloid, or at the Houghton Visitors Center prior to your departure. Perhaps the best option is to pay in advance online at www.pay.gov.

The National Park Service has long discussed charging admission fees to national parks as a way to compensate for shortfalls in federal funding. In the past, all gate fees were fed back into the federal government's general treasury, eliminating an incentive to levy a fee. With the new user-fee program, however, 80 percent of the monies gathered is spent at the collecting park. The remaining 20 percent is spent at national parks with priority maintenance projects. In Isle Royale's case, that means hundreds of thousands of dollars that will be spent maintaining trails and repairing or replacing docks.

Getting There

If getting there is half the fun, you'll be very excited by the time you arrive at Isle Royale. Travel to the island is not particularly convenient or cheap, which is probably why the average visitor stays are considerably longer than at most other national park destinations. The average length of visit to Rocky Mountain National Park is just a few hours, where at Isle Royale it's three days; that average even accounts for day-trippers who wander around the harbor for a few hours and leave that afternoon.

Many, however, come to appreciate even the trip to and from Isle Royale, a mental decompression chamber of sorts that eases the passage between island wilderness and the civilized world.

Your options for travel to Isle Royale are seaplane, ferry, or personal boat.

Ferry

The National Park Service operates the largest ferry, the 165-foot *Ranger III,* which has been in service since 1958. It departs from Houghton for the six-hour passage to Rock Harbor twice a week at 9am Tuesday and Friday from late May to mid-September, except for three Tuesdays—one each during June, July, and August—when the ship heads to Windigo. The ship makes the return trip on Wednesdays and Saturdays, also departing at 9am (except the Wednesdays following the Tuesday Windigo trips). The one-way cost is $80 adults and $40 ages 1-15; infants are free. Canoes and kayaks are an additional $35-70 if they're longer than 20 feet (6 meters) or weigh more than 90 pounds (41 kg). Make reservations through the **National Park Service** (906/482-0984, www.nps.gov/isro).

If you'd rather see more of the Keweenaw and spend less time on the ferry, drive another hour up the peninsula to Copper Harbor, where you can catch the *Isle Royale Queen IV* for a three-hour trip to Rock Harbor. It operates from mid-May through the end of September, with a varying schedule, adding additional departures as needed in July and August. The one-way cost is $80 adults, $57.50 under age 16. Canoes and kayaks are an additional $60. The *Isle Royale Queen IV* is highly reliable and has happily surprised weary backpackers by showing up to retrieve them on even the stormiest of days. But the ship richly deserves its nickname, "The Queasy." In heavy seas, its hull can rock and roll at a fairly good pitch. To check the schedule and make reservations, contact the **Isle Royale Line** (906/289-4437, www.isleroyale.com).

A third and fourth ferry run from Grand Portage, Minnesota: the 65-foot (19-meter) MV *Voyageur II* (outbound Mon., Wed., and Sat., inbound Tues., Thurs., and Sun.). Departures are at 7:30am central daylight time outbound and at 8am inbound. On its way to Rock Harbor, it circumnavigates the island, offering drop-off and pickup service along the way. This makes for a slow but interesting trip. Rates start at $87 one way but vary depending on your selected destination. *Voyageur II* can also carry canoes and kayaks for an additional $37 each way.

For those interested in a simple day trip, the **Sea Hunter III** departs from Grand Portage, Minnesota, for Windigo at 8:30am central daylight time and departs from Windigo at 2pm central daylight time. The trip takes 1.5 hours each way, and there is only one round-trip per day. Rates start at $87.

Reserve a spot on the *Voyageur II* or *Sea Hunter III* through **Grand Portage-Isle Royale Transportation Line** (651/653-5872 or 888/746-2305 Nov.-Apr., 218/600-0765 May-Oct., www.isleroyaleboats.com).

Seaplane

Seaplane service by **Isle Royale Seaplanes** (21125 Royce Road, Hancock, 906/483-4991, http://isleroyaleseaplanes.com, $360 pp round-trip, $250 pp one-way) in Hancock is the most expensive but the quickest way to the park, although the 35-minute flight can be delayed by wind and fog. The plane, a Cessna 206 amphibious seaplane, flies Thursday to Tuesday and can carry up to four passengers. The plane cannot carry stove fuel, but you can purchase it on the island at the park store. Luggage is limited to 50 pounds (23 kg) per passenger.

Private Boat

Arriving by private boat is popular in midsummer—perhaps a bit too popular for those who treasure the island's solitude and resent the whine of powerboat engines. The Rock Harbor and Windigo marinas offer docking and refueling for powerboats and sailboats; boats also are allowed to drop anchor in a secluded bay overnight and save the marina fee. Protected harbors are plentiful on the east end of the island (although most remain exposed to an east wind) but are nonexistent on the west end. Every boat arriving at the island must first stop at a ranger station in Windigo or Rock Harbor to obtain a permit and pay the park user fee.

Those with boats under 20 feet (6 meters)

should not attempt a Lake Superior crossing. Even if you have a larger vessel, consider the passage only if you possess strong navigation skills and an adequate marine radio. Lake Superior has many ocean-like characteristics, and storms can appear with little notice.

TOP EXPERIENCE

★ HIKING

The park's website (www.nps.gov/isro) is a good resource for finding more information about the following trails.

Day Hikes from Rock Harbor

Several day hikes are possible if you choose to "motel camp" in Rock Harbor.

Don't miss **Scoville Point,** a 4.2-mile (6.8-km) relatively easy loop with interpretive signs that traces a rocky finger of land east of Rock Harbor.

Another popular short hike is the moderately challenging 3.8-mile (6.1-km) loop to Suzy's Cave, formed by the wave action of a once much-deeper Lake Superior. Suzy's Cave is southwest of Rock Harbor, which puts it in between Rock Harbor and Siskowit Mine.

Lookout Louise, north of Tobin Harbor, offers one of the island's most spectacular views, gazing over its ragged northeastern shoreline. If you have a canoe, it's a short paddle and then a moderately challenging 2-mile (3.2-km) hike. Without a canoe, it's a fine but lengthier hike along lovely Tobin Harbor and the eastern end of the Greenstone Ridge. You'll have to retrace your steps to return to Rock Harbor, making the trek a total of about 20 miles (32 km). The longer hike is considerably more taxing, but there's a campground at Three Mile Point (about halfway through your trek) so you can break it up.

For another all-day hike, follow the Lake Superior shoreline to the Daisy Farm campground and the Ojibway Trail, which heads north and brings you to the **Ojibway Tower,** an air-monitoring station. The tower marks the highest spot on the eastern end of the island, and you can climb its steps (but not enter the tower room) for an unmatched view of the island's interior lakes and bays on both the north and south sides of the island. Travel back via the Greenstone Ridge and along Tobin Harbor for a varied and considerably challenging 18-mile (29-km) hike that will take you through blueberry patches, wildflower meadows, and serene shorelines. For a similar, shorter (and only moderately difficult) hike of about 10 miles (16.1 km), turn north at the Three Mile campground to ascend **Mount Franklin,** another high point on the Greenstone Ridge. Follow the Ojibway Trail from Rock Harbor to Three Mile Point (a distance of 3 miles/4.8 km), then follow the sign for Mount Franklin, another 2 miles (3.2 km). Return by following the same path in reverse.

Day Hikes from Windigo

If you'd prefer not to haul your possessions on your back, it's possible—but a little more difficult—to do day hikes out of Windigo. Because fewer trails exist here, most hikes will be of the out-and-back variety.

The best loop option is to **Huginnin Cove,** a 9.7-mile (15.6-km) moderately challenging route that passes through prime moose habitat before emerging onto the Lake Superior shore.

There's a campground if you choose to make it an overnighter. The east side of the trail passes an old mine, which was last active in 1892.

Another excellent, but significantly challenging, option is the **Feldtmann Lake Trail,** which winds along Washington Harbor before heading inland to one of the island's least visited lakes. You can hike the 17-mile (27-km) route out and back in a day, but you'll enjoy your adventure more if you plan it as an overnight. Set up camp here and you'll likely be treated to moose sightings, unmatched fishing, and maybe the howl of a distant wolf. Plus, if you stay overnight, you'll have the time and energy for the short side trip to Lake Superior's pretty Rainbow Cove.

Longer Hikes

With 165 miles (265 km) of trails, Isle Royale has far more outstanding hiking options than is possible to outline here. Consider a comprehensive guide like Jim DuFresne's excellent *Isle Royale National Park: Foot Trails and Water Routes* (5th ed.), published by Michigan Trail Maps (www.michigantrailmaps.com). If you prefer to avoid the busier areas of Windigo and Rock Harbor, consider arranging for the *Voyageur II* **ferry** (218/475-0024 or 218/475-0074) or the island's **water taxi**

hiker surveys the horizon from Greenstone Ridge

service (906/337-4993) to drop you off and pick you up at another location.

In general, the **Greenstone Ridge** is the main route to traverse the island, a 42.2-mile (67.9-km) trail (one-way) of mostly high and dry terrain. It slices a horizontal path along the length of the island, beginning at Lookout Louise near Rock Harbor and ending at the Windigo Visitors Center. It is also the most popular, but only among members of the serious backpacking community, which thins out the number of people considerably. (Note: The trail is rated as moderately challenging for intermediate backpackers, not the novice.) On this four-day, three-night adventure, seeing moose is not uncommon; if you're lucky, you may even see a gray wolf. In addition to wildlife, the scenic views on this hike are exceptional, given its route along the highest elevation on the island. Campgrounds are strategically located every 10 miles (16.1 km) along the route. Greenstone Ridge represents the highest portion of the park, which affords a panoramic view of Lake Superior from any direction.

The park's second-longest, the 26-mile (42-km) one-way **Minong Ridge Trail,** easily ranks as its most challenging. Traversing the north side of the island from near Windigo to McCargoe Cove, the rough and lightly used trail meanders over a rocky ridge and disappears through bogs and includes the abandoned Minong Mine near its terminus. If you like surroundings that are primitive and peaceful, and don't get nervous about some poorly marked stretches, this trail is for you. Wildlife sightings, especially moose, are likely here. Though campgrounds are spaced far apart on this trail, they're worth the effort. Little Todd Harbor and Todd Harbor are some of the nicest on the island.

Finally, the **Feldtmann Ridge Trail** follows along the southwestern shore, beginning and ending at Windigo. It's a well-marked but lightly used route of 22 miles (35 km) one way. The trail offers outstanding variety, from the shoreline of Washington Harbor, through gentle bogs, up the high Feldtmann Ridge, and finally to the open wildflower meadows and waters of Siskiwit Bay. Campgrounds are located at either end of the Feldtmann Ridge at the one-third and two-thirds marks along the route. Because of the uphill climb involved, this trail is considerably challenging.

PADDLING

For paddlers, Isle Royale is a dream destination, a nook-and-cranny wilderness of rocky islands, secluded coves, and quiet bays interrupted only by the low call of a loon. First-time visitors can't do better than the **Five Fingers,** the collection of fjord-like harbors and rocky promontories on the east end of the island. Not only is it well protected (except from northeasters), it offers some of the finest and most characteristic Isle Royale scenery and solitude. Though Isle Royale is generally better suited to kayaks, open canoes can handle these waters in calm weather.

For kayaks, the entire island offers paddling opportunities, though some areas have little shoreline access, requiring long stretches of paddling. Note that open-water passages on Lake Superior should be attempted by experienced paddlers only, and should *not* be attempted in a canoe or other open boat. Capsizing in Lake Superior is not merely an unfortunate experience; it's a life-threatening one. Water temperatures rarely exceed the 40s (4-9°C), and hypothermia can set in within minutes.

You can avoid open-water passages and still explore other areas of the island by making use of the *Voyageur II* **ferry** (218/475-0024 or 218/475-0074) or the island's **water taxi service** (906/337-4993), which will transport you and your boat to various docks on the northeastern half of the island.

Ferries can transport your boat, provided it is less than 20 feet (6 meters) long. You also can rent canoes, 14-foot (4-meter) fishing boats, and outboard motors at Windigo and Rock Harbor (906/337-4993). For Rock Harbor visitors, a wonderful day can be spent exploring Tobin Harbor, where rental canoes await.

Exploring the inland lakes is a remarkable experience on Isle Royale. Fishing is often superb, and moose often loiter near the shore, unaware of your presence. Plan your routes carefully to avoid grueling portages. Again, your best bet is to arrange for the water taxi or the *Voyageur II* ferry to drop you and your boat at a mid-island spot like Malone Bay, Chippewa Harbor, or McCargoe Cove. From there you'll have manageable, even easy portages to several lakes, including Siskiwit, Wood, Whittlesey, Intermediate, Richie, LeSage, Livermore, and Chickenbone. There's nothing quite like drifting across a wilderness lake in the middle of a wilderness island.

Marquette and the Lake Superior Shore

Home to the Upper Peninsula's largest city, the

Lake Superior shore is deserving of a good portion of your time. Marquette is modern and cosmopolitan, especially for a city located in Michigan's most remote region. The presence of Northern Michigan University makes it a college town, which means there's plenty to do, whether you're a fan of bars or live performances, college-level sports, or the arts and culture scene. If you're here for the great outdoors, you'll find plenty of it just over Marquette's doorstep: The rugged and undeveloped Huron Mountains lie to the west, while Presque Isle is one of the U.P.'s most precious gems.

And while Lake Superior may not have the sandy beaches or be as swimmable as Lake Michigan or Lake Huron, it's almost impossible

Highlights

Look for ★ to find recommended sights, activities, dining, and lodging.

★ **Downtown Marquette:** Take a break from nature to enjoy the Upper Peninsula's most cosmopolitan city (page 205).

★ **Presque Isle Park:** Admire some of the area's most beautiful scenery by taking a drive, cycling, hiking, or skiing through this preserved park (page 207).

★ **Lakenenland Sculpture Park:** This quirky outdoor display of "junkyard art" is part artwork, part political commentary, and continually changing (page 208).

★ **Hiawatha Water Trail:** The 120-mile (193-km) journey from Big Bay to Grand Marais is beautiful and adventurous (pages 214 and 248).

★ **Grand Island:** Take a ferry 10 minutes off the shore of Munising and spend a day or a weekend exploring this isolated island (page 232).

★ **Hiawatha National Forest:** Several hundred acres of national forest provide endless recreational opportunities in every season (page 233).

★ **Shipwreck Dives and Tours:** Whether viewed from behind a scuba mask or from a glass-hulled boat, the ruins of Lake Superior nautical lore are unforgettable (pages 237 and 238).

★ **Pictured Rocks National Lakeshore:** These colorful, scenic rocks rank among the top tier of U.P. attractions. Venture slightly inland, and you'll find some of the most dramatic waterfalls in the Upper Peninsula (page 242).

★ **Iverson Snowshoe Company:** One of the very few manufacturers of snowshoes that still produce their wares by hand, Iverson offers fascinating factory tours (page 254).

to be unmoved by its rough, wild coast. The rocky shoreline and its ocean-like feel make the largest of the Great Lakes unquestionably the most awesome.

Munising and Grand Island are located on a picturesque bay that would rival any in the world for sheer beauty. Continue east and it only gets better, as the remarkable colors, cliffs, and rock formations of Pictured Rocks National Lakeshore stretch out like an artistic masterpiece being unveiled. If you've never kayaked before, this is a wonderful place to start. The national lakeshore is bookended on the opposite side by Grand Marais.

Don't forget to venture inland, where many of the U.P.'s renowned outdoor recreational activities await. Of particular interest is the Seney National Wildlife Refuge, which has 95,000 acres of wetlands, boglands, and wilderness. The refuge is an ideal summertime destination for hunting, fishing, berry picking, and photographing wildlife. In the winter, cross-country skiing and snowshoeing are hugely popular.

PLANNING YOUR TIME

You'll probably want to spend at least two or three days in Marquette. The city's touch of urban sophistication is the perfect tonic to melt away any "wilderness fatigue." Marquette can also serve as an ideal launching pad for hub-and-spoke explorations of the surrounding areas. Set aside a day each for Munising and Pictured Rocks, longer if you plan to explore the lakeshore by foot. Try to get out onto Lake Superior, whether by sea kayak, charter boat, or a tour. Two or three days will do just fine. Book a nice hotel, make some dinner reservations, and spend your days exploring.

Accommodation Price Key

$	Less than $100 per night
$ $	$100-200 per night
$ $ $	More than $200 per night

HISTORY

Marquette and the Lake Superior shore weren't immune to the influence of trade and industry that shaped the rest of the Upper Peninsula. Indeed, its history is remarkably similar, albeit a bit tamer. French missionaries, including the city namesake, Jacques Marquette, explored the area in the mid-1600s. Fur trappers arrived several decades later, while the mining industry started up in the mid-1800s. But it took more than just mining to put the city on the map; a combination of enterprises gave Marquette its prosperity. Shipping, a stream of wealthy vacationers, and the mining of iron ore each contributed to the diverse local economy.

But not all of the Lake Superior shore was exploited, as the Huron Mountains remained largely untouched. Beginning around the 1880s, the Hurons became the wilderness retreat of choice for several millionaire industrialists. Cyrus McCormick, head of the lucrative farm implement company that would become International Harvester, amassed a huge wilderness estate around White Deer Lake, now part of the Ottawa National Forest's McCormick Tract Wilderness Area. Frederick Miller of Miller Brewing acquired his piece of wilderness at Craig Lake, now a wilderness state park. Dozens of others established "camps" at the Huron Mountain Club, an organization so exclusive that even Henry Ford was turned down for membership when he first applied. The members easily had enough clout to stop construction of a road that was to link L'Anse with Big Bay. County Road 550 unceremoniously ends just west of Big Bay—its terminus marked by a gate and a security guardhouse.

Today, the 25,000-acre enclave is shared mostly by the descendants of those original members, who quietly protect and preserve this spectacular landholding. Though locals grumble about the lack of access to the

---

Previous: Miners Castle at Pictured Rocks National Lakeshore; downtown Marquette; Pictured Rocks National Lakeshore.

Marquette and the Lake Superior Shore

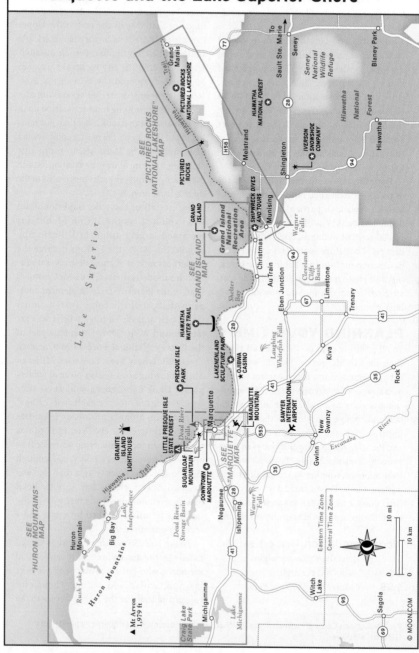

Lake Superior

To Sault Ste. Marie

77

Seney

Blaney Park

Grand Marais

Seney National Wildlife Refuge

PICTURED ROCKS NATIONAL LAKESHORE

HIAWATHA NATIONAL FOREST

28

Hiawatha National Forest

94

Hiawatha

"PICTURED ROCKS NATIONAL LAKESHORE" MAP

PICTURED ROCKS

H58

Melstrand

Shingleton

IVERSON SNOWSHOE COMPANY

SHIPWRECK DIVES AND TOURS

Munising

Wagner Falls

GRAND ISLAND

Grand Island National Recreation Area

"GRAND ISLAND" MAP

Christmas

Au Train

94

Cleveland Cliffs Basin

Limestone

67

Trenary

41

Shelter Bay

HIAWATHA WATER TRAIL

28

Eben Junction

Laughing Whitefish Falls

Kiva

35

Rock

PRESQUE ISLE PARK

LAKENENLAND SCULPTURE PARK

OJIBWA CASINO

MARQUETTE MOUNTAIN

SAWYER INTERNATIONAL AIRPORT

41

New Swanzy

Escanaba River

GRANITE ISLAND LIGHTHOUSE

LITTLE PRESQUE ISLE STATE FOREST

Dead River Falls

Marquette

SUGARLOAF MOUNTAIN

DOWNTOWN MARQUETTE

"SEE MARQUETTE MAP"

553

Gwinn

35

"SEE HURON MOUNTAINS" MAP

Hiawatha Trail

Lake Independence

Huron Mountain

Big Bay

Dead River Storage Basin

Negaunee

Ishpeming

28

Warner Falls

Eastern Time Zone

Central Time Zone

10 mi

10 km

Rush Lake

Huron Mountains

▲ Mt Arvon 1,979 ft

Craig Lake State Park

Michigamme

Lake Michigamme

41

Witch Lake

95

Sagola

69

© MOON.COM

property, it's clear that the Huron Mountain Club has been an exceptional steward of the land. It has kept away loggers, miners, and developers, leaving what some consider the most magnificent wilderness remaining in the state, perhaps in the entire Midwest.

Pictured Rocks National Lakeshore joined the Huron Mountains as an exceptional specimen of nature in 1966 after areas of the Great Lakes shore were considered for inclusion in the National Park System. The 43 miles (69 km) of scenic shoreline between Munising and Grand Marais became the first national lakeshore in the United States.

Marquette and Vicinity

With a population of just over 20,000, Marquette ranks as the largest city in the Upper Peninsula. Tucked in a well-protected natural harbor midway across the U.P.'s northern shore, it thrives due largely to its central location, placing it as the axis for U.P. government and commerce, including its status as a central port for the iron industry.

Don't be deterred by the succession of strip malls and chain motels along US 41. Head toward downtown for a much more urban feel where you'll discover the city's rich architectural heritage, a U.S. Olympic Training Center, Northern Michigan University, and a beautiful setting along the high, rocky Lake Superior shoreline. Marquette has never really promoted itself as a tourist destination, but this may be to the visitor's benefit. Lodging and good restaurants are plentiful, the downtown and lakefront are ideal for strolling, and the U.P.'s natural attractions—rugged hills, waterfalls, wildlife, and wild rivers—all await just outside the city limits, often without the crowds and typical tourist-trap blight.

SIGHTS
★ Downtown Marquette
Third Street, running north-south, and Washington Street, running east-west, represent Marquette's main cross streets, and where they meet is a good area to begin an exploration of downtown. This puts you in the heart of the shopping and historic district. Buildings like the 1902 **Marquette County Courthouse** (3rd St. and Baraga Ave.) and the 1927 **MFC First National Bank** (101 W. Washington St.) display the city's affinity for beaux arts architecture. Step inside the courthouse for a better look, and also to check out a display about Michigan Supreme Court Justice and author John Voelker, better known by his pen name, Robert Traver. An Ishpeming native, Traver wrote on widely diverse topics—the popular novel *Anatomy of a Murder* as well as a series of books on fly fishing. Based on a real murder in nearby Big Bay, *Anatomy* was made into a movie of the same name in 1959. Scenes from the film, starring Jimmy Stewart and George C. Scott, were filmed in the third-floor courtroom and in Big Bay. The **Marquette Regional History Center** (145 W. Spring St., 906/226-3571, www.marquettehistory.org, 10am-5pm Mon.-Tues. and Thurs.-Fri., 10am-8pm Wed., 10am-3pm Sat., $10 adults, $8 seniors and military, $4 students, $3 under age 13) offers a walking tour brochure.

The old redbrick waterworks building now houses the **Marquette Maritime Museum** (300 Lakeshore Blvd., 906/226-2006, http://mqtmaritimemuseum.com, 11am-4pm Tues.-Sun. mid-May-mid-Oct., $8 adults, $7 seniors and retired military, $6 students with I.D., $5 children 3-12, free under age 3, active military free). This worthwhile stop includes exhibits on everything from Native American birch-bark canoes to Great Lakes shipwrecks and lighthouses, an interactive display of a freighter's pilot house, and a working submarine periscope. Admission to the Marquette Harbor Lighthouse is available at an extra charge.

Marquette

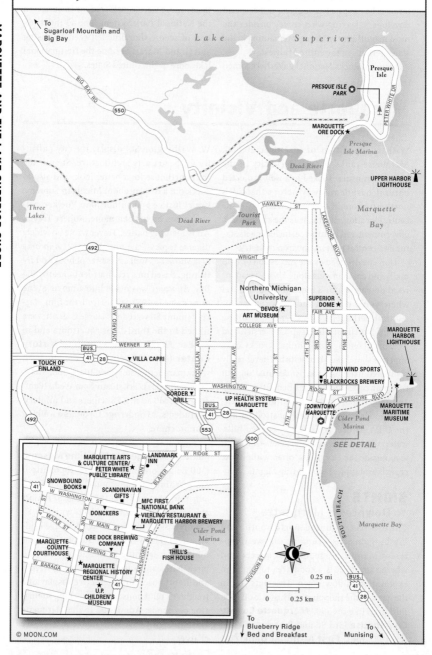

To Sugarloaf Mountain and Big Bay

Lake Superior

BIG BAY RD

(550)

Three Lakes

Dead River

Tourist Park

Presque Isle

PRESQUE ISLE PARK

PETER WHITE DR

Presque Isle Marina

MARQUETTE ORE DOCK ★

UPPER HARBOR LIGHTHOUSE

Dead River

HAWLEY ST

LAKESHORE BLVD

Marquette Bay

(492)

WRIGHT ST

Northern Michigan University

DEVOS ART MUSEUM ★

SUPERIOR DOME ★

FAIR AVE

FAIR AVE

COLLEGE AVE

ONTARIO AVE

WERNER ST

MCCLELLAN AVE

LINCOLN AVE

7TH ST

5TH ST

4TH ST

3RD ST

FRONT ST

PINE ST

MARQUETTE HARBOR LIGHTHOUSE

BUS.
(41) (28)

■ TOUCH OF FINLAND

▼ VILLA CAPRI

DOWN WIND SPORTS

▼ BLACKROCKS BREWERY

WASHINGTON ST

BORDER ▼ GRILL

UP HEALTH SYSTEM MARQUETTE ■

BUS.
(41) (28)

RIDGE ST

LAKESHORE BLVD

MARQUETTE MARITIME MUSEUM

DOWNTOWN MARQUETTE ✪

Cider Pond Marina

SEE DETAIL

(492)

(553)

(500)

SOUTH BEACH

Marquette Bay

To Blueberry Ridge Bed and Breakfast

To Munising

DIVISION ST

BUS.
(41) (28)

0   0.25 mi
0   0.25 km

Detail

(41)

W RIDGE ST

MARQUETTE ARTS & CULTURE CENTER/ PETER WHITE PUBLIC LIBRARY ★

LANDMARK INN ●

FRONT ST

BLAKER ST

SNOWBOUND BOOKS ■

W WASHINGTON ST

SCANDINAVIAN GIFTS ■

MFC FIRST NATIONAL BANK ★

VIERLING RESTAURANT & MARQUETTE HARBOR BREWERY ▼

DONCKERS ▼

W MAIN ST

ORE DOCK BREWING COMPANY ▼

W SPRING ST

S LAKESHORE BLVD

Cider Pond Marina

THILL'S FISH HOUSE ▼

W 4TH ST

3RD ST

MAPLE ST

MARQUETTE COUNTY COURTHOUSE ★

MARQUETTE REGIONAL HISTORY CENTER ★

W BARAGA AVE

(41)

U.P. CHILDREN'S MUSEUM ●

© MOON.COM

If you're traveling with children, head for the **U.P. Children's Museum** (123 W. Baraga Ave., 906/226-3911, www.upchildrenmuseum. org, 10am-5pm Tues.-Sun., closed major holidays, $6 adults and children ages 2 and up, free 1 and under), where they can climb into a tree habitat to learn about its root system, crawl into a replica wasp nest, or explore life in the aquifer under a pond.

The **Marquette Arts and Culture Center** (217 N. Front St., 906/228-0472, www.marquettemi.gov, 9:30am-8:30pm Mon.-Thurs., 9:30am-5:30pm Fri., 9:30am-4:30pm Sat., free), located on the lower level of the **Peter White Public Library,** offers a gallery featuring the work of local artists that changes each month. You'll also find a museum shop offering many of the pieces for sale, as well as occasional informal concerts and plays.

Superior Dome

Where would you expect to find the world's largest wooden dome? In the heart of logging country, of course, and along Lake Superior, where hostile weather regularly foils outdoor sporting events. In 1991, Northern Michigan University completed the 8,000-seat **Superior Dome** (1401 Presque Isle Ave., 906/227-2850), affectionately known as the "Yooper Dome." Enclosing some five acres, the dome is fashioned from a framework of 781 huge fir beams, strong enough to withstand extreme accumulations of snow. Along with hosting a variety of school sporting events and practices, the dome is open to the public for walking and running on weekday mornings. Call or stop by for specifics.

DeVos Art Museum

Although it had its beginnings in the 1975 Lee Hall Gallery, the **DeVos Art Museum** (1401 Presque Isle Ave., 906/227-2235, http:// art.nmu.edu/museum, noon-5pm Mon.-Wed. and Fri., noon-8pm Thurs., donation), part of Northern Michigan University's School of Art and Design, got a facelift with its 2005 reopening, complete with a new, larger building, made possible by a grant from the DeVos

Foundation of Grand Rapids. The museum's permanent collection, which represents work from numerous well-known artists, including Salvador Dalí, is displayed on a rotating basis, while other areas of the museum host temporary exhibits. You'll also enjoy the sculpture walk, where an inviting pathway snakes through one of the university's wooded areas.

★ Presque Isle Park

A thumb of land thrust out into the big lake, **Presque Isle Park** (pronounced "presk ile," which translates from French as "almost an island" or "peninsula"), about 4 miles (6.4 km) north of downtown off Lakeshore Boulevard, is a microcosm of the area's beauty: rocky red bluffs, tall pines, and lovely Lake Superior vistas. You can drive through the 323-acre park, but you'd do better to get out and stroll or ski along its many trails. Watch for albino white-tailed deer that survive in this protected setting. Near the park's entrance, there's a playground, a picnic area, tennis courts, and a marina.

Marquette Ore Dock

Presque Isle Park is the perfect spot to watch 600-foot-long freighters being loaded at the towering **Marquette Ore Dock**—a unique type of Upper Peninsula experience. Trains carrying pellets of taconite (an iron-clay mixture) from one of the nearby open-pit iron mines chug out onto the 70-foot-high (21-meter) elevated track and empty their loads into the hold below. Chutes transfer the taconite into the bellies of the ore freighters, which transport their cargo to the industrial centers of the southern Great Lakes. It's a noisy spectacle, and a pleasant reminder that a small part of the U.P.'s mining heritage still survives today. Check www.boatnerd.com for a schedule of vessel passages.

The ore dock is located on Lakeshore Boulevard, shortly before the entrance to the park.

Lighthouses

The **Marquette Harbor Lighthouse**

(300 Lakeshore Blvd., 906/226-2006, http://mqtmaritimemuseum.com, tours 11:30am, 1pm, and 2:30pm Tues.-Sun. mid-May- mid Oct., $8 adults, $4 under age 13) is one of Lake Superior's most attractive. The light and some of the land surrounding it was recently acquired by the Marquette Maritime Museum under a lease from the Coast Guard. The lease will expire in 2032, so there's plenty of time to make it to the beautiful red light for a tour. As part of the lease agreement, all tours must be escorted by a member of the museum staff. Built in 1866 and expanded in 1906, the Marquette Harbor Lighthouse serves as an interpretive display and an extension of the museum.

To see another, slightly less scenic lighthouse, head to Presque Isle Park for a look at the **Presque Isle Upper Harbor Lighthouse.** The light is still guiding ships into the railroad ore docks nearby. **Granite Island Lighthouse** is 6 miles (9.7 km) offshore; it's a little more than 10 miles (16.1 km) northeast of Marquette.

Stannard Rock Lighthouse is a little harder to get to, since it's located in Lake Superior, about 50 miles (80 km) from Marquette's shoreline. Due to its considerable distance from land, charter services will usually only sail to the lighthouse in conjunction with a fishing trip. One such operator is **Kimar's Charters** (E3216 M-28, Au Train, 906/892-8277, www.kimarscharters.com).

★ Lakenenland Sculpture Park

Be sure to check out **Lakenenland Sculpture Park** (http://lakenenland.com), a free outdoor sculpture display located on M-28 about 15 miles (24 km) east of Marquette. Artist Tom Lakenen specializes in "junkyard art" and has moved many of his creations to this site. The 100 sculptures vary in size, but many are large, some as tall as 15 feet (5 meters). Examples include rebar alligators, elephants, space aliens, and even political figures. Outdoor art exhibits are a rarity in much of the nation, and even rarer in Michigan's Upper Peninsula. Seeing these intriguing sculptures in a forested rural setting makes for an interesting diversion. This compelling exhibit can be viewed at any time. There is a secure box for those who wish to leave a donation, but Lakenen stresses that visitors should not feel obliged. The funds raised defray the cost of maintaining the site.

Ishpeming and Negaunee

In many ways, these twin towns 15 miles (24 km) west of Marquette represent the heart of the iron range. One of the Upper Peninsula's earliest iron mines, the Jackson Mine, opened here in 1847. The Empire and Tilden Mines, in nearby Palmer, continue to operate today, and represent the Upper Peninsula's last link to the signature industry of its past.

Today, Ishpeming and Negaunee are tarnished versions of their former selves. The economy never recovered from the closing of most of the area's mines in the 1960s, and the once vital downtowns were further displaced by the commercial strips along US 41, which passes just north of Ishpeming. But anyone who enjoys history will find these towns intriguing, with their vintage ornate storefronts, ramshackle antiques shops, and fenced-off cave-in areas, where the land has succumbed to decades of tunneling.

One of the finest museums in the Upper Peninsula, the state-run **Iron Industry Museum** (73 Forge Rd., Negaunee, 906/475-7857, www.michigan.gov/ironindustrymuseum, 10am-4pm Tues.-Sun. May-Sept., 10am-4pm Wed.-Sat. Oct.-Apr., donation, Michigan Recreation Passport required for parking) is located along the Carp River off US 41. The spot wasn't chosen for its scenery; it marks the site of one of the area's earliest iron forges, built in 1848. This small facility packs a lot of information and several expertly designed displays into a single exhibit hall. It tells the story of Michigan's $48 billion iron mining and smelting industry, which

1: Presque Isle Park 2: Snowbound Books 3: Lake Superior shore 4: Marquette Harbor Lighthouse

1

2

SNOWBOUND
est. BOOKS 1984
New & Used

3

4

dwarfed the California gold rush ($955 million), Michigan's lucrative logging industry ($4.4 billion), and even Michigan's venerable copper mining ($9.6 billion). You'll learn how iron prompted the development of dozens of port towns and the giant ore freighters that still ply the Great Lakes today. The Technology Timeline traces advancements in exploration, working conditions, and mining methods.

Few people think of Ishpeming as the center of the U.S. ski industry, but many of the large resorts in the Rockies can trace interest in the sport to Michigan. In 1887 residents of northern Michigan, many of them Scandinavian immigrants, established the Ishpeming Ski Club, one of the oldest continuously operating clubs in the nation. In 1888 they organized the country's first ski jumping competition. Everett Kircher, visionary founder of Michigan's Boyne Mountain resort, invented the first successful snowmaking machine. As a result, Ishpeming was chosen as the site of the **U.S. National Ski Hall of Fame and Ski Museum** (610 Palms Ave., Ishpeming, 906/485-6323, www.skihall.com, 9am-4pm Mon.-Fri. Sept.-May, 9am-4pm Mon.-Sat. June-Aug., $5 adults, $3 students through college, ages 12 and under free), the sport's official hall of fame.

The museum, on US 41 between 2nd and 3rd Streets, covers the sport from *way* back, beginning with a replica of a 4,000-year-old ski and pole found in Sweden. Most interesting are the displays of early ski equipment, including early poles, which "often doubled as weapons," an examination of the evolution of chairlifts, and an account of the skiing soldiers of the 10th Mountain Division, who played an important role in the mountains of Italy during World War II. The hall of fame plaques offer insightful short biographies of those who shaped the sport, from racers to resort owners.

SHOPPING
Downtown Marquette is home to distinctive shops that are worth browsing. **Snowbound Books** (118 N. 3rd St., 906/228-4448, www. snowboundbooks.com, 10am-6pm Mon.-Fri., 10am-5pm Sat.-Sun.) offers a good selection of local and regional titles. Follow Main Street down to the waterfront, where **Thill's Fish House** (250 E. Main St., 906/226-9851, 8am-5:30pm Mon.-Fri., 9am-3pm Sat.) sells fresh catch and smoked whitefish from a little shop at the marina, in the shadow of the old wooden ore dock. Expect to pay around $10 per pound for whitefish and perch, and $15 per pound for walleye and other varieties, depending on market conditions.

The U.P.'s Scandinavian heritage looms large in Marquette. **Scandinavian Gifts** (1025 N. 3rd St., 906/225-1993, 10am-5:30pm Mon.-Fri., 10am-5pm Sat., 11am-4pm Sun.) showcases the sleek and simple lines of classic Scandinavian design in its selection of glassware and silver, plus lots of Norwegian sweaters too. Back on US 41, **Touch of Finland** (2853 US 41, 906/226-2567, www. touchoffinland.com, 10am-7pm daily) has a bit of almost everything in its 4,000 square feet, including housewares, textiles, and a complete sauna department. They also do a robust online business.

ENTERTAINMENT
Ojibwa Casino
If you're looking for gaming, look no farther than the **Ojibwa Casino** (105 Acre Trail, 906/249-4200 or 800/560-9905, www. ojibwacasino.com) in Marquette. Table games include blackjack, roulette, craps, and poker, while more than 300 reel video and video poker machines play from a penny to $5. There are seven sites available at the Ojibwa Casino RV Park and free shuttle service to and from a number of chain hotels in the area. The Snack Bar serves up all sorts of food right on the casino floor, from soup, pizza, and burgers to shrimp and fish dinners, all at very reasonable prices. Be sure to check with the casino for Snack Bar specials.

Microbreweries
Blackrocks Brewery (424 N. 3rd St.,

Marquette, 906/273-1333, www.black rocksbrewery.com, 4pm-11pm Mon., noon-11pm Tues.-Sun.) began in 2010 when two friends who found themselves out of work decided to transform their longtime hobby into a business. Beginning as a "nano brewery"—a facility with very minimal capacity—the fledgling enterprise later opened a separate production facility with greater capabilities. Their pub, however, continues to operate out of their original location on 3rd Street. Blackrocks offers year-round and seasonal varieties. Examples of the latter include Hiawatha Ale, an American wheat ale with a dash of ginger and orange peel, and 3rd Street Stout, a dark stout variety with a hint of chocolate.

Ore Dock Brewing Co. (114 W. Spring St., Marquette, 906/228-8888, www.oredock brewing.com, noon-11pm Sun.-Thurs., noon-midnight Fri.-Sat.) was inspired by the founders' trip to the American West, where they became enamored of the variety of local brewpubs in many of the small towns they visited. Deciding to do the same thing for their hometown, they set up shop in a historic (1864) building in downtown Marquette. While some of the selections are local takes on the classics (porter and Belgian strong ale), others are real exercises in creativity, with clever names and descriptions to match: Low Hanging Fruit ("an outerworldly blueberry invasion") and Uncle Drew's Flying Machine ("with lifting wings of tangerine and plumes of pineapple").

FESTIVALS AND EVENTS

For more information on events in the area, contact **Travel Marquette** (117 W. Washington St., Marquette, 906/228-7749 or 800/544-4321, www.travelmarquette michigan.com).

U.P. 200

The **U.P. 200** (www.up200.org) is a sled-dog race held in mid-February that begins with a nighttime start in Marquette, heads to Grand Marais, and then returns to Marquette—a distance of 220 miles (354 km). At the checkpoints in Wetmore, Grand Marais, and again in Wetmore on the return leg, each participant is required to rest a minimum of five hours, making the race roughly a 36-hour event. An estimated 30,000 people watch the annual race, which has quickly grown into one of the U.P.'s most beloved spectator events. The start and finish are the big draws, but the race has prompted a weeklong calendar of activities, from broomball tournaments (hockey played with boots instead of skates, balls instead of pucks, and brooms instead of sticks) to fireworks. Serious mushers will be interested to know that the U.P. 200 is an Iditarod qualifying event.

Hiawatha Traditional Music Festival

Summertime brings the **Hiawatha Traditional Music Festival** (906/226-8575, www.hiawathamusic.org) during the second-to-last full weekend of July. Featuring traditional music such as bluegrass, acoustic blues, folk, old time, and more, the Hiawatha is the only festival of its type and size in the Upper Peninsula.

Pine Mountain Music Festival

The **Pine Mountain Music Festival** (906/482-1542, www.pmmf.org) runs during the first three weeks of June and is a celebration of opera, symphony, and chamber music that takes place at venues around the Upper Peninsula, usually in Marquette, Iron Mountain, and Houghton.

Harbor Fest

During the fourth weekend of August, Marquette plays host to its annual **Harbor Fest** (https://marquettewestrotary.org), two days and nights of quality free music sponsored by the Marquette West Rotary. Representing different genres, the selections include bluegrass, classical, pop, and a series of "tribute bands"—groups that impersonate famous musical acts that most of

Northern Michigan University

NMU's Superior Dome

Hail Northern, we thy sons and daughters
Now bring thee tribute long deserved
Thou beacon light 'mid nature's grandeur
Through passing decades well preserved
Oh, may we labor with untiring zeal
That when these golden days have flown
We may with honor face the future
And match thy courage with our own.

Students at Northern Michigan University (NMU) are a rare and special breed. Not everyone can tolerate spending their winters in Marquette, on the frozen shores of Lake Superior, where the

the audience will remember: Chicago, James Brown, and Sly and the Family Stone, to name a few. Harbor Fest is held at Mattson Lower Harbor Park (Lakeshore Dr. and Pine St.) near the campus of Northern Michigan University.

Annual Marquette Blues Fest

During Labor Day weekend, Mattson Park is the site for the **Annual Marquette Blues Fest** (www.marquetteareabluessociety.com), three days of performances by both local and nationally known blues artists, which have included Johnny Rawls, Lurrie Bell, and Jeff Daniels with his Ben Daniels Band. Visit the

website in the weeks prior to the next festival to view the lineup.

Art on the Rocks

Head to Presque Isle Park for the annual **Art on the Rocks** (http://marquette artontherocks.com) held during the last weekend of July. The event is an art festival featuring a juried exhibition and sales.

North of the 45th Parallel

The name of the **North of the 45th Parallel** exhibition at NMU's **DeVos Art Museum** (1401 Presque Isle Ave., 906/227-2194, http://art.nmu.edu, noon-5pm Mon.-Wed., Fri., average daytime high temperature drops into the mid-20s (-5 to -3°C) each January. (In 2019, a new record low was set—a shockingly frigid -15°F/-26°C.) It's a place where class is more often canceled for cold than for snowfall. Michigan has other options for higher education, including the University of Michigan and Michigan State University, that are located in the warmer climate of the Lower Peninsula. But the hardy Northern students are here because they like it here.

Founded in 1899 with just 32 students, NMU is the largest university in Michigan's Upper Peninsula, with an enrollment of over 9,000 (quite small compared to most downstate schools). The school offers 180 academic majors and 120 minors in such subjects as business, technology, education, and sociology. Northern Michigan takes special pride in its technology programs, which envision providing a "learning environment that embraces technology to enhance student access, promote the development of independent learners, and encourage greater student faculty communication and collaboration." It was this vision that led the school to become the first state university in Michigan to become a "laptop campus," providing each of its students with a laptop computer and a standard set of software tools for use during the school year. The university upgrades students' computers every two years.

NMU's campus consists of more than 50 facilities located on the shores of Lake Superior. The most interesting of these is undoubtedly the Superior Dome, which has the distinction of being the world's largest wooden dome structure. A fascinating sight, the dome is 14 stories high with a diameter of 563 feet (172 meters), and covers more than 5 acres (2 hectares). It's impressively built from Douglas fir, a natural choice considering its location. Containing 781 beams and more than 100 miles (160 km) of fir decking, the dome can support up to 60 pounds (27 kg) of snow per square foot. Inside, removable artificial turf (also the largest of its kind in the world) can host football, soccer, and field hockey. Beneath the turf are three basketball or volleyball courts, two tennis courts, and a 200-meter track.

The real action takes place at the Berry Events Center. An Olympic-size ice sheet, 200 by 100 feet (60 by 30 meters), hosts ice hockey, the sport of choice here, where long winters and proximity to Canada make the sport popular. While NMU competes in NCAA Division II for most sports—basketball, football, and the like—hockey is a Division I sport, and is an experience that shouldn't be missed if you're in town.

There are other reasons to visit NMU's campus too. The school's drama department stages several theatrical productions each year, and the DeVos Art Museum offers scores of intriguing pieces by regional artists.

noon-8pm Thurs., donation) explains its eligibility criterion: Only artists residing north of that line, which represents the midway point between the north pole and the equator, are permitted to display their work in the juried competition. The restriction is designated to emphasize the breadth of artists who call northern Michigan home. The 45th parallel crosses Michigan around Gaylord, in the northern portion of the Lower Peninsula, and is often recognized as the dividing line between "up north" and "downstate."

International Food Festival
The **International Food Festival** (www.travelmarquettemichigan.com) happens each year for three days around the 4th of July and is held at Ellwood Mattson Lower Harbor Park (200 Lakeshore Blvd., Marquette). Tempting arrays of foods from the German, Asian, Mexican, and Cajun traditions are on offer. The event includes live entertainment and fireworks at dusk on July 4.

SUMMER RECREATION
Hiking and Biking
Range Mountain Bike Trail System
The trail system in the greater Marquette area is complex and can lend itself to confusion. Before setting out, a good first step is to visit

www.travelmarquettemichigan.com for a series of interactive online maps of all the hiking and biking trails in the greater Marquette area. The entire Ishpeming-Negaunee area is part of the comprehensive **Range Mountain Bike Trail System,** with more than 25 miles (40 km) of trails stretching from Teal Lake to Lake Sally, south of Suicide Bowl. Routes are detailed in the online maps.

Sugarloaf Mountain

As County Road 550 runs north out of Marquette toward Big Bay, you'll travel just 6 miles (9.7 km) before a sign and parking area for **Sugarloaf Mountain** lures you to pull over for a moderately challenging 30-minute hike (1.2 miles/1.9 km round-trip). A series of stairways will facilitate your gradual ascent up the rock. At the summit, you'll be rewarded with a sweeping view of Lake Superior to the north, the city of Marquette to the east, and the undulating landscape of the wild Huron Mountains stretching all the way to the western horizon. For the more intrepid hikers, there is an alternative route marked "difficult."

Another worthwhile hike here is a section of the North Country National Scenic Trail. The north shore of the Upper Peninsula is fortunate to be a part of the North Country Trail, a 4,600-mile-long (7,400-km-long) trail administered by the National Park Service that begins in western Vermont and meanders through seven additional states before ending in central North Dakota. In the Marquette area, a stretch of the NCT begins at the Sugarloaf Mountain trailhead and straddles the Lake Superior shore for 2 miles (3.2 km), culminating at Little Presque Isle, an especially scenic point that juts out into the lake.

Little Presque Isle State Forest Recreation Area

There's great hiking and mountain biking in the surrounding terrain, much of it part of the **Little Presque Isle State Forest Recreation Area.** Several miles of trails wind around nearby Harlow Lake, up Hogsback Mountain, and along the Lake Superior shore. Parking is available in the unmarked lot on the west side of County Road 550; it's near an old gravel pit, about 1 mile (1.6 km) north of the Sugarloaf Mountain lot.

Noquemanon Trail Network

The **South Marquette Trails** are part of the **Noquemanon Trail Network** (906/228-6182, www.noquetrails.org), ranked among *Bike* magazine's top 10 trails in 2005, and provide miles of hiking and biking. The Mount Marquette Loop is a 5-mile (8-km) trail, while the Carp River and Pioneer loops run a combined total of 9 miles (14.5 km). The organization has introduced a handy **smartphone app** (http://marquette.ifindtrail.com) featuring interactive maps of the whole trail network.

Canoeing and Kayaking
★ Hiawatha Water Trail

One of Lake Superior's greatest kayaking destinations, the **Hiawatha Water Trail** (www.hiawathawatertrail.org) runs from Big Bay to Grand Marais, a total of 120 miles (193 km), and passes by Marquette and Presque Isle. The most beautiful portion of the trail lies to the east, along Pictured Rocks National Lakeshore between Munising and Grand Marais, but getting there will take some hard paddling. Access points and campgrounds are available along the way; get a copy of the official Hiawatha Water Trail Map at **Down Wind Sports** (514 N. 3rd St., Marquette, 906/226-7112, www.downwindsports.com).

Presque Isle is one of Marquette's most beautiful destinations, and visitors who only see it from land are missing out: This is the ultimate kayak trip. More than 2 miles (3.2 km) of jagged shoreline is dotted with rugged crags, towering sandstone cliffs, rocks, and an undeveloped shore. Put in and take out at the Presque Isle Marina. For guided tours, contact **Uncle Ducky Outfitters** (1331 W. Munising Ave., Munising, 906/387-1695, www.paddlingmichigan.com). The six-hour

Paddlers Choice tour runs $169 for adults, $155 for children under 16.

The **Dead River Storage Basin** offers some nice paddling opportunities on the long, narrow surface. To get there from Marquette, take US 41 west for approximately 1.5 miles (2.4 km) before turning right onto Midway Drive. In about 0.5 miles (0.8 km), take the right fork in the road (County Road 510). Continue for approximately 2 miles (3.2 km) before crossing the 501 Bridge. Proceed an additional mile (1.6 km) before coming to Hoist Dam Road. Turn left and continue to the Dead River Boat Ramp, where you can put in.

A source for renting kayaks and related gear is Marquette Outdoors (2145 Sugarloaf Ave., Marquette, 980/549-1070, https://marquetteoutdoors.com).

Golf

Marquette holds a few surprises for visitors searching out a round of golf. Try a visit to the Greywalls course at the **Marquette Golf Club** (1075 Grove St., 906/225-0721, www.golfgreywalls.com, nonmembers $56, cart $18 per rider, June-Sept., cheaper spring and fall). Greywalls opened in 2005 to wide acclaim, earning high marks in *Golf Digest* and other magazines. The course's 18 holes are complemented by Marquette's natural terrain, featuring views of Lake Superior, rocky crags, and evergreen forests. Another 18 holes at the Heritage Course round out the semi-private facility, the only 36-hole club in the Upper Peninsula.

Beaches

Although there are beaches near Marquette, few people are brave enough to actually dive in, as Lake Superior isn't well suited for swimming. Among the impediments are cold water temperatures, an often rocky shoreline, and sudden drop-offs just offshore. That said, you're still welcome to go for a dip if you're daring enough. Of course, there's more to do than swim: You can grill, sunbathe, play a game of volleyball, or toss a Frisbee. **South Beach,** just off Lake Street in Marquette,

and **McCarty's Cove,** on Lakeshore Drive, are two of the city's most popular. Both are equipped with playground equipment and restrooms, and each offers pleasing views and sandy beaches perfect for an afternoon by the lake.

Off-Road Vehicles

For an off-road trail that's part of the state system, head south toward Gwinn. About 5 miles (8 km) west of Gwinn, the **Bass Lake Motorcycle Trail** (www.riderplanet-usa.com) is open to vehicles less than 50 inches (127 cm) wide. The long loop, just under 25 miles (40 km), circles several lakes, including Bass, Crooked, Spring, and Pike. Take M-35 to Crooked Lake Road and head southwest to a parking area, which is near the Pike Lake and Bass Lake Campgrounds. The **Porterfield Lake Motorcycle Trail** is on the border of Marquette and Dickinson Counties, where more than 20 miles (32 km) of trail split into several loops. Porterfield Lake Trail is 8 miles (12.9 km) southwest of Gwinn. Additionally, ORVs are allowed on all trails and forest roads on state land. Contact the **Michigan Department of Natural Resources** (DNR, www.michigan.gov/dnr) for more information.

Waterfalls

Among the most scenic of the Marquette region's waterfalls is **Warner Falls,** a 20-foot (6-meter) drop into the relatively still waters of the Warner Creek, which seems to be more a pond. Warner Falls is reasonably accessible: About 8 miles (12.9 km) west of Marquette, take M-35 south past Palmer and pull off less than 1 mile (1.6 km) past the M-35/County Road 565 intersection. The falls are on the right and can easily be seen from the road.

The **Dead River Falls,** just west of Marquette, are beautiful but difficult to find and even harder to get to. Take US 41 west of town to Wright Street and head north. Turn left at Forestville Road and drive to a powerhouse about 2.5 miles (4 km) up. From there, park and take the gravel road to a clear trail on

the left. Follow it down a steep hill, then turn right; stay on the path until you reach the falls.

For a map of additional falls in the area and detailed instructions on how to get to them, contact **Travel Marquette** (117 W. Washington St., 906/228-7749 or 800/544-4321, www.travelmarquettemichigan.com).

WINTER RECREATION
Downhill Skiing

Marquette Mountain (4501 M-553, 906/225-1155, www.marquettemountain. com, lift tickets $36-72) gets a nod for its 600-foot (185-meter) vertical drop, one of the highest in the state. The 23 trails may not be exceptionally long, but they offer good variety, including bumps and tree runs. The half pipe and terrain park grow and improve every year. Located just 3 miles (4.8 km) south of Marquette on County Road 553, this place is popular all week long with college students and locals. Night skiing is offered Tuesday-Sunday in season, usually mid-November to early April. Rental equipment is available.

You'd hardly guess that the 300-acre **Al Quaal Recreation Area** (501 Poplar St., Ishpeming, 906/235-6861, www. ishpemingcity.org), on the north shore of Ishpeming's Teal Lake, is a city park. To get there, take Deer Lake Road north from US 41. You can make a winter day of it, with a few downhill runs served by a rope tow, a 1.9-mile (3-km) cross-country loop, an outdoor ice rink, and especially the 1,200-foot (365-meter) iced toboggan run where a small hourly fee includes a rental toboggan. The park is open daily, except for the downhill runs, which are open on weekend afternoons only. Check the website for admission cost.

Ski and Snowshoe Trails

For cross-country skiing, take M-553 south from Marquette for about 10 miles (16.1 km) to the **Blueberry Ridge Ski Trails** (free), 15 miles (24 km) of groomed and tracked trails looping through the Escanaba River State Forest, including one lighted 1.7-mile (2.7-km)

circuit. Another option is the **Anderson Lake Pathway,** 5 miles (8 km) south of Gwinn on County Road 557, with four hilly loops ranging 2-4.3 miles (3.2-6.9 km) in length. Both networks are open to mountain bikes in summer months.

Cross-country skiers looking for a challenge should head for the ominous-sounding **Suicide Bowl** trail network between Ishpeming and Negaunee. Groomed for skating and diagonal stride, it offers more than 18 miles (29 km) of trails and a map dotted with phrases like "hairpin curve," "bad downhill," and "exceedingly difficult trail." The parking area is on Cliff Drive, south of Business M-28; follow it past downtown Ishpeming. This area is also the site of **Suicide Hill,** a ski jump used in international competitions.

Visit Wilderness Sports (107 E. Division St., Ishpeming, 906/485-4565, www. wildernesssportsinc.com) to rent cross-country skis and equipment as well as snowshoes.

Luge

If ski jumping isn't wild enough for you, you might want to try luge. Just south of Negaunee on M-35, **Lucy Hill** (www.upluge. org, 906/250-1813) is operated by the Upper Peninsula Luge Club. The course meets International Luge Federation standards as an official luge track, dropping 300 feet (90 meters) with 29 turns. It's open to the public most weekend afternoons, with instruction and equipment available.

Snowmobiling

Marquette County is one of the largest counties in Michigan, and is home to a bevy of snowmobile trails. The main trail in and out of Marquette is **Trail 8,** which presses west toward Baraga along US 41/M-28, and then south to Gwinn. To get to Au Train or Munising, take **Trail 417,** which more or less follows M-28 east, before dipping south for a bit and rejoining with Trail 8. If you're

1: paddling the Hiawatha Water Trail 2: Warner Falls 3: view from Sugarloaf Mountain

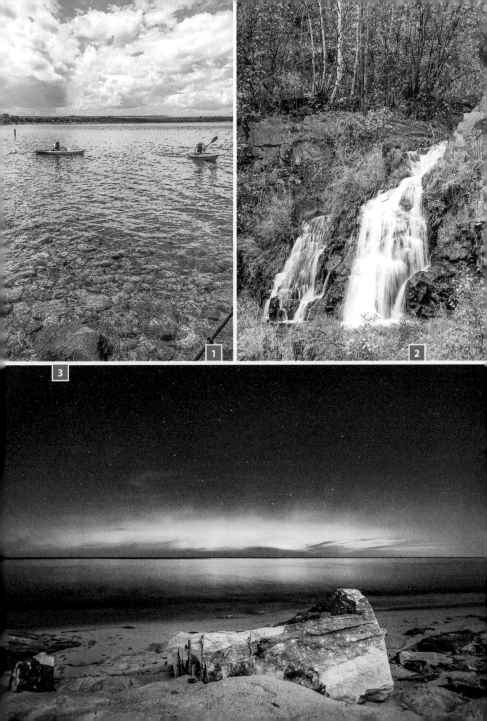

heading up to Big Bay, take **Trail 310** out of town. For a detailed snowmobile trail map, contact **Travel Marquette** (117 W. Washington St., 906/228-7749 or 800/544-4321, www.travelmarquettemichigan.com).

Additionally, snowmobiles are allowed to travel with the flow of traffic on the right side of all plowed roads in Marquette County—provided that they stay single-file and travel at a reasonable speed. For everyone's mutual safety, be careful, stop at intersections, and pay attention to all traffic. All snowmobiles are required to be registered and have a state trail permit, available through the **Michigan DNR** (www.michigan.gov/dnr) and at snowmobile shops throughout the state.

Snowmobiles can be rented from Marquette Powersports (241 US 41 E., Negaunee, 906/401-0444, www.polaris.com).

FOOD

For a city its size, Marquette has a surprisingly good selection of high-quality, locally owned restaurants. The ★ **Vierling Restaurant and Marquette Harbor Brewery** (119 S. Front St., 906/228-3533, https://marquette-now.com/the-vierling, 11am-9pm Mon.-Sat., $18-35) stands out for its good food, century-old decor, and interesting views of the Marquette Harbor ore docks. Ask for a table near the large windows in back. The menu offers lots of variety, including vegetarian and Italian dishes and whitefish served five ways. Excellent breakfasts, soups, and sandwiches are available too. A microbrewery downstairs features British-style ales and stouts.

If you're craving an extra-special breakfast (or any other meal) while in town, head over to **Donckers** (137 W. Washington St., 906/226-9603, www.donckersonline.com, 8am-7pm Tues.-Sat., 8am-4pm Sun., $7-13). Signature omelets, waffles and pancakes (which they refer to as flapjacks), and a variety of breakfast sandwiches dominate the early morning offerings. Lunch items include grilled chicken and cheese sandwiches, burgers, and more. Topping it all off is the

tempting candy counter, guaranteed to give you an overdose of sugar.

Locals will also point you to one of the locations of the no-frills **Border Grill** (1145 W. Washington St., 906/228-5228; 800 N. 3rd St., 906/228-0100, www.bordergrill.net, 11am-9pm daily, under $12) for savory Tex-Mex with fresh salsa.

Wedged between chain eateries on US 41 you'll find a local: **Villa Capri** (2100 US 41, 906/225-1153, www.thevillacapri.com, 3pm-10pm daily, $9-29). This Italian establishment offers a quality menu at reasonable prices. Gnocchi and tortellini, plus some generously sized steaks, make this a place to go out of your way for.

Marquette is home to a number of LGBTQ-friendly businesses, including **Bodega** (517 N. 3rd St., 906/226-7009, www.cafebodegamqt.com, 8am-4pm Sun., 8am-3pm Mon. and Wed., 8am-8pm Thurs.-Sat., $8-16), a woman-owned restaurant offering an eclectic menu of local U.P. favorites, plus several Mexican dishes.

ACCOMMODATIONS

The best spot in Marquette is easily the ★ **Landmark Inn** (230 N. Front St., 906/228-2580, 888/752-6362 reservations, www.thelandmarkinn.com, $$$). Built in the 1930s as the Northland Hotel, it hosted such luminaries as Amelia Earhart and Abbott and Costello. After falling into disrepair and eventually closing in the 1980s, it has been beautifully restored and reopened as the Landmark. Paying not much more than you would for a basic chain motel room, you get a taste of history, a touch of elegance, and a prime location, with Lake Superior on one side and downtown Marquette on the other.

South of Marquette, check in to **Blueberry Ridge Bed-and-Breakfast** (18 Oakridge Dr., 906/251-0219, http://blueberryridgebedandbreakfastmqt.com, $$) for a quiet stay in the north woods. Many of the major hotel and motel franchises are also represented in Marquette, especially along the US 41/M-28 strip.

219

MARQUETTE AND THE LAKE SUPERIOR SHORE
MARQUETTE AND VICINITY

Camping

You can't pitch a tent at the **Little Presque Isle State Forest Campground** (906/339-4461, www.michigan.gov/dnr), north of Marquette on County Road 550, but the six rustic cabins ($74)—no electricity, no running water, no roads all the way in—make for great camping, and they're available year-round. A 0.5-mile (0.8-km) hike from the parking area will get you to your cabin, and once you're there, it's all hand-pumped water, wood-burning stoves, and vault toilets. There are 18 miles (29 km) of hiking trails, along with miles of Lake Superior beach, fishing, and other recreational opportunities. Cabins sleep up to six, and reservations are required.

More traditional camping, either in a tent or at an RV site, can be found at **Marquette Tourist Park** (2145 Sugarloaf Rd., 906/228-0460, www.marquettemi.gov/departments/community-services/parks-and-recreation/tourist-park, tent sites $25, with electricity $40, full hookup $50). The 40-acre in-town park has 110 rustic tent-only campsites; public restrooms, showers, and water and electrical hookups are also available. You'll also find fire rings, picnic tables, a ball field, and a playground. Advance reservations are strongly recommended. There are another 100 or so campsites at **Gitche Gumee RV Park** (2048 M-28 E., 906/249-6123, www.gitchegumeepark.com), which features amenities such as 70 cable TV channels, a movie theater, and a fudge factory.

There are four **state forest campgrounds** in nearby Gwinn: Anderson Lake West (19 sites, $17), Bass Lake (22 sites, $15), North Horseshoe Lake (11 sites, $15), and Pike Lake (10 sites, $16), each accommodating tents and a few small trailers. There are no reservations and just a few rustic amenities, including vault toilets and drinking water from a hand pump. Contact the **Michigan DNR Gwinn Field Office** (410 W. M-35, Gwinn, 906/346-9201, www.michigan.gov/dnr). Gwinn is approximately 10 miles (16.1 km) due south of Marquette on County Road 553.

INFORMATION AND SERVICES

Get visitor information from the friendly folks at **Travel Marquette** (117 W. Washington St., 906/228-7749 or 800/544-4321, www.travelmarquettemichigan.com).

For local medical attention, **UP Health System Marquette** (850 W. Baraga Ave., 906/449-3000, www.mgh.org) has a high-quality emergency room and trauma care center.

Marquette has plenty of banks and ATMs. Try **Huntington Bank** (1930 US 41, 906/228-8000, www.huntington.com), **IncredibleBank** (1140 W. Washington St., 906/226-0293; 1101 3rd St., 906/226-0300, www.incrediblebank.com), or **First Bank** (1502 W. Washington St., 906/228-7300, www.first-bank.com).

Note that Marquette and its surrounding areas are in the eastern time zone.

GETTING THERE AND AROUND
Car

Getting to Marquette by car is especially easy: US 41 runs from the south and west; from the east, M-28 and US 2 lead to US 41, a better option than smaller roads such as M-553. US 41 also runs through Ishpeming and Negaunee, west of Marquette. The three cities are beginning to blend into one long stretch of shops and services.

Air

If you're flying into town, **Sawyer International Airport** (MQT, 125 G Ave., Gwinn, 906/346-3308, www.sawyerairport.com) has scheduled flights from Detroit on **Delta Airlines** (800/221-1212, www.delta.com) and Chicago O'Hare on **American Airlines** (800/433-7300, www.aa.com).

You'll most likely want to rent a car; Sawyer has **Alamo** (800/462-5266, www.alamo.com), **Avis** (800/831-1212, www.avis.com), **Budget** (800/527-7000, www.budget.com), **Enterprise** (800//736-8227), and **National** (800/227-7368, www.nationalcar.com). Bus

Best Breweries

Keweenaw Brewing Co.

For those who love to sit and enjoy a cold, refreshing pint, Upper Michigan is a destination not to be missed. Microbreweries have emerged nationally, closely tying into the culture of their area and reflecting local tastes and preferences. Featured brews like Presque Ale and Cold Iron Cream Ale speak to the rugged northern spirit characteristic of Upper Peninsula breweries. The ingredients used are often seasonal, so the varieties may not be available at all times.

MICROBREWERIES

Since microbreweries are both production facilities and taprooms, the days and hours they open to the public may be more limited than a traditional bar, as the staff has additional responsibilities. Be sure to call ahead.

Here's a taste of some noteworthy establishments:

- **Blackrocks Brewery** (424 N. 3rd St., Marquette, 906/273-1333, www.blackrocksbrewery. com)

service runs to Marquette and Gwinn on **Marq-Tran** (906/225-1112, www.marq-tran. com).

Boat

Marquette has two marinas: The **Cinder Pond Marina** (906/228-0469, www. michigan.gov/dnr) is located near Marquette's distinctive ore dock. There are 91 seasonal slips and 10 transient slips, as well as full amenities like electricity, showers, pump-out, gasoline, and day-use dockage. Cinder

Pond Marina is open early May through late October, can be reached on radio channel 71, and is located at 46°31.56 N, 87°22.26 W. The Ellwood Matson Lower Harbor Park, a 22-acre open space with park benches, picnic tables, and a playground, stretches out to the west. The **Presque Isle Marina** (906/228-0464, www.michigan.gov/dnr) has 87 seasonal and 10 transient slips and is located at Presque Isle Park. As at Cinder Pond Marina, there are plenty of amenities. The marina is located at 46°34.20 N, 87°22.25 W. It's open early May

- **Brickside Brewery** (64 Gratiot Ave, Copper Harbor, 906/289-4772, www.bricksidebrewery.com)
- **Cold Iron Brewery** (104 S. Lowell St., Ironwood, 906/285-7020, https://coldironbrewing.com)
- **East Channel Brewing Co.** (209 Maple St., Munising, 906/387-3007, www.eastchannelbrewery.com)
- **Keweenaw Brewing Co.** (408 Shelden Ave., Houghton, 906/482-5596, www.keweenawbrewing.com)
- **Ore Dock Brewing Co.** (114 W. Spring St., Marquette, 906/228-8888, www.oredockbrewing.com)

RESTAURANT/BREWERY

Some microbreweries in the U.P. double as restaurants. After all, what better way to enjoy the work of a master brewer than with a great meal? Here are a few places that offer the best of both worlds:

- **Hereford and Hops** (624 Ludington St., Escanaba, 906/789-1945, www.herefordandhops.com)
- **Lake Superior Brewing Company** (14283 Lake Ave., Grand Marais, 906/494-2337)
- **The Library** (62 N. Isle Royale St., Houghton, 906/481-2665, www.thelibraryhoughton.com)
- **Soo Brewing Company** (100 W. Portage Ave., Sault Ste. Marie, 906/259-5035, http://soobrew.com)
- **Tahquamenon Falls Brewery and Pub** (24019 Upper Falls Dr., Paradise, 906/492-3300, www.tahquamenonfallsbrewery.com)
- **Vierling Restaurant and Marquette Harbor Brewery** (119 S. Front St., Marquette, 906/228-3533, http://thevierling.com)

through late October and can be reached on channel 9.

Bus

Bus service to Marquette is available on **Indian Trails** (989/725-5105 or 800/292-3831, www.indiantrails.com) on a route that stretches from Chicago to Calumet, stopping in Marquette as well as Escanaba, Houghton, and Hancock along the way.

The same public bus that shuttles visitors from Sawyer International Airport to Marquette runs a daily circuit around the area with regular stops in Marquette, Negaunee, Ishpeming, and Gwinn. **Marq-Tran** (906/225-1112, www.marq-tran.com) also offers door-to-door service for a small fee that increases with distance (though it won't be more than $5.60). Contact Marq-Tran for regular schedules and fees.

Taxi

For taxi service, try **Checker Transport** (906/226-7772, http://checkertransport.com).

Huron Mountains

Ask 10 people where the Huron Mountains begin and end, and you're likely to get 10 different answers. But everyone will agree that they fall within the vague boundaries of Lake Superior to the north and east and US 41 to the south and west. It's over 1,000 square miles (2,600 sq km) where the terrain rises to rugged hills and even mountains. Mount Arvon, about 15 miles (24 km) due east of L'Anse, tops out at 1,979 feet (604 meters), the highest point in the state.

On a map you'll see it's an intriguing parcel of real estate, virtually devoid of towns and roads. What the Huron Mountains do have, however, is peaks and valleys, white pine forests, hundreds of lakes, dazzling waterfalls that don't appear on maps, the headwaters of several classic wilderness rivers, and total quiet—all in a place where animals far outnumber people. Even by U.P. standards, it's a remote and rugged place. If the Huron Mountain Club should ever come up for sale, government officials would no doubt clamor to turn it into a state or national park.

In the meantime, we can be content in knowing that such stunning natural beauty is being lovingly protected. Although much of the Huron Mountains is inaccessible to the public, a few areas can be explored.

BIG BAY AREA

Many visitors approach the Huron Mountains from the east, where County Road 550 climbs 30 miles (48 km) out of Marquette to the tiny town of **Big Bay** (pop. 257). The town provides convenient access to the Huron Mountains, Lake Superior harbor, Lake Independence fishing, and unique lodgings.

Sited above Lake Independence and close to Lake Superior, Big Bay is sandwiched between wilderness and inland sea. The town has swung from prosperity to near ghost town status more than once. It was first a bustling logging outpost, then one of Henry Ford's company towns, humming with busy sawmills. Local lore relates a story of a bank that was wary of the town's volatile economy and was loath to loan money to town businesses. This overly conservative stance proved to be the bank's undoing, and while the town's 20 businesses were thriving, the bank closed down.

From Big Bay, the best way to venture into the backcountry is County Road 510, which branches off County Road 550 on the southeast edge of Big Bay and continues south to US 41 west of Marquette. Another option is the Triple A Truck Trail, which branches off County Road 510. Both are usually well-maintained dirt and gravel roads, although wet or snowy weather can quickly render them impassable. Dozens of old logging roads and single-tracks branch off these main routes. To find your way around, you'll need either a topographic or the very good local map (sometimes called the "waterfall map") available for free from **Travel Marquette** (906/228-7749 or 800/544-4321, www.travelmarquettemichigan.com).

SIGHTS
Craig Lake State Park

Craig Lake State Park is probably unlike any state park you've ever visited. The entrance is nearly 7 miles (11.3 km) down a rugged truck trail that often requires a 4WD vehicle and is periodically "improved" with sharp old mining rock that can inflict lethal wounds on tires. Once you arrive at the Craig Lake parking area, you can access the 7,000-acre park on foot or, with a short portage, by canoe or kayak. No wheeled vehicles or boat motors are permitted anywhere within the park. The access road to the park is north from US 41/M-28 about 8 miles (12.9 km) west of Champion.

Huron Mountains

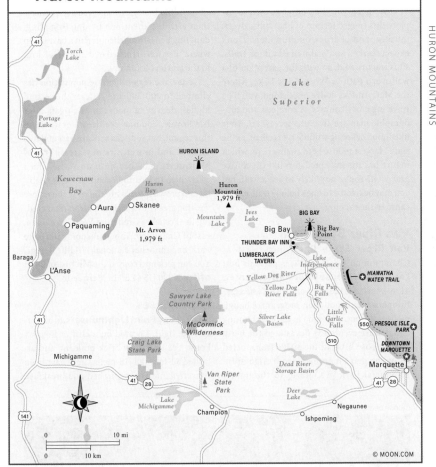

McCormick Wilderness

Once the private wilderness retreat of Cyrus McCormick, whose father invented the reaping machine, the 27-square-mile (70-sq-km) **McCormick Wilderness** was willed to the U.S. Forest Service by his family in 1967. Today it remains in pristine wilderness condition: remote, undeveloped, and largely unused. In other words, it's perfect for backcountry hiking and camping. No-trace camping is permitted throughout the wilderness area. For more information, contact the

Ottawa National Forest Ranger District (4810 E. M-28, Kenton, 906/852-3500, www.fs.fed.us).

To access the McCormick Tract, follow US 41/M-28 west from Marquette for about 50 miles (80 km) to Champion. Continue until you cross the Peshekee River, then follow the first paved road north (County Rd. 607, also called the Peshekee Grade or the Huron Bay Grade). In about 10 miles (16.1 km), you'll see a sign for Arfelin Lake; make a left turn at the next road (N. Arfelin Rd.). After about 1 mile

(1.6 km) look for an "Arfelin Lake" sign and a small parking area.

Once here, you'll be on your own to explore this rugged terrain of high hills, rivers, muskeg, and bedrock outcroppings. Don't expect marked and maintained hiking trails. This tract is wild, so with the exception of a well-worn path to White Deer Lake, where the McCormicks' lodge once stood, you'll be traveling cross-country. A compass and topographic map are absolute necessities. Your likelihood of seeing wildlife is excellent, as the state's largest moose herd roams here, which in turn has attracted predators like the elusive gray wolf. You're not likely to see a wolf, but you may be treated to one's hollow wail at your camp in the evening.

Van Riper State Park

Van Riper State Park, just west of Champion on US 41/M-28, is perhaps best known for its **Moose Information Center,** a kiosk that tells the story of the U.P.'s successful moose reintroduction program. Though moose were once common in the U.P., hunting and disease eventually devastated the herd. Two "moose lifts" in the 1980s transported 59 of the giant mammals from Algonquin Provincial Park in Ontario to the lightly traveled wilderness along the Peshekee Grade near the McCormick Tract. It was quite a project: wildlife biologists captured each moose, then airlifted them one by one in a sling, dangling beneath a helicopter, to a base camp where they were trucked 600 miles (965 km) to the Huron Mountains.

Today, the region's moose population has climbed to 200-300 and reflects the second highest density of moose in Michigan, after Isle Royale. You may see them anywhere in this region, but your chances are best at dawn or dusk and in wet, swampy areas. **Travel Marquette** publishes *Michigan Moose*, which offers help in locating occupied moose habitat and provides maps highlighting the moose viewing areas in Van Riper State Park, including the Peshekee Grade and Wolf Lake Road, east of Champion; Tahquamenon Falls State Park; and the Seney National Wildlife Refuge. You can pick up a copy at the **Michigan DNR office** (1990 US 41 S.) in Marquette.

Lighthouses

The **Big Bay Point Lighthouse** is an above-average light. Located on a cliff at Big Bay Point, the two-story brick building and attached 60-foot-tall (18-meter) light have been converted into a charming bed-and-breakfast.

moose near Big Bay

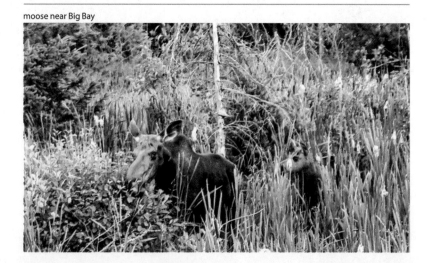

The 1868 **Huron Island Lighthouse,** located northwest of Big Bay and 3 miles (4.8 km) offshore, is only accessible by private boat. The island, part of the Huron National Wildlife Refuge, is open to the public during daylight hours. You can charter a sightseeing trip to the Huron Islands with **Uncle Ducky Charters** (434 E. Prospect St., Marquette, 877/228-5447 www.paddlingmichigan.com).

SUMMER RECREATION
Hiking and Biking

Though it's situated right on busy US 41, **Van Riper State Park** is worthy of mention. It has an amenity-rich modern campground on the eastern shore of Lake Michigamme that rarely fills up. Here you'll find a boat launch, great walleye fishing, and a fine swimming beach with unusually warm water and a sandy bottom. Many campers overlook the property on the north side of the road, the park's largest and most appealing acreage. It includes a rustic campground on the Peshekee River and 4 miles (6.4 km) of hiking trails. Climb the **Overlook Trail,** a loop that ascends a rocky outcrop, for a great view of rolling forest land and Lake Michigamme. In addition, Van Riper is less than a dozen miles from the gated entrance to the McCormick Tract, so you can take advantage of modern comforts while spending your days in the rugged backcountry that begins just across the highway.

Visitors that make their way into **Craig Lake State Park** will be rewarded with the seclusion and backcountry hiking of Michigan's most remote state park. If you're going to make the journey to the park, you should take a vehicle with a high ground clearance for the 7-mile (11.3-km) trek off paved roads, especially after a rainfall, when it's best to have a 4WD vehicle. The park has nearly 7,000 acres and two main trails that total more than 15 miles (24 km), half of which is part of the North Country National Scenic Trail. Trails are rugged, often steep, and are frequently blocked by streams or other obstacles. There are six full lakes, several smaller ponds, and plenty of wildlife, including black bears,

moose, and the more common deer. Adequate backcountry practices should be followed; make sure you go in well prepared. The access road to Craig Lake State Park is north from US 41/M-28 about 8 miles (12.9 km) west of Champion. For backcountry preparation tips, maps, and directions, contact the **Michigan DNR** (906/339-4461, www.michigan.gov/dnr).

In the town of Big Bay, take the **Big Bay Pathway,** part of the Noquemanon Trail Network. Only one of its loops is for hiking and cycling, the relatively flat 4-mile (6.4-km) Hidden Grin Loop. The other three loops, totaling nearly 6 miles (9.7 km), are more appropriate for cross-country skiing in the winter. Take County Road 550 into Big Bay, then turn left on Dump Road and take it less than 1 mile (1.6 km) to the trailhead, which is on the right.

The Commercial Forest Reserve Act gives property owners a tax break in exchange for allowing others access to their property, so trespassing isn't an issue as you explore most of the Huron Mountains. There is a wide array of possibilities for hiking and mountain-biking on old logging roads and various foot trails. Two spots worth exploring are **Gobbler's Knob,** also known as the Thomas Rock Scenic Overlook, and the **Elliott Donnelley Wilderness Area. Thomas Rock** is a rock outcrop off County Road 510 that overlooks Lake Independence and Lake Superior. To get there from Big Bay, take County Road 550 (Big Bay Rd.) south out of town until you reach County Road 510, a distance of about a mile (1.6 km). Turn right and continue for 0.5 miles (0.8 km). You'll see the overlook on your right.

Elliott Donnelley Wilderness Area can best be reached from Marquette. Simply take County Road 550 (Big Bay Rd.) west from Marquette and continue for approximately 10 miles (16.1 km). Just after you pass the Little Garlic River, you'll see a 4-mile (6.4-km) trail that winds along the river and continues past Little Garlic Falls.

Keep in mind that the Huron Mountains can be a confusing place. It can be frustrating to drive down one dead-end logging road after

another, or worse, to get hopelessly lost on one of hundreds of unmapped, unmarked trails. Before you head off into the woods, make sure you're equipped with a detailed map, a compass, and a GPS unit, and that you're proficient in their use. Otherwise, it's best to find a local guide who can show you around on foot, mountain bike, or snowshoe. For personally guided tours, contact **MQT Adventures and Guide Services** (263 County Road BI, Marquette, 906/362-7916, 6am-midnight daily).

Canoeing and Kayaking

In addition to its backcountry hiking trails, much of **Craig Lake State Park** is accessible by nonmotorized watercraft. There's a 0.25-mile (0.4-km) portage from the parking lot to one of several boat landings on the lakes, though Crooked Lake is perhaps the most appealing, with lots of interesting bays and inlets. To reach it, paddle across the southeastern corner of Craig Lake and follow the 0.5-mile (0.8-km) portage east. Be aware that many of the lakes are large enough to become rough during windy or stormy weather. You'll need a state park pass and a vehicle suitable for rough, unpaved roads. Contact the **Michigan DNR** (906/339-4461, www.michigan.gov/dnr) for more information.

Other large lakes in the area are suitable for canoeing or kayaking. A good example is **Lake Independence** in Big Bay; try taking the Iron River from the lake to Lake Superior. There are plenty of smaller lakes scattered throughout the Huron Mountains. Ask an outfitter for more information and advice. If you're looking for a good river, put in the **Yellow Dog River** at County Road 510 and take out 5 miles (8 km) downriver at County Road 550 for an easy-to-middling white-water trip; this section is rated Class II-V.

Of course, experienced kayakers will want to spend some time paddling along the Lake Superior shoreline. Big Bay is the westernmost

end of the **Hiawatha Water Trail** (www.hiawathawatertrail.org), more than 120 miles (193 km) of Lake Superior shoreline that take paddlers all the way to Grand Marais to the east. There are at least 20 public access points and 23 water-accessible campsites along the way. Trail maps for the Hiawatha Water Trail are available for a fee at **Big Bay Outfitters** (308 Bensinger St., Big Bay, 906/250-2457), where you can also rent kayaks and canoes. Big Bay and the shoreline between L'Anse and Marquette aren't as spectacular as Pictured Rocks to the east, but as with most of the Great Lakes shorelines, you'd be hard-pressed to find a stretch that doesn't make a good place to get your paddle wet. Pay particular attention to the shore on either side of Big Bay Point, and be sure to check the weather reports, as Lake Superior can produce sudden storms.

Fishing

Big Bay's **Lake Independence** has a reputation as a good fishing spot. Anglers can find walleye, yellow perch, and smallmouth bass. Put in at the boat launch at Perkins Park Campground, just off Big Bay Road/County Road 550. For a more remote, secluded experience, head to **Craig Lake,** a little north of US 41/M-28. There you'll find northern pike, smallmouth bass, and muskie. To get there, enter the park by taking Keewaydin Road north off US 41/M-28. Proceed for about 2 miles (3.2 km) until you reach Craig Road. Turn left and continue for 2.5 miles (4 km) until you arrive at Craig Lake.

You can also find suitable rivers and streams virtually everywhere. Try the **Yellow Dog River** for trout. And head to the **Little Garlic River,** about 10 miles (16.1 km) northwest of Marquette on Big Bay Road/County Road 550, for steelhead.

Charters on Lake Superior, as well as inland lakes and rivers, can be arranged through a number of area companies, many of them in Marquette. **Uncle Ducky Charters** (434 E. Prospect St., Marquette, 906/228-5447, www.paddlingmichigan.com) is one of

---

1: Big Bay Point Lighthouse 2: the Peshekee River in Van Riper State Park the best all-around charters, while **Rivers North Guide Service** (906/458-8125, www.riversnorth.net, half day from $325, full day $525) specializes in fly-fishing.

Beaches

Perkins Park Campground on the west side of Lake Independence has a nice, family friendly beach—and the water will be more comfortable than chilly Lake Superior too. **Lake Michigamme,** just off US 41, has a pleasant swimming beach along the 0.5-mile (0.8-km) frontage of Van Riper State Park. To get there, simply take US 41 west from Marquette. Continue for approximately 20 miles (32 km), just past the town of Champion, and look for the signs indicating Van Riper State Park. If it's late enough in the season and you don't mind Superior's bite, there's a small beach by the **Big Bay Harbor of Refuge.**

Off-Road Vehicles

For such a wide expanse of undeveloped land, there are disappointingly few trails marked for off-road vehicles. In fact, one of the only DNR trails for ATVs near the Huron Mountains is the **Champion Trail,** which runs south from Champion on US 41/M-28 to Republic, a 7-mile (11.3-km) ride.

Waterfalls

The waterfall map, which you can get from **Travel Marquette** (117 W. Washington St., Marquette, 906/228-7749 or 800/544-4321, www.travelmarquettemichigan.com), will point you toward many of the region's falls. Some of the finest and most accessible include **Little Garlic Falls,** which is on the Little Garlic River, 11 miles (17.7 km) northwest of Marquette, about a 20-minute drive.

Yellow Dog Falls (sometimes known as Hills Falls) is just off of County Road 510, about 8 miles (12.9 km) south of Big Bay. Look for the Yellow Dog River Falls trailhead and a small parking area. From here, it's about a 1-mile (1.6-km) hike to the falls. When you're finished, continue on County Road 510 for 3 more miles (4.8 km) and look for signs announcing **Big Pup Falls,** which is on Big Pup Creek, a tributary of the Yellow Dog River. This waterfall is well hidden by trees and brush, but it's located just off the road.

WINTER RECREATION
Ski and Snowshoe Trails

The loops of the **Big Bay Pathway** are great for cross-country skiing once the snow falls. Meditation Loop is 2 miles (3.2 km) long and suitable for beginners, while the Hidden Grin Loop, at 4 miles (6.4 km), is a longer intermediate-level loop. The other two paths, the 3-mile (4.8-km) Bear Mountain Loop and its 1-mile (1.6-km) Ridgeline Extension Loop, are more difficult. The trailhead for the Big Bay Pathway is at 301 Deutsch Avenue in Big Bay, just on the edge of a residential neighborhood. If you're coming from Marquette, take County Road 550 to Big Bay. Turn left at County Road KT/Deutsch Avenue and continue for two blocks to the trailhead.

The **Saux Head Trails,** part of the Noquemanon Trail Network like Big Bay Pathway, have about 7.5 miles (12 km) of two-way groomed trails. The loops range from intermediate to advanced. Saux Head Trails are about 11 miles (17.7 km) southeast of Big Bay. Take County Road 550 from Marquette, turn right on Saux Head Lake Road, and then turn left about 1 mile (1.6 km) later. Parking areas are on the left.

To ski or snowshoe any of these trails, you'll need a trail pass from the **Noquemanon Trail Network** (906/235-6861, www.noquetrails.org). Visit Wilderness Sports (107 E. Division St., Ishpeming, 906/485-4565, www.wildernesssportsinc.com) to rent cross-country skis and equipment as well as snowshoes.

Snowmobiling

Trail 310 winds some 54 miles (87 km) from Marquette west and north to Big Bay. From the other direction, **Trail 14** connects L'Anse and Big Bay over a distance of 56 miles (90 km). The two trails merge south of Big Bay via

Alternate Trail 310; otherwise they meet up in Big Bay. The **Clowry-Big Bay Trail** (Trail 5) heads north into the Huron Mountains from Clowry, near Champion on US 41/M- 23, and joins Trail 14.

Snowmobiles are allowed on the plowed surface of any of Marquette County's roads, provided you stay on the right-hand side and move with the flow of traffic. When operating a snowmobile on a public road, be especially careful, stop at all intersections, and watch for traffic. Stay off the state highways, and double-check the laws for riding on paved roads within individual towns and cities.

FOOD

★ **Thunder Bay Inn** (400 Bensinger St., 906/345-9220, https://bigbayinn.wordpress. com, 4pm-10pm Mon.-Tues., noon-9pm Wed.-Sun., $13-25) is known as the iconic hotel where scenes in the movie *Anatomy of a Murder* were filmed in 1959. The pub, added to the building for the production of the movie, endures as a cornerstone of the community. The menu rotates depending on the day of the week but typically features classic American fare and Mexican specialties, available daily. Homemade pizza is available on Mondays and Tuesdays only.

There are a few other dining choices in Big Bay. Lunch and breakfast are served at **Hungry Hollow Café** (County Rd. 550, 906/345-0075, www.cramsgeneralstore.com, 8am-2pm Mon.-Thurs. and Sat., 8am-8pm Fri., 8am-4pm Sun., under $10), part of Cram's General Store. Try the homemade pasties and soups, or visit on Friday for the fish fry. For dinner, go to the ★ **Lumberjack Tavern** (202 Bensinger St., 906/345-9912, noon-2am daily, $11-26), where you'll find earnest, friendly people, great service, and good food. Many people come for the history, not the menu: In 1952, Mike Chenoweth was murdered here, providing the inspiration for Judge John Voelker's bestselling novel *Anatomy of a Murder,* which was later made into an iconic motion picture of the same name directed by Otto Preminger.

ACCOMMODATIONS

There's a surprisingly good and varied choice of lodgings in tiny Big Bay. Probably the best known is the ★ **Thunder Bay Inn** (400 Bensinger St., 906/345-9220, https:// bigbayinn.wordpress.com, May-Mar., $$), re-opened in 2008 after new owners restored it to its former glory. Built in 1910, the hotel was purchased by Henry Ford during the 1920s as a place for him and his executives to stay when visiting his numerous U.P. sawmills. The inn offers a quiet, unhurried style of lodging characteristic of a bygone era—which means there are no TVs, radios, or telephones in the rooms. Along with their simplicity, the rooms are comfortable and very clean. Most have a full bath. All have full or twin beds, except Room 201, which was occupied by Henry Ford and has a king bed.

As a lighthouse, the ★ **Big Bay Point Lighthouse Bed-and-Breakfast** (4674 County Road KCB, 906/345-9957, www. bigbaylighthouse.com, $$$) naturally occupies a dramatic position on a rocky point just a few miles from the town of Big Bay. The redbrick keeper's home, attached to the 1896 light, has been restored and fitted with seven very comfortable guest rooms, all with private baths. Five rooms have Lake Superior views. The inn has extensive grounds, comprising more than 43 acres and 0.5 miles (0.8 km) of shoreline, set far back from busy roads. Guests can use the sauna, climb the light tower, or relax in the living room, where owners Linda and Jeff Gamble have collected lighthouse lore and history. Spa services are also available. Reserve well in advance.

There are two budget choices in Big Bay, both in good locations. The **Big Bay Depot** (301 Bensinger Rd., 906/345-9350, $) occupies an old train depot overlooking Lake Independence. The five refurbished suites include full kitchens, two double beds, and lake views; pets are welcome and weekly rates are available. The independent **Picture Bay Motel** (8750 Big Bay Rd., 906/345-9820, $) is neat as a pin. Two units have basic cooking

Anatomy of a Murder

Lumberjack Tavern

Every small town has its share of interesting local lore, but the hamlet of Big Bay in the Huron Mountains can boast a special distinction. In 1952 attorney John Voelker, a former Marquette County prosecutor, received a call from Charlotte Peterson asking him to represent her husband, who had been charged with murder. A short time earlier, Army lieutenant Coleman Peterson had been arrested and held after confronting and shooting bar owner Mike Chenoweth at the Lumberjack Tavern. The motive? Charlotte's credible allegation that Chenoweth had raped her at the bar during her husband's recent deployment. The case quickly became the talk of the town.

The fact of Peterson's guilt was not in dispute, yet Voelker agreed to take the case and used an unusual defense—a then-novel interpretation of an insanity defense then called "irresistible impulse," which had not been used in Michigan since the late 19th century. The tactic worked and resulted in the lieutenant's acquittal by mental disease or defect.

The unusual circumstances of this episode (a murder in an unlikely location, the unusual defense, combined with heavy media attention) later inspired Voelker, who had a part-time vocation as a writer, to pen a novel on the incident: *Anatomy of a Murder*, written under the pen name Robert Traver and published in 1958. The next year there was a motion picture of the same name, directed by Hollywood legend Otto Preminger and starring Jimmy Stewart, Lee Remick, and Ben Gazzara. The historical events are accurately reflected in both the book and the movie, and their exceptional quality has led to their inclusion in many law school curricula for demonstrating a variety of legal strategies. The American Bar Association has ranked the movie as one of the 12 best trial films ever.

Today the **Lumberjack Tavern** still operates and enjoys considerable notoriety due to its place in history. A local cottage industry capitalizing on the town's fame has emerged in the form of souvenir shops and the like. Despite this small amount of commercialization, many visitors find the trip to the legendary bar a fun way to spend an afternoon.

facilities. Pets are welcome for an additional $5 per night.

Camping

Backcountry campers will find nearly unlimited options in the **Huron Mountains** and **McCormick Wilderness**. Respect private property, observe backcountry camping principles, and travel with a map, compass, GPS unit, and other essentials. If you're not experienced in the backcountry, it might be wise to plan your first trip by first stopping at **Downwind Sports** (514 N. 3rd St., Marquette, 906/226-7112, http://downwindsports.com) for information, maps, gear, and other essentials.

Straddling the highway, **Van Riper State Park** (851 County Rd. AKE, 906/339-4461, www.michigan.gov/dnr, $17-25) offers easily accessible modern and rustic campsites, although it's within earshot of US 41. The park also rents out a cabin near the modern campground, which has a refrigerator-freezer, a toaster, a microwave, basic furniture, and sleeping space for six. Reserve well in advance.

At 7,000-acre **Craig Lake State Park** (906/339-4461, www.michigan.gov/dnr, $15), you essentially get an organized campsite tucked in the backcountry wilderness. A rough 7-mile (11.3-km) drive and a 1- or 2-mile (1.6- or 3.2-km) hike brings you to many lovely and often empty campsites. Choose from sites that sit on beds of pine needles above the east shore of Craig Lake, or follow the portage trail east to sites on a small peninsula in Crooked Lake. There are also a couple of rustic cabins on the northwestern shore of Craig Lake. Originally built by Frederick Miller of Miller Brewing fame, these barebones cabins have bunks for your sleeping bag, some utilitarian furniture, and protection from the bugs and cold. The larger cabin includes a huge gathering room with a stone fireplace and sleeps 14. The other cabin sleeps six. Both have a water pump, firewood, and a rowboat. Reservations are necessary for the campsites and cabins. It's best to reserve six months in advance.

INFORMATION AND SERVICES

For information about Big Bay and the Huron Mountains, contact **Travel Marquette** (117 W. Washington St., Marquette, 906/228-7749 or 800/544-4321, www.travelmarquettemichigan.com), which has advice and trail maps for hiking and cross-country skiing.

Although there are no hospitals in Big Bay, there are two within 30 miles (48 km) of the city. **The UP Health System Marquette Hospital** (850 W. Baraga Ave., Marquette, 906/449-3000, www.mgh.org) has an emergency room and trauma center, or you can go to **UP Health System Bell Hospital** (901 Lakeshore Dr., Ishpeming, 906/486-4431, www.uphealthsystem.com/bell) just south of US 41. A third hospital is farther away in L'Anse; take Broad Street from US 41 to Main Street and turn right to the **Baraga County Memorial Hospital** (18341 US 41, L'Anse, 906/524-3300, www.bcmh.org).

You'll want to do your banking in the bigger cities outside Big Bay and the Huron Mountains.

GETTING THERE AND AROUND
Car

The Huron Mountains aren't as easily accessible as the U.P.'s other areas; there are only two roads in. The best is Big Bay Road/County Road 550, which heads directly northwest from Marquette toward Big Bay. County Road 510 is an alternative and somewhat more meandering route. If you're planning on getting off the main roads, be warned that some of these smaller byways are little more than old logging roads. You'll want to have a 4WD vehicle or, at the very least, a vehicle with high clearance.

Air

The closest airport to the region is **Sawyer International Airport** (MQT, 125 G Ave., Gwinn, 906/346-3308, www.sawyerairport.com), which has scheduled flights from

Detroit on **Delta Airlines** (800/221-1212, www.delta.com) and from Chicago O'Hare on **American Airlines** (800/433-7300, www. aa.com). To rent a car, Sawyer has a bevy of rental services: **Alamo** (800/462-5266, www. alamo.com), **Avis** (800/831-1212, www.avis. com), **Budget** (800/527-7000, www.budget. com), **Enterprise** (800/736-8227, www. enterprise.com), and **National** (800/227-7368, www.nationalcar.com).

Boat

If you're boating to Big Bay, you can put in at the **Big Bay Harbor of Refuge** (906/345-9353, www.co.marquette.mi.us). With only 10 transient and 4 seasonal slips, space is limited, especially for day-use dockage. The Big Bay Harbor has the usual amenities: water, electricity, pump-out, and gas, as well as restrooms, showers, and a picnic area. The harbor location is 46°49.45 N, 87°43.27 W.

Munising and Grand Island

When it comes to attracting visitors, nature dealt Munising a royal flush. The town of 2,700 curves around the belly of protected Munising Bay. The Grand Island National Recreation Area beckons just offshore. Pictured Rocks National Lakeshore begins just east of town and stretches more than 40 miles (64 km). The Hiawatha National Forest protects the woodlands to the south and west.

M-28 leads to the heart of Munising, where you'll find most restaurants, independent motels, and the ferry dock for cruises to Pictured Rocks.

SIGHTS
★ Grand Island

Although it's just a 10-minute ferry ride from Munising, Lake Superior effectively isolates Grand Island. Part of the Hiawatha National Forest since 1989, the heavily wooded 13,000-acre island is a national recreation area. Roughly the size of Manhattan (save for 40 acres that are privately owned), Grand Island offers opportunities for hiking, beachcombing, mountain biking, and camping.

Don't miss the **historic cemetery** near Murray Bay. Here you can visit the resting places of shipwreck victims and the island's first nonnative settlers. Grand Island had long been a summering ground for the Ojibwa people when a man named Abraham Williams arrived in the 1840s to establish a trading post. Williams was the first European

settler to permanently reside on the island; he raised a family and died there in 1873 at the then-amazing age of 81. Today, only the descendants of Williams and their spouses can be buried here.

Automobiles are not allowed on the island except with special permission or those owned by island landholders. Van tours now operate under special permit, bumping along a few dirt roads on the island's southern half. ATVs are allowed from October 1 to April 15, and mountain bikes are allowed anytime on all trails on public land. Dogs are allowed if leashed. Drinking water is not available on the island. The $5 daily user fee is collected by the ferry service. For more information, contact the Hiawatha National Forest's **Munising Ranger District** (400 E. Munising Ave., 906/387-3700, www.fs.fed.us).

Grand Island Ferry Service (906/387-2600, www.grandislandup.com, round-trip $23 for adults, $15 for children 6-12, ages 5 and under free) provides daily round-trip transportation to the island from Memorial Day through October 10. Transporting a bike to the island is $10. Fares include the $5 recreation-area user fee.

Grand Island Ferry Service also offers **bus tours** of Grand Island (Memorial Day-early Oct., $30 adults, $15 children ages 11 and under). The tour makes 10 stops on the island, including Echo Lake, the Trout Bay Overlook, and Mather Beach, an excellent swimming

Grand Island

(Map labels:)
Lake Superior
NORTH LIGHT
Grand Island
Grand Island National Recreation Area
Alger Underwater Preserve
Echo Creek
Echo Lake
Mather Beach
GRAND ISLAND
TROUT BAY OVERLOOK
DRIFTWOOD CAMPSITE
Trout Bay
HISTORIC CEMETERY
MURRAY BAY GROUP CAMPSITE
Murray Bay
Ice Cave
WILLIAMS LANDING
Passenger Ferry
POWELL LANDING
EAST CHANNEL LIGHT (ON PRIVATE PROPERTY)
HIAWATHA WATER TRAIL
28
SHIPWRECK DIVES AND TOURS
Munising Bay
Munising
Bayshore Park
H13
28
0   1 mi
0   1 km
© MOON.COM

beach where Echo Creek empties into Lake Superior. Unless you have limited mobility, outdoors enthusiasts will likely grow frustrated with the amount of time spent inside a vehicle. Tour prices include the ferry fee but not the $5 recreation-area user fee.

★ Hiawatha National Forest

A huge swath of the massive 860,000-acre Hiawatha National Forest sprawls out south of Munising, stretching all the way to Lake Michigan. It offers almost endless opportunities for hiking, mountain biking, and camping. Get information at the **Hiawatha National Forest Visitors Center** (400 E. Munising Ave., 906/387-3700, www.fs.fed.us), which shares a building and staff with the Pictured Rocks National Lakeshore. The Forest Service also maintains a very comprehensive network of cross-country skiing and snowshoeing trails throughout the West and East zones of the forest. Their website (www.fs.usda.gov/activity/hiawatha/recreation/wintersports) offers detailed maps and up-to-date report on the condition of each trail. The Forest Service also works with the Michigan DNR (www.michigan.gov/dnr) to maintain the many snowmobile trails that crisscross the forest.

Alger County Heritage Center

In Munising, a short way east of downtown on Washington Street, the **Alger County Heritage Center** (1496 Washington St., 906/387-4308, www.hsmichigan.org, noon-4pm Tues.-Sat., donation) keeps a fine collection of local historical artifacts that document the region's past. Visitors can peek at personal artifacts, Grand Island artifacts that include a log cabin from John Jacob Astor's American Fur Company, and Munising woodenware, including serving pieces, barrels, and other types of wood products.

Bayshore Park

At Munising's waterfront, the pleasant **Bayshore Park** provides a place for travelers to stretch their legs, enjoy a relaxing picnic, and admire the marina. In addition to the views of Grand Island just offshore and plenty of picnic tables, take time to visit the lovely Alger County Veterans Memorial Park, where the walkway bricks are engraved with names and messages honoring American soldiers; you can see artillery, a statue, and a monument.

Christmas

If you're driving into Munising from the west along M-28, you'll pass through Christmas, a small hardscrabble town that is most notable for Kewadin Casino and the world's tallest Santa, the tallest Old Woman in the Shoe, and the largest concrete Frosty the Snowman.

Kewadin Casino

Thankfully, there's more in Christmas than a year-round gift shop and a huge Santa. The **Kewadin Casino** (N7761 Candy Cane Lane, 906/387-5475, www.kewadinchristmas.com) is located in Christmas, only a few miles west of Munising. With table games like blackjack, three- and four-card poker, and Let It Ride, in addition to slots, the Kewadin has some of the best U.P. gaming. Enjoy a bite to eat at Frosty's Pub 'n Grub, a moderately priced bistro.

Lighthouses

Most of Grand Island's private property is on the thumb, including the unique **East Channel Light,** an 1867 wooden lighthouse made of hand-hewn timbers. Although the lighthouse has suffered from vandalism and neglect over the decades, recent years have proved more promising. In 1999 the Alger County Historical Society raised money to save the structure. To date, the timber sill and floor joists have been replaced, and the exterior walls have been strengthened. With the assistance of Northern Michigan University, restoration work is continuing. The lighthouse and the surrounding land are privately owned, so no tours or public access is allowed, but you can view it at a distance from Sand Point on the mainland, or from your tour boat as you explore Pictured Rocks National Lakeshore.

On North Point, the **North Light** has just a 25-foot (8-meter) tower, but since it rises from a 175-foot (53-meter) cliff, it earns the honor of being the highest above sea level. The 1867 building is now a well-cared-for private summer residence. Respect the owner's privacy and stay off the property. The two **Munising Range Lighthouses** were built in 1908 to help ships navigate the passage to the east and south of Grand Island; both are still operating today. The front tower is 58 feet (18 meters) tall, while the rear light is 33 feet (10 meters)

tall. The lights and station building are not open to the public. The two **Grand Island Harbor Range Lights** serve the same purpose for the west passage.

ENTERTAINMENT
Microbrewery

East Channel Brewing Co. (209 Maple St., Munising, 906/387-3007, www.eastchannelbrewery.com, noon-10pm daily) is an unpretentious, no-nonsense place where their pub beers, as they call them, take center stage. Offerings range from classics, like their Old Tru's IPA and their Shack Happy Maple Brown Ale, to some more creative concoctions, such as Bucket Brigade Maple Coffee Blend and Powell's Point Punch. From late May through mid-October, their partner The Cooking Carberry offers a selection of freshly baked pizzas in the outdoor beer garden.

SUMMER RECREATION
Hiking and Biking Trails
Rock River Canyon Wilderness Area

A favorite spot in **Hiawatha National Forest** is the **Rock River Canyon Wilderness Area.** In this undisturbed corner of the national forest, about 12 miles (19.3 km) west of Munising, the Rock River and Silver Creek have carved deep crevices in the sandstone, forming dark, narrow canyons. Adding to the area's wild beauty is **Rock River Falls,** which pours 20 feet (6 meters) over a sandstone ledge. There are a few developed hiking trails in the area, but you can also make your way along old logging roads and railroad grades. The canyons themselves require some scrambling for the adventurous. If you plan to explore the area, be sure to bring a compass and a topographic map, which are available from the visitors center.

To reach the wilderness area, take M-28 west from Munising. About 5 miles (8 km) west of Au Train, watch for Rock River Road, also called County Road H-01, on the left. Follow it to Forest Road 2276 and turn right (west). Within 4 miles (6.4 km), you'll arrive at Forest Road 2293; turn south and travel 0.75

miles (1.2 km) to a small parking area. A short trail leads down to the canyon and falls.

Grand Island

About 50 miles (80 km) of trails crisscross **Grand Island,** mostly old roadbeds. If you're just visiting for a day, a mountain bike is the only way you'll have time to see the entire island; it's a 23-mile (37-km) trip around the perimeter. It's probably one of the best mountain bike routes in the U.P. for nontechnical riders, with wide, grassy paths cutting through hardwood forests, passing under towering pines, snuggling up against Lake Superior shorelines, and providing spectacular views of wilderness bays and the distant Pictured Rocks.

Both hikers and bikers can reach **Murray Bay,** about 2 miles (3.2 km) from the ferry dock at the southern end of the island. Murray Bay has a nice day-use area and a sand beach nestled in a grove of pines. There are also two campsites here, but the location near the ferry dock will limit your privacy.

North of Murray Bay, the island sprouts a tombolo, known as "the thumb," off its southeastern corner. This landmass wraps north and forms **Trout Bay,** a lovely spot ringed with honey-hued beaches and sandstone cliffs. Watch for the low profile of loons bobbing in calm waters. Trout Bay is home to the island's four other developed campsites, some of the most attractive you'll find. From Wick Point off Murray Bay on the southern tip of the island, a diagonal hiking trail leads to the shore of Trout Bay, where it intersects with a shared hiking/biking trail that continues west from Little Dunes I and II before terminating at the Trout Bay Overlook, where you can see directly across the bay to Cobbler Cove. The combined length is approximately 4.5 miles (7.2 km).

Farther north, the island's most interesting trails follow the eastern and western shorelines. The **eastern shore** climbs high above lake level, offering occasional outstanding views of Pictured Rocks and the Grand Sable Dunes. The **western shore** provides ample opportunities to reach the fine sand beaches that line much of this side of the island. The island's interior trails are largely wooded and somewhat less interesting, unless you're hoping to spot a black bear. This shouldn't be too difficult as they're quite plentiful. Hiking the full length of the eastern shore is approximately 10.5 miles (16.9 km). The western shore is slightly longer at 11 miles (17.7 km).

Canoeing and Kayaking

Paddlers will enjoy **Trout Bay** on Grand Island, which features some sea caves along its eastern shore and interesting paddling around the thumb. It's a full two-day journey around the entire island—a trip you'll remember and an outstanding way to experience this superlative parcel of the Upper Peninsula.

The **Hiawatha Water Trail** (www.michiganwatertrails.org) is another excellent way to explore the Lake Superior shoreline in a sea kayak. Bookended by Big Bay to the west and Grand Marais to the east, the water trail stretches in either direction away from Munising and Grand Island. Get a map from **Northern Waters Adventures** (712 Munising Ave., 906/387-2323, www.northernwaters.com) in Munising. You can also rent sea or recreational kayaks from Northern Waters, as well as sign up for a guided day trip or overnight trip.

Fishing

Echo Lake is near the center of **Grand Island.** It offers great bass and northern pike fishing for anyone with a Michigan fishing license, but access can be a little tricky, since it is largely ringed with marshy grasses. You can also fish areas of **Munising Bay** such as Sand Point and the Anna River.

Ice fishing is particularly good on Grand Island too. The more remote northern end of the island is perhaps its most impressive part, with high cliffs, creeks, and untouched beaches. In recent years, peregrine falcons have nested nearby.

Golf

The **Pictured Rocks Golf and Country**

Club (10240 County Rd. H-58, 906/387-3970, $29 for 18 holes, cart $14) is an 18-hole, 6,246-yard course in Munising. Pictured Rocks is the county's only golf course, and it's a good one. The clubhouse has a restaurant and a well-stocked pro shop. Take M-28 to East Munising Avenue before continuing on Munising-Van Meer-Shingleton Road (County Rd. H-58) to the golf course.

Another type of golfing adventure can be had at Munising's **Miners Falls Mini Golf** (E9558 M-28 E., Munising, 906/387-4653, 4pm-10pm Mon.-Thurs., noon-10pm Sat., noon-9pm Sun. May-Sept., $10) on M-28.

Off-Road Vehicles

Even though there are no state ORV trails near Munising, there's still plenty of opportunity for off-roading, thanks to the vast stretch of **Hiawatha National Forest** (400 E. Munising Ave., 906/387-2512, www.fs.fed.us) that blankets the U.P. all the way down to St. Ignace. You can't ride on any road you choose, however. Contact the U.S. Forest Service for a Motor Vehicle Usage Map, which details miles of forest roads open to ORVs. Bear in mind that there are numerous patches of privately owned land scattered throughout the forest. Please respect private property and stay on federal forest roads.

Waterfalls

The Munising area sports an incredible density of waterfalls, which run the gamut from easy to difficult to reach. Among the latter, **Rock River Falls,** located about 25 miles (40 km) from Munising in the Rock River Canyon Wilderness, is especially worthwhile. **Munising Visitors Bureau** (500 E. M-28, 906/387-1717, www.munising.org) prints a helpful waterfall map that will direct you to all 17 waterfalls in Alger County. Nearby **Pictured Rocks National Lakeshore** also contains several notable falls.

1: Laughing Whitefish Falls 2: great white trillium growing in Hiawatha National Forest 3: East Channel Light

Just on the edge of town near M-28 is **Horseshoe Falls.** Follow M-28 to Prospect Street, turn left, proceed two blocks to Bell Avenue, and turn left again. Farther south on M-28 you'll see **Alger Falls,** which spills down along the highway. The impressive and serene **Wagner Falls** is nearby, just off M-94 near the junction with M-28. A perennial favorite, it's in a well-marked spot and is operated by the state park system as a scenic place. Though it feels secluded, 20-foot (6-meter) Wagner Falls is just a five-minute walk from the parking area. Continue up the streamside trail past the main falls to the second cascade. About 20 miles (32 km) west of Munising, you'll find picturesque **Laughing Whitefish Falls,** which enjoys protection as a state park scenic site. Water plunges 30 feet (9 meters) over hard dolomite rock ledges, then continues rolling and frothing twice that distance to the bottom of a gorge. To reach Laughing Whitefish Falls, follow M-94 west from Munising to Sundell, then go north on Dorsey Road for 2.5 miles (4 km).

TOP EXPERIENCE

★ Diving
Alger Underwater Preserve

When loggers were felling the vast stands of pine across the central Upper Peninsula in the 1800s, Munising grew into a busy port, with schooners carrying loads of timber to the growing cities of the southern Great Lakes and iron ore to an ever-growing number of factories. The narrow and shoal-ridden passage between the mainland and Grand Island and along the Pictured Rocks shoreline was the ruin of many ships; their skeletons litter the lake floor here.

The **Alger Underwater Preserve** covers 113 square miles (293 sq km), from just west of Grand Island to Au Sable Point near the east end of Pictured Rocks National Lakeshore. Visit www.michiganpreserves.org to download *A Diver's Guide to Michigan Underwater Preserves* for invaluable advice on planning your expedition, including information on equipment and proper safety precautions. The preserve is home to 15 ships, all well pre-served in the cold freshwater of Lake Superior. Some wrecks, like the 19th-century *Bermuda* and the 145-foot *Smith Moore*, stand upright and nearly intact. Many of the dive sites in the preserve are marked with buoys to help ensure that they are protected from poachers. Removing or disturbing artifacts in any Great Lakes underwater preserve is a felony under Michigan law.

Several factors make the Alger Underwater Preserve one of the finest sport diving locations in the Midwest, including excellent visibility of the wreckage of 15 wrecks from depths of 6-105 feet (2-32 meters). While the water is certainly cold, the presence of Grand Island moderates the temperatures slightly, making the dive a bit more comfortable. "It's one of the best wreck diving sites for beginners that I can imagine," notes Pete Lindquist, who operates a dive charter in Munising.

There are also preserves in Whitefish Point, Marquette, Keweenaw, and the Straits of Mackinac. The Keweenaw Underwater Preserve has several wrecks, but they're spread farther apart than in Alger, and are located at greater depths, some more than 200 feet (60 meters) down.

Just offshore from Munising High School, an **underwater museum** among dock ruins includes submarine signs that interpret large maritime artifacts. The Alger Underwater Preserve also attracts divers for its **sea caves** in about 20 feet (6 meters) of water, where sandstone cliffs have been eroded by wave action.

Charter Services

To arrange a dive charter, contact **Lake Superior Shipwreck Diving** (1204 Commercial St., Munising, 906/387-4477, www.shipwrecktours.com, $100 per diver for a trip to two shipwreck sites, with a two-diver minimum). Open Water certification is required.

These charter services cover eastern Lake Superior but can also rent equipment to divers headed to other parts of the U.P.: **Abyss Dive Charters** (616/295-6542, www.abyssdivecharters.com) in Mackinaw City services divers in northern lower Michigan and in Whitefish Bay. **Great Lakes Divers** (400 Cedar St., Alpena, 989/916-9990) in Alpena offers charters to the Straits of Mackinac Shipwreck Preserve and to the Thunder Bay National Marine Sanctuary in Lake Huron. You'll want to dive in the warmer months with scuba gear and a full wetsuit, as the waters can be cold, and get even colder as you descend. For both companies, prices and schedules vary widely; call for details.

★ Shipwreck Tours

If you do just one thing in the Munising area, do a fascinating two-hour tour with **Grand Island Shipwreck Tours** (1204 Commercial St., 906/387-4477, www.shipwrecktours.com, $38 adults, $34 seniors, $14 ages 6-12, $1 children under 6). The boat glides directly over shipwrecks, some in as little as 28 feet (9 meters) of water. The view through the 8- to 10-foot-long windows is truly remarkable, with the ships filling the windows like historic paintings, perfectly visible in the clear water and looking close enough to touch. On the *Bermuda*, you can easily make out deck lines, hatches, and even piles of iron ore lying on the deck. Weather permitting, the tour visits three shipwrecks dating from 1860 to 1926. Along the way, the knowledgeable crew also shares history and points out other sights, including the wooden East Channel Light along the shore of Grand Island. Contact **Grand Island Shipwreck Tours** for schedules and to make reservations, which are recommended.

WINTER RECREATION
Ski and Snowshoe Trails

Four miles (6.4 km) south of Munising, in the **Hiawatha National Forest,** the **Valley Spur** ski trail system (E8017 M-94, 906/387-4918, www.valleyspur.org, day pass $10, 3-day pass $25, free under age 19) has some 27 miles (43 km) of groomed trails ranging in difficulty from easy to expert. Loops range 1-7 miles

(1.6-11.3 km). The Valley Spur lodge is open most weekends for warmth and a hot beverage. To get to Valley Spur, take M-94 south.

The **Munising Ski Trail** begins a few miles east of town and skirts close to the Superior shoreline in Pictured Rocks National Lakeshore. Most of the loops on the nearly 12-mile (19.3-km) trail are rated for easy to intermediate skiing. Lengths vary from less than 1 mile to 2.5 miles (1.6-4 km). You'll want to be careful to stay on the trails too, as many sections are located along the tops of sheer cliffs. These make for beautiful sightseeing, but be sure to exercise caution. For more information, contact the **National Park Service** (906/387-3700, www.nps.gov/piro).

Another year-round trail option is **Bruno's Run,** which lies just south of Wetmore on Federal Forest Highway 13. The trailhead is on the eastern shore of Moccasin Lake. From this starting point, the trail runs in a circular loop for about 12 miles (19.3 km) and offers a diversity of views—forest, shoreline, and lakes. Bruno's Run is rated as moderately challenging.

An excellent source to rent cross-country skis and other winter sports gear is **South Bay Outfitters** (120 Superior St., Munising, 906/387-4004, 10am-5pm Tues.-Fri., 10am-1pm Sat.).

Snowmobiling

Trail 417 leaves Marquette and takes you east to Au Train before hooking south to catch **Trail 8** (heading west, 8 will take you to Gwinn). Take Trail 8 east to follow the Pictured Rocks National Lakeshore all the way into Paradise and Whitefish Point. To get to Munising, head north on **Trail 7** or **419.** If you're interested in heading south, Trails 7 and 41 will take you there, connecting you to the miles upon miles of U.P. snowmobile trails. There are more than 300 miles (480 km) of trails in Alger County alone, so you won't need to leave the county unless you want to. To get a state trail permit, contact the **Michigan DNR** (www.michigan.gov/dnr).

An excellent source to rent snowmobiling and other winter sports gear is **South Bay Outfitters** (120 Superior St., Munising, 906/387-4004, 10am-5pm Tues.-Fri., 10am-1pm Sat.).

Ice Fishing

Many of the locations that provide good summertime fishing do just as well for ice fishing when the water freezes over. Try **Anna River** and the rest of **Munising Bay,** where you can break through the ice and angle for whitefish, lake trout, northern pike, and more.

An excellent source to rent ice fishing and other winter sports gear is **South Bay Outfitters** (120 Superior St., Munising, 906/387-4004, 10am-5pm Tues.-Fri., 10am-1pm Sat.).

Ice Sports

For winter recreation that's less conventional than skiing or snowmobiling, try **ice climbing** on **Grand Island.** Ice formations form on the sandstone cliffs on the east side of the island, and once the channel and bay begin to freeze over, ice climbers can tackle the 20- to 90-foot-high (6- to 27-meter) ice sheets. The **ice caves** just north of Eben Junction and west of Munising make for tamer recreation, but they're still impressive in their own way. Take snowmobile Trail 8 out of town to the caves that form when water seeping through the walls of Rock River Gorge freezes over. Ice climbing does carry some risk, so exercise appropriate caution.

FOOD

For a town on the edge of a national lakeshore that presumably gets a fair amount of tourist traffic, Munising has surprisingly little in the way of dining. One destination for classic choices is the **Driftwood Deli** (231 E. Superior St., 906/387-1443, www.driftwood-deli.com, 9am-3pm Sun.-Thurs., 9am-8pm Fri.-Sat., $12-20). This is a great place to find pastrami and Italian grinders, basically submarine sandwiches. There's also a variety of paninis. **Muldoon's Pasties** (1246 W. M-28, 906/387-5880, www.muldoonspasties.com,

10am-7pm daily, $10-13) is the best spot in town for a fresh, authentic taste of the pasty, a potpie-type meal that's a true U.P. classic.

Looking for something a bit out of the ordinary? Try **The Duck Pond Eatery** (E7974 M-28, Munising, 906/387-1689, https://duckpondeatery.com, $8-16), which features a mostly meatless menu. Examples include Lake Superior whitefish tacos blackened or deep fried, and a black bean burger. Meat options are offered, including a barbecue pulled pork sandwich.

If pizza is on your mind, there are two attractive options. **Main Street Pizza** (113 Maple St., 906/387-3993, 11am-11pm Mon.-Thurs., 11am-midnight Fri.-Sat., noon-11pm Sun., under $10) offers a tempting array of pizza with various toppings and salads, as well as a few Mexican items. **Pictured Rocks Pizza** (106 Birch St., 906/387-5700, noon-9pm Tues.-Sun., $10-20) makes fresh oven-baked pizza right before your eyes in either traditional or "personal" (nine-inch) sizes. Almost any topping imaginable is offered.

If you're willing to take a little drive, one of the better restaurants in the Upper Peninsula is about 15 miles (24 km) west of Munising in Au Train. Along the curve of Lake Superior's Au Train Bay on M-28, the ★ **Brownstone Inn** (E4635 W. M-28, Au Train, 906/892-8332, 11am-8pm Tues.-Thurs., 11am-9pm Fri.-Sat., noon-8pm Sun., $17-40) serves up original and ever-changing dishes, including delicious versions of the ubiquitous Lake Superior whitefish, Canadian salmon, extra jumbo gulf shrimp, and choice Angus steaks. There are good vegetarian options and an excellent Friday-night fish fry too.

ACCOMMODATIONS

The ★ **Sunset Motel on the Bay** (1315 E. Bay St., 906/387-4574, www.sunsetmotelonthebay.com, $$) has a great location right on Munising Bay at the east end of town. There are 15 rooms, and the motel's three suites ($$$) have kitchenettes; each of the rooms faces the bay. It's a great find with great rates. Wireless Internet access is

free, and pets are welcome. The downtown **Munising Motel** (332 E. Onota St., 906/387-3187, https://munisingmotel.com, $$) has 12 recently renovated rooms within walking distance of the city dock and Pictured Rocks Cruises. Another good option is the **Terrace Motel** (420 Prospect St., 906/387-2735, www.exploringthenorth.com/terrace/terr.html, $), close enough to downtown to easily access its restaurants and other amenities, but far enough to provide a secluded atmosphere.

Most lodgings along M-28 on Munising's near east side are within walking distance of downtown and the waterfront. The are has some nice and tidy small motels like the **Superior Motel and Suites** (500 E. M-28, 906/387-1600, www.superior-motel.com, $$) and the **Pictured Rocks Inn and Suites** (420 M-28, 906/387-2493, www.picturedrocksinn.com, $$), which is close to the center of town and offers an indoor pool. Two miles (3.2 km) east of Munising, the **Alger Falls Motel** (E9427 M-28, 906/387-3536, www.algerfallsmotel.com, $$) has 16 rooms and a housekeeping cottage. Dogs under 30 pounds (13.6 kg) are allowed for a small additional charge.

Camping

There are no reservations, fees, or permits required for camping on **Grand Island.** The island has two designated campgrounds at **Murray Bay** (two sites) and **Trout Bay** (four sites), offering the relative luxury of pit toilets and fire rings. Backcountry camping is permitted throughout the island as long as you stay off the tombolo and private property and are at least 100 feet (30 meters) away from lakes, streams, cliffs, trails, roads, and natural research areas. No ground fires are permitted. And remember, drinking water is not available anywhere on the island, so come prepared.

For ultimate convenience—and the luxury of seclusion—**Bay Furnace** (no reservations, $20) in **Hiawatha National Forest** is a good choice. Just west of Munising and north of M-28, it offers 50 rustic sites with a very nice setting next to Lake Superior and overlooking Grand Island. Some sites almost have their own private stretch of beach, and a short cross-country ski trail at the campground's north end gives campers a little extra breathing room. Near the day-use area, you can examine the remains of the old charcoal furnace that at one time produced 20 tons of iron a day. During its heyday in the 1870s, as many as eight steamers at a time would line up at docks, bringing in wood to fuel the furnace and hauling away iron. Take M-28 west from Munising to Christmas and turn north at the Forest Service campground sign.

The Hiawatha National Forest has several other designated campgrounds nearby. Contact the **Hiawatha Visitors Center** (400 E. Munising Ave., 906/387-3700, www.fs.fed.us) for more information and directions.

Families gravitate to the **Munising/Pictured Rocks KOA** (906/387-3315, https://koa.com/campgrounds/pictured-rocks, from $45) on M-28, 3 miles (4.8 km) east of Munising. It has 89 sites in a nice wooded setting. What you lose in wilderness you gain in kid-friendly amenities like an outdoor pool, basketball courts, and a recreation room.

INFORMATION AND SERVICES

You can get all of the visitor information you need from the **Munising Visitors Bureau** (422 E. Munising Ave., 906/387-1717, www.munising.org).

For immediate medical care, make your way to **Munising Memorial Hospital** (1500 Sand Point Rd., 906/387-4110, www.munisingmemorial.org), a small community hospital just north and east of town. Take East Munising Avenue where it splits from M-28 and follow it northeast to Washington Street; turn left and follow Washington to the hospital.

There aren't as many banks in Munising as in Marquette, but you shouldn't have trouble finding one if you urgently need cash. In the center of town is the main office of **Peoples**

State Bank of Munising (100 E. Superior St., 906/387-2006, www.psbup.com).

GETTING THERE AND AROUND
Car

To get to Munising by car, take M-28 from Marquette and points west. You'll pass through Au Train and Christmas along the way, and you'll be continuously rewarded with views of Lake Superior and Munising Bay, some of the more picturesque locations in the Upper Peninsula. If you're coming from the east, M-28 merges with M-94, which heads north from Manistique and the Lake Michigan shore. It's more of a back road, but you can take Forest Highway 13 (H-13) north from Nahma Junction on US 2.

Air

Munising's closest commercial airport is **Sawyer International Airport** (MQT, 125 G Ave., Gwinn, 906/346-3308, www.sawyerairport.com), just south of Marquette, a little less than an hour away, which has scheduled flights from Detroit on **Delta Airlines** (800/221-1212, www.delta.com) and from Chicago O'Hare on **American Airlines** (800/433-7300, www.aa.com). There's no scheduled ground transportation from the airport, so you'll need to rent a car; try **Alamo** (800/462-5266, www.alamo.com), **Avis** (800/831-1212, www.avis.com), **Budget** (800/527-7000, www.budget.com), **Enterprise** (800/736-8227, www.enterprise.com), or **National** (800/227-7368, www.nationalcar.com).

Boat

Consider yourself fortunate if you're arriving in Munising by boat. You'll be able to sail past the Pictured Rocks National Lakeshore, an unbelievably scenic stretch of shoreline with plunging cliffs and, in places, very shallow waters. And then you'll sail past beautiful Grand Island into Munising Bay on your way to **Munising-Bayshore Marina** (906/387-3445, https://cityofmunising.org/marina, mid-May–mid-Oct.). The marina's 24 floating slips have access to potable water, electricity, and restrooms. Nearby, there's a pleasant park with picnic tables and benches and plenty of lawn. Contact the harbormaster on channel 16 or 18. The marina is located at 46°24.52 N, 86°39.06 W.

The Grand Island Ferry Service (906/387-2600, http://grandislandup.com, daily Memorial Day–early Oct., $23 adults, $15 children, free under age 6) provides transit between Munising and Grand Island. There's a $10 additional charge for bicycles. Call for a current schedule. The ferry's departure point is about 2 miles (3.2 km) west of downtown near Powell Point; follow M-28 west and watch for the signs. Even if you're planning just a day trip, you'd be wise to pack some warm clothing and a method for purifying water. Rough weather can cancel ferry service at any time. It's also easy to lose track of time and miss the last ferry. There is a ship-to-shore radio at Williams Landing in the event of an emergency. **Private boats** may be pulled ashore at Williams Landing and Trout Bay, and moored offshore in Murray Bay and Trout Bay.

Bus

Although there is no bus service to Munising, regional **Alger County Transit** buses (Altran, 906/387-4845, www.altranbus.com, $8) run between Munising and Marquette. Altran also provides dial-a-ride service for a fee. Call at least 24 hours in advance for reservations.

Pictured Rocks and Grand Marais

Lake Superior takes center stage at Pictured Rocks National Lakeshore. Although the national lakeshore is just 3 miles (4.8 km) wide, it sports a length of 42 miles (68 km), showcasing a huge swath of magnificent shoreline from Munising to Grand Marais. Pictured Rocks derives its name from the sandstone bluffs that rise directly from the water's surface, washed in shades of pink, red, and green from the mineral-rich water that seeps from the rock. These photogenic cliffs stretch for more than 15 miles (24 km), occasionally forming sculptures of crazy castle-like turrets, caves, and arches. The national lakeshore also features a lesser-known but equally spectacular stretch of shoreline called the Grand Sable Banks, where 200-foot (60-meter) sand dunes are hemmed by a 12-mile (19.3-km) ribbon of sand and pebble beach. You'll also find lakes, forest trails, waterfalls, a lighthouse, and other historic attractions.

Pictured Rocks' season is short. Most of the park's 300,000 annual visitors arrive in July and August, when they're most likely to enjoy summer weather and daytime temperatures in the 70s (21-26°C). Visit in June and you'll share the park with fewer people, but the blackflies and mosquitoes can be onerous. September may be the park's finest month, but it can be cold.

No matter when you go, pack plenty of warm clothing along with shorts. Even at the height of summer, evenings are almost always cool, dipping into the 50s (10-15°C). The giant refrigerator that is Lake Superior, where the water temperature rarely climbs out of the 40s (4-9°C), can put a chill in the air near the shoreline. In fact, a Lake Superior beach on a sweltering August afternoon may be the most refreshing place on earth.

SIGHTS
★ Pictured Rocks National Lakeshore

Most people never lose their fascination with beautiful displays of nature. Hugging the Lake Superior coastline for 42 miles (68 km), **Pictured Rocks National Lakeshore** (906/387-3700, www.nps.gov/piro) is an archetypical example. Generations of writers,

Pictured Rocks National Lakeshore

0   4 mi
0   4 km

Lake Superior

Grand Marais

GRAND SABLE VISITOR CENTER (SUMMER ONLY)

WOODLAND PARK

Sable Falls

Grand Sable Dunes

AU SABLE LIGHT STATION

Grand Sable Banks

Grand Sable Lake

Au Sable Point

LOG SLIDE OVERLOOK

HURRICANE RIVER

Hurricane River

TWELVEMILE BEACH

Lake Superior State Forest

Alger Underwater Preserve

Lakeshore Trail

KINGSTON LAKE

H58

Twelvemile Beach

PICTURED ROCKS NATIONAL LAKESHORE

Little Beaver Lake

Beaver Lake

LITTLE BEAVER LAKE

HIAWATHA NATIONAL FOREST

Spray Falls

Spray Creek

Chapel Beach

Chapel Lake

Grand Portal Point

Chapel Falls

CHAPEL RD

Mosquito Falls

Melstrand

Mosquito River

H58

MINERS CASTLE

Miners Falls

Alger Underwater Preserve

MINERS CASTLE RD

Miners Creek

Grand Island National Recreation Area

Sand Point

NATIONAL LAKESHORE HEADQUARTERS

GRAND ISLAND

MUNISING FALLS INTERPRETIVE CENTER

28

Munising Falls

PICTURED ROCKS CRUISES

MUNISING/ PICTURED ROCKS KOA

Munising Bay

Alger Falls

Munising

MUNISING INFORMATION CENTER

SHIPWRECK DIVES AND TOURS

Hiawatha National Forest

28

94

© MOON.COM

artists, and photographers have been inspired by the colorful hues of its escarpments. In 1820 the geologist Henry Rowe Schoolcraft visited Pictured Rocks and described it as having "some of the most sublime and commanding views of nature." In 1966 Congress saw the need to protect this prized area and established Pictured Rocks National Lakeshore—the first such property in the nation—under the authority of the National Park Service.

For a full 15 miles (24 km), massive sandstone cliffs tower over the lake, some reaching heights of 200 feet (60 meters). Because of the multidimensional geology of the area, the colors of various minerals combine with the groundwater to create streaks of red (from iron), yellow-brown (limonite), and pink-green (copper). Other physical features lie within the park's borders, including sand dunes and waterfalls, but for most visitors, the colorful cliffs are the main attraction. With a few exceptions, however, they can only be viewed from the water.

Mindful of this, local operators offer visitors of all abilities the opportunity to see and enjoy the cliffs. These include boat tours, sea kayaking, and hiking.

Pictured Rocks Cruises (906/387-2379, www.picturedrocks.com, Memorial Day-mid-Oct., $42 adults, $14 ages 4-12, $1 under age 4) offers three-hour trips up the shoreline from Munising, sidling up practically close enough to touch the rock formations while giving you the perspective to comprehend the turreted shapes like Miners Castle. Though trips are offered up to seven times a day, plan for either the late afternoon or sunset cruises, when the sinking sun shows off the multicolored sandstone in its best light, providing the best conditions for photographs. The boats depart from the Munising City Pier.

Kayaking offers the skillful paddler-photographer the chance to get some truly remarkable shots from otherwise impossible angles.

Munising Falls Area

The highlight of this spot used to be the trail that led hikers behind the 50-foot (15-meter) **Munising Falls,** but erosion problems prompted its closure. It's still worth a stop, though, for the falls and the adjacent **interpretive center,** which offers a glimpse of the history of this peaceful area, home to a belching pig-iron furnace in the 1860s.

Munising Falls also marks the west trailhead for the **Lakeshore Trail.** A 43-mile (69-km) segment of the North Country National Scenic Trail, the Lakeshore Trail runs the length of the Pictured Rocks National Lakeshore. The eastern trailhead lies near Sable Falls.

Past Munising Falls, the paved access road ends at **Sand Point,** home of the **National Lakeshore Headquarters** (N8391 Sand Point Rd., 906/387-2607, www.nps.gov/piro). While the headquarters houses offices and not visitor services, it displays some interesting Coast Guard and shipwreck artifacts on its grounds. Sand Point has a small beach and a boat ramp, a good spot to launch a small craft for exploring nearby Grand Island.

Miners Castle

For whatever reason, many people choose to assign synthetic names to natural geographic features. The sandstone cliffs 5 miles (8 km) northeast of Munising Falls are known as **Miners Castle** for the turret-like shapes caused by wind and wave erosion. The nine-story-high rock formation is most impressive and ranks as one of the park's most popular attractions. Boardwalks and steps lead to two viewing platforms out on the rock, where you can peer down into the gloriously clear waters of Lake Superior. If that entices you to do a little beachcombing and wading, a nearby trail leads down some steps through the pines to the inviting **Miners Beach.**

To reach Miners Castle, follow County Road H-58 east from Munising to the well-marked turnoff for Miners Castle Road. Before you reach the Miners Castle formation itself, you'll see another sign on Miners Castle Road directing you to **Miners Falls.** It's a fairly easy 1-mile (1.6-km) round-trip walk to these pleasant falls, where Miners Creek tumbles 40 feet (12 meters) over a rocky escarpment.

Chapel Basin Area

Continuing northeast on County Road H-58, the next auto-accessible route into the heart of the park is at Melstrand, where the gravel-and-dirt Chapel Road bumps 6 miles (9.7 km) toward the shore and another park highlight, the Chapel Basin area. Park your car here, and you'll find plenty to entertain you during a long day hike or weekend: three waterfalls, a deep inland lake, Superior beaches, and a good loop hiking trail. **Chapel Falls** is the key attraction, as evidenced by the 1.5-mile (2.4-km) paved pathway that leads to it.

If you turn left instead of right at Chapel Beach, you can make a 10-mile (16-km) loop around **Chapel Basin.** Along the way, you'll pass **Grand Portal Point,** another significant Pictured Rocks landmark, before returning to the parking area. Don't leave Chapel Basin without a visit to **Mosquito Falls,** which is a bit farther inland off Chapel Road. The Mosquito River spills over a series of ledges, creating an accessible waterfall calm enough for wading and soaking fatigued hiking feet. A trail leads to various sections of the falls and links up with the Lakeshore Trail.

Beaver Lake

Located near the center of the park, 800-acre **Beaver Lake** is the largest inland lake in Pictured Rocks. Anglers are drawn to the lake and the tributaries that feed it, especially for trout. **Little Beaver Lake,** connected by a small channel, has a boat launch. Boats are limited to 10 hp or less, making this a pleasant waterway for paddlers. Little Beaver also has one of the park's three auto-accessible campgrounds, with eight sites available on a first-come, first-served basis. Be aware that

1: Twelvemile Beach 2: Miners Falls 3: Pictured Rocks National Lakeshore at dusk

wetlands cover much of the terrain between Beaver Lake and Lake Superior, so bugs can be a problem, especially in June and early July.

Lighthouse

It's a 1.5-mile (2.4-km) walk along the Lakeshore Trail from the Hurricane River campground to the **Au Sable Light Station** at Au Sable Point. Built in 1874, the 87-foot (27-meter) brick light and its keepers did yeoman's duty for decades—warning ships away from the rock shoals that extend out for nearly a mile and create shallows of just 6-30 feet (2-9 meters). Nonetheless, at least 10 steamers met their demise here. As you walk the trail from the campground, look for parts of the **shipwrecks** just offshore, which often poke out of the sandy bottom and are easily visible in the crystal-clear water. The light was automated in 1958.

Several recent restoration projects involved renovating the lightkeeper's quarters, rehabilitating the landscape, and installing a photovoltaic (solar-powered) system to power the site. **Tours** are offered from mid-June through September (906/387-3700, 11am-4:30pm Wed.-Sun. July-mid-Aug., $3, free under age 6).

North Country National Scenic Trail

As part of its trek across the Upper Peninsula, the **North Country National Scenic Trail** runs the full length of Pictured Rocks, paralleling the Lakeshore Trail. One especially beautiful portion is a 2-mile (3.2-km) stretch running from the Log Slide to the **Au Sable Light Station.** After emerging from Pictured Rocks at Munising, the trail continues, generally hugging the Lake Superior shore.

Grand Sable Dunes

Just east of Au Sable Point, the **Log Slide Overlook** marks the site of a once busy logging operation. In the late 1800s, loggers used this high point—some 300 feet (90 meters) above Lake Superior—to send freshly cut logs down to the water's edge, where they were loaded onto Great Lakes schooners. Today,

you can stand on a platform and simply marvel at the view, with the lighthouse to the left, the great dunes to the right, and the brilliant blue of the big lake filling the horizon.

Grand Marais

Though not part of Pictured Rocks National Lakeshore, the little town of Grand Marais marks the park's eastern boundary and is an excellent jumping-off point for a visit to the national lakeshore. This sleepy New England-like village is worth a visit for its simple windswept beauty. With an outstanding natural harbor, rare on Lake Superior's southern shore, Grand Marais was originally settled by fishers. Loggers soon followed, when sawmills were built here in the 1860s and 1870s to handle the logging that went on just to the south.

While commercial fishing remains a component of the local economy, its fortunes have declined due to overharvesting and the arrival of invasive species. Instead, tourism has become the primary industry. The downtown straddles the harbor, which is a good spot to entice kayakers to play in the surf on a north-to-east wind. The few streets here also offer charming arts and crafts shops and a small number of clean, inexpensive motels and restaurants.

Follow the bay around to its western point to reach the pier. The adjacent Lake Superior shoreline offers a nice sand and pebble beach, which is closed if endangered piping plovers are nesting (Apr.-Aug.). Rock hounds should continue west along the beach, past the Woodland Park city campground, to reach a good spot for **hunting agates.**

Lake Superior State Forest

Traveling east from Beaver Basin, several dirt roads spiral south off County Road H-58 into the woods. These lead into the **Lake Superior State Forest,** part of the buffer zone protecting Pictured Rocks. Here you'll find plenty of inland lakes, hiking and biking trails, and rustic campgrounds. Many of these are overlooked by the summer visitors to the national lakeshore. For more information on the state forest, contact the **Michigan DNR** (www.michigan.gov/dnr). Topographic maps ($5) of the area are available at the **Hiawatha Visitors Center** (400 E. Munising Ave., Munising, 906/387-3700, www.fs.fed.us).

FESTIVALS AND EVENTS
Annual Grand Marais Music and Arts Festival

The second weekend of August is the time slated for the annual **Grand Marais Music and Crafts Festival** (906/494-2447, www.grandmaraismichigan.com), a much anticipated event that showcases local artists, talented bands of various genres, and an array of food vendors. The festival is held at Woodland Park, near Braziel and Millen Streets.

SUMMER RECREATION
Hiking and Biking

Pictured Rocks National Lakeshore (906/387-3700, www.nps.gov/piro) offers a variety of trails, ranging from short and easy to long and challenging.

Little Beaver Lake

Two good hiking trails leave from the campground at Little Beaver Lake. The short and pleasant 0.7-mile (1.1-km) **White Pine Trail** is a self-guided nature trail that circles through a 300-year-old pine forest. The 5-mile (8-km) **Beaver Basin Loop Trail** makes a lap around Little Beaver and Big Beaver Lakes, and then follows the Lake Superior shore past sea caves cut by the lake's pounding waves. Boardwalks skirt the wetlands before returning to the trailhead.

Grand Sable Banks and Dunes

The **Grand Sable Banks and Dunes** (*grand sable* is French for "great sands") stretch for nearly 5 miles (8 km) from the overlook, with glacial banks of gravel supporting the huge mounds of sand. They are magnificent when viewed from a distance, glowing gold and rising abruptly from the cobalt waters of Lake Superior. In many areas, especially near the overlook, the dunes are free of grasses and plants, so you can play around on them without fear of damaging fragile plant life or causing erosion.

Most people, however, choose to explore the dunes from the eastern end. Near the **Grand Sable Visitors Center** (E21090 County Rd. H-58, 906/494-2660, www.nps.gov/piro, 9am-5pm daily late May-Labor Day), a trail winds across the top of the dunes, where marram grass, beach pea, and sand cherry grow. Each plant binds to the sand and prevents shoreline erosion. Be careful to stay on the trail here. Interpretive signs discuss the plants' tenuous hold on the environment.

Miners Falls

A short, easy walk that can be tackled by almost any visitor is the **Miners Falls Trail.** This flat 1-mile (1.6-km) trek takes the hiker from a parking area to the majestic **Miners Falls.** It's a great way for a visitor with somewhat limited mobility to enjoy Pictured Rocks. Follow County Road H-58 east from Munising to the well-marked turnoff for Miners Castle Road. Before you reach the Miners Castle formation itself, you'll see another sign on Miners Castle Road directing you to Miners Falls.

Lakeshore Trail

The **Lakeshore Trail** is a 43-mile (69-km) segment of the **North Country National Scenic Trail** that spans seven states from New York to North Dakota. Running the length of the Pictured Rocks National Lakeshore, the trail never strays far from the water's edge.

Hikers typically take 4-5 days for the full **backpacking** trip. Backcountry camping permits (877/444-6777, www.recreation.gov) are essential. In addition to backcountry camping, there are three primitive campgrounds offer tent sites along Lakeshore Trail as it transits the park: Hurricane River, Twelve Mile Beach, and Little Beaver. The western trailhead is at Munising Falls Visitors Center (1505 Sand Point Rd., Munising); the eastern trailhead is at Grand Sable Visitors Center (E21090 County Rd. H-58). A shuttle specifically for backpackers runs to and from the two trailheads twice a day, stopping at a few parking areas en route.

TOP EXPERIENCE

Canoeing and Kayaking

Paddlers can get the best view of **Pictured Rocks National Lakeshore** by **sea kayak.** This will allow you to avoid the rather touristy narration of the Pictured Rocks Cruises tour and really experience the true grandeur of this shoreline. Safety concerns cannot be overemphasized, however. Only experienced paddlers should venture out on their own, and only in a closed cockpit (not a canoe) after carefully monitoring weather conditions. Paddlers can get themselves into serious trouble at Pictured Rocks if caught in sudden summer squalls along the 15-mile (24-km) rock wall without shelter. Having said that, sea kayaking along Pictured Rocks ranks as one of the finest paddles on the Great Lakes.

★ Hiawatha Water Trail

The stretch of Pictured Rocks and Lake Superior shoreline leading into Grand Marais is also the easternmost stretch of the **Hiawatha Water Trail** (www. hiawathawatertrail.org), which ends here, 120 miles (193 km) from its starting point in Big Bay. If you're heading in the opposite direction, it's the beginning of a long and satisfying journey in a sea kayak. Either way, the Pictured Rocks portion between Munising and Grand Marais is the trail's most beautiful stretch. There are at least 20 public access points and 23 water-accessible campsites along the way. The Hiawatha Water Trail has an official map, which can be obtained at **Down Wind Sports** (906/226-7112, www. downwindsports.com) in Marquette or at the **Pictured Rocks/Hiawatha National Forest Visitor Center** (1505 Sand Point Rd., Munising, 906/387-3700).

Kayak Tours

If you're unsure of your abilities, hook up with **Northern Waters** (129 E. Munising Ave., Munising, 906/387-2323, www. northernwaters.com). The company offers outstanding guided trips (full-day $169 adults, $149 ages 8-11, half-day $129 adults, $109 ages 8-11, minimum guest weight 75 pounds), ferrying guests and boats to a departure point at Miners Castle. Beginners are welcome, since the day includes some basic instruction and you'll be traveling in a tandem kayak with an experienced guide. Kayak rentals (and longer trips to Grand Island and Isle Royale) are also available.

Another potential partner is **Pictured Rocks Kayaking** (1348 Commercial St., Munising, 906/387-5500, www. paddlepicturedrocks.com, $168 adults, $158 children 5-12), which offers paddlers the opportunity to launch from their host ship and safely explore the rocks. The four- to five-hour tour includes two hours of kayaking. They also offer shorter tours of Miners Castle and Grand Island.

Beaches

A sign near the **Twelvemile Beach** campground says it all. It displays an icon of a swimmer not in the usual crawl position, but with water lapping at their ankles. In other words, the water here is bone-chilling cold; swim if you dare, but wading is really more realistic. It's this cold water that keeps Twelvemile Beach the pristine, stunning ribbon of sand that it is. If such a perfect beach boasted 75°F water, it would be overrun with Jet Skis and zinc oxide. Instead, this is a place where you can stroll for hours with only the company of peregrine falcons, bald eagles, and deer wandering down for a drink. You might even catch the occasional black bear snorting around in the sand.

The Twelvemile Beach campground is easy to reach, just a short drive off County Road H-58 through a pretty birch forest. Use the well-placed stairs to reach the lake. The campground has a nice **day use area** at its east end.

Just about 5 miles (8 km) farther up the beach (or County Rd. H-58) lies the **Hurricane River** campground, where the Hurricane River empties into Lake Superior. Hurricane Beach is combination of rock and sand that is continually shaped by the weather and therefore takes on a different persona each year. If water levels are sufficiently low, it's possible to walk 1.5 miles (2.4 km) east all the way to the Au Sable Light Station.

Farther west, across County Road H-58 near the **Grand Sable Visitors Center** (E21090 County Rd. H-58), the sandy shores and often warm waters of **Grand Sable Lake** are a wonderful spot for a swim or picnic.

Fishing

Fishing in the **Pictured Rocks National Lakeshore**—both in Lake Superior and the inland lakes and rivers—is a bit different from fishing elsewhere in the Upper Peninsula. Specifically, angling has been permitted by Congress for more than 40 years. It's not just an opportunity; it's your right. You'll be able to cast a line for a large selection of game fish, including walleye, northern pike, whitefish, smelt, smallmouth bass, coho salmon, and brook, rainbow, and lake trout. Try Lake Superior, Grand Sable Lake, Beaver Lake, and Little Beaver Lake for the greatest variety of fish. For rivers, it's best to try at Sable Creek, Hurricane River, Beaver Basin Streams, and Miners River, among others. Contact the staff at the **National Lakeshore Headquarters** (N8391 Sand Point Rd., 906/387-2607, www. nps.gov/piro) for guidelines, regulations, maps, and tips.

For fishing on state land near Grand Marais, try **North and South Gemini Lakes** for bass, bluegill, perch, and walleye. **Ross Lake,** 2 miles (3.2 km) east, is a source for bass, bluegill, perch, and pike. And **Canoe Lake,** 2.5 miles (4 km) south, offers perch and pike. Contact the **Michigan DNR** (906/452-6227, www.michigan.gov/dnr) for more info.

Off-Road Vehicles

East of Grand Marais, near Lake Superior between Blind Sucker Flooding and Muskallonge Lake, the first of two DNR ATV trails has an impressive 46 miles (74 km) in three large loops. **Pine Ridge Trail** has parking at the intersection of County Road 416 and County Road 407; there's also access from Holland Lake Campground if you continue west on County Road 416. The **Two Heart Trail** actually connects to the Pine Ridge Trail, adding almost 34 miles (55 km), for a total of some 80 miles (129 km). Use the same trailhead parking as Pine Ridge, or you can get access to Two Heart from the Mouth of Two-Hearted River Campground (gas is available) or Pike Lake Campground. The **Michigan DNR** (906/452-6227, www.michigan.gov/dnr) has more information and maps.

Waterfalls

Just inside the western boundary of **Pictured Rocks National Lakeshore,** a short trail leads to 50-foot (15-meter) **Munising Falls,** which spills into a narrow gorge before emptying into Lake Superior's Munising Bay. Head east to the Chapel Basin Area where, amid a pale birch forest some 1.5 miles (2.4 km) from the parking area, a stream of frothing water drops like a horsetail 90 feet (27 meters) into a deep gorge and Chapel Lake below. Continue past the falls another 1.75 miles (2.8 km) to reach Chapel Beach, where you'll find a backcountry campground. From here, you can turn right to Chapel Rock and follow the Lakeshore Trail 1.5 miles (2.4 km) to **Spray Falls,** one of the least visited and loveliest waterfalls in the park, where Spray Creek drops over the sandstone cliffs right into Lake Superior.

The trail to **Sable Falls** leaves from the **Grand Sable Visitors Center** (E21090 County Rd. H-58, 906/494-2660, www.nps. gov/piro, 9am-5pm daily late May-Labor Day), a 0.5-mile (0.8-km) walk largely composed of steps. As you work your way downhill, you'll be treated to several views of this exceptionally pretty falls, which drop in tiers through a narrow canyon and out to a rocky Lake Superior beach.

Perhaps the most dramatic waterfall in the park is **Miners Falls,** near Munising. A fairly narrow gorge gives way to a 40-foot (12-meter) drop, rewarding the visitor with a powerful thunder and the sensation of mist on their face. To get here, take County Road H-58 east from Munising until you come to Miners Castle Drive, where you'll turn left and continue for 3.5 miles (5.6 km). On your right, you'll come to a dirt parking area. From there it's an easy 15-minute walk to the falls.

WINTER RECREATION
Ski and Snowshoe Trails

The **Grand Marais Ski Trail** has several loops on the extreme east end of **Pictured Rocks National Lakeshore,** where County Road H-58/Au Sable Point Trail passes near Sable Falls and the Lake Superior shoreline. In fact, the E Trail loops close to the shore on an intermediate 2-mile (3.2-km) journey out and back. All of the loops here range from easy to intermediate, and vary in distance from less than 1 mile to nearly 2.5 miles (1.6-4 km), for a total of 10.4 miles (16.7 km). Parking is on either side of County Road H-58, just west of William Hill Road. Be sure to watch for both car and snowmobile traffic when crossing the highway. For trail maps and additional information, the staff at the **National Lakeshore Headquarters** (N8391 Sand Point Rd., 906/387-2607, www.nps.gov/piro) are more than happy to help. You can jump on the North Country National Scenic Trail as well.

An excellent source to rent ski equipment, snowshoes, and other winter sports gear is South Bay Outfitters (120 Superior St., Munising, 906/387-4004, 10am-5pm Tues.-Fri., 10am-1pm Sat.).

Snowmobiling

There are more than enough snowmobile trails in the Pictured Rocks-Grand Marais region. The most important one is **Trail 8,** which cuts east-west from Munising to Sault Ste. Marie. At Pictured Rocks National Lakeshore, **Trail 89** bends away from Trail 8 and takes you north to the Superior shoreline. South of town, **Trails 443** and **43** connect to the rest of the U.P.'s snowmobile trails—south to St. Ignace and west to Escanaba, Ironwood, and the Keweenaw Peninsula. There's also a web of smaller trails that weaves around the city: **Trails 88, 888, 9,** and **492** will take you between the main trails and to other places in the region. Contact **Grand Marais Sno-Trails** (906/494-2300) for more information and a detailed map. And remember: Under Michigan law, snowmobiles are allowed on the shoulders of plowed roads, and on any unplowed road. Follow the speed limits and drive with care.

An excellent source to rent snowmobile and other winter sports gear is South Bay Outfitters (120 Superior St., Munising, 906/387-4004, 10am-5pm Tues.-Fri., 10am-1pm Sat.).

FOOD

Grand Marais has a few good dining spots, both right downtown on County Road H-77. The **Grand Marais Tavern and Restaurant** (14260 Lake Ave., 906/494-2111, 11am-10pm Mon. and Wed.-Sat., noon-10pm Sun., $9-18) is a great place to stop for lunch after hiking or time behind the wheel. There are great burgers, beer, and pizza, with a pleasant outdoor dining area overlooking Lake Superior.

Down the street, ★ **Lake Superior Brewing Company** (14283 Lake Ave., 906/494-2337, www.lakesuperiorbrewing.com, noon-2am daily, $10-15) does the microbrewery tradition proud, with homemade beers like Sandstone Pale Ale and Granite Brown, as well as sandwiches, soups, and great homemade pizzas. For a summer treat, stop in the retro **Superior Hotel** (Lake Ave. and Randolph St.), where a soda fountain still sells phosphates and penny candy.

ACCOMMODATIONS

The **Beach Park Motel** (21795 Randolph St., 906/494-2681, http://beachparkmotel.com,

$) has large rooms, each with a view of the water. A block east of County Road H-77 on Randolph Street, it's within walking distance to everything in town. Small dogs are allowed for an additional $10.

East of County Road H-77 on Wilson Street, **Voyageur's Motel** (21914 Wilson St., 906/494-2389, www.voyageursmotelmi. com, $$) sits atop a ridge overlooking Grand Marais Harbor. Nice newer rooms, each with two queen beds, a mini fridge, and a coffee maker, plus a sauna-whirlpool facility, make this a good choice. There's also a three-bedroom cottage available with a three-night minimum stay required.

The historic **Superior Hotel** (14245 Lake Ave., 906/494-2539, www.grandmarais michigan.com, $) is an old-fashioned hotel along the lines of a European-style hostel. Rooms are clean but very Spartan and do not include a TV or private bath. The rates, however, make it an attractive option. There's a $5 fee for each additional person.

The affordable **Hilltop Cabins** (14176 Ellen St., 906/287-1377, www.hilltopcabinsmi. com, $$) rents one- to three-bedroom cabins, each with a full living room, kitchen, and bath. Motel rooms with views of the bay are available, but the cozy cabins are much more desirable.

For more information and other lodging options, contact the **Grand Marais Chamber of Commerce** (906/494-2447, www.grandmaraismichigan.com).

Camping

Pictured Rocks National Lakeshore has three auto-accessible campgrounds: Little Beaver Lake, Twelvemile Beach, and Hurricane River. Each is equipped with water and pit toilets. No reservations are accepted, and fees are $25 per night.

The **Little Beaver Lake Campground** is located at the terminus of Little Beaver Lake Road, which is 3 miles (4.8 km) north of County Road H-58. With only eight sites, this is the smallest of Pictured Rock's campgrounds, which offers a better chance for a quiet experience. Because of the narrow access road, single unit vehicles of over 36 feet (11 meters), and combined units of over 42 feet (13 meters) are prohibited.

The **Twelvemile Beach Campground** is a short drive off County Road H-58. Many of the 37 campsites string out along a bluff over the beach. Arrive at midweek (or early on Saturday, often a turnover day) for one of the choice spots. Some are larger than the average house lot and undoubtedly have better views. Well-placed stairs allow campers and picnickers to reach the lake.

Just about 5 miles (8 km) farther up the beach (or County Rd. H-58) lies the **Hurricane River Campground,** where the Hurricane River empties into Lake Superior. This is also an exceptionally scenic campground, with 21 sites and a good location near the water and Au Sable Point.

Backcountry camping at the national lakeshore is permitted only at designated hike-in sites, mostly along the Lakeshore Trail. Reservations (877/444-6777, www. recreation.gov) are required, and the website will issue you the required permit ($15, plus $5 pp per night). Most sites do not have water or toilets.

With an excellent location just outside the national lakeshore boundary, **Woodland Park** (906/494-2613, www.burttownship. com/recreation/woodland-park-campground, mid-Apr.-mid-Oct., $30-45) has 125 sites, all of which offer water and electricity. There's a bevy of other amenities, including two bathhouses, laundry, wireless Internet, and fire pits. Opt for a more secluded site that requires you to get some exercise and walk up the beach a bit.

Camping is also available in Munising, Grand Marais, and in Lake Superior State Forest, which borders Pictured Rocks to the south.

INFORMATION AND SERVICES

You'll find visitors centers at both ends of the national lakeshore. One is in Munising;

the other is located inside the park at the Grand Sable Dunes, just a few miles from Grand Marais. Be sure to stop at one of these centers before beginning your visit. They have rangers on duty and excellent maps, displays, and historical information that will enhance your visit. Both also offer small but comprehensive bookstores. The **Munising Information Center** (100 E. Munising Ave., Munising, 906/387-1900, www.nps.gov/piro, 9am-5pm daily summer, 9am-4:30pm Mon.-Sat. mid-Sept.-Memorial Day), serving both the Pictured Rocks National Lakeshore and Hiawatha National Forest, is open year-round. The **Grand Sable Visitor Center** (E21090 County Rd. H-58, 906/494-2660, www.nps.gov/piro, 9am-5pm daily) is open from late May to Labor Day only. The **Munising Falls Visitor Center** (1505 Sand Point Rd., Munising, www.nps.gov/piro, 9am-5pm daily Memorial Day-mid-Sept.) is geared primarily to issuing backcountry permits and also has a bookstore.

The two closest hospitals are **Helen Newberry Joy Hospital** (502 W. Harrie St., Newberry, 906/293-9200, www.hnjh.org) in Newberry and **Munising Memorial Hospital** (1500 Sand Point Rd., Munising, 906/387-4110, www.munisingmemorial.org) in Munising. To access either hospital, head south on M-77 until you get to M-28. For Helen Newberry Joy Hospital, turn left and follow M-28 to M-123; turn left again and travel north on M-123 to Harrie Street, then turn left to the hospital. For Munising Memorial Hospital, turn right onto M-28 from M-77, then turn right on Connors Road. Make a left at Munising/Shingleton Road, then another right at Washington Street to the hospital.

In Grand Marais, you can do banking at the **Peoples State Bank of Munising** (N14264 Lake St., Grand Marais, 906/494-2265, www.bankatpsb.com). You'll find more banking options in Newberry and Munising.

GETTING THERE AND AROUND

Car

The easiest route between Munising and Grand Marais will bring you well south of Pictured Rocks. Take M-28 east from Munising, then M-77 north to Grand Marais.

County Road H-58 offers closer access to the area around the national lakeshore. From the Grand Marais end, you'll be able to get as far as the Kingston Lake Campground. From Munising and the west, you can get to the Little Beaver Lake Campground.

As a linear park, Pictured Rocks perennially struggles with auto accessibility versus invasiveness. There have been sporadic discussions for decades about a "Beaver Basin Rim Road" that would weave through the park nearer to Lake Superior, offering easier auto access to park attractions but undeniably changing the spirit and peacefulness of the largely road-free preserve.

Air

The closest commercial airport is **Chippewa County International Airport** (CIU, 5019 Airport Dr., Kincheloe, 906/495-5631, www.airciu.com), nearly 80 miles (129 km) away, south of Sault Ste. Marie. **Delta Airlines** (800/221-1212, www.delta.com) offers scheduled flights from Detroit and Minneapolis-St. Paul, and car rentals are available from **Enterprise** (906/203-7122, www.enterprise.com).

If you're traveling from other major cities, it may be easier to fly into **Sawyer International Airport** (MQT, 125 G Ave., Gwinn, 906/346-3308, www.sawyerairport.com) instead, about a two-hour drive away. Sawyer has scheduled flights from Detroit Metro on **Delta Airlines** and Chicago O'Hare on **American Airlines.** There's no scheduled ground transportation from the airport, so you'll need to rent a car; try **Alamo** (800/462-5266, www.alamo.com), **Avis** (800/831-1212, www.avis.com), **Budget** (800/527-7000, www.budget.com), **Enterprise** (800/736-8227, www.enterprise.com), or **National** (800/227-7368, www.nationalcar.com).

Boat

The **Burt Township Marina** (906/494-2613, 906/494-2381 off-season, www.burttownship.com/recreation/marina, May 1-Oct. 15) in Grand Marais is Lake Superior's only natural harbor of refuge between Munising and Whitefish Point. You'll find a boat launch, fuel, electricity, water hookups, a pump-out station, and transient dockage. The marina is open seasonally and is located at 46°41.05 N, 85°58.15 W.

Bus

The **Altran Shuttle** (906/387-4845, www.altranbus.com/backpacker) is a county bus that makes daily runs during the high season to Munising Falls and Grand Marais and will drop off hikers at any point along County Road H-58. Fare is $35 per person. It's the perfect way for backpackers to enjoy the park without contributing to the growing vehicle problem. Call to make a reservation, at least one day in advance.

Seney and Vicinity

> The train went up the track and out of sight, around one of the hills of burnt timber. Nick sat down on the bundle of canvas and bedding the baggage man had pitched out of the door of the baggage car. There was no town, nothing but the rails and the burnt over country. The thirteen saloons that had once lined the one street of Seney had not left a trace.
>
> Ernest Hemingway,
> "Big Two-Hearted River"

Applied to the small town of Seney, Hemingway's quote may be a bit of an exaggeration. Seney is still there, a small dot on the map at the crossroads of M-77 and M-28. But by the time Hemingway's protagonist, Nick Adams, was exploring the central U.P., the town of Seney was indeed just a shadow of its former self.

"Hell town in the Pine," loggers once called it, the new center of a logging trade that had crept northward into the U.P. after depleting the lucrative stands of red and white pine in the northern Lower Peninsula. Seney was the center of the action in the 1880s, both in and out of the woods. Situated along a railroad siding and the shores of the Fox River—used to transport the logs—the city became an important transit point. Besides logging, the local economy thrived on drinking, gambling, and womanizing. Seney didn't lack for local color: legendary characters included P. K. "Snap Jaw" Small, who entertained barroom crowds by biting the heads off live toads and birds, and "Protestant" Bob McGuire, who sharpened his thumbnails into miniature bowie knives. Seney was romanticized in the national press, in a manner similar to Tombstone, Arizona, and other towns of the Wild West.

Seney never had the huge fertile forests so common elsewhere in Michigan. Glaciers scrubbed this swath of the central U.P. flat, creating a patchwork of rivers, wetlands, and rocky, sandy soil. The red and white pines that did grow here were leveled in just a few short years. Soon loggers were settling for the less valuable hardwoods and small conifers, burning the scrub as they went. Shortly after the turn of the 20th century they moved on, leaving behind the now barren land and vast "stump prairies."

Optimistic farmers followed the quickly departed loggers. They burned the brush and went to great lengths to drain the wetlands, digging miles of 20-foot (6-meter) ditches. Their hopes were quickly dashed by the area's poor soil and short growing season. Soon, they too departed, but the fires had a more lasting effect, deeply scarring the fragile soil.

These days humans are finally trying to help instead of harm this beleaguered land. The immense Seney National Wildlife Refuge now manages and protects 150 square miles (390 sq km) immediately west of M-77, restoring the wetlands with an intricate series of dikes and control ponds that began as a 1930s Civilian Conservation Corps project. Today, the refuge is an important sanctuary and nesting place for a rich variety of waterfowl.

The area's rivers remain a wonderful resource as well. The Fox, Manistique, and Driggs all snake through this area, along with countless creeks and lesser branches. Henry Ford, Calvin Coolidge, and Ernest Hemingway all fished these legendary trout waters, as do anglers today. Here too Hemingway used a bit of literary license: it was really the Fox that he so eloquently chronicled in his Nick Adams stories. He merely borrowed the more romantic sounding name of the Big Two-Hearted River, which in fact flows just east of here.

SIGHTS
★ Iverson Snowshoe Company

Aluminum snowshoes now dominate the sport, but for beauty and tradition, they simply can't match white ash and rawhide snowshoes. In Shingleton, 25 miles west of Seney on M-28, Anita Hulse and her two sons operate this wonderful factory, where workers hand-shape strips of local ash into classic snowshoe frames.

Visitors are welcome at **Iverson Snowshoe Company** (E9664 M-28, Wetmore, 906/452-6370, www.iversonssnowshoes.com, 7:30am-3pm Mon.-Fri.), one of just two wooden snowshoe manufacturers in the nation. You can watch workers shave and saw strips of ash, steam them, bend them around a form, and send them to a drying kiln overnight. Finished frames are laced with gummy strips of rawhide or newer-style neoprene. All of this happens in a small building, where

visitors practically lean over the shoulders of the workers.

Iverson manufactures about 11,000 snowshoes a year, about a third of which go to L.L.Bean. Other customers include REI, the Norwegian army, park rangers, and utility workers. Iverson also makes rustic chairs and tables to order. It's best to call ahead if you're interested in a tour; groups of more than five or six should definitely call.

TOP EXPERIENCE

Seney National Wildlife Refuge

The **Seney National Wildlife Refuge** (1674 Refuge Entrance Rd., 906/586-9851, www.fws.gov/refuge/seney) has more than 95,000 acres in the area known as the Great Manistique Swamp. Established for resident wildlife, the area provides protection for endangered and threatened species and a habitat for migratory birds. The refuge is one of the U.P.'s most pristine wildlife viewing areas.

While people can walk or bike much of this preserve via an extensive network of maintenance roads, the refuge offers plenty of seclusion for its inhabitants. More than 200 species of birds and nearly 50 species of mammals have been recorded here, including bald eagles, trumpeter swans, loons, deer, and occasionally, moose or wolves. Whether you're an experienced bird-watcher or just a casual observer, the refuge is a wonderful place to see a fascinating array of wildlife.

Start your visit at the excellent **National Wildlife Refuge Visitors Center** (M-77, www.fws.gov/refuge/seney, 9am-5pm daily May 15-Oct. 20), 5 miles (8 km) south of the town of Seney on M-77. A 15-minute audiovisual program, informative displays, and printed materials will provide a good overview of what you can expect to see in the refuge. Some of the handouts will increase your chances of spotting birdlife, pinpointing things like eagle nests and ponds frequented by loons. Sightings are often best in the early morning and evening.

The **Pine Ridge Nature Trail** departs

from the visitors center and allows for a quick 1.4-mile (2.3-km) foray into wetland habitat. The self-guided trail circles a pool, and a stretch of boardwalk spans a marshy area.

The one-way **Marshland Wildlife Drive** (May 15-Oct. 20) also departs from the visitors center and makes a 7-mile (11.3-km) auto-accessible loop through the refuge, with several interpretive signs placed along the way. The route includes three observation decks equipped with spotting scopes. You can borrow binoculars from the visitors center. An eagle's nest is visible from the road, as are several pools frequented by herons and swans. Trumpeter swans were hand-raised and released here and are now seen regularly. Tundra swans also migrate through in spring and fall. An adjacent 3-mile (4.8-km) **fishing loop** accesses a fishing platform and is also open to autos.

Strangmoor Bog

One of Seney's most unusual features, **Strangmoor Bog** lies deep in the wetlands near the refuge's western boundary, and unfortunately is not easily accessible to visitors. Strangmoors, or string bogs, are finger-like bogs alternating with sand ridges that are remnants of ancient beaches. They are typically found only in arctic and subarctic regions, and Seney's bog is one of the southernmost examples in North America.

ENTERTAINMENT
End of the Road Winery

One of the growing list of wineries in the Upper Peninsula can be found in the oddly named town of Germfask. Despite being a small operation, **End of the Road Winery** (6917 Burns Rd., Germfask, 906/450-1541, www.endoftheroadwinerymi.com, 11am-5:30pm Tues.-Sat. mid-May to mid-Oct.) offers a surprisingly diverse selection of wines, including classic cabernets and chardonnays, plus a creative variety that use blueberry, peach, raspberry, and cranberry. Their on-site vineyard is the source for many of their creations.

SUMMER RECREATION
Seney National Wildlife Refuge
Hiking and Biking

Unfortunately, most visitors to Seney rarely leave their cars to venture beyond the Marshland Wildlife Drive. But to access the balance of what **Seney National Wildlife Refuge** has to offer, a bicycle is best. Bikes are welcome on more than 100 miles (160

trumpeter swans at Seney National Wildlife Refuge

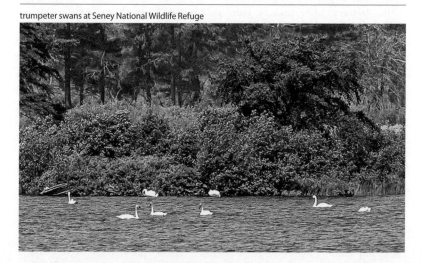

km) of dirt and gravel maintenance roads, which are closed to motorized traffic except refuge vehicles. You won't find any exciting or technical rides, as the land is flat, but a bicycle allows you to cover far more ground than you could hiking and it's quiet enough that it won't frighten the wildlife. There's also something magical about spinning down a gravel road amid all the chirping, twittering, and honking, with nothing but waving grasses and glinting ponds surrounding you for miles.

Easy terrain, easy access, and well-marked trails make Seney a great choice for families or less active cyclists. You will want a mountain bike or hybrid bike, since the gravel can be tough on skinny tires. No off-road riding is permitted in the refuge. There are three main access points for the refuge. One is at the visitors center on M-77, where trails sprout off the Marshland Drive. This area is the most heavily visited, but trails here weave between many different pools, so the ride is interesting, and waterfowl sightings can be particularly good. Note that Loops 1 and 2 are part of the Marshland Drive and are open to motor vehicles.

A second access point is about 3 miles (4.8 km) south of the visitors center, near the Grace Lutheran Church. Turn west at the sign for the Northern Hardwoods cross-country ski area, referred to as Smith Farm by locals. You'll soon reach a small parking area and a gate across the road. The trail begins just a few hundred yards/meters west. This is a more lightly visited area of the refuge. From here, Loop 5 makes a 12.2-mile (19.6-km) circle, including a stretch that runs parallel to the Driggs River.

If you stay on the trail that follows the Driggs, rather than swinging back east to complete Loop 5, after about 9 miles (14.5 km) you'll emerge onto M-28 west of the town of Seney. This is the third access point, called Driggs River Road. It's a well-defined road for the first 1.5 miles (2.4 km) south of M-28, until it arrives at the refuge boundary.

Canoeing and Kayaking

Paddling is an excellent way to explore the western reaches of **Seney National Wildlife Refuge,** and it happens that the **Manistique River** is an easily navigable canoeing river, with a sand bottom and just enough twists and turns to keep things interesting. It can be popular at the height of summer, so it's best to go off-season or early in the day for optimal solitude and wildlife watching. Put in at the roadside park on M-77, 1 mile (1.6 km) south of Germfask, or arrange a trip through Northland Outfitters. If you have your own boat, you can opt for the lightly traveled Driggs or Creighton River. Both cross M-28 west of Seney. Paddling is not permitted on any refuge pools or marshes.

Northland Outfitters (8174 M-77, 906/586-9801, www.northoutfitters.com) is located on M-77 in Germfask, just south of the refuge entrance. The company rents canoes, kayaks, and camping gear, and offers paddling trips on the Manistique.

Fishing

The **Seney National Wildlife Refuge** allows some fishing within its boundaries. Pick up information on its special regulations at the visitors center. Fishing can be quite good on the area's major rivers, including the Fox River, which merges with the Manistique just east of M-77 and continues into the refuge. Bass, northern pike, and walleye are especially plentiful. You'll need to move to the eastern branch of the Fox River if you're looking for trout.

The Fox River

In 1919, Ernest Hemingway stepped off a train in Seney, asked for directions to a good trout stream, and was directed up an old railroad grade to the east branch of the Fox River. Where truth meets fiction we'll never know, but Hemingway's U.P. travels resulted in "Big Two-Hearted River," his Nick Adams tale about fishing what was really the Fox. Consequently, the Fox has always carried a special cachet in the U.P. and among trout fishing enthusiasts.

Fishing

Michigan has dozens of superb **trout fishing** streams, but most anglers seem to agree that the Fox belongs on the A-list. According to Jerry Dennis, author of several Michigan fishing books, it has produced some gargantuan brook trout. "The Fox even today has a reputation for brook trout of a size rarely encountered elsewhere in the United States. Fish 15 to 20 inches long are taken with fair regularity," he writes. The east branch still is considered the river's prime stretch, partly because it's more difficult to reach. To get here, you can hike in from M-77 north of Seney, where it flows just west of the road. A state forest campground 8 miles (12.9 km) up M-77 from Seney offers public access. Many locals simply cast near the bridge at Seney, where the main river flows under M-28. Because of the Fox's allure, the DNR is considering instituting special fishing regulations. Check with authorities before heading out.

Hiking and Biking

The **Fox River Pathway** was no doubt prompted by perennial interest in Hemingway's narrative. The route stretches 27 miles (43 km) north from Seney to just shy of Pictured Rocks National Lakeshore, and by U.P. standards, it's somewhat bland. Its most appealing stretch—especially for anglers looking for fishing access—is the southern end, where the trail parallels the main river for 10 miles (16.1 km). Farther north, it follows the Little Fox and the west branch. Heading north, the trail traverses the Kingston Plains, where loggers left behind stump prairies. Markers along this route offer information about the area's logging history.

Because it passes through a good deal of cutover land, the trail can be extremely hot and dry. If you plan to hike it, be sure to carry a water purification system. You'll find rustic campgrounds at both trailheads, and just one along the route, about 6 miles (9.7 km) from the southern end.

For hikers, another much shorter option is the trail that heads north from the Fox River Pathway's northern terminus at the Kingston Lake Campground. Not considered part of the pathway, this trail winds through pines and hardwoods in the Lake Superior State Forest for 4 miles (6.4 km) before spilling out onto a particularly deserted and delightful stretch of Twelvemile Beach on Lake Superior, inside Pictured Rocks National Lakeshore.

WINTER RECREATION
Ski and Snowshoe Trails

It seems that as soon as the snow falls, **Seney National Wildlife Refuge** is open for cross-country skiing and snowshoeing. The largely flat trails are groomed from mid-December through mid-March and make for a pleasant way to pass an afternoon. The trailhead for six different skiing loops is located just off Robinson Road west of M-77. Half of the trails are easy and suitable for beginners. The others will present a bit of a challenge, but given the relatively flat terrain, experienced skiers shouldn't have any problems. Loops range from less than 1 mile (1.6 km) to 2 miles (3.2 km) in length. You can snowshoe anywhere in the refuge except on the groomed ski trails.

Snowmobiling

The best part about snowmobiling in Seney is its proximity to the trails that spread across the Grand Marais region north of town. The **Seney Trail** (Trail 43) cuts diagonally through Seney before connecting to the remaining miles of the Upper Peninsula's trails. Unplowed roads and the shoulders of plowed roads are open to snowmobiles as well.

FOOD AND ACCOMMODATIONS

If you're hungry, stop at any of the smattering of restaurants that have gathered along M-28 as you approach town from either direction.

There is lodging in Seney, but you'll find better choices elsewhere. Newberry,

Manistique, Munising, and Grand Marais are all within 30 minutes' drive. If you'd like to stay in town, try a room at the affordable **Fox River Motel** (1588 M-28, 906/499-3332, www.thefoxrivermotel.com, $), downtown at the corner of M-77 and M-28. Wi-Fi is included.

Camping

Even if overnight camping isn't allowed in the refuge, there are plenty of campgrounds to choose from. The **East Branch Fox River State Forest Campground** (906/341-2355, www.michigan.gov/dnr, $15) has 19 sites for tents or small trailers. Take M-77 north of Seney about 7 miles (11.3 km). To get to the **Fox River State Forest Campground** (906/341-2355, www.michigan.gov/dnr, $15), take County Road 450 northwest of Seney, to find the seven rustic campsites for tents and small trailers only. Both of these campgrounds work on a first-come, first-served basis.

You'll find small and rustic **Mead Creek Campground** (906/341-2355, www.michigan.gov/dnr, $15) just off County Road 436 about 15 miles (24 km) west of M-77 near Germfask. Mead Creek has nine sites with vault toilets and water from a hand pump, and it is first come, first served.

For more camping options, ask at the **National Wildlife Refuge Visitors Center** (M-77, www.fws.gov/refuge/seney, 9am-5pm daily May 15-Oct. 20).

INFORMATION AND SERVICES

Visitor information for the **Seney National Wildlife Refuge** can be obtained from the **U.S. Fish and Wildlife Service** (1674 Refuge Entrance Rd., 906/586-9851, www.fws.gov/refuge/seney). When you first arrive, stop by the visitors center to view an orientation slide show, see exhibits, and obtain information. The center is located on M-77 a few miles north of Germfask.

For medical care or the hospital, head east along M-28 to Newberry and the **Helen Newberry Joy Hospital** (502 W. Harrie St., Newberry, 906/293-9200 or 800/743-3093, www.hnjh.org). Take M-28 to M-123 and turn left; take another left on Harrie Street to the hospital.

GETTING THERE AND AROUND
Car

Getting to Seney by car is simple. The town is at the intersection of M-77, the north-south highway that runs between US 2 and Grand Marais, and M-28, the main artery that cuts east-west through the middle of the peninsula. Seney is 40 miles (64 km) from Manistique, 35 miles (56 km) from Munising, and 25 miles (40 km) from Grand Marais.

Air

Unfortunately, Seney is a fairly long drive from either **Chippewa County International Airport** (CIU, 5019 Airport Dr., Kincheloe, 906/495-2522, www.airciu.com), south of Sault Ste. Marie, or **Sawyer International Airport** (MQT, 125 G Ave., Gwinn, 906/346-3308, www.sawyerairport.com), near Marquette. Both airports have plenty of car rental options, and it's easy to get to Seney via M-28. Driving time from either airport is about 1.5 hours.

Public Transportation

Currently there is no public transportation serving Seney.

Whitefish Bay to the Lake Huron Shore

On the northwestern tip of its namesake bay,

Whitefish Point boasts the oldest active lighthouse on Lake Superior, but it's probably best known for its proximity to Tahquamenon Falls, the largest and arguably most beautiful waterfall in the Upper Peninsula. Whitefish Bay is also the place to go for Lake Superior swimming, since the water tends to be warmer here than in Marquette. The pleasantly named community of Paradise, just to the south, can serve as a strategic base of operations.

The quickest way to Sault Ste. Marie from the west is to take M-28 to I-75, but then you'll miss out on the drive along Whitefish Bay, where Lake Superior narrows to become the St. Mary's River. To enjoy this

Highlights

Look for ★ to find recommended sights, activities, dining, and lodging.

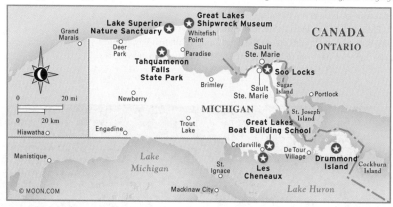

★ **Lake Superior Nature Sanctuary:** This remote sanctuary is home to several endangered and rare species (page 263).

★ **Great Lakes Shipwreck Museum:** This museum commemorates ships that succumbed to the lakes and honors those who were lost while sailing them (page 264).

★ **Tahquamenon Falls State Park:** This *grand dame* of Upper Peninsula waterfalls is unquestionably one of the most photographed and widely loved landmarks in the entire state (page 264).

★ **Soo Locks:** Watching giant freighters navigate the locks is a fascinating experience (page 274).

★ **Drummond Island:** Snowmobile trails, hiking paths, and unmatched golf courses are only a few of the reasons to head to this relaxing out-of-the-way destination (page 285).

★ **Les Cheneaux:** Located only 30 miles (48 km) from the Mackinac Bridge, these 36 islands are worth a visit for their sightseeing and seclusion (page 287).

★ **Great Lakes Boat Building School:** Tour this pillar of the boating community and you'll be both amazed and inspired at the skills and dedication of the students and staff (page 289).

beautiful scenery, take a leisurely ride along the Lake Shore Drive/Whitefish Bay Scenic Byway.

You'll no doubt want to spend time at Sault Ste. Marie, watching the big ships make their way through the locks or strolling along quaint Portage Avenue. Don't forget to cross into Canada and visit the other Sault Ste. Marie. You'll love what America's friendly northern neighbor has to offer.

Les Cheneaux and Drummond Island are perfect for pure relaxation. These quiet isles are close to both Sault Ste. Marie and busy Mackinac Island but feel like they're hundreds of miles away. Get out on the water and explore the islands and channels.

PLANNING YOUR TIME

Sault Ste. Marie is the largest city in the eastern U.P. and is certainly worth a day of your time. In fact, you can easily spend the entire afternoon at the locks. If you include a trip to Tahquamenon Falls and a visit to Les Cheneaux, you'll want to spend about two or three days in the region. Serious hikers, bikers, or boaters should plan on a longer stay, since there are plenty of outdoor attractions— Hiawatha National Forest, state parks galore, and the placid waters of Lake Huron. If you have time, head out to Drummond Island for some secluded hiking.

Accommodation Price Key

$	Less than $100 per night
$$	$100-200 per night
$$$	More than $200 per night

HISTORY

The Ojibwa people were the first settlers of the area, migrating here in the 1500s. They discovered a rich supply of whitefish in the area's turbulent waters and established a permanent settlement at the edge of the rapids, making this one of the oldest continuously settled areas in the Midwest. *Addik-kim-maig,* the Ojibwa name for whitefish, means "deer of the waters," a reference to the fish's importance as a food source. The Ojibwa lived off the river's riches here for more than 300 years, but in a sad and often repeated tale, the arrival of Europeans put an end to the Ojibwa way of life and took away this important fishing ground. For in addition to a new European settlement at the Soo, the Iroquois had also arrived, as they had been driven from their homeland in the New York region by European immigrants. As tensions and battles occurred between the parties, eventually the Ojibwa were forced out.

French immigrants lived off the area's riches for many years, after establishing a major fur trading post here in the mid-1600s, then a Jesuit mission. By the early 1800s, Michigan's northern reaches were thoroughly settled by the French, British, and the Ottawa people, and the bounty of the area's natural resources ringing the shores of Lake Superior were being discovered.

The only problem was the rapids. For decades, ship cargo had to be unloaded by hand, portaged around the rapids by horses and mules pulling carts, then reloaded onto another vessel. In 1839, the American Fur Company built a short railroad line, which eased the job, but transport remained backbreaking and exceedingly slow. Great Lakes shipping was booming on the lower Great Lakes, but the resources of the Lake Superior region remained underutilized, its cargo backed up by the rapids.

Eastern industrialists then began lobbying for government-funded locks as a solution. But the portaging business had become the lifeblood of Sault Ste. Marie's economy, and the community opposed such a project. Locals managed to stave off the inevitable until 1852, when President Millard Fillmore signed a bill authorizing construction of the first lock at Sault Ste. Marie.

In 1855, the State Lock opened, which was

Previous: the Tahquamenon River; ship in the Soo Locks; autumn in Tahquamenon Falls State Park.

Whitefish Bay to the Lake Huron Shore

CANADA

USA

DRUMMOND ISLAND

Johnswood

SEE "DRUMMOND ISLAND" MAP

Lake Huron

ONTARIO

Portlock

Echo Bay

DeTour Village

Drummond Island

DETOUR REEF LIGHT STATION

Richards Landing

St. Joseph Island

134

46

Sugar Island

Cedarville

GREAT LAKES BOAT BUILDING SCHOOL

Les Cheneaux Islands

23

Cheboygan

Sault Ste. Marie

SOO LOCKS

Sault Ste. Marie

Oak Ridge

46

LES CHENEAUX

17

SEE "SAULT STE. MARIE AND VICINITY" MAP

POINT IROQUOIS LIGHT

129

LES CHENEAUX CULINARY SCHOOL

Hessel

Bois Blanc Island

Bay Mills

Brimley

CHIPPEWA COUNTY INTERNATIONAL AIRPORT

48

North Lake Huron Paddle Trail

Mackinac Island

Mackinac Island

75

GREAT LAKES SHIPWRECK MUSEUM

Whitefish Point

WHITEFISH POINT LIGHTHOUSE

Bay Mills RESORT CASINO

H40

Mackinaw City

Whitefish Point Underwater Preserve

SEE "TAHQUAMENON FALLS STATE PARK" MAP

Whitefish Bay

PENDILLS CREEK NATIONAL FISH HATCHERY

75

31

Straits of Mackinac

St. Ignace

CRISP POINT LIGHTHOUSE

LAKE SUPERIOR NATURE SANCTUARY

CURLEY LEWIS MEMORIAL HIGHWAY

SOLDIER LAKE CAMPGROUND

Hiawatha National Forest

Cross Village

W Lakeshore Dr

Paradise

123

Eckerman

Trout Lake

123

2

Lake Superior

TAHQUAMENON FALLS STATE PARK

Upper Tahquamenon Falls

Soo Junction

THREE LAKES CAMPGROUND

Caffey

Lake Michigan

Tahquamenon River

Four Mile Corner

H40

Muskallonge Lake State Park

BODI LAKE STATE FOREST CAMPGROUND

Newberry

Hog Island

123

Deer Park

H37

Garden Island

St. James

BLIND SUCKER RIVER

OSWALD'S BEAR RANCH

117

Beaver Island

Grand Marais

PRETTY LAKES QUIET AREA

Curtis

Engadine

Whiskey Island

Pictured Rocks National Lakeshore

MICHIGAN

Manistique Lake

Trout Island

High Island

Hiawatha Trail

77

END OF THE ROAD WINERY

77

Seney

Blaney Park

Milakokia Lake

Gull Island

Gulliver

28

2

To Marquette

© MOON.COM

10 mi

10 km

0

actually a pair of locks, each 350 feet (107 meters) long. They were an instant success. In their first year, they facilitated the transit of nearly 12,000 tons of iron ore. Within a decade, the annual figure soared to more than 120,000 tons. By World War I, the nation's hunger for iron and copper, coupled with the opening of vast iron mines in Minnesota's Mesabi Range, made the Soo Locks the busiest shipping canal in the world. Even today, the freight transported each year across Lake Superior and through the Soo Locks exceeds that of the Panama and Suez Canals combined.

Soon after the completion of the State Lock, the sudden burgeoning of commercial traffic demonstrated that more locks were needed. The 515-foot (157-meter) Weitzel Lock opened in 1881, and, since then, several additional locks have been built to handle both the increased traffic and the ever-expanding size of Great Lakes freighters. Today, three American locks are in operation, including the 1,200-foot (365-meter) Poe Lock, built in 1968 to accommodate the huge transport ships now common on the Great Lakes. (A fourth lock, the Sabin Lock, has been placed in "caretaker" status and is no longer used.) There is also one lock operating on the Canadian side of the strait.

The oldest city in Michigan, Sault Ste. Marie is inseparable from the locks that have both shaped its past and continue to define it today. However, the community has experienced little growth in recent years. The area's largest employers include the Ojibwa-owned Kewadin Casino, Lake Superior State University, and a prison complex south of town. Sault Ste. Marie also has some state government administrative jobs. But tourism reigns as the local economic lifeblood, with many visitors coming specifically to see the parade of goods that pass through town via a miracle of nautical engineering.

Paradise and Vicinity

"The searchers all say they'd have made Whitefish Bay if they put 15 more miles behind her . . ." Singer-songwriter Gordon Lightfoot immortalized the ill-fated ore carrier *Edmund Fitzgerald* for the masses, but locals here need no reminders. During a fierce November squall in 1975, the huge ore carrier vanished, taking the lives of all 29 hands, just 20 miles (32 km) from **Whitefish Point** and the safety of **Whitefish Bay.**

On Lake Superior, the largest and fiercest of the Great Lakes, northwest storms can build over 200 miles (320 km) of cold, open water. They most often unleash their full fury on an 80-mile (129-km) stretch of water from Grand Marais to Whitefish Point, earning the area its nickname, "Graveyard of the Great Lakes." Not surprisingly, Whitefish Point has long served as a beacon for mariners, a narrow finger of land reaching toward Canada and the gateway to Whitefish Bay, one of the few safe havens on this unpredictable inland sea.

SIGHTS
★ Lake Superior Nature Sanctuary
The Lake Superior Nature Sanctuary is wild and undeveloped, even by Upper Peninsula standards. Situated about 12 miles (19.3 km) north of Paradise, the 369-acre plot of land straddles the Lake Superior shoreline and is filled with endangered, threatened, and rare plant species in addition to common Upper Peninsula wildlife: bears, deer, and coyotes. The shifting weather patterns from winter to winter raise or lower the water level and continually alter the land. The property is preserved by the **Michigan Nature Association** (866/223-2231, www. michigannature.org), which recommends guided visits and organizes field trips to the

sanctuary that include docents sharing information on the flora and fauna. It's difficult to get to, and only foot traffic is allowed within the sanctuary. If you decide to make a visit, plan on it being a full-day affair.

To get there, drive about 11 miles (17.7 km) north from Paradise along M-123 (Whitefish Point Rd.). Look for West North Shore Road and turn left. The drive is rough, so it's best to use an SUV. As you get closer to the Lake Superior shore, the road dead-ends at a clearing/parking area. From there, it's strictly walking. Continue north to the lakeshore, then turn left to experience the sanctuary. There are some pieces of private property, so please respect the residents' privacy.

★ Great Lakes Shipwreck Museum

To commemorate the many ships that failed to round that point of safety, Whitefish Point is now the appropriate home of the **Great Lakes Shipwreck Museum** (18335 N. Whitefish Point Rd., 888/492-3747, www. shipwreckmuseum.com, 10am-6pm daily May-Oct., $14 adults, $10 children 1-6, free under age 6, $45 families). With dim lighting and appropriately haunting music, this fine compact museum traces the history of Great Lakes commerce and the disasters that sometimes accompanied it. Several shipwrecks are chronicled here, each with a scale model, photos or drawings, artifacts from the wreck, and a description of how and why the ship went down. Most compelling is the *Edmund Fitzgerald* display, complete with a life preserver and the ship's bell, recovered in a 1995 expedition led by museum founder Tom Farnquist, an accomplished diver and underwater photographer.

Housed in the former Coast Guard station, the museum, which occupies a complex of buildings, also includes the restored lightkeeper's home, a theater showing an excellent short film about the *Fitzgerald* dive, and an interesting gift shop with nautical charts, prints, books, and more. To reach the museum, take

M-123 to Paradise and follow Whitefish Point Road 11 miles (17.7 km) north. This absorbing museum makes Whitefish Point a most worthwhile destination.

Whitefish Point Underwater Preserve

For experienced divers, the **Whitefish Point Underwater Preserve** (www. michiganpreserves.org) offers a fantastic array of wrecks—30 steamers and schooners are littered all around the point. Check the website for a complete list, but be aware that the *Edmund Fitzgerald* is not among them. Good visibility is a hallmark of this 376-acre preserve. Most wrecks lie 40-270 feet (12-82 meters) deep and are located in areas unprotected by harbors. Only very experienced divers and boaters should dive here. Contact the **Paradise Area Tourism Council** (906/492-3319, www.michigansparadise.com) for information on area dive services.

★ Tahquamenon Falls State Park

West of Newberry, the headwaters of the Tahquamenon River bubble up from underground and begin a gentle roll through stands of pine and vast wetlands. Rambling and twisting northeast through Luce County, the river grows wider and more majestic by the time it enters **Tahquamenon Falls State Park** (41382 M-123, 906/492-3415, www. michigan.gov/dnr). Then, with the roar of a freight train and the power of a fire hose, it suddenly plummets over a 50-foot (15-meter) drop, creating a golden fountain of water 200 feet (60 meters) wide.

As many as 50,000 gallons of water per second gush over the Upper Tahquamenon, making it the second-largest waterfall by volume east of the Mississippi, eclipsed only by Niagara. Adding to Tahquamenon's majesty are its distinctive colors: bronze headwaters from the tannic acid of decaying cedars and hemlocks that line its banks, and bright white foam from the water's high salt content.

Tahquamenon Falls State Park

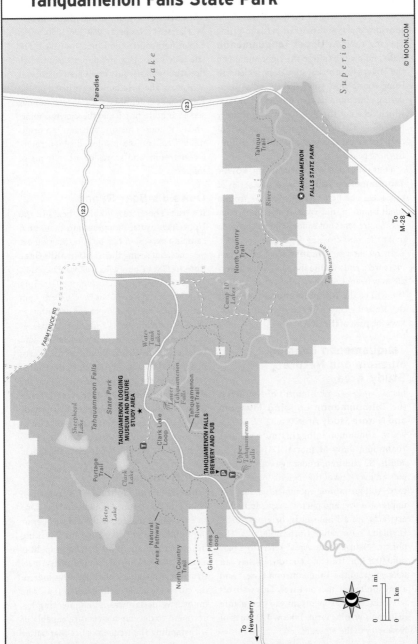

Accessing Tahquamenon Falls is easy, since both the Upper Falls and Lower Falls lie within Tahquamenon Falls State Park, which provides short, well-marked paths to prime viewing sites. At **Upper Tahquamenon Falls,** follow the trail to the right and down the 74 steps to an observation deck, which will bring you so close you'll feel the falls' thundering power and its cool mist on your face, which on a hot summer day is wonderfully refreshing. The deck offers a stunning view of both the placid waters above and the furious frothing below.

Four miles (6.4 km) downstream, **Lower Tahquamenon Falls** consists of a series of cascades. The best vantage point is from a small island in mid-river. A state park concessionaire rents out canoes and rowboats to make the short crossing.

In recent years, **moose** have been seen more frequently within the park. They generally stay near water, so your best chance to see one will be the **Tahquamenon River Trail** that links the Upper and Lower Falls and follows the path of the river.

Tahquamenon Logging Museum and Nature Study Area

Just 1.5 miles (2.4 km) north of Newberry, the **Tahquamenon Logging Museum and Nature Study Area** (41382 W. M-123, www.tahquamenonloggingmuseum.org, 10am-5pm daily Memorial Day-Sept., $5 adults, $2 children, under age 6 free) presents an overview of the region's logging history. Antique mining equipment, old logs of impressive size, and photos, maps, and other artifacts are all housed in original rustic Civilian Conservation Corps buildings. The phrase "Nature Study Area" refers to a 0.5-mile (0.8-km) trail and boardwalk that can take you into the Tahquamenon Forest and along the Tahquamenon River. This walk offers an exceptional opportunity to view nature in its most pristine form. Take M-123 north of Newberry to the museum.

Luce County Historical Museum

The **Luce County Historical Museum** (411 W. Harrie St., Newberry, 989/306-1860, www. exploringthenorth.com, 1pm-4pm Wed.-Fri. late June-Labor Day, by appointment in fall, donation) doesn't just retell area history; it *is* history. The 1894 building is listed on the National Register of Historic Places and has served as both the jail and the sheriff's home. Today, it houses historic artifacts, an original jail cell, an old-fashioned schoolroom, a courtroom, and scores of other items of interest.

Oswald's Bear Ranch

It's true: There are wild black bears in the Upper Peninsula. Bumping into them on a camping excursion can be a frightening experience, but seeing them at **Oswald's Bear Ranch** (13814 County Rd. 407, 906/293-3147, www.oswaldsbearranch.com, 9:30am-5pm daily Memorial Day-Labor Day, 9:30am-4pm daily Sept.-Oct. 10, $25 per car or motorcycle, $15 individuals), is a much more peaceful experience. Twenty-nine black bears roam four habitats here, safe for visitors to observe in a natural setting. This is one of the United States' largest bear ranches and once held the largest captive black bear in the world. Tyson Bear, who died in 2000, weighed 880 pounds (400 kg). You can observe the bears on a walking tour. North of Newberry, take M-123 to County Road 407 and head west to the ranch.

Lighthouses

Whitefish Point Light (18335 N. Whitefish Point Rd.) first beamed in 1849, and has done so ever since, making it the oldest operating lighthouse on Lake Superior. Marking the bay's entry, the Whitefish Point Light is a utilitarian-looking 80-foot (24-meter) steel structure. Though it looks relatively modern, the current tower actually dates to 1861. The innovative design was an engineering experiment to develop a structure capable of withstanding the frequent gales that batter

Whitefish Point. The light was automated in 1971. Guided tours of the lighthouse are available (10am-6pm daily May-Oct.) for $5 per person but cost $4 when purchased along with admission to the adjacent Great Lakes Shipwreck Museum.

If you're an especially passionate lighthouse buff, you'll find a truly obscure one to add to the list. The 58-foot (18-meter) **Crisp Point Light** sits on a tiny arc of land 14 miles (23 km) west of Whitefish Point, on an isolated, unbroken stretch of Lake Superior shoreline. Though an automated light took over duty decades ago, the handsome 1904 tower and adjacent home still stand. A much-needed restoration project took place 2022-2023. You'll need a map or the *DeLorme Gazetteer* to find the light; a 4WD vehicle will also be helpful. Don't attempt the last couple of miles if the ground is wet and muddy. The light is about 9 miles (14.5 km) east of the mouth of the Two-Hearted River. Reach it from the west on County Road 412, or from the east via the Farm Truck Road truck trail off M-123. The lighthouse is open for tours (906/658-3600, http://crisppointlighthouse.org). Hours vary (but are generally 10am-6pm daily late May-late Oct.) with the availability of volunteers; check the website for current hours. The grounds are always open, but "quiet hours" are from 11pm to 6am.

FESTIVALS AND EVENTS
Wild Blueberry Festival

Traverse City has its Cherry Festival, and Paradise, not to be outdone, has its very own **Wild Blueberry Festival** (www.wildblueberryfestival.org). Observed during the third weekend of August, the annual event celebrates the area's heritage as a place where wild blueberries once grew in great abundance. The festival is held right off M-123 in the heart of Paradise and features arts and crafts vendors (where the exhibitors are required to be the actual artists), plenty of music, including the Blueberry Jamboree, held during the evenings, and, of course, blueberry pie-eating contests, blueberry pie sales, and more.

SUMMER RECREATION
Hiking

Wedged on a 0.25-mile (0.4-km) strip of land between Lake Superior and Muskallonge Lake, **Muskallonge Lake State Park** (30042 County Rd. 407, Newberry, 906/658-3338, www.michigan.gov/dnr) occupies the site of the old Deer Park township. It was once home to a sawmill, a hotel, and no doubt a saloon or two. Today, a couple of fishing resorts represent the only commerce in this remote area, about 18 miles (29 km) east of Grand Marais. The North Country National Scenic Trail passes through here, and a few feeder trails let you connect to and hike a section of the historic path.

The trails at **Pretty Lakes Quiet Area** (906/293-3293) also connect to the North Country Trail. The five beautiful lakes are connected by a short trail. Take M-123 to County Road 407 north of Newberry and go left on County Road 416 to the campground. There's another short 1.25-mile (2-km) trail at nearby **Bodi Lake State Forest Campground** (906/293-3293). M-123 connects with County Road 500 near Tahquamenon Falls State Park; take County Road 550 north to County Road 437 and follow it to Bodi Lake.

The dominance of Tahquamenon Falls themselves makes it easy to overlook the balance of the 40,000-acre **Tahquamenon Falls State Park** (41382 W. M-123, 906/492-3415, www.michigan.gov/dnr), Michigan's second largest. In contrast to the heavy crowds at the falls—over 500,000 visitors per year, the most of any U.P. state park—the vast majority of the parkland remains peaceful and is etched with 25 miles (40 km) of little-used **hiking trails.** From the Upper Falls, the **Giant Pines Loop,** a 3.8-mile (6.1-km) trail, passes through a stand of white pines before crossing M-123. Once on the north side of the highway, you can link up with the **Clark Lake Loop,** a 5.6-mile (9-km) hike that traces the southern

shoreline of the shallow lake. Another worthwhile option is the **Tahquamenon River Trail,** which begins on the north side of the Tahquamenon River at the Lower Falls. For 4 miles (6.4 km) it hugs the river's edge until it ends at the Upper Falls.

Canoeing and Kayaking

The **Two-Hearted River,** clean and clear and usually quite mellow, is well suited for canoeing. In spring, however, rapid snowmelt can cause it to produce a serious amount of white water. A state designated wilderness river, the Two-Hearted winds through pine and hardwood forest; the only signs of civilization you're likely to see are a handful of cottages at the river's mouth. There are several low banks and sandbars, so picnic spots are easy to find. The Two-Hearted is also a widely regarded blue-ribbon trout stream, so be prepared for plenty of anglers when the season opens in April.

Put in at the High Bridge State Forest Campground on County Road 407 for a 23-mile (37-km) trip to the mouth. You'll find two state forest campgrounds and other camping sites along the route.

It's possible to paddle nearly all 94 miles (151 km) of the **Tahquamenon River.** A popular put-in is off County Road 415 north of McMillan, but you'll start off through several miles of bug-infested wetlands. A better choice is about 10 miles (16.1 km) downstream, off County Road 405 at Dollarville, where you'll also avoid portaging around the Dollarville Dam. Beyond Newberry, you'll be treated to a trip with a nice natural feel, since no roads come anywhere near the river. Watch the banks for bears, deer, and other wildlife. Naturally, you'll have to portage around the falls, but then you can follow the river to its mouth without any other interruptions.

A great source for rental kayaks and other equipment is **The Woods Tahquamenon River Canoe and Kayak Rental** (19184

1: Upper Tahquamenon Falls 2: Oswald's Bear Ranch 3: Whitefish Point Light 4: Great Lakes Shipwreck Museum

M-123, Newberry, 906/203-7624, www.thewoodscanoerental.net). Besides renting equipment, they also offer guided tours on the Tahquamenon River and other area waterways.

Fishing

Water is the draw at **Muskallonge Lake State Park** (30042 County Rd. 407, 906/658-3338, www.michigan.gov/dnr). The park's 2 miles (3.2 km) of Lake Superior frontage are wonderfully secluded, with low grass-covered dunes stretching off to the east and west and no visible development in either direction. Muskallonge Lake is stocked by the DNR and produces good fishing opportunities for northern pike, walleye, smallmouth bass, and perch. Because the lake is relatively shallow, it warms up enough for comfortable swimming—a rarity in the U.P. that explains this park's somewhat surprising popularity in summer. A modern campground offers several sites overlooking the water. Sites are usually available even in summer, but you can always reserve one by phone or online.

The final 16 miles (26 km) of the Tahquamenon River wind through the park, emptying into Whitefish Bay at its eastern terminus. Fishing for muskie and walleye is usually quite good in the pools below the Lower Falls. Also consider joining the fleet of runabouts and anglers in waders near the mouth of the river, where trout often school.

There is no outfitter in the Paradise area from which to rent fishing gear. However, **Superior Charters** (22272 S. Mackinac Trail, Rudyard, 906/322-6851, www.superiorchartersup.com) offers full- and half-day fishing trips on the Tahquamenon River and Whitefish Bay that include all necessary equipment.

Bird-Watching

A vital resting spot for migratory birds crossing Lake Superior, **Whitefish Point** is a birdwatcher's dream. Beginning with the hawk migration in April, and continuing through late fall, the point attracts an amazing variety of birds. Eagles, loons by the thousands, songbirds, water birds, owls, and unusual species like arctic loons and arctic terns all pass through, some 300 species in all. Even if you're not a bird enthusiast, plan to spend some time at this remarkable site, where you can wander the sand beaches, watch the birds, and keep an eye out for the big lake freighters that pass quite close to shore as they round the point. Bring along binoculars and an extra jacket. For more information, contact the **Whitefish Point Bird Observatory** (6914 N. Whitefish Point Rd., 517/580-7364, www.wpbo.org), staffed by the Michigan Audubon Society.

Golf

For golfing in the area, head to **Newberry Country Club** (5073 M-123, 906/293-8422, www.newberrycountryclub.com, $45 for 9 holes, $62 for 18 holes peak season, includes cart), a challenging 18-hole championship course at the corner of M-28 and M-123. The Newberry Country Club has been around for more than 80 years—not as long as some clubs up here, but it's not new either—and offers a driving range, a pro shop, and a bar and restaurant. Contact the country club to ask about packages, special rates, and events.

Off-Road Vehicles

Choices are limited for driving off-road in the Whitefish Point area. Some DNR trails aren't too far away, but you'll need to head west or south to find them. You can, however, ride on any state forest road that hasn't been specifically marked as off-limits, several of which are nearby. Try Lake Superior State Park or many of the roads in the nearby Hiawatha National Forest. Contact the **Sault Ste. Marie Ranger District** (4000 I-75 Business Spur, Sault Ste. Marie, 906/635-5311, www.fs.fed.us) for motor vehicle usage maps.

Waterfall Tour

For another look at Tahquamenon River and Falls, you may want to plan a day for the **Tahquamenon Falls Train and Riverboat Tour** (7195 County Road 381, Soo Junction, 888/778-7246, www.trainandboattours.com, mid-June-Labor Day, $55 adults, $51 over age 61, $32 ages 4-15, under age 4 free). The train departs from Soo Junction, 15 miles (24 km) east of Newberry (watch for the company's billboard on M-28). GPS devices often don't recognize their address; see the website for detailed driving directions. A narrow-gauge train crawls its way 5 miles (8 km) along an old logging route, through a spruce and maple forest, tamarack lowlands, and peat bogs. In about half an hour, the train sighs to a stop deep in the woods at the Tahquamenon River's banks, where you'll transfer to a large tour boat and cruise downstream nearly two hours toward the falls. Just as the river begins to roil, the boat docks on the river's south shore and guests walk the last 0.5 mile (0.8 km) to the falls. It's an entertaining 6.5-hour trip that has been in operation long before a state park provided easy access to the falls. Trains leave at 10:30am; reservations at least 24 hours in advance are required. Days of operation vary—check the website for details.

WINTER RECREATION
Ski and Snowshoe Trails

The exciting thing about Paradise is that it feels very much like a paradise, even when it's buried under several feet of snow. Cross-country skiers will find a couple of well-groomed loops just off M-123 about a mile west of town. Paradise Pathway's loops range 1.5-3 miles (2.4-4.8 km) long. Contact **Tahquamenon Country** (906/492-3319, www.michigansparadise.com) for more information.

Nearby, **Tahquamenon Falls State Park** (41382 W. M-123, 906/492-3415, www. michigan.gov/dnr) has several miles of groomed ski trails, and countless more if you're interested in backcountry skiing. The River Trail leaves the parking area and runs about 4 miles (6.4 km) to the ranger station. This trail isn't a loop, so you'll have to backtrack. There's also the 1-mile-long (1.6-km) Nature Trail. The Giant Pines Loop is 3.5 miles (5.6 km) and closest to the parking area;

farther away are the Wilderness Loop, at 7.4 miles (11.9 km), and the 5.6-mile (9-km) Clark Lake Loop. A number of these loops and trails connect to the North Country National Scenic Trail, so you have an additional 4,400 miles (7,100 km) of trails available.

In Newberry, try the **Canada Lakes Pathway** (906/492-3415) for 14 miles (23 km) of groomed ski trails near Natalie State Forest Campground, southeast of Newberry.

Snowmobiling

If you want to snowmobile up to the very end of Whitefish Point, take **Trail 453,** which will eventually get you there, although there's a network of trails that you'll need to navigate first. If you're heading east from Grand Marais, **Trail 8** will get you to Paradise before it curves south and east to Sault Ste. Marie. Several miles before Paradise, however, Trail 8 intersects with **Trails 452** and **451,** which head north and hit 453 and continue to the tip of Whitefish Point. Heading down to Newberry, take **Trail 49.**

Snowmobiles can be rented from **North Store Follow Me Outfitters** (18549 County Rd. 407, Newberry, 906/658-3450, https://northstorefmo.com).

FOOD

If you want to cut loose, head to **Timber Charlie's** (101 Newberry Ave., Newberry, 906/293-3363, 11am-9pm Sun.-Thurs., 11am-10pm Fri.-Sat., $16-23), a family-friendly place that serves basic fare. Try selections of Mexican, Italian, seafood, steak, and burgers; there's also a full bar.

In Tahquamenon Falls State Park, you can't do much better than the ★ **Tahquamenon Falls Brewery and Pub** (24019 Upper Falls Dr., 906/492-3300, www.tahquamenonfallsbrewery.com, 9am-10pm daily, $16-29), a microbrewery and restaurant with great food and a relaxed brewpub atmosphere. Best of all, it's just steps away from the viewing area for the Upper Falls. Selections of steak, fresh fish, hefty burgers, and other sandwiches give way to that Yooper classic, the pasty. If you haven't stopped for one at a roadside diner, you'll want to get one here. The beer offerings vary but typically include Harvest Wheat, Black Bear Stout, Honey Brown Ale, and Porcupine Pale Ale.

ACCOMMODATIONS

There are some nice hotels in and around Paradise and Newberry, but for more selection, including plenty of chains, it's worth the drive to Sault Ste. Marie. One of the best hotels up here is the **Paradise Inn** (8359 N. Whitefish Point Rd., 906/492-3940, www.exploringthenorth.com/paradiseinn/motel.html, $$), at the junction of M-123 and Whitefish Point Road. Two of the 36 rooms at this modest but well-kept motel are suites with jetted tubs. Continental breakfast and guest laundry are available as well.

Another excellent option is the **Magnuson Grand Hotel Lakefront** (8112 N. M-123, 906/492-3770, http://magnusongrandlakefront.com, $$). The waterfront views, indoor pool, and superb breakfast make this a great place for travelers desiring something a bit more upscale.

There are additional lodging options in Newberry. For a historical feel, try the elegant, intimate bed-and-breakfast **The MacLeod House** (6211 County Rd. 441, 906/293-3841, $).

Camping

About 11 miles (17.7 km) east of Grand Marais on County Road H-58 is **Blind Sucker River,** a deceptively terrible name for such an appealing place to camp. There are three state forest campgrounds in this area: along the Blind Sucker River, along the Blind Sucker Flooding, and near Lake Superior (all $15). If you choose to camp along the Superior shore, be prepared for cold nights, even in August.

Even more attractive may be the state forest's **Pretty Lakes Quiet Area** ($15), about 8 miles (12.9 km) to the southeast of Grand Marais. Here you'll find five small clear lakes, ringed with sand and linked together by short portages. There are canoe campsites on Beaverhouse, Camp Eight, and Long Lakes, along with an 18-site rustic campground near the approach road at Pretty Lake. No motors are allowed on Pretty, Brush, Beaverhouse, or Long Lake. This is indeed a pretty, secluded spot where you'll listen to loons and other wildlife rather than the whine of powerboats and automobiles. To reach it, it's easiest to stay on County Road H-58, which becomes County Road H-37/County Road 407 when it swings south at Muskallonge Lake State Park. About 5 miles (8 km) south, turn west on County Road 416 and follow it 2.5 miles (4 km) to the campground. If you have a good map, you can also follow County Road 416 from the Blind Sucker area.

There are dozens of other lakes and camp-sites in the Lake Superior State Forest. Pick up a good topographic map and contact **Lake Superior State Forest** (906/293-3293, www. michigan.gov/dnr) for more information.

On the northwest shore of Bodi Lake, **Bodi Lake State Forest Campground** (906/492-3415, $20 per night, first come, first served) is another camping option. Situated in a quiet, secluded location, the small facility (12 sites) can accommodate tents or small trailers. There's also a boat launch to get out on the water, where there is excellent walleye and pike fishing.

INFORMATION AND SERVICES

For tourism and visitor information for the area, contact the friendly people at the **Newberry Area Tourism Association** (906/293-5562, www.newberrytourism.com) or **Tahquamenon Country** (906/492-3319, www.michigansparadise.com).

Since the stretch of land between Grand Marais and Sault Ste. Marie is relatively se-cluded, most essential services are located in the bigger cities west and east of Whitefish Point. Although Newberry is small, with just 1,550 people, there's a good community hos-pital, the **Helen Newberry Joy Hospital** (502 W. Harrie St., Newberry, 906/293-9200 or 800/743-3093, www.hnjh.org). Take M-123

into Newberry and continue west on Harris Street to the hospital. The hospital also of-fers weekly clinic services in Paradise, with a physician or nurse practitioner visiting the **Paradise Community Health Center** (7321 N. M-123, Paradise, 906/492-3881) 11am-10pm, Sunday-Thursday.

Most of the area's easily accessible banks are located in Newberry. The **Tahquamenon Area Credit Union** (www.tacumi.com) has branches in Newberry (7693 M-123, 906/293-5117 or 800/575-5117), Engadine, and Rudyard. Other banks in Newberry in-clude **Nicolet Bank** (414 Newberry Ave., 906/293-5165, www.nicoletbank.com) and **First National Bank of St. Ignace** (1014 S. Newberry Ave., 906/293-5160, www.fnbsi. com).

GETTING THERE AND AROUND

Car

If you're driving from Grand Marais, the quickest and easiest route is south on M-77 to M-28 east until you reach M-123. Left onto M-123 takes you through Tahquamenon Falls State Park into Paradise. The trip should take 1.5 hours. The other option is more time-consuming, but it hugs Lake Superior and is more scenic than the alternative stretch of flat, uninspired scenery along M-28. It's about a two-hour drive if you head east out of Grand Marais on the Grand Marais Truck Trail, which bends south after Muskallonge Lake State Park as County Road 407. Continuing south, follow the leftward bend to the east, then turn left on M-123 and follow it to Paradise. Past Paradise, M-123 continues south until it reconnects with M-28 east of Newberry.

From Sault Ste. Marie, take I-75 south to M-28 and head west until you come to M-123; proceed north.

Air

The closest airport to Paradise, Tahquamenon Falls, and the rest of Whitefish Point is **Chippewa County International Airport** (CIU, 119 Airport Dr., Kincheloe,

906/495-2522 or 906/495-5631, www.airciu.com), south of Sault Ste. Marie, which offers two daily flights from Detroit on Delta Airlines. You'll need to rent a car if you fly in because there's no public transportation to Paradise. Car rentals at the airport are by **Avis** (906/495-5900, www.avis.com). The drive to Paradise takes a little more than an hour via M-80 toward I-75 (follow the signs); take I-75 north to M-28. Take M-28 west for 30 miles (48 km) before you hit M-123, which will take you north to Whitefish Point.

Boat

The small **Whitefish Point State Dock** (906/492-3415, www.michigan.gov/dnr), near the tip of Whitefish Point at 46°45.32 N, 84°57.52 W, has only a handful of slips and limited amenities, but it's one of only two harbors between Grand Marais and Sault Ste. Marie. The other is **Little Lake State Dock** (906/658-3372, www.michigan.gov/dnr), about halfway between Grand Marais and Paradise at 46°43.06 N, 85°21.48 W and with even fewer amenities than Whitefish Point.

Sault Ste. Marie

At the foot of Whitefish Bay, mighty Lake Superior gradually narrows to form the St. Mary's River, the waterway that links it to Lake Huron, Lake Michigan, and their counterparts to the south. Because Lake Superior is 21 feet (6 meters) higher than the other lakes, the St. Mary's River is a series of falls and rapids near Sault Ste. Marie. *Sault,* pronounced "soo" and often used as a nickname for the city, means "falling water," a name bestowed by early French explorers.

Sault Ste. Marie is the U.P.'s second-largest city, with a population of 13,000. This historic place is well worth a visit, especially to view the boat traffic through the famous Soo Locks, which link Lakes Superior and Huron. But don't overlook the area to the south and east, where the lovely blue-green waters of Lake Huron wrap around the end of the peninsula, a scalloped shoreline of quiet bays and a scattering of isolated and picturesque islands.

SIGHTS
Curley Lewis Memorial Highway

The twisting, scenic **Curley Lewis Memorial Highway,** also called **Lake Shore Drive,** follows the curve of Lake Superior's Whitefish Bay from M-123 east about 37 miles (60 km) to Sault Ste. Marie. It's almost an attraction in

itself, passing through the eastern unit of the Hiawatha National Forest and offering views of the far end of Lake Superior and a few other worthwhile stops.

About 15 miles (24 km) from the beginning of the Memorial Highway is the federally run **Pendills Creek National Fish Hatchery** (21990 W. Trout Ln., 906/437-5231, www.fws.gov, 7am-noon and 12:30pm-3pm Mon.-Fri., free), which raises thousands of lake trout that grow up to tempt anglers in Lakes Superior, Michigan, and Huron. Visitors can wander around the tanks to peer down at the hundreds of wriggling trout fry and the breeder trout that weigh in at 15 pounds or more. The raceways are covered to keep birds and other predators at bay. Outdoor areas are also accessible on weekends.

About 2 miles (3.2 km) past the hatchery are the **Big Pine Picnic Grounds,** a day-use area in the Hiawatha National Forest that is a wonderful spot to take a break. It offers a pleasant, shaded area under a canopy of huge white pines and a pretty sand and pebble beach along Whitefish Bay.

Continuing about 2 miles (3.2 km) east, don't miss the chance to climb the tower at the **Point Iroquois Light Station** (906/437-5272, hours vary, generally 10am-3:30pm Thurs., Fri., and every other Saturday June 15-Oct.), where Whitefish Bay narrows into

Sault Ste. Marie and Vicinity

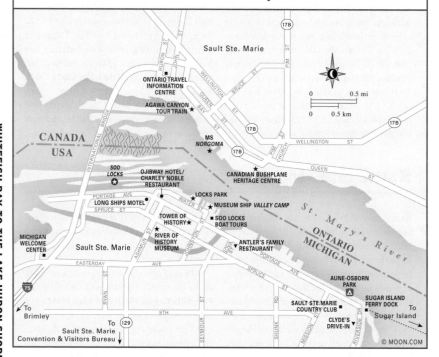

the St. Mary's River. Since 1855 a beacon here has helped guide ships through this extremely difficult passage, where reefs lurk near the Canadian shore and the rock walls of Point Iroquois threaten on the U.S. side. In 1870, the original wooden light tower was replaced with the present one, a classic white-painted brick structure. A keeper's home was added in 1902.

With fewer and fewer lighthouses open to the public, it's fun to climb the iron spiral staircase for a freighter captain's view of the river, the bay, and the frequent shipping traffic. Stop in the adjacent lightkeeper's home, where the local historical society has restored some rooms to illustrate the life of a lightkeeper; other rooms feature displays and old photos. The lighthouse and adjacent beach are now part of the Hiawatha National Forest, which should help ensure its continued preservation.

This is the kind of road where every view is better than the last. As the highway curves south, watch for the turnoff to the west marking the terrific **Mission Hill Overlook.** Drive up the sand and gravel road for grand sweeping views of the river and bay, Ontario's Laurentian Mountains, the cityscape of Sault Ste. Marie, and freighters that look like toy ships. Closer by, the Point Iroquois light is just 1 mile (1.6 km) away on the opposite side of Monocle Lake. Just to the south is Spectacle Lake.

TOP EXPERIENCE

★ Soo Locks

Nearly every visitor to the Soo makes a pilgrimage to the locks, right in the heart of downtown Sault Ste. Marie along Portage Street. The city has beautified this area with

Locks Park, an esplanade that invites a peaceful stroll. Blue freighter signs mark the **Locks Park Walkway,** which wanders along Water Street and is dotted with interpretive plaques that explain the city's heritage and other objects of historical interest. These include a former U.S. Weather Bureau Building, a Japanese *torii* (ceremonial gateway), and an obelisk commemorating the 1905 dedication of the Soo Locks.

In the heart of Locks Park, the U.S. Army Corps of Engineers manages the locks and a **visitors center** (906/253-9290, www.saultstemarie.com, 9am-9pm daily mid-May-mid-Oct.) next to a raised **viewing platform** that allows visitors to see the locks in action. Inside the visitors center are several exhibits that provide background on how the locks work. A moving model shows how ships are lowered and raised by opening and closing the gates of a lock chamber and allowing water to rush in or out. No pumps are required; the locks are gravity-fed, which means the water simply seeks its own level. Other displays explain the construction of the locks. A knowledgeable staff with a PA system, along with video cameras upriver, notify you as vessels approach. In summer months, you can usually count on a ship coming through about once an hour. You can also call the visitors center to get the day's shipping schedule, but times can change depending on weather conditions and other factors.

It's easy to spend an hour or two watching the ships as they crawl through the locks with seemingly just inches to spare. Summer evenings are especially pleasant, when you'll likely have the platform to yourself to watch the illuminated ships. If you're lucky, you might see a "saltie," an oceangoing vessel that's likely hauling grain to foreign ports. Overall, the three most common Great Lakes shipments are iron ore for steelmaking; limestone, which is a purifying agent for steelmaking and is used in construction as well as papermaking; and coal for power plants.

The locks and viewing platform are open through the Great Lakes shipping season, which is year-round except for January 15 to March 25. Those are the official dates when the locks terminate operations for winter maintenance, although ice buildup on Lake Superior can affect the length of the shipping season.

After viewing the locks, you can "lock through" yourself on the extremely popular **Soo Locks Boat Tours** (800/432-6301, www.soolocks.com, early May-mid-Oct., $32 adults, $13 ages 5-12). The two-hour trip takes you through both the American and Canadian locks and travels along both cities' waterfronts. Also offered are lunch, dinner, and various special cruises to see lighthouses, Fourth of July fireworks, etc. At busy times, you'll be in the midst of freighter traffic, dwarfed by their enormous steel hulls. The large passenger boats have both heated and open deck areas. Boats depart as early as 9am from two docks on Portage Avenue. Although the tour does cross into Canadian waters, you do not need to bring a passport or other travel documents since you won't actually be disembarking in Canada.

Museums

After you've watched the big Great Lakes boats, the **Museum Ship *Valley Camp*** (501 Water St., 906/632-3658 or 888/744-7867, www.saulthistoricsites.com, 10am-5pm Mon.-Sat. and 11am-5pm Sun. mid-May-mid-June, 9am-6pm Mon.-Sat. and 10am-5pm Sun. mid-June-early Sept., 10am-5pm Mon.-Sat. and 11am-5pm Sun. early Sept. 4-late Oct., $16 adults, $8 ages 5-17) gives you a chance to see what it was like to live and work aboard a giant steamer. This 550-foot (170-meter) steamship logged more than 1 million miles (1.6 million km) on the Great Lakes hauling ore, coal, and stone from 1907 to the mid-1970s. Now it's permanently docked five blocks east of the Soo Locks. Visitors can tour the pilothouse, engine room, main deck, crew quarters, coal bunker, and more. The ship has a number of aquariums and maritime displays, some better than others. The most popular is a display on the sinking of the *Edmund Fitzgerald,*

The History of the Soo Locks

The rapids on the St. Mary's River have been an impediment to water transportation for as long as people have lived in the area. Faced with a 20-foot (6-meter) drop on the journey from Lake Superior to Lake Huron, the indigenous Ojibwa people would take their canoes out of the water and portage around the rapids. Early European settlers did the same until the fur trade and an increased European presence required them to use ships. Since the ships were too large to portage, they solved the problem by having two sets of ships, one on the Lake Superior side and one on the Lake Huron side. After reaching Lake Superior's rapids, goods would be unloaded and transported to ships waiting on the Lake Huron side. This proved to be a workable but inefficient solution.

The Northwest Fur Company built the first locks in the 1790s on the Canadian side of the river. Though small, at 38 feet (12 meters), the locks remained in use until they were destroyed in the War of 1812, forcing a return to the old system.

The next undertaking wasn't until 1853-1855, when the Fairbanks Scale Company agreed to construct two locks in exchange for 250,000 acres of public land, which the company hoped to exploit for mining. Upon completion, the two 350-foot (105-meter) locks were turned over to state control. In 1881, demand for newer and larger facilities prompted a transfer of control to the United States Army Corps of Engineers, which continues to operate and maintain the water gates to this day.

The locks are an amazing feat of engineering, consuming enormous amounts of power and requiring regular maintenance. To meet the challenge, the U.S. Hydroelectric Power Plant, just south of the locks, is part of the overall facility. The plant generates more than 150 million kilowatt-hours of electricity each year, with the locks receiving first priority. Any remaining electricity is distributed to Sault Ste. Marie in Michigan and to the surrounding eastern U.P. communities.

The Poe and MacArthur Locks are capable of handling the largest ships and see the most use; the Poe is 1,200 feet (365 meters) long and can accommodate ships with up to 72,000 tons of cargo. The Davis Lock, one of the two smaller locks, handles smaller ships, while the Sabin Lock is currently dormant and in "caretaker" status.

The locks' operations are quick and efficient, with each capable of draining and filling in a matter of minutes. Some 10,000 ships pass through the locks each year despite their annual winter closure. During winter, the Army Corps works on maintenance and repairs.

You can watch the daily operations of the Soo Locks from the visitors center, which lets you get fairly close to the massive freighters as they make their way along the St. Mary's River. You'll also find several informative displays about the history and operation of the locks. Try a trip through the locks with Soo Locks Boat Tours. On the last Friday in June, the Army Corps of Engineers host its annual open house, known as **Engineers Day** (www.saultstemarie.com/soo-locks-engineers-day), which allows the public to see facilities that are normally off-limits. The event is free; no tickets required.

including two tattered lifeboats found empty and drifting on the lake. All in all, it's well worth a couple of hours. Make sure to stop at the museum shop, housed in a separate building next to the parking lot. It has an excellent selection of maritime books and videos.

Like most observation towers, the **Tower of History** (326 Portage Ave., 906/632-3658, www.saulthistoricsites.com, 10am-5pm Mon.-Sat. and noon-5pm Sun. mid-May-mid-June, 9am-6pm Mon.-Sat. and 10am-5pm Sun. mid-June-early Sept., 10am-5pm Mon.-Sat.

1: St. Mary's River as seen from the Tower of History
2: Soo Locks Boat Tours

and noon-5pm Sun. early Sept.-late Oct., $8 adults, $4 children ages 5-17), four blocks east of the Soo Locks, is an ugly blight on the landscape: a 21-story stark concrete monolith, but with a wonderful 360-degree view of the twin Soo locks, the St. Mary's River, Lake Superior, and forests rolling off in the distance. Rather than being stuck behind windows, you get to enjoy the views from an open-air deck. Bring a jacket, as it can get chilly. The tower also includes a few small exhibit areas and a theater showing documentary videos. Luckily, there is an elevator to the top. Interestingly, the tower was originally built as a bell tower for the neighboring church. Intended as part of a larger church complex, financial difficulties caused the project to be abandoned. In 1980 the tower was donated to Sault Historic Sites.

The **River of History Museum** (531 Ashmun St., 906/632-1999, www.riverofhistory.com, 11am-5pm Mon.-Sat. early June-late Sept., $7.50 adults, $3.75 ages 5-17) uses the St. Mary's River as the framework for telling the story of the region's history. Life-size dioramas depict things like Native Americans spear fishing in the rapids and a French fur trapper's cabin (the French were the first European settlers in the region). The museum incorporates lots of sound in its displays: dripping ice from melting glaciers, roaring rapids, Ojibwa elders passing down legends. One hopes the museum will keep building on this idea.

The Museum Ship *Valley Camp*, Tower of History, and River of History Museum can all be visited by purchasing a **combination ticket** (www.saulthistoricsites.com, $28.50 adults, $13.75 ages 5-17), providing a significant savings off the individual admission prices.

Lighthouses

Soo Locks Boat Tours (1157 E. Portage Ave. and 515 E. Portage Ave., 906/632-2512 or 800/432-6301, www.soolocks.com) offers the option of extending their popular locks tour with the **St. Mary's River Lighthouse Cruise** ($65 pp, $1 children 4 and under).

After riding through the Soo Locks, you'll get a short tour of the St. Mary's River and a float-by of a number of picturesque lighthouses. See the unoccupied but intact keeper's residence at **Cedar Point** and the remains of the original light on **Round Island.** You'll cross into Canadian waters (a passport is not necessary) and see the **Gros Cap Reefs Lighthouse** and the **Point Louise Range Lights.** Each ship includes a concession bar offering snacks and coffee. Box lunches are available with advance reservations. During the trip, you'll be able to see the **Point Iroquois Lighthouse** from the boat, but this one is worth going out of your way to visit on land.

Sault Ste. Marie, Ontario

Just across the International Bridge lies the Soo's sister city in Ontario, also named Sault Ste. Marie. With a population of 75,000, it's the larger of the two cities, with a more diversified economy, which includes a huge steel plant and a paper company. Aside from these industries, Sault Ste. Marie, Ontario, also has a great deal to offer visitors. Downtown, a lovely **boardwalk** rambles along the river for about a mile, beginning at the bridge and extending east past fishing platforms, shops, and the MS *Norgoma,* the last passenger cruise ship built for the Great Lakes, now a museum. On Wednesday and Saturday, there's a farmers market near the tented pavilion.

One of the most advertised and popular visitor attractions is the once-daily **Agawa Canyon Train Tour** (129 Bay St., 705/946-7300 or 800/242-9287, www.agawatrain.com, late July-mid-Oct., C$140 adults, C$104 over age 59, C$70 under age 19, 2 and under free), a full-day (8am-6pm) round-trip through the scenic wooded gorge of the Agawa Canyon. The tour includes a 90-minute stopover in the canyon, where you can hike to lookouts, visit waterfalls, wander along the river, or just enjoy the grassy picnic area. The train trip is even more popular, although slightly more expensive (C$155 per person, except children 2 and under), in the fall color season, which usually runs mid-September to mid-October. Tours depart at 8am from the station; reservations are recommended.

As in Alaska, bush planes are an integral part of life in the wilds of the Canadian north. A small plane with pontoons can get you where no land vehicle can, since almost any remote lake can serve as a landing strip. The **Canadian Bushplane Heritage Centre** (50 Pim St., 705/945-6242 or 877/287-4752, www.bushplane.com, 9am-6pm Tues.-Sun. mid-May-mid-Oct., 10am-4pm Tues.-Sun. mid-Oct.-mid-May, C$17 adults, C$15 seniors, C$9 students, C$5 children), near Pim and Bay Streets on the waterfront, chronicles the history of Canada's bush planes, which began with the Ontario Air Service in the 1920s and was established to fight forest fires. Even if you're not an aviation buff, you'll enjoy this unique museum, housed in the Air Service's old waterfront hangar.

You can reach Ontario via the 3-mile-long (4.8-km) **International Bridge** (934 Bridge Plaza, 906/635-5255 U.S., 705/942-4345 Canada, www.saultbridge.com, toll $4/C$5.10 for passenger car, one-way). You can exchange money and pick up maps and other useful area information at the **Ontario Travel Information Centre** (705/945-6941, www.ontariotravel.net) at the foot of the bridge. Documentation required to enter Canada is proof of citizenship, typically a passport. To reenter the United States after visiting Canada you need either a valid passport or an enhanced driver's license issued by one of the states that participate in the Western Hemisphere Travel Initiative (WHTI).

ENTERTAINMENT
Bay Mills Resort and Casino
Bay Mills Casino (11386 W. Lakeshore Dr., Brimley, 877/229-6455 or 888/422-9645, www.baymillscasinos.com, 10am-2am daily) offers the usual gaming standbys—blackjack, roulette, craps, three-card poker, Texas hold 'em, and more. It also has something that few other U.P. casinos provide: free alcoholic drinks while actively gaming. If that's

not enough to bring you to their doors, there are more than 1,000 slot and video poker machines and Royal Ascot video horse racing. You'll also find several varied dining options. Black Bay Grille and Games is located right on the waterfront, Sacy's Restaurant offers a fine-dining environment, and there are also two lounges and a café. Bring your clubs for a round of golf (you can also rent some from the pro shop), or stay the night in the hotel, with 140-plus rooms.

Brimley's other casino, **Kings Club Casino** (12140 W. Lakeshore Dr., Brimley, 906/248-3227, 10am-2am daily), is actually part of the Bay Mills Resort. Shuttle service is offered between the two casinos. Unlike most gaming venues, Kings Club is not open 24 hours. Kings Club is one story and has more than 280 slot and video poker machines. That's a far cry from the casino's beginning, when Kings Club was the first Native American-operated blackjack casino in the country and the first in Michigan to offer slots and keno.

FESTIVALS AND EVENTS
International 500 Snowmobile Race
The **International 500 Snowmobile Race** (www.i-500.com) has been held in Sault Ste. Marie since 1969. The I-500 was conceived as a snowmobiling version of the Indianapolis 500. The 500 miles (800 km) are handled by a team of drivers, although someone will occasionally go it alone, on a 1-mile (1.6-km) iced track, while Sno-Cross races are held concurrently at the same venue. Races are usually held in late January and early February, after several warm-up events.

International Bridge Walk
The **International Bridge Walk** is held each summer on the last Saturday of June as a symbol of friendship between two cities and two nations. It's similar to the annual Labor Day walk across the Mackinac Bridge, except that the 2.8-mile (4.5-km) walk is about half the

distance, and you actually get to stroll into Canada. Be sure to bring your passport or enhanced driver's license.

SUMMER RECREATION
Hiking

West of town, the **Algonquin Pathway** has more than 9 miles (14.5 km) of trails for hiking and biking and, in the winter, cross-country skiing. Two miles (3.2 km) of the path are lighted. Take I-75 to 3-Mile Road and head west, turning right on 20th Street and left on 16th Avenue to the trailhead. Another good spot is the **Pine Bowl Pathway,** 19 miles (31 km) southwest of Sault Ste. Marie. Pine Bowl has nearly 8 miles (12.9 km) of trails and rolling terrain. To get here, take I-75 south to the Kinross/Tone Road exit and head east on Tone Road, then turn right onto Wilson Road.

You'll be able to find some good trails at a number of area campgrounds. **Monocle Lake Campground** (Forest Rd. 3699, 906/635-5311), in Hiawatha National Forest 21 miles (34 km) west of Sault Ste. Marie and near the Point Iroquois Light, has an inviting 2-mile (3.2-km) loop accessible from its day-use parking lot. A viewing platform overlooks an active beaver pond before the trail heads uphill to another overlook, which has views to the St. Mary's River and beyond, before returning to the parking lot.

At **Soldier Lake Campground** (Forest Rd. 3138, 906/635-5311), in Hiawatha National Forest 30 miles (48 km) west of the city, there's a 4-mile (6.4-km) footpath that winds its way around the 15-acre lake and a spur that connects to the North Country National Scenic Trail. Slightly farther out, 38 miles (61 km) west of Sault Ste. Marie and a few miles south of M-28 in Hiawatha National Forest, **Three Lakes Campground** (Forest Rd. 3142) has an easy 1-mile (1.6-km) loop around Walker Lake.

Fishing

Sault Ste. Marie is uniquely positioned for some of the Upper Peninsula's finest fishing. With Lake Superior above and Huron below, the Soo sits on the wide ribbon of the St. Mary's River that links the two and offers the chance to snag walleye, perch, pike, trout, salmon, and, of course, whitefish. Contact the **Sault Ste. Marie Convention and Visitors Bureau** (225 E. Portage Ave., 906/632-3366 or 800/647-2858, www.saultstemarie.com) for more detailed information and a fishing guide.

For inland lake fishing, try a visit to **Monocle Lake,** a 172-acre inland lake with walleye, smallmouth bass, pike, and perch. The lake is 40-45 feet (12-14 meters) deep and has two reefs near Hiawatha National Forest's **Monocle Lake Campground** (Forest Rd. 3699, 906/635-5311). There's a boat launch between the campground and the day-use area. **Soldier Lake Campground** (Forest Rd. 3138, 906/635-5311) is on the shores of a much smaller 15-acre lake in Hiawatha National Forest, with bass and perch for the catching. Consider **Lake George** and **Munuscong Lake** as well.

A great local partner for charter fishing is **Northwind Charters** (908 7 Mile Rd., Sault Ste. Marie, 906/748-1980, www. northwindcharters.wixsite.com). The company offers five-hour trips on a sliding scale depending on the number of guests ($400 for one person, $450 for two, $500 for three). Best of all, they provide all the needed gear—poles, lures, etc. All that guests are required to bring is a Michigan fishing license, snacks and drinks, and a cooler to store your catch, although this can be left in your vehicle until needed at the end of the trip.

Another local charter service is **Young Buck Fishing Charters** (1225 Riverside Dr., Sault Ste. Marie, www.fishingbooker.com, five-hour trip $550, multiday options available). Your day begins early (5:30am). The boat can accommodate up to three anglers. All equipment is provided. Just be sure to bring your Michigan fishing license. They can take their guests to lake or river destinations.

Golf

The 18 holes at the **Sault Ste. Marie**

Country Club (1520 Riverside Dr., 906/632-7812, http://saultstemariecc.com, $25 for 9 holes, $45 for 18 holes, includes cart) are among the choicest of the Upper Peninsula, and some of the oldest as well. The course opened more than 100 years ago and was expanded into an 18-hole course in the 1980s. Visit the pro shop or have an evening dinner at the Grillroom 1901, located in the clubhouse. Take Portage Avenue east out of the city to the country club.

There are another 18 holes at **Tanglewood Marsh** (2600 W. 16th Ave., 906/635-7651, www.upga.com, $20 for 9 holes, $37 for 18 holes, includes cart). Take I-75 to exit 392 and head west on 3-Mile Road. Turn right on 20th Street and left on Oak Street, then curve right on 16th Avenue to the clubhouse.

Brimley has one of the U.P.'s top-rated golf courses at **Wild Bluff Golf Course** (11335 W. Lakeshore Dr., 906/248-5860 or 888/422-9645, www.wildbluff.com, $40 for 9 holes, $75 for 18 holes, includes cart), which is part of the Bay Mills Resort. The 18-hole championship course received an impressive 4.5 stars from *Golf Digest*, and it's easy to see why. A fine pro shop and an elegant player's lounge complete the golf experience.

Bird-Watching

Like Whitefish Point, the Sault Ste. Marie area is a popular spot for bird-watching. Among the best places to scout for avian life is **Sugar Island**, the large island east of Sault Ste. Marie between Michigan and Ontario. The 15-mile-long (24-km) island and the St. Mary's River both attract migratory birds, particularly snowy and great gray owls. Both the Little Traverse Conservatory and the Osborn Preserve, which is owned by the University of Michigan Biological Station, help conserve and preserve the island's wildlife and make the southern part of the island a great place for bird-watching. Look for spruce grouse, black terns, sedge wrens, and long-eared owls. Access to the island is by ferry from Sault Ste. Marie. For schedules and rates, visit the **Eastern Upper Peninsula**

Transportation Authority website (www.eupta.net/ferry-system).

Beaches

One of the finest beaches in the area is on the edge of **Monocle Lake** (906/635-5311, www.fs.fed.us) in Hiawatha National Forest, 20 miles (32 km) west of Sault Ste. Marie on Lake Shore Drive. The large lake makes for some great swimming, certainly better than chilly Lake Superior. This swimming area is easily accessible from the day-use parking area and is equipped with grills and picnic tables. To get here, take the Whitefish Bay National Scenic Byway (Lake Shore Dr.) as it follows the shoreline west of St. Ignace to Forest Road 3699. If you're determined to swim in Lake Superior, head over to **Brimley State Park** (9200 W. 6 Mile Rd., 906/248-3422, www.michigan.gov/dnr) on the shores of Whitefish Bay. The water here is generally Lake Superior's warmest.

Off-Road Vehicles

Off-road trails are scarce in this area. The only one in Chippewa County is the 29-mile (47-km) **Kinross Motorcycle Trail,** about 20 miles (32 km) south of Sault Ste. Marie near Kinross and the Chippewa County International Airport. As its name implies, the trail is open only to motorcycles. The trail's three main loops all extend from a central parking area. Take Tone Road east from I-75 to Wilson Road and turn right to the parking area. Although there are no other designated trails in the county, all state forest roads are open to off-road vehicles unless specifically marked otherwise. More than 2,000 miles (3,200 km) of roads in the Hiawatha National Forest are open to ATV/ORV use. For motor vehicle usage maps and more information, contact the **Sault Ste. Marie Ranger District** (4000 I-75 Business Spur, 906/635-5311, www.fs.fed.us).

WINTER RECREATION
Ski and Snowshoe Trails

On the west side of the city, the trails at the

Algonquin Pathway offer cross-country skiers a series of loops that total 9 miles (14.5 km), with the longest 2-mile (3.2-km) loop illuminated for night skiing. To get here, take I-75 to 3-Mile Road, then head west to 20th Street and turn right. Take 20th Street to the intersection with 16th Avenue.

The **Pine Bowl Pathway** is about 20 miles (32 km) southwest of the city and has nearly 8 miles (12.9 km) of groomed trails. To get to Pine Bowl from Sault Ste. Marie, head south on I-75 to the Kinross/Tone Road exit (exit 378) and take Tone Road east to Wilson Road; turn right on Wilson to the pathway.

A source for both ski and biking equipment in Sault Ste. Marie is Foxhole Bike and Ski (107 E. Portage, 906/632-8161).

Downhill Skiing

You could go to **Sault Seal Recreation Area** (2601 Minneapolis St., 906/635-6961, www.saultcity.com, 4pm-8pm Tues.-Fri., 1pm-8pm Sat.-Sun., adults $10, children $6) for some downhill skiing, but the big draw here is tubing, with seven downhill runs. If you're looking for better skiing, head elsewhere in the U.P., or consider crossing the border into Canada for the **Searchmont Resort** (103 Searchmont Resort Rd., Searchmont, 705/781-2340 or 800/663-2546, www.searchmont.com) in Ontario. Remember to bring the proper travel documents for crossing the border. The latter option will require several hours of driving.

Snowmobiling

The main drags into and out of Sault Ste. Marie by snowmobile are **Trail 8,** which heads west and north to Whitefish Point, Manistique, and Marquette, and **Trail 49,** which drops south toward Les Cheneaux before connecting to the rest of the Upper Peninsula's network of trails. In the city itself, Trails 8, 49, and others (449 and 497) run parallel to many of the streets. After crossing Power Canal near the Soo Locks, you must stay on the trail or risk a fine.

There are no options for snowmobile rentals in Sault Ste. Marie. The nearest source is in Newberry at **North Store Follow Me Outfitters** (18549 County Rd. 407, Newberry, 906/658-3450, https://northstorefmo.com).

FOOD

For an old-fashioned "service at your car" burger place, cruise on over to ★ **Clyde's Drive-In** (1425 Riverside Dr., 906/632-2581, noon-7pm Sun., Mon., and Thurs., noon-8pm Fri.-Sat., under $12), at the Sugar Island ferry dock, for the great grilled hamburgers they've been making since 1949. Inside, seating and a menu of fried items are also available.

Antler's Family Restaurant (804 E. Portage Ave., 906/253-1728, www.saultantlers.com, 11:30am-8pm daily, $8-18) serves up burgers, ribs, fresh fish, and steaks, in a setting with more than 300 game heads mounted on the ceiling. Don't go when you have a headache—they have a strange habit of setting off sirens and whistles for no particular reason. Kids will naturally love this place.

Seafood, steaks, and just about everything else are on the menu at the **Lockview Restaurant** (329 Portage Ave., Sault Ste. Marie., 906/632-2772, www.thelockviewrestaurant.net, 7am-8pm Sun.-Thurs., 7am-9pm Fri.-Sat., dinner entrees $14-28). This place excels at all times of the day, offering creations like steak and eggs at breakfast, sweet sea clams at lunch, and walleye and a 12-ounce ribeye for dinner.

In late 2020, Soo Brewing Company owner Ray Bauer decided to move the brewery and consolidate it with his winery a few blocks down Portage Street, creating **Soo Brewing Company and 1668 Winery** (100 W. Portage Ave., Sault Ste. Marie, 906/259-5035, http://soobrew.com, http://1668winery.com, 4pm-9pm Mon.-Thurs., noon-10pm Fri.-Sat., $10-18). He also expanded the business to offer food, making the establishment a full-service restaurant. The combination of a brewery and winery under the same roof has proven to be a big hit. The winery side specializes in fruity offerings, such as Black Raspberry and Sweet Peach. Beer offerings include Gingerbread

Blonde Ale, Family Harvest Weizenbock, and House Apple Cider—the hard variety. Food offerings include burgers, salads, and wrap sandwiches, plus some creative appetizers like smoked whitefish dip and fried cheese curds.

ACCOMMODATIONS

The ★ **Hotel Ojibway** (240 W. Portage Ave., 906/632-4100, www.wyndhamhotels.com, $$), now part of the Trademark Collection by Wyndham, has the nicest accommodations in town and the best location, overlooking the St. Mary's River and the locks. For the very best view, ask for an upper level room facing north. The elegant 1928 building has been beautifully restored, with large rooms, an indoor pool, and a whirlpool. Ask about packages for a better deal.

For the same good location but for less money, try the ★ **Long Ships Motel** (427 W. Portage Ave., 906/632-2422 or 888/690-2422, www.longshipsmotel.com, $), a clean and comfortable independent motel with a fine spot across from Locks Park. A little farther east, but still within walking distance of the river and downtown, is the **Mid-City Motel** (304 E. Portage Ave., 906/632-6832, https://midcityssm.com, $).

Much of Sault Ste. Marie's lodging is gradually transitioning to chain establishments, which tends to boost the number of available beds (good for tourism) but sacrifices the charm and uniqueness of the independents. Currently the Soo area has the highest concentration of chains in the eastern U.P., as it is the region's largest city and most popular tourist draw. Most, however, are not within walking distance of the locks.

Camping

Right in Sault Ste. Marie, there's a modern 65-site municipal campground at **Aune-Osborn Park** (1225 Riverside Dr., 906/632-3268, www.saultcity.com, $32-35) on the St. Mary's River near the Sugar Island ferry dock. Just east of Brimley, **Brimley State Park** (906/248-3422, www.michigan.gov/dnr, $25-29) offers about a mile of sandy Lake Superior beach and a large modern campground. It's a good choice for anyone looking for an easy place to set up camp to enjoy the Soo and other nearby attractions. Although it's just a campground, Brimley is a popular park, so consider making reservations if you're aiming for a summer weekend. For a little more seclusion, head farther west to the **Hiawatha National Forest** (906/635-5311, www.fs.fed.us, $18). Within 30 minutes' drive of the Soo, you can find pretty and private tent sites next to the Lake Superior shore at Bay View, or near the great fishing point at Monocle Lake. Reservations are not possible.

INFORMATION AND SERVICES

For more information on the Sault Ste. Marie area, contact the **Sault Ste. Marie Convention and Visitors Bureau** (225 E. Portage Ave., 906/632-3366 or 800/647-2858, www.saultstemarie.com). For regional information and maps, stop by the **Michigan Welcome Center** (943 Portage Ave. W., 906/632-8242, 8am-4:30am daily) near the International Bridge.

When you plan to **cross the border** to enter or leave the United States, make sure you have a passport, a passport card, or other required travel documents. For a complete list of acceptable documents, visit the U.S. Department of State's travel website (http://travel.state.gov), but for most visitors the required documents are simply a passport and, for foreign visitors, perhaps a visa or visa waiver as well. At the border crossing you'll be asked to show your documents, followed by a few simple questions. Be prepared and respond truthfully and respectfully. Refrain from making any kind of humorous remark to the customs agents, as they're instructed to take everything a traveler says seriously.

There are a few situations when things can get a bit more complicated. Be prepared to declare all goods, particularly items purchased or left abroad (gifts) and any firearms you're carrying. You'll be required to pay duty on larger amounts of certain items: wine and liquor (more than 40 ounces), beer (more than 23 cans or bottles), and cigarettes (more than 200). If you're traveling with children and are not their parent or legal guardian, you'll need to have a letter from their parents or guardian giving their permission to leave the United States and enter Canada with their child. If the child is a naturalized U.S. citizen you'll also need her or his U.S. Certificate of Citizenship. Make certain a contact phone number is included. For more information, contact **U.S. Customs and Border Protection** (906/632-7221, www.cbp. gov) or **Canada Border Services Agency** (204/983-3500, www.cbsa-asfc.gc.ca).

Medical care in Sault Ste. Marie is readily available. For more than a century, **War Memorial Hospital** (500 Osborn Blvd., 906/635-4460, www.warmemorialhospital. org) has been providing the eastern Upper Peninsula with quality health care. To get there, take Ashmun Street to Spruce Street and head west to the hospital.

You won't have a problem finding a bank or ATMs in Sault Ste. Marie. **Huntington Bank** (511 Ashmun St., 906/635-5251, www. huntington.com) is downtown right near Portage Street. There are several other banks near the Soo's waterfront, including **Central Savings Bank** (511 Bingham Ave., 906/635-6250, www.centralsavingsbank.com).

GETTING THERE AND AROUND
Car

If you're coming north over the Mackinac Bridge from the Lower Peninsula, Sault Ste. Marie is a short, easy 45-minute drive on I-75. If you're going to Portage Avenue and downtown, get off at exit 394 and turn left onto Easterday Avenue. Take the next right, onto Eureka Street, which quickly becomes Portage Avenue and takes you along the riverfront to the locks. There's a very helpful visitor information center as soon as you turn onto Eureka Street. Stop here for maps, brochures, and additional information.

Exit 394 is the last before the border crossing. If you don't get off here, you'll soon find yourself on the International Bridge crossing into Canada. Make sure you have your passport or other travel documents. If you're entering the United States from Canada, King's Highway 17 (the Trans-Canada Highway) will get you to the International Bridge.

If you're arriving from the western Upper Peninsula, take M-28 to I-75, then follow I-75 north to Sault Ste. Marie.

Air

The closest commercial airport is **Chippewa County International Airport** (CIU, 5315 Airport Dr., 906/495-5631 or 800/225-2525, www.airciu.com) in Kincheloe, about 20 miles (32 km) south of Sault Ste. Marie. Scheduled flights run daily from Detroit and Minneapolis on Delta Airlines, and car rentals are available from **Enterprise** (906/495-1035, www.enterprise.com).

Boat

There are two marinas in Sault Ste. Marie. The **Charles T. Harvey Marina** (2442 Riverside Dr., 906/632-6741, www.michigan. gov/dnr), located on the lower St. Mary's River, has more than 30 boat slips and the usual amenities: electricity, water, showers, and pump-out service. It is located at 46°28.15 N, 84°18.00 W. The harbormaster can be reached on channel 9.

The **George Kemp Marina** (485 E. Water St., 906/635-7670, www.michigan.gov/dnr) is in downtown Sault Ste. Marie. It has more than 50 slips with electricity, water, showers, and pump-out service. Kemp Marina is located at 46°29.57 N, 84°20.21 W. The harbormaster can be reached on channel 9.

Bus and Shuttle

To get to Sault Ste. Marie on public transportation from elsewhere in the United States, **Indian Trails** (989/725-5105 or 800/292-3831, www.indiantrails.com) has regular service to the Soo. Call for current schedules and rates, or use the convenient fare finder tool on the website. You can also access the **Mackinaw Shuttle** (231/539-7005, https://mackinawshuttle.com) if you're already in northern Michigan.

The Huron Shore

East of I-75, the Upper Peninsula gradually narrows into a series of smaller peninsulas, points, and islands in Lake Huron. The area has a simple, pretty, and tranquil feel, the kind of place where casual cycling, beachcombing, and picnicking set the pace for a summer day. While there's plenty to explore for the casual, time-rich visitor, there are few true destinations. In fact, the whole area is often overlooked by guidebooks, which suits the locals and summer cottage owners just fine. So don't get too excited about sightseeing; just pack a lunch, put on a pair of comfortable shoes, and while away the day along a rocky shoreline.

SIGHTS

DeTour Village

DeTour Village marks the end of the road and the end of the Upper Peninsula mainland. This small village has long served an important navigational role for ships heading up and down the St. Mary's River. Many ships squeeze through DeTour Passage, the narrow waterway between the point and Drummond Island. They make a turn, or detour, to chart a course from the St. Mary's River to the Straits of Mackinac. DeTour Village is a very old community that has guided ships with its navigational light since 1848. It remains a pleasant place to watch the ship traffic from public parks and gardens along M-134.

Nearby Lime Island marks the centerpiece of the **Island Explorer Water Trail,** a boating route that travels from Lime to Mackinac Island along a linked network of islands. For more information, contact the **DeTour Area** Chamber of Commerce (625 N. Ontario St., 906/297-5987). You can also stay at cabins and cottages on state forest land on Lime Island. For more information on rates and availability, contact the **Sault Ste. Marie Forest Management Unit** (906/635-5281, www.michigan.gov/dnr).

★ Drummond Island

Drummond Island is about 250 square miles (645 sq km), some 65 percent of which is state-owned land. The rest is owned mostly by summer residents, who swell the island's population to about 5,000 in July and August—but you'd never know it. Life on this idyllic island is geared toward fishing, so most residents cluster along the shorelines, although these cloistered places can rarely be seen from the island's few roads.

With rocky shorelines, inland lakes, marshy lowlands, hardwood forests, and open meadows, Drummond Island boasts remarkably diverse animal and plant habitats. More than 24 different kinds of orchids grow wild on the island. Loons, bobcats, moose, and a pack of wolves all roam the island along with more common species.

Drummond and its neighboring islands are actually composed of above-ground deposits of limestone, part of the Niagara escarpment that stretches from Door County, Wisconsin, and across northern Lake Michigan. In an area called the Maxton Plains at the island's north end, this slab of limestone bedrock lies near the surface, covered by just a thin layer of alkaline soil. This unusual combination supports one of the world's foremost examples of

Drummond Island

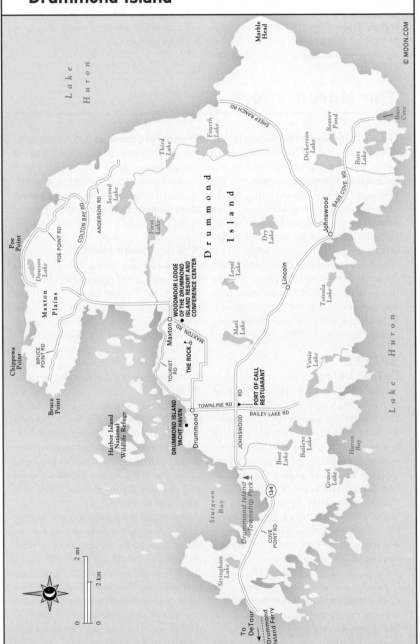

© MOON.COM

Lake Huron

Marble Head

Bass Cove

SHEEP RANCH RD

Beaver Pond

Bass Lake

BASS COVE RD

Dickerson Lake

Fourth Lake

Third Lake

Second Lake

ANDERSON RD

First Lake

Drummond Island

Dry Lake

Johnswood

COLTON BAY RD

Poe Point

POE POINT RD

Dawson Lake

Maxton Plains

Loyal Lake

Lincoln

Toivola Lake

WOODMOOR LODGE OF THE DRUMMOND ISLAND RESORT AND CONFERENCE CENTER

Chippewa Point

BRUCE POINT RD

Maxton

MAXTON RD

Marl Lake

THE ROCK

TOURIST RD

Vanio Lake

Bruce Point

Lake Huron

Harbor Island National Wildlife Refuge

DRUMMOND ISLAND YACHT HAVEN

TOWNLINE RD

PORT OF CALL RESTUARANT

RD

BAILEY LAKE RD

Drummond

JOHNSWOOD

Boot Lake

Baileys Lake

Huron Bay

Drummond Island Township Park

134

Gravel Lake

Sturgeon Bay

COVE POINT RD

Stringham Lake

To DeTour
Drummond Island Ferry

2 mi

2 km

0   2 km
0   2 mi

alvar grassland, a rare mix of arctic tundra and Great Plains plants, including Hill's thistle, false pennyroyal, and prairie dropseed. The Nature Conservancy owns more than 800 acres of the Maxton Plains. The preserve is open to the public, so you can explore this moon-like landscape where large boulders of conglomerate flecked with red jasper, called puddingstone, punctuate the barren expanses of the limestone bedrock.

For more information on Drummond Island, contact the **Drummond Island Tourism Association** (906/493-5245 or 800/737-8666, www.visitdrummondisland.com).

★ Les Cheneaux

"The Snows," everyone calls them, though the real name for these islands is Les Cheneaux (lay shen-O), French for "The Channels." And there are channels aplenty. Like shards of glass, 36 long and narrow islands lie splintered just off the U.P.'s southeastern shore, forming a maze of calm channels and protected bays in northern Lake Huron. Not surprisingly, it's a delight for boaters. Tall sailboats, small runabouts, classic cabin cruisers, and simple canoes all share these waters, as they have for more than a century.

Les Cheneaux first attracted boaters in the 1880s for the area's renowned fishing. Early enthusiasts came here from nearby Mackinac Island, already a popular vacation getaway for the wealthy. At first, these resort dwellers from Mackinac arrived on daylong excursions. Before long, they built their own cottages to revel in the solitude not found in the other Great Lakes resort areas. Because its summer guests were predominantly wealthy industrialists from southern Michigan, Indiana, and Illinois, Les Cheneaux maintained a tactful, understated style. Cottages were elegant and not ostentatious. Boats were sleek, not showy.

The islands of Les Cheneaux still maintain that genteel, simple air. If you're the kind of person who doesn't want or need to be entertained, you'll enjoy this charming area, free of crass commercialism. Nautical pastimes rule here, but in proper Les Cheneaux style, they rarely take the form of a powerboat or a screaming Jet Ski. Boating here is best exemplified by the amazing array of classic wooden craft you'll see puttering and purring through the channels. The nation's first (and now oldest) Chris Craft franchise was founded in Hessel in 1926. Today many survive thanks to the area's crystal-clear water, the short boating season, and careful maintenance, which all help preserve the tender wooden hulls.

"Life Is Better with Water," proclaims the website of the **Les Cheneaux Islands Chamber of Commerce** (680 W. M-134, Cedarville, 888/364-7526, www.lescheneaux.net). For detailed information about this idyllic place, a visit here is a must.

Harbor Island National Wildlife Refuge

About 1.5 miles (2.4 km) off the shore of Drummond Island, the comparatively small **Harbor Island National Wildlife Refuge** (www.fws.gov/refuge/harbor_island) is far enough to be remote, but still close enough that it isn't hard to get to. You can access the 695-acre island by private boat. Some popular recreational activities include offshore fishing and hunting. There's also a small swimming beach. Wildlife includes foxes, snowshoe hares, grouse, and sparrows. During the winter the refuge has been known to welcome timber wolves from Ontario's nearby St. Joseph Island. The refuge is managed by **Seney National Wildlife Refuge** (1674 Refuge Entrance Rd., Seney, 906/586-9851, www.fws.gov).

Lighthouses

Lighthouse lovers won't want to miss a tour of **DeTour Reef Light Station,** over 80 feet (24 meters) tall and listed on the National Register of Historic Places. Stationed between Drummond Island and the village of DeTour, the 1931 light underwent extensive restoration and reopened for tours in 2005. It's a bold, boxy lighthouse, with sharp lines

that seem suited to the job of warning ships of the dangerous reef below the surface. The **DeTour Reef Light Preservation Society** (906/493-8169, www.drlps.com) arranges tours of the lighthouse (Sat. Father's Day-Labor Day, advance reservations required, $100 nonmembers, $80 members). The two-hour tour, limited to six people, begins with a boat ride to the light, then climbs a 20-foot (6-meter) ladder and continues through the lighthouse and to the top of the watch room.

★ Great Lakes Boat Building School

It might seem almost natural, given the strong boating tradition of the Les Cheneaux area, that the community is home to a highly re-garded school devoted to boat construction. Housed in a handsome boathouse-style build-ing, the **Great Lakes Boat Building School** (485 S. Meridian St., Cedarville, 906/484-1081, www.glbbs.edu) teaches students in their choice of three one-year programs: tra-ditional wooden boat construction, marine service technology, and small engine technol-ogy. This fascinating school offers free public tours (10am and 2pm Mon.-Fri. year-round), an excellent way to learn about the area's nautical traditions. The 1.5-hour tour is led by a senior faculty member and offers visitors the opportunity to see students at work. The guide is able to answer questions, which tend to be rather numerous.

ENTERTAINMENT
Kewadin Casino

The eastern U.P. seems to have a high den-sity of casinos. There are gaming parlors in St. Ignace, Sault Ste. Marie, Christmas, Brimley, and elsewhere, all within a couple of hours of Les Cheneaux and Drummond Island. But that hasn't stopped the small **Kewadin Casino** (3395 N. 3-Mile Rd., Hessel, 906/484-2903, www.kewadin.com) from opening in Hessel. Gaming is limited to slots and some

1: Les Cheneaux Islands **2:** Les Cheneaux Culinary School **3:** sandhill crane on Drummond Island **4:** dock at the Great Lakes Boat Building School

blackjack. There are no hotel rooms, and a deli is the best among the casino's few amenities.

FESTIVALS AND EVENTS

During the second weekend of August, Hessel is home to the **Les Cheneaux Islands Antique Wooden Boat Show** (906/484-2821, http://lciboatshow.com, $10 per person, free under age 12), believed to be the larg-est such show in the country, featuring more than 100 wooden-hulled vessels. Wooden boat owners and aficionados from around the country show up in the small U.P. town to celebrate wooden boats of all types. The boat show takes place in conjunction with **The Festival of Arts,** so even if you're not interested in wooden boats, there's plenty to do browsing the vendor booths in search of handmade crafts and artwork. For informa-tion, contact the **Les Cheneaux Historical Association** (906/484-2821).

SUMMER RECREATION
Hiking and Biking

A mountain bike is a fun way to explore **Drummond Island,** since M-134 dissolves into a variety of double-tracks and, eventu-ally, single-track roads. Don't expect techni-cal riding, as the island is quite flat. When you venture into state land, you'll likely end up sharing some of the designated DNR trails with ATVs, which can be both irritat-ing and potentially dangerous. But with 76 miles (122 km) of trail, you're sure to find stretches with little or no traffic. For spe-cific trails, ask about **Marble Head View Point** (4 miles/6.4 km) as well as **Warners Cove** (4 miles/6.4 km), one of several coves on the island's south shore due south of Pats Lake, and **Gravel Lake** (3 miles/4.8 km) on the south shore. Trail information is avail-able from the **Drummond Island Tourism Association** (906/493-5245 or 800/737-8666, www.visitdrummondisland.com).

An eastern Upper Peninsula road bik-ing map is available from the Michigan Department of Transportation or from the

Les Cheneaux Chamber of Commerce (680 W. M-134, Cedarville, 906/484-3935, www.lescheneaux.net). The map highlights major biking roads in the area, including Hessel, Cedarville, DeTour, and other cities. It also offers advice on traffic levels, shoulder width, and other issues of concern to bikers. For mountain bikers, there are plenty of double-tracks, trails, and back roads. You can get detailed information from the visitors center on the island, located at the corner of M-134 and Townline Road.

The island is also an idyllic place for hiking. The **Drummond Island Resort Trail** is a 15-mile (24-km) loop that runs near the Drummond Island Resort. During the winter, the trail is groomed for cross-country skiing. The **Heritage Hiking Trail** is a short 1-mile (1.6-km) loop in Drummond Island Township Park.

Canoeing and Kayaking

A canoe or kayak is a great way to explore the waters of **Les Cheneaux.** The fjord-like bays and 150 miles (240 km) of ragged shoreline make this a magical place to paddle. One of the best routes to take is the **North Lake Huron Paddle Trail,** which extends for some 75 miles (121 km) from DeTour nearly to St. Ignace, passing among the islands of Les Cheneaux on the way. It's best to get a guide while paddling the islands, since the ins and outs of the waterways make it easy to get lost. For kayak tours, rentals, and advice, pay a visit to **Woods and Waters Tours** (20 Pickford Ave., Hessel, 888/502-8373, www.woodsandwaters.eco), an outfitter and guide company in Hessel. Guided day trips of the North Lake Huron Paddle Trail are offered, as well as half-day, full-day, and sunset kayak trips. Custom tours can also be arranged.

Fishing

Anglers aren't going to spend much time in **Les Cheneaux** before the channels start calling. It's easy to see why. The diversity of its ecosystem makes it a place unlike any other; there is an exceptional variety of fish, including northern pike, brook trout, steelhead, and salmon. Book a fishing charter with **Island Charters** (117 N. Greenwood Dr., Cedarville, 906/235-3825, https://islandchartersmi.com). Tours can run either a full day (8 hours) or half day (4 hours) and start at $550. Custom tours to any destination between Mackinac and Drummond Islands can be arranged for $100 per hour.

One of the popular spots for inland fishing

kayaking the North Lake Huron Paddle Trail

is **Munuscong River State Forest** (906/635-5281, www.michigan.gov/dnr), where you can cast at the river for walleye, pike, bass, and perch, or head 1 mile (1.6 km) east to Lake Munuscong for more fishing. For additional fishing spots and information about fishing seasons, contact the **Les Cheneaux Islands Chamber of Commerce** (680 W. M-134, Cedarville, 906/484-3935, www.lescheneaux.net).

Boating

The best way to see **Les Cheneaux,** of course, is to get out on the water. Aside from the pretty wooded islands, part of the fun is eyeing the beautiful old boathouses that dot the shorelines, especially on Marquette Island. If you have your own craft, you'll find launches in Hessel and Cedarville, the only two towns in the area. Though the waters are protected and normally quite safe, be sure to bring a chart, or at least a map provided by local businesses. The various bays, channels, and points can be rather confusing. Many area cottages rent boats or include them in their rates.

Golf

For such a mellow place as **Drummond Island,** you might be surprised to run across **The Rock** (33494 S. Maxton Rd., 906/493-1000 or 800/999-6343, www.drummondisland.com, $35-59 for 18 holes), a spectacular designer golf course completed in 1990. The first-rate course makes fine use of the natural environment, its holes weaving through woods and limestone outcroppings. In 2008 The Rock earned a four-star rating from *Golf Digest* as part of the magazine's "Best Places to Play." Contact The Rock for specials and packages.

The nine-hole **Les Cheneaux Club Golf Club** (1407 Golf Links Rd., 906/493-1000, www.lescheneauxgolfclub.org, $18 for 9 holes, $25 for 18 holes, $11-20 pp gas-powered cart) in Cedarville is the oldest still playable and continuously played links in Michigan. It was first played in May 1898 on natural forest, sand, water, and rock. In Hessel, try the

Hessel Ridge Golf Course (2061 N. 3-Mile Rd., 888/660-9166, www.hesselridge.com, $16 for 9 holes, $22 for 18 holes, $22 for 9 holes with cart, $34 for 18 holes with cart, reduced rates after 3pm). The 18-hole, 6,415-yard course is located on a ridge overlooking Hessel, with tree-lined boundaries, well-manicured greens, and beautiful views.

Off-Road Vehicles

Three off-road trails are maintained within the **Les Cheneaux** area. The farthest west is **Bay City Lake Trail,** a short distance north of Hessel. The 50-inch (127-cm) trails here consist of three loops that total nearly 8 miles (12.9 km) around Bay City Lake. To get here, take 3-Mile Road north of Hessel to Bay City Lake Road, just past Hessel Ridge Golf Course, and turn left to the parking area. The 8.4-mile (13.5-km) **Birch Hill Trail** is for motorcycle use only, and is located east of Cedarville. Take M-134 to Prentiss Bay Road and continue north to the parking area. Nearby, the **Foreman Lake Trail** has several additional miles of trails. Continue north on Prentiss Bay Road, turn right on Traynor Road, and then right again on Springer Road. Closer to DeTour, **Cranberry Lake Trail** runs for 8 miles (12.9 km) from M-48 to Caribou Lake. This trail is for vehicles less than 50 inches (127 cm) wide, and there's parking at the trailheads on M-48, just north of M-134, and on M-134 itself, near the turnoff for DeTour Campground.

Drummond Island, with its vast stretches of state-owned land, is an ideal place to take ATVs. There are more than 65 miles (105 km) of trails, many of them looped and much of them through old-growth boreal forests. Pay special attention to the island's northern shore, which has plenty of stunning Lake Huron views. Also, with the exception of M-134 between the ferry and Channel Road, all of Drummond Island's roads, paved and unpaved, are ATV friendly. Ask for a full-color map from the **Drummond Island Tourism Association** (906/493-5245, www.visitdrummondisland.com) or local businesses. But it doesn't stop there: Drummond Island is also home to **Turtle Ridge Off-Road Terrain Challenge Park** (906/493-1000, www.drummondisland.com/off-road-michigan-turtle-ridge-park, $35 per day, multiple-day discounts), which has rock crawls, hill climbs, mud, and more.

WINTER RECREATION
Ski and Snowshoe Trails

On **Drummond Island,** cross-country ski trails include 4.5 miles (7.2 km) at the **Rainbow Trail,** a groomed, mostly flat trail on Maxton Cross Road. No snowshoeing is allowed at the Rainbow Trail. The **Drummond Island Resort and Conference Center** (http://drummondisland.com) has 15 miles (24 km) of groomed trails for cross-country skiing. Skis are available for resort guests to use for free.

Visitors interested in snowshoeing can head to a section of trails specifically set aside by Drummond Island Resort, and there are 2 miles (3.2 km) of snowshoe trails available on the Island Heritage Trail at Drummond Island Township Park. Additionally, all 76 miles (122 km) of the island's designated DNR trails are accessible by snowshoe. Contact the **Drummond Island Tourism Association** (906/493-5245, www.visitdrummondisland.com) for additional information.

Back on the mainland, skiers can try the 5 groomed miles (8 km) at the **Peek-A-Boo Hill Cross Country Ski Trail,** maintained by the Les Cheneaux Nordic Ski Club. To get to the trail, take Blindline Road north of M-129, then go west on State Avenue to the Les Cheneaux Community Schools' running track, where you'll find the trailhead. The **Search Bay Backcountry Ski Trail** is a good option, located 5 miles (8 km) west of Hessel. The two 1.5-mile (2.4-km) loops make a figure eight. They're groomed and easy to ski, taking you out onto the small peninsula of St. Martin's Point. The trailhead is accessible south of M-134.

Snowmobiling

Drummond Island Resort and Conference Center is a good place to start when snowmobiling on the island. It's a good place to gain access to Drummond Island's astonishing 100 miles (160 km) of groomed snowmobile trails. As for rentals, Drummond Island Resort rents snowmobiles ($199-225 per day) and requires a $500 damage deposit. Free snowmobile maps are available from local businesses and the tourism association.

The trails in **Les Cheneaux** connect with the hundreds of miles of trails that crisscross the Upper Peninsula. **Trail 47** extends from DeTour and will take you to **Trail 2** near St. Ignace, making stops in Cedarville and Hessel along the way. **Trail 491** splits north from 47, taking you to Pickford, while **Trail 49** will take you north to Kinross and Sault Ste. Marie. Additionally, you can operate your snowmobile on all unplowed roads in Mackinac County, as well as on the far-right side of paved roads and the unpaved portions of highways. Obey traffic laws and speed limits, and be careful.

FOOD

For such a small town, Cedarville actually has a nice selection of restaurants. ★ **Cattail Cove Restaurant and Lounge** (22 Hodeck St., 906/484-2995, 11:30am-11pm Mon.-Thurs., 11:30am-2am Fri.-Sat., 9am-10pm Sun., $13-31) is a good example. It's no surprise to see fresh local fish on the menu, since the restaurant owns its own fish market; try a Great Lakes catch while you're in the area. You can get good char-grilled prime rib too. The outdoor deck overlooks Cedarville Bay, making it the perfect place for a cocktail or two in good weather.

If you're in the mood for some Italian, head over to **Ang-Gio's** (232 W. M-134, 906/484-3301, 11am-8:30pm Tues.-Sun., $11-21) for some tasty pizza, plus a number of other Italian and American favorites. Despite the Italian cuisine, the atmosphere is decidedly northern Michigan. Knotty pine walls and contemporary furniture leave no doubt that the visitor is in the U.P., which takes nothing away from its charm.

One of the most noteworthy dining destinations in the area is the ★ **Les Cheneaux Culinary School** (186 S. Pickford Ave., Hessel, 906/484-4800, www.lcculinary.org, 5pm-9pm Wed.-Sun. late May-early Sept., $14-48). As the name implies, the institution is primarily a school. It teaches aspiring chefs through a yearlong apprentice-based program, inspired by the Great Lakes Boat Building School in Cedarville. Instruction lasts from September through May, after which the students operate the facility as a restaurant. The kitchen sources ingredients from local farms, so the menu frequently changes. Commonly featured items include salmon poke and braised lamb shoulder tacos, plus small-plate items like leaf lettuce salad and grilled cucumber.

In DeTour, stop by ★ **Mainsail Restaurant and Saloon** (410 N. Ontario St., 906/297-2141, 11am-10pm Mon.-Tues. and Thurs.-Sat., 10am-8pm Sun., $17-29), a casual restaurant that serves three hearty meals daily. Examples include steak, shrimp, fresh fish, salads, and burgers—solid American food plus a few burritos. Stop by the saloon for draft beer and mixed drinks. As an added bonus, Mainsail is home to the original blueprints for the *Edmund Fitzgerald,* the freighter that met with tragedy and was immortalized by Gordon Lightfoot.

Drummond Island has a fair handful of restaurants too. The **Port of Call Restaurant** (30420 E. Johnswood Rd./M-134, 906/493-5507, www.drummondislandfudge.com, 8am-10pm Mon.-Sat., 8am-9pm Sun. mid-Apr.-late Nov., $17-32) is an establishment that prides itself on offering a selection of international items that aren't usually found in U.P. restaurants. Traditional breakfast items like eggs Benedict and bagel sandwiches give way to Belgian waffles, Greek gyro omelets, and European bakehouse breads like Russian pumpernickel and Jewish rye. Lunch and dinner menus feature Asian vegetable noodle soup, Greek gyros, English fish-and-chips,

and pierogi with Polish sausage. You'll find plenty of traditional Midwestern American food too. Port of Call features an impressive wine selection.

At the Drummond Island Resort and Conference Center, try **Pins Bar & Grill** (33494 S. Maxton Rd., 906/493-1004, www.drummondisland.com, 8am-9pm daily, $18), where you'll find burgers, pizza, wings—and bowling.

ACCOMMODATIONS

On Drummond Island, stay in luxury at ★ **Woodmoor Lodge of the Drummond Island Resort and Conference Center** (33494 S. Maxton Rd., 906/493-1000, https://cabinsandresorts.com, $$), a grandiose retreat with a handsome log lodge. Guests have access to all Drummond Island Resort facilities, including an outdoor pool, tennis courts, bowling, and even sporting clays. You can also rent some Frank Lloyd Wright-style cottages, many overlooking Potagannissing Bay.

Another good lodging choice is ★ **Drummond Island Yacht Haven** (33185 S. Water St., 906/493-5232 or 800/543-4743, www.diyachthaven.com, $$$), with large cabins overlooking island-studded Potagannissing Bay. The larger three-bedroom cabins have limestone fireplaces. Weekly rates are available. The property also offers sandy beaches, boat rentals, and other amenities. Contact the **Drummond Island Tourism Association** (906/493-5245, www.visitdrummondisland.com) for more choices.

Along the Lake Huron shore near Cedarville, **Spring Lodge and Cottages** (916 Park Ave., Cedarville, 906/484-2282 or 800/480-2282, www.springlodge.com, $$) has a wonderful location in the heart of Les Cheneaux, right on the Snows Channel. It has large and well-kept house cottages, most overlooking the water. Rates are by the week only. Boat rentals are also available on-site. Boat rentals are available for guests only.

For nicer-than-average motel rooms and an indoor pool, try the **Cedarville Lodge** (M-134, Cedarville, 906/484-2266, http://

cedarvillelodge.net, $$). Another affordable choice is the **Islands Inn Motel** (90 E. M-134, 906/484-2293, $). And the **Les Cheneaux Motel** (769 M-134, 906/484-2581, www. lcmotel.com, $) offers superb rates and includes a kitchenette in each unit.

Camping

Drummond Island's best camping is at **Drummond Island Township Park** (no reservations, $10, $12.25 with electricity), just north of M-134, not far from the ferry dock. This rustic campground (no showers) has pretty sites tucked in the woods on Potagannissing Bay. There's a sand beach and a boat launch.

Camp along the Lake Huron shore and under the pines in a former state park now managed by the **Lake Superior State Forest** (906/293-5131, www.michigan.gov/dnr). The marked beach and picnic area is on M-134, 6 miles (9.7 km) west of DeTour Village. For more seclusion, boaters should head for **Government Island,** the only publicly owned island in Les Cheneaux. Once a Coast Guard station, it's now part of the **Hiawatha National Forest** (906/643-7900, www.fs.fed. us). Outhouses and picnic tables are available at a couple of primitive sites on the northeastern and southern ends of the small island; no-trace camping is free and permitted anywhere on the island. Groups of more than four people are required to register with the ranger station.

INFORMATION AND SERVICES

There are a few sources for helpful visitor information. Among the finest are **Les Cheneaux Islands Chamber of Commerce** (680 W. M-134, Cedarville, 906/484-3935, www.lescheneaux.net) and the **Drummond Island Tourism Association** (906/493-5245, www.visitdrummondisland. com).

The nearest hospital is St. Ignace's **Mackinac Straits Hospital** (1140 N. State St., St. Ignace, 906/643-8585, www.mackinac

straitshealth.org), about a 30-minute drive from Cedarville and an hour from DeTour. Take M-134 to I-75, then head south, exiting at the I-75 Business Loop (exit 348). Continue south for about 2 miles (3.2 km) and look for the hospital on the right just after you pass the Mackinac County Airport. Another option is **War Memorial Hospital** (500 Osborn Blvd., Sault Ste. Marie, 906/635-4460, www. warmemorialhospital.org), a bit farther away.

Most of the area's banks are in Cedarville, where you'll find a **Central Savings Bank** (143 W. M-134, 906/484-2036, www. centralsavingsbank.com), on M-134 as you pass through town; **First National Bank of St. Ignace** (192 S. Meridian, 906/484-2262, www.fnbsi.com); and the **Soo Co-Op Credit Union** (90 Beach St., 906/484-2073, www. soocoop.com) downtown.

In DeTour, go to the **Central Savings Bank** (109 Elizabeth St., 906/297-6901, www.centralsavingsbank.com) near the Drummond Island Ferry dock. While on the island, go to **Detour Drummond Community Credit Union** (34857 S. Townline Rd., 906/493-5263, www.ddccu. com).

GETTING THERE AND AROUND
Car

One of the Huron Shore's draws is its convenient accessibility. If you're taking the bridge up from the Lower Peninsula, Cedarville is a short 30-minute drive up I-75 and along M-134. It's another 30 minutes along M-134 to DeTour and Drummond Island. From Sault Ste. Marie, head south on I-75 and catch M-134 or take M-129 straight down. M-129 is a shorter distance, but the interstate is fast and convenient and won't add much time to your drive.

The 1-mile-long (1.6-km) auto crossing is managed by the **Drummond Island Ferry** (906/235-3170, $14 per vehicle, plus $2 pp) for a 10-minute trip across the St. Mary's River. Ferry service is offered year-round. Fares and schedules can change without notice; see www.visitdrummondisland.com

for current schedules and additional pricing for trailers, snowmobiles, camper units, and other details. Additional information can be obtained from the **Drummond Island Tourism Association** (906/493-5245, www.visitdrummondisland.com).

Air

Most air passengers to the eastern U.P. fly into **Chippewa County International Airport** (CIU, 5019 Airport Dr., Kincheloe, 906/495-5631 or 800/225-2525, www.airciu.com), which has scheduled flights from Detroit on Delta Airlines and rental cars from **Enterprise** (906/495-1035, www.enterprise.com). Driving time to DeTour from Chippewa County Airport is 60-90 minutes.

About a 90-minute drive from DeTour, **Pellston Regional Airport** (PLN, US 31, Pellston, 231/539-844, www.pellstonairport.org), south of Mackinaw City in the Lower Peninsula, has scheduled flights from Detroit on Delta Airlines. Car rental is offered through **Avis** (213/539-8302, www.avis.com) and **Budget** (231/539-8160, www.budget.com).

Boat

Les Cheneaux's 36 islands, sheltered channels, and bays make this a boater's dream. If you're one of the fortunate ones boating here, you'll want to head to the **Hessel/**

Clark Township Marina (906/484-3917 or 906/484-2672, www.michigan.gov/dnr, late May-early Sept.), which has 30 transient slips and a boatload of amenities. Along with the expected water, electricity, pump-out, and showers, Hessel Marina is close to marine-repair supplies, a fish-cleaning station, and a laundry. The marina is located at 46°00.05 N, 84°25.30 W. Use radio channel 9.

Farther east, you can go to **DeTour State Dock** (906/297-5947, www.michigan.gov/dnr, mid-May-late Sept.), with basic amenities and a harbormaster on duty. Use radio channel 16, then switch to 71. It's located at 45°59.43 N, 83°53.50 W. For other marinas, consider **Cedarville Marine** (100 E. Hodeck St., 906/484-2815, www.cedarvillemarine.com) in Cedarville or Hessel's **E. J. Mertaugh Boat Works** (296 S. Hessel Pt. Rd., 906/484-2434, www.ejmertaughboatworks.com). Additionally, there are a number of private marinas on Drummond Island. Contact the **Drummond Island Tourism Association** (906/493-5245, www.visitdrummondisland.com) for more information.

Public Transportation

There is no regularly scheduled public transportation to Les Cheneaux, so you'll need your own vehicle.

Background

The Landscape

GEOLOGY AND GEOGRAPHY

Michigan is, without question, one of America's most geographically peculiar states, consisting of two enormous peninsulas surrounded by four of the five Great Lakes. While for many the image of the mitten-shaped Lower Peninsula represents the state as a whole, the Upper Peninsula also deserves recognition for its landmass large enough to hold the combined area of New Jersey, Connecticut, Rhode Island, and Delaware—all within its scalloped borders.

A combination of cataclysmic volcanic eruptions and soupy tropical seas initially formed what we call Michigan. In the northeastern part of the state, near Lake Superior and northern Lake Huron, volcanoes erupting roughly one billion years ago laid down thick layers of basalt, which later tilted and faulted, forming the area's rugged, rocky topography of ancient mountain ranges and steep sawtooth shorelines.

Much later, a series of powerful glaciers carved out the Michigan landscape, the most recent occurring just 12,000 years ago. Four separate ice sheets scraped across the region, scouring out depressions that became lakes, lowlands, and ragged shorelines. When the ice melted and the glaciers retreated, the meltwater filled the vast basins and created the modern Great Lakes.

Michigan's Upper Peninsula is made up of two distinct geographic regions, the Superior Upland and the Northern Highlands. The Superior Upland, the region formed by ancient volcanic activity, spans the western two-thirds of the Upper Peninsula. It offers a landscape of dramatic beauty, characterized by rugged basalt cliffs and thick boreal forests of fir, spruce, and birch—all parts of the vast Canadian Shield that dips down from the Canadian arctic, across portions of the northern Great Lakes region, and back up the west side of Hudson Bay in a giant horseshoe. Much of the region rises more than 1,000 feet (305 meters) above sea level, including the state's highest point, Mount Arvon—which tops out at 1,979 feet (603 meters). The Superior Upland was also the location of some of the nation's richest sources of minerals, most notably copper and iron ore. Most of the known deposits have been depleted by aggressive mining during the 20th century.

South and east of the Superior Upland lie the Northern Highlands, covering the eastern Upper Peninsula and extending down into the northern half of the Lower Peninsula. Here basalt bedrock gives way to sandstone and limestone, and boreal forests segue into pine

and hardwoods. Once heavily logged for vast and valuable stands of white and red pine, the Northern Highlands today are prized for the recreation opportunities offered by abundant woods, water, and wildlife.

The western Upper Peninsula borders northeastern Wisconsin and stretches east for 334 miles (538 km) between Lakes Superior and Michigan. The eastern U.P. reaches a third Great Lake, Lake Huron, where it terminates at Drummond Island. Also recognized as part of the U.P. is Isle Royale, a 45-mile-long (72-km) archipelago in Lake Superior, and Michigan's only national park. It's one of the remotest and least visited properties in the National Park System.

Although the U.P.'s landmass covers more than 16,000 square miles (41,000 sq km), water shapes its character—1,700 miles (2,700 km) of shoreline on three of the Great Lakes account for more than half of Michigan's total of 3,288 shoreline miles (second only to Alaska among U.S. states). In addition, the U.P. includes more than 4,000 inland lakes, 12,000 miles (19,000 km) of rivers, and over 300 named waterfalls. It also boasts 11 federally designated Wild and Scenic Rivers and is home to America's first national lakeshore, Pictured Rocks.

The Great Lakes State, Land of Hiawatha, Water Winter Wonderland—many of these Michigan nicknames are especially descriptive of the Upper Peninsula. But for many, the land north of the bridge is known simply as God's Country.

CLIMATE

Weather patterns in the U.P. can be unpredictable, as the presence of the Great Lakes exerts considerable influence. Temperatures can be surprisingly moderate, since the lakes tend to cool the hot air of summer and, to a lesser degree, warm the cold winds of winter. Except near the shores, afternoon highs during July and August average in the 70s (21-26°C). From

Previous: the natural harbor at Grand Marais.

December through February, they drop into the 20s (-6 to -2°C) and can often get much colder.

Although the area has four well-defined seasons, temperatures can nonetheless vary widely. You can enjoy spring-like skiing conditions in February or experience temperatures in the single digits at Thanksgiving. In summer you may swelter on a hike through the woods but soon feel the need to don a jacket when visiting a Lake Superior beach. None of this should deter you from visiting the Upper Peninsula—just make sure you're prepared for all the possibilities.

The Lake Effect

The Great Lakes often act like large insulators—slow to warm up, slow to cool down—and can have a dramatic effect on snowfall. Dry winter air travels over the Great Lakes as prevailing westerly winds, absorbing moisture. When this air hits land, it dumps its precipitation in the form of **lake-effect snow.** This phenomenon affects the Superior Highlands more severely, which explains why many of the U.P.'s successful ski resorts are clustered near Iron Mountain along the western edge of the peninsula.

The prevailing western breezes also affect the Great Lakes' water temperatures, most noticeably on Lake Michigan. During summer, the winds warm surface waters that blow east toward Lake Michigan beaches in the northwestern Lower Peninsula. While the lake is rarely warm enough for swimming on the Wisconsin side, it can be exceedingly pleasant in the Lower Peninsula (the lake's eastern shore) and at least tolerable in the U.P. —evidenced by the scores of popular beaches along US 2 from Escanaba to St. Ignace and lining the western side of the Lower Peninsula. This peculiarity has earned the region the nickname "the banana belt."

Lake Superior is altogether different. Water temperatures in this northern lake rarely climb out of the 40s (4-9°C), save for the occasional shallow bay. "No one ever drowns in Lake Superior," the saying goes. "They all die of hypothermia first."

Freshwater freezes more quickly than saltwater, and the Great Lakes often ice over several miles out from shore. Commercial shipping shuts down from January 15 to March 25, but persistent ice can force an early end or a late start to the season. During the especially severe winter of 2013-2014, ice clogged the Straits of Mackinac well into April, making it difficult for Mackinac Island to prepare for the upcoming tourism season. Ice floes on Lake Superior persisted into May.

Commercial ships can regularly cut through up to a foot of ice, but anything thicker requires the U.S. Coast Guard's *Mackinaw,* a 240-foot (75-meter) heavily reinforced ship specifically designed for ramming a passage through ice. The *Mackinaw* can "back and ram" its way through ice as thick as 10 feet (3 meters).

A Few Words About Winter

The Upper Peninsula's winter is long and cold. Snow and cold temperatures are virtually constant from Thanksgiving to Easter. In an average season, the U.P. receives some 160 inches (405 cm) of snow.

This, however, represents an average. U.P. snows are legendary, especially in the Keweenaw Peninsula, where 300-inch (760-cm) winters are not unusual. In summer, curious pier-like devices can be seen sprouting from front doors and leading to sidewalks on Keweenaw homes, usually a few feet off the ground. These serve as a guide for show shoveling. The accepted standard is not to do so until at least 24 inches (61 cm) are on the ground. Ladders nailed to roofs are there for a specific reason as well. When accumulated snow threatens to collapse the roofs, the ladders provide a foothold from which to clear it.

It's important to be aware of the **wind chill factor,** the effect of the cold temperatures combined with biting winds. When it's 5°F (-15°C) outside, a 15-mph (24 kph) wind will

What's So Great About These Lakes?

In a word, plenty. By any standard, the Great Lakes are enormously impressive. Carved away by receding glaciers several thousand years ago, the five lakes are beautiful, useful, recreational—and massive. The combined lakes (Superior, Michigan, Huron, Erie, and Ontario) cover more than 94,000 square miles (243,000 sq km) and hold an estimated 6 *quadrillion* gallons (23 quadrillion liters) of water, nearly one-fifth of the earth's freshwater and enough to cover the nation's 48 contiguous states to a depth of nearly 10 feet (3 meters). Four out of the five lakes touch the State of Michigan.

Here are some more interesting facts about the lakes you'll encounter in the U.P.:

Measured by surface area, **Lake Superior** is the largest body of freshwater in the world, at 31,700 square miles (82,100 sq km), roughly the size of Maine. Its shoreline stretches an amazing 1,826 miles (2,939 km), farther than the distance from Houghton to Miami. Superior is also the deepest of the Great Lakes (1,332 feet/406 meters at its deepest point), but if measured by volume, there are two lakes that are larger: Lake Tanganyika in East Africa and Lake Baikal in Siberia. Lake Superior, however, is large enough to hold each of the other Great Lakes, as well as all the water from Lake Erie an additional three times. The lake holds 3 quadrillion gallons (11.5 quadrillion liters) of water (the numeral 3 followed by 15 zeros), accounting for a full 10 percent of the world's freshwater. The water from Lake Superior alone is sufficient to submerge North and South America to a depth of 1 foot (0.3 meters).

The second largest, and the only one that lies entirely within the United States, **Lake Michigan** is 307 miles (494 km) long and 118 miles (190 km) wide, and holds just shy of 1,180 cubic miles (4,920 cubic km) of water. With an average depth of 279 feet (85 meters), Lake Michigan plunges to 925 feet (282 meters) at its deepest point. Its surface area is 22,300 square miles (57,800 sq km), and it has more than 1,600 miles (2,600 km) of shoreline. Technically, Lake Michigan and Lake Huron are hydrologically inseparable, which means they have the same surface elevation and are not separated by a river. The Straits of Mackinac connect the two lakes.

Lake Huron is the third largest of the Great Lakes by volume, holding some 849 cubic miles (3,539 cubic km) of water, but the second largest by surface area at 23,010 square miles (59,595 sq km). Manitoulin Island is the largest island in a freshwater lake in the world, with an area of more than 1,000 square miles (2,600 sq km). The island also has more than 100 lakes of its own, including Manitou Lake, the world's largest lake on an island in a lake. And if the collective perimeters of the lake's 30,000 islands were added to its mainland coastline, Lake Huron could boast the longest shoreline of any of the Great Lakes.

make it feel like -25°F (-32). Not only is this exceedingly uncomfortable, it also elevates the risk for frostbite or hypothermia. Owing to its importance, weather forecasts usually warn about the wind chill factor. Remember to take into consideration both the actual temperature and the wind chill when dressing for the outdoors.

Despite these concerns, many people welcome the Upper Peninsula's winter, as it accounts for a huge portion of the state's tourism revenue. Few other areas in the nation can offer as reliable a season for skiing, snowboarding, snowmobiling, ice fishing, and snowshoeing.

ENVIRONMENTAL ISSUES

The Upper Peninsula's primary environmental concern is the safeguarding of the area's prized natural resources. Thankfully, citizens have traditionally been more than willing to step in and oppose those who would abuse the land. Throughout history, there have been various threats to the region's ecosystem, beginning with the fur trade, followed by mining and logging, and more recently by asbestos dumping, nuclear waste, and water-use issues. A new economic opportunity, metallic sulfide mining, is potentially lucrative but controversial, since it can cause severe environmental damage. Despite these risks, it is now being permitted in a limited number of Upper Peninsula locations. Whether it will continue is still undetermined.

In sum, much of the Upper Peninsula is still relatively unspoiled but may not stay that way. The Upper Peninsula Environmental Coalition and similar organizations continue to work diligently to keep this land the natural paradise that it is today.

PRESERVATION

Beginning in the 1920s, as the mining and timber industries began their declines, modern concepts of land and resource preservation became a priority, beginning with the establishment of the Ottawa and Hiawatha National Forests in the late 1920s. In 1931, Isle Royale became part of the National Park System. The 1940s saw the addition of the Porcupine Mountains and Tahquamenon Falls State Parks. Still more land acquisitions would follow, including Pictured Rocks National Lakeshore in 1966. This recent history of the Upper Peninsula tells the story of a region once exploited for its resources gradually becoming a natural domain protected from the excesses of industry.

Plants and Animals

TREES

There's a reason the **white pine** is Michigan's state tree. Vast stands of the magnificent trees once covered the northern portions of the state, making Michigan the nation's leading lumber center. Pines from the Great Lakes State rebuilt much of Chicago after the Great Fire and supplied a hungry nation as it expanded westward across the treeless plains.

Today, a few tracts of these magnificent species remain—scraping the sky with towers of virgin white pine, red pine, hemlock, and cedar. Much of the U.P.'s original prime logging land is now second-growth pines, with many now reaching considerable heights. Today's logging operations still clear-cut, but in much smaller sections, and are increasingly shifting to selective cutting methods.

ANIMALS
Mammals

Though it's called the Wolverine State, only meager evidence exists of wolverines ever having lived in Michigan, even in the Upper Peninsula. A possible explanation for the unexpected name might lie with the early fur traders, who may have brought wolverine pelts to the numerous trading posts in the Upper Peninsula. In February 2004, however, a wolverine was sighted and photographed in Huron County, at the tip of the thumb in the Lower Peninsula. It was the first confirmed sighting in some 200 years and was a shock to biologists at the state's Department of Natural Resources.

With an estimated 85 percent of its area forested, the U.P. is habitat for a considerable number of gray and red foxes, skunks, squirrels, beavers, minks, muskrats, and other small mammals. The entire state has a large, and often problematic, population of white-tailed deer. Of all the large mammals, this is the one you'll see most frequently—and often not until one suddenly leaps out in front of your car. The U.P. is also home to more seldom seen mammals: a healthy number of black bears, moose, bobcats, cougars, and some 200 to 300 wolves.

Birds

Some 300 varieties of birds live in the state, including such notable species as bald eagles, peregrine falcons, hawks, loons, swans, herons, and dozens of songbirds. Hunting for game birds such as ducks, geese, grouse, and pheasant is a popular sport. Michigan lies on a major migratory pathway, offering excellent bird-watching during both spring and fall. Of

Michigan State Symbols

- State tree: white pine
- State bird: American robin
- State fish: brook trout
- State flower: apple blossom
- State gem: Isle Royale greenstone
- State stone: Petoskey stone
- State reptile: painted turtle
- State fossil: mastodon
- State soil: Kalkaska sand
- State wildflower: dwarf lake iris
- State game mammal: white-tailed deer

special note is the hawk migration, as thousands fly between Canada and the southern Lower Peninsula.

Aquatic Life

An abundance of fish thrive in both the Great Lakes and inland waters. Sportfishing remains popular on the Great Lakes, especially for chinook salmon, coho, steelhead, lake trout, and brown trout. Commercial fishing has decreased dramatically over the last few decades, due to overfishing and the accidental introduction of the lamprey eel and zebra mussel into the Great Lakes.

On inland waters, walleye and yellow perch are prized for flavor, while muskie and northern pike are considered a top sport fish. Bass, trout, and panfish can also be found in inland waters. Michigan has several blue-ribbon streams (www.trailstotrout.com), especially in the eastern U.P.

Reintroduction and Management Programs

Two of the Upper Peninsula's mammals are testimonies to the effectiveness of reintroduction and management programs. The **gray wolf** is believed to have been present in each of Michigan's counties at some point, but by 1910 they were relegated to just the Upper Peninsula. Before their reappearance in the 1990s, Michigan's last wolf pups were born in the mid-1950s near Pictured Rocks. Wolves were first protected in 1965, and were listed as endangered in 1973. Four of the animals were relocated to the U.P. from Minnesota in 1974, only to be killed. Today the wolves are thriving. In 1991 a pair of wolves produced the first pups born in the state's mainland in more than four decades. That population, estimated at about 20 animals in 1992, is believed to have descended from animals that wandered to the U.P. from Minnesota, Wisconsin, or Ontario. In 2009, the wolf was removed from Michigan's list of threatened species.

In the 1980s, **moose** were reintroduced to a remote area south of the U.P.'s Huron Mountains, with officials releasing a total of 61 moose from Ontario in two separate operations. Most interesting was the method of reintroduction: wildlife biologists airlifted the moose one by one in a sling dangling beneath a helicopter to a base camp, from where they were trucked 600 miles (970 km) to the Huron Mountains. Van Riper State Park in Michigamme has an interesting display with photos of the famous "moose lifts." The reintroduction worked, though not as well as hoped, as the moose population failed to meet the projected goal of 1,000 animals by 2000. Today, several hundred moose roam the western U.P., and their population continues to grow.

The programs of wolf and moose management in the Upper Peninsula don't involve Isle Royale, which is under the direct control of the National Park Service. A separate and ongoing study of the predator-prey relationship between the species on the island has been conducted since 1958, the longest continuous study of its kind anywhere. Although island populations rise and fall periodically, a variety of factors have affected the populations of both animals in recent years. According to the study's 2016-2017 annual report, the moose population had spiked to some 1,500, while the number of wolves had declined to only two. Scientists believe the decline in the wolf population may have been due to a lack of genetic diversity. In 2018, the National Park Service reintroduced new wolves to the island. As of February of 2022 the population stood at 28, according to the 2021-2022 annual report. This resurgence has helped restore a balance to the predator/prey relationship with the moose population, which peaked around 1,900 in 2020 but was under 1,400 in 2022.

History

MICHIGAN'S NATIVE PEOPLES

Buried under layers of glacial ice until about 10,000 years ago, the land that is now Michigan was inhospitable to many of the Indigenous people that thrived in much of the Midwest, such as the Paleo and Archaic Indians. Some of the first signs of Michigan civilization can be found in the Upper Peninsula's Keweenaw Peninsula, where the Copper Culture people of about 5000-500 BCE left evidence of their skill as prehistoric miners, devising ways to extract copper from bedrock and fashioning it into tools. Some archaeologists believe these people may have been the very first toolmakers anywhere.

The **Algonquin** people migrated to the Great Lakes region from the St. Lawrence River region sometime after 1000 CE. The Algonquians are divided into three tribes: the **Ottawa** (or Odawa), the **Ojibwa** (or Chippewa), and the **Potawatomi.** Collectively, they identified as the **Anishinabe,** or "First People." They named their new land "Michi Gami," meaning "Large Lake." In and around the Great Lakes they found sustenance from the abundant wildlife, including white-tailed deer, fish, moose, elk, and black bears. The rich natural resources nourished them for centuries before the arrival of the Europeans.

The three groups coexisted peacefully, each moving to a different area. The Ottawa settled around the Straits of Mackinac, Sault Ste. Marie, and the Leelanau Peninsula; the Ojibwa moved west, along the shores of Lake Superior; and the Potawatomi headed south, to the southern half of the Lower Peninsula. They communicated regularly, and their peaceable relationship proved valuable when invaders came to their lands. Together, they successfully fought off the warring Iroquois who arrived from the east in the 1600s. They also presented themselves as a strong, unified people when Europeans arrived.

THE FRENCH

Étienne Brûlé, the first European to arrive in what is now Michigan in 1615, was more interested in exploiting the land than conserving it. Brûlé was sent by Samuel de Champlain, lieutenant governor of New France, who hoped to find copper and a shortcut to the Far East. Brûlé sent back reports recounting the land's untamed beauty and its previously unknown flora and fauna.

Other opportunists soon followed. Some were after the region's rich supply of furs, others after the people of what they viewed as a godless land. Among the most famous of these early explorers was the Roman Catholic missionary Jacques Marquette, who established the state's first permanent settlement, at Sault Ste. Marie in 1668, followed by a second outpost at the straits of Michilimackinac in 1671. The arrival of the French coureurs de bois, a loose term referring to unlicensed traders, provided a sharp contrast to the priests and ruling class. Rugged individualists, they lived among the Native Americans, respected their customs, and hunted and trapped the region's rich stores of game.

Marquette's 17th-century writings attracted more settlers, mostly fur traders,

Two States in One

Is it a case of simple sibling rivalry or a marriage of irreconcilable differences? The relationship between the Upper and Lower Peninsulas of Michigan is a paradox. While the two Michigans are physically linked by a 5-mile-long (8-km) bridge, culturally they remain a world apart. Many Lower Peninsula residents dismiss the Upper Peninsula as a collection of bug-infested backwoods filled with yokels. U.P. residents (who proudly call themselves "Yoopers") find these generalizations insulting, especially when those very same Lower Peninsula people often flock north to enjoy the U.P.'s woods, wildlife, and beaches.

An accident of history is responsible for the two peninsulas being formed into a single state. In 1837, as Michigan was petitioning for admission to the Union, a dispute developed with Ohio over the "Toledo Strip," a strip of land that included Toledo, a valuable port on Lake Erie. For Michigan to enter the Union, Congress demanded that the Michigan Territory relinquish all rights to the Toledo Strip in exchange for a "barren wasteland"—the western three-quarters of the Upper Peninsula. What at the time seemed unfortunate for Michigan, however, proved to be a boon when priceless quantities of iron ore and copper were discovered.

Today, most of the rivalry is good-natured. U.P. residents like to joke about blowing up the Mackinac Bridge and are given to displaying bumper stickers portraying a giant U.P. with a tiny Lower Peninsula dangling from its eastern end. Yet there is a kernel of seriousness to the squabble. Upper Peninsula residents feel they pay taxes to a distant state capital but receive very little in return, save for government-protected land and wildlife programs. From time to time, residents launch quasi-serious drives to declare sovereignty from the rest of Michigan and create the state of Superior. As a musical group from Ishpeming, Da Yoopers, satirically sings, "Dear Mr. Governor, you better turn us loose / We asked you for some rest stops, instead you sent us moose / The honeymoon is over, the declaration's written / We'll take what's above the bridge, and you can keep the mitten."

including John Jacob Astor. By the early 1800s, Astor's American Fur Company, headquartered on Mackinac Island, had made him the wealthiest man in the United States.

THE BRITISH

As European colonization continued, the area's peacefulness was shattered. The lucrative fur trade attracted British traders who, by the late 1600s, began traveling from New York and across Lake Huron to St. Ignace. They began bartering their goods for pelts and thus interfered with the established trade alliances between the French and the Indigenous people. Before long, animosity between the British and French reached a peak, resulting in the French and Indian War in the mid-1700s.

The war effectively ended the 150-year French era and ushered in British rule by 1759. Occasional skirmishes among the French, British, and Native Americans continued, especially around the Straits of Mackinac. In one of region's more exciting historical moments, a group of Ojibwa successfully raided the British-run Fort Michilimackinac in 1763 as part of Pontiac's Rebellion. Today, museums and historic state parks in the area chronicle these events.

The British ruled the colony with an iron fist. While the French had treated the Native Americans with a certain amount of respect, the British allied themselves with tribes that were traditional enemies of those indigenous to the area. After Pontiac's Rebellion, the Native Americans negotiated slightly better terms for their relationships with the ruling British, who made peaceable changes to some of their policies. The British actively discouraged settlement of Michigan's interior to protect their rich fur empire. In 1783, the Treaty of Paris gave the lands to the newly independent United States.

STATEHOOD FOR MICHIGAN

In 1825 New York's Erie Canal opened, which connected Albany on the Hudson River to Buffalo on Lake Erie. This new water route enabled more and more people to move westward and settle in the Michigan Territory. From 1820 to 1830, the population more than tripled to just over 31,000. In 1837 the burgeoning territory was awarded statehood, making Michigan the 26th state admitted to the Union. For the first 10 years of its existence, Detroit served as the new state's capital. Michigan's original constitution mandated that by 1847 the legislature was to determine a new location for the seat of government. After considering various candidate cities, Lansing was chosen, primarily for reasons of security. By locating the capital farther from the international frontier it would be safer from potential British attacks.

The Upper Peninsula, however, was almost left out of the new state. Due to poor surveying at the time, a feud ignited between Ohio and the Territory of Michigan over the 468-square-mile (1,212-sq-km) section of land known as the Toledo Strip. The Toledo War—a bit of a misnomer, as there was virtually no physical fighting—ensued and remained unresolved until 1836, when Congress awarded the strip to Ohio and gave Michigan the western three-quarters of the Upper Peninsula in compensation, which would have otherwise likely gone to Wisconsin. The arrangement paved the way for Michigan's admission to the Union. Since the added territory seemed worthless, Michigan took little consolation. But soon after, the seemingly unimportant frontier of the Upper Peninsula began to yield its bounty of copper and iron, making the deal an economic bonanza.

By 1840 more than 200,000 people had migrated to Michigan. Early industries revolved around farming and agriculture, with lumber becoming a hugely successful enterprise by the latter part of the 19th century. Altogether, more than 160 billion board feet of pine were cut and hauled from Michigan's north woods by the 1890s—enough to build 10 million six-room houses. While the southern part of the state grew increasingly urbanized, the north woods and the Upper Peninsula remained largely a land of mining towns and logging camps.

INDIAN REMOVAL ACT

In one of the most heartbreaking chapters in American history, President Andrew Jackson signed the Indian Removal Act in 1830, giving the U.S. government permission to "trade" Native American lands east of the Mississippi for unspecified lands out west. The federal government claimed it was for the protection of the Native Americans, correctly predicting that settlers would continue to surge into their ancestral homelands in the name of frontier expansion.

Native Americans did not want to leave, let alone be removed from what had been their homelands for centuries. At first, Indigenous people in northern Michigan and Wisconsin were largely passed over by the federal Indian Bureau—possibly because the federal government considered this land undesirable, unlike the farmland in southern Michigan where the Potawatomi had lived before being forcibly removed.

Sadly, the federal government's persecution of the Native Americans did eventually reach northern Michigan. By the mid-1800s, treaties had "legally" confiscated much of their land in both the Upper and Lower Peninsulas and established many of the reservations that still exist today.

The government of the new State of Michigan, however, did treat the Indigenous people with a modicum of decency. In 1850, Native American men were given the right to vote and even to run for office in counties where the population was predominantly Indigenous, a concession then unheard of elsewhere.

THE COPPER RUSH

In 1840, state geologist Douglass Houghton confirmed the presence of copper in the

Historical Highlights

The region's prolific history is quite noticeable throughout the Upper Peninsula, with virtually every community boasting a local history museum and a variety of state-recognized sites. The state's Michigan History Center operates the Michigan Historical Marker Program, which has designated 128 noteworthy sites scattered among the U.P.'s 15 counties.

MINING HISTORY

- **Fayette Historic State Park** (page 94): Perhaps the best preserved "ghost town" in America, Fayette serves as a three-dimensional window to the 19th century, when belching blast furnaces turned raw iron ore into pig iron.

- **Iron County Heritage Trail** (page 130): This complex of attractions is a great destination for history buffs. The Iron County Historical Museum is its centerpiece.

- **Keweenaw National Historical Park** (page 165): This park is made up of sites throughout the Keweenaw that were seminal to the area's copper mining heritage. Don't miss the Quincy Mine!

- **Downtown Calumet** (page 165): This town offers a dynamic reminder of the once prosperous copper industry.

MARINE HISTORY

- **Marquette Maritime Museum and Marquette Harbor Lighthouse** (page 205): This fascinating nautical museum emphasizes the role lighthouses have played in Great Lakes shipping.

- **Great Lakes Shipwreck Museum** (page 264): This haunting yet intriguing museum pays tribute to those lost while working in commercial shipping on the Great Lakes.

MILITARY HISTORY

- **Fort Mackinac** (page 48): A massive fortress perched on a bluff overlooking the Straits of Mackinac and the village below, Fort Mackinac best exemplifies the quintessential 19th-century military fort. Interesting programming featuring interpreters in period dress makes this a "must visit" destination.

- **Colonial Michilimackinac State Park** (page 72): The site of the original fort, built in 1715, is the location of an archaeological dig ongoing since 1959, summertime reenactments, and a big wooden replica fort.

- **Fort Wilkins Historic State Park** (page 178): An example of excessive 19th-century military spending, Fort Wilkins was built to combat trouble that never occurred. Today it's a historically accurate display of military life during the era, complete with costumed interpreters.

Upper Peninsula's Keweenaw Peninsula. These were vast deposits of pure native copper, much of it near the surface. The federal government acquired the western half of the U.P.—along with its mineral rights—from the Ojibwa in 1842, just as prospectors began flooding toward the wild and remote Keweenaw. The young United States had an insatiable appetite for the metal, first for new industrial machinery, later for Civil War munitions, and eventually for electrical wiring and other innovations. Houghton's discovery proved to be of incalculable value.

The copper rush began almost overnight,

first with prospectors, then with large mining enterprises swarming the Keweenaw. Lucky prospectors secured deck space on Great Lakes vessels and sailed up Lakes Huron and Michigan, then along the southern shore of Lake Superior. At the same time, hundreds of others straggled through the roadless wilderness, trudging overland through northern Wisconsin by snowshoe or following rivers through thick forests to reach the fabled riches. It was the nation's first mineral rush.

The burgeoning copper industry employed thousands of immigrant laborers, built cities, made millionaires, and made possible extravagant luxuries like opera houses and mansions, many still standing today in Calumet and Laurium. Before it was over, King Copper had generated more than $9.6 billion in wealth—some 10 times the amount of the more famous California gold rush.

The entire nation turned to northern Michigan for its copper. During much of the 19th century, the Keweenaw Peninsula produced 75 percent of all U.S. copper; during the Civil War, it rose to 90 percent. More than 400 mining companies operated in the Keweenaw during copper's heyday. The constant demand for labor drew immigrants from more than 30 countries, most notably the British Isles and Scandinavia. With multiple cultures sharing the same mine shafts and communities, Copper Country served as one of the nation's first examples of ethnic diversity.

But by the mid-20th century virtually all the larger mines had closed due to depletion and poor economic conditions, leaving behind tattered homes, abandoned commercial districts, and empty streets. Soon after, newer mines emerged in the southwestern United States and South America, which proved more productive and cost-effective. Today, lumber and tourism stand as the primary economic pillars of the Upper Peninsula.

Economy and Government

ECONOMY

For almost two centuries, Michigan has been a microcosm of the country's great industrial transition. As the state's primary industries—mining, logging, and (in the Lower Peninsula) automobile manufacturing—have slowly declined, Michigan has been forced to confront its rocky road of economic instability and find ways to diversify its economic base. In recent years that effort has begun to bear fruit. However, the effects of the initial downturn were more pronounced in the Upper Peninsula and continue to be felt today.

When the mines closed, many U.P. communities were left without new sources of jobs and income, leaving them a shell of their former selves. Driving through Escanaba's historic downtown, for example, it's almost impossible to not notice the city's decline and realize that its streets are an echo of more prosperous times.

Many of the smaller former mining towns also display significant deterioration, which ironically contributes to their unassuming small-town charm. At the same time, residents of the U.P. are not the sort to surrender to tough times, whether it's a particularly bitter winter or a rough economy. In any case, the reason most people come to the U.P. is precisely because of its decidedly rugged atmosphere.

Logging and Mining

The Upper Peninsula's economy was long based on logging and mining. Great fortunes were made in logging in the late 1800s, as Michigan's vast stands of virgin timber produced enough wood to lay an inch-thick plank across the entire state with enough left over to cover Rhode Island.

It's difficult to gain an appreciation of the riches harvested from Michigan's copper and iron mines. Michigan produced more than $9.6

billion worth of copper and a staggering $48 billion worth of iron, in contrast to just $955 million produced from the California gold rush. But as the most accessible deposits were exhausted and global economics began to play a role, these riches and the miners disappeared.

Tourism

The gradual decline of the mining industry was followed by a rise in tourism, which emerged as the U.P.'s economic salvation. Today, the entire U.P. subsists on tourism and a reduced, but still viable, timber industry—successfully marketing its recreational opportunities and natural resources as its most attractive assets. In 2005, *Sherman's Travel* cited the "majestic wildlife, unspoiled rivers, waterfalls, and dense forests" as just one of the reasons for putting the Upper Peninsula on its list of Top 10 Summer Destinations, an honor it shared with London, the Hamptons, and the Greek Islands. On Mackinac Island, tourism is a well-established tradition, and it was regarded as one of America's prime vacation spots even before the iconic Grand Hotel was built.

Shipping

Just as tractor-trailers rumble down the nation's highways, commercial ships transport commodities across the Great Lakes. Officially designated as the nation's "Fourth Seacoast" by Congress in 1970, the Great Lakes serve as a vital transportation artery for much of the nation's commerce.

With its hundreds of miles of Great Lakes shoreline and deepwater ports, Michigan's Upper Peninsula is a key player in the Great Lakes transportation network. In addition, the Soo Lock system that links Lakes Superior and Huron at Sault Ste. Marie ranks among the largest and busiest in the world.

Iron ore forms the foundation of the Great Lakes trade. In Upper Peninsula ports like Escanaba and Marquette, huge lake carriers, some as long as 1,000 feet (305 meters), load iron ore from nearby mines, then transport it to steelmaking centers in the southern Great Lakes, which supply industrial manufacturers, including the nation's auto industry. The Great Lakes fleet hauls up to 125 million tons of cargo each year, including more than 58 million tons of iron ore—nearly twice the "float" of any other commodity. Transit by ship is a highly economical method of moving heavy and bulky commodities such as ore.

Great Lakes shipping is primarily affected by global competition. Each year, increasing levels of durable goods ranging from refrigerators to automobiles regularly arrive in the United States from overseas, which translates to decreased domestic steel production and, in turn, reduces the demand for iron ore. Trains and trucks also compete with the shipping industry for certain commodities. Overall, however, transport via ship has proven to be a stable industry.

GOVERNMENT

During the early 20th century, Michigan was traditionally a stronghold of the Republican party. Beginning with the Great Depression, however, a competitive two-party political system emerged, as the Democratic Party made major inroads throughout the state.

Since then, Michigan has proven influential in determining the direction of presidential elections. Michigan's vote has dovetailed with the winner of the popular vote in six out of the last eight presidential elections, while Democratic candidates have carried Michigan in each presidential race from 1992 to 2020, with the exception of 2016.

But all this talk of Republicans and Democrats seems rather passé when compared to the Upper Peninsula's relatively recent and occasionally serious talks of seceding from Michigan to form its own autonomous state. It would be called Superior, clearly a reference to Lake Superior. To date, little has come from these efforts, and is unlikely to in the future, considering the Upper Peninsula accounts for only three percent of Michigan's total population of 10 million. The movement was most popular back in the 1960s and 1970s, and occasionally lives on today in half-joking comments and a few satirical bumper stickers.

People and Culture

The residents of Michigan's Upper Peninsula today reflect a diversity of backgrounds due to the region's multilayered history. The French "empire builders" were the first Europeans to arrive, and in due time the British replaced the French. Early American settlers included large and diverse groups from western New York and New England. During the 19th century, immigrants from Europe came seeking a better life, particularly Finns, Swedes, Italians, and Cornish people who worked in the Upper Peninsula mines and lumber camps. Many of today's residents are directly descended from these pioneers.

Today, Upper Peninsula residents number around 311,000, slightly more than 3 percent of Michigan's approximately 10 million citizens, ranking Michigan as the nation's 10th most populous state. According to the U.S. Census Bureau, the U.P.'s five largest cities contain about 20 percent of its people: Marquette's population is 20,561, Sault Ste. Marie's 13,523, Escanaba's 12,439, Menominee's 8,449, and Houghton's 7,675.

NATIVE AMERICANS

In most books of Michigan history, the land's first inhabitants are given little more than a cursory nod, a line or two that identifies the approximately 100,000 early Native Americans as belonging to the tribes of the "Three Fires," the **Ojibwa, Ottawa,** and **Potawatomi.** The three tribes collectively called themselves the Anishinabe, or "First People." Another tribe with a significant presence in the Upper Peninsula during the 1700s was the **Menominee,** who lived in northern Wisconsin and parts of the Upper Peninsula.

Arriving at a precise population figure can be difficult, since the term "Native American" can be defined in several ways, such as politically (tribal membership), ethnically (genealogy), or culturally (personal identification). According to the Office of Tribal Justice

of the U.S. Department of Justice, a Native American "is a person who is of some degree Indian blood and is recognized as an Indian by a Tribe and/or the United States." Today, Michigan is home to one of the largest Native American populations in the country, currently 57,785 (according to the U.S. Census Bureau), with many residing in the Upper Peninsula. It's been estimated that Michigan may have the largest Native American population east of the Mississippi. Today, only a small percentage of Native Americans live on reservations.

There are several reservations throughout the peninsula, including the Sault Ste. Marie Tribe of Chippewa Indians, the largest federally recognized tribe in the Great Lakes area. Of the tribes in the area that are federally recognized, five have been authorized by the U.S. government to operate their own police agencies and courts, which exercise exclusive jurisdiction over particular laws involving Native Americans and events that occur within their boundaries. Tribal courts have broad powers in matters involving child welfare and other civil matters involving tribal members. Jurisdiction extends to nonmembers while present on the reservation. In addition, Native American tribal councils throughout the state provide a variety of outreach services, economic development initiatives, and cultural activities.

Most reservations have cultural centers with museums or displays open to the public. Many communities also host powwows (native dance ceremonies) and festivals. Check with local convention and visitors bureaus, or inquire at tribal headquarters, which are prominent and well-marked buildings on most reservations.

THE IMMIGRANTS

As early as the 1600s, early French fur traders, missionaries, and voyageurs became the area's first European settlers, traversing Michigan's numerous rivers and establishing posts in far-flung areas. Most of these immigrants, however, didn't arrive until over a century later. They turned up in great waves during the early 1800s, with more settlers following in the 1830s and over the subsequent two decades in response to widespread famines in Europe.

The Lower Peninsula today is home to descendants of immigrants from many foreign lands, including Holland, Germany, Canada, India, the Middle East, Somalia, and Liberia. By contrast, the cultural makeup of the Upper Peninsula is less diverse. Immigrants from Sweden, Finland, Italy, and the Cornwall region of England arrived during the 1900s, responding to promises of steady work and decent wages in the iron and copper mines.

Newcomers from Sweden and Finland in particular took to the U.P., perhaps because the U.P.'s woods and rushing rivers held resemblance to their native Scandinavia.

Significant Scandinavian influences remain in the U.P., including active Finnish- and Swedish-speaking communities. Finnish names, foods, and the ubiquitous sauna can be found throughout the Keweenaw Peninsula. The community of Hancock today remains largely Finnish, reflected even in its street names. Some 16 percent of the Upper Peninsula population is Finnish, with the northwest Upper Peninsula containing the largest population of Finnish Americans in the nation. Finnish influences can also be found in Marquette, while Escanaba reflects a noticeable Swedish character.

Arts and Entertainment

HISTORICAL MUSEUMS

Not surprisingly, many of the peninsula's museums are devoted to the lore and legends of the Great Lakes and the state's maritime industry. Paradise, located near the eastern U.P.'s Whitefish Point, is home to the **Great Lakes Shipwreck Museum,** which includes artifacts from 13 shipwrecks, including an exhibit that features the bell from the *Edmund Fitzgerald,* the Great Lakes ore carrier that mysteriously sank in 1975, and whose memory was immortalized in a song by folk singer Gordon Lightfoot. The museum does an excellent job of telling the tales of the hundreds of ships that met their demise in the area's frigid, turbulent waters. Also in the U.P., the **National Ski Hall of Fame** in Ishpeming chronicles the downhill and cross-country versions of the sport, while neighboring Negaunee is home to the **Michigan Iron Industry Museum,** an excellent state-run facility on the site of one of the state's first iron forges.

ENTERTAINMENT

Due to its more rural character, the Upper Peninsula lacks much of the cultural entertainment common to more populated areas, such as theater, music, dance, and nightlife. However, several towns host summertime music festivals, the largest of which is the Pine Mountain Music Festival, as well as opera, symphony, and chamber music. These happen at various locations across the peninsula each summer. You'll be able to find theatrical productions and musical performances in the peninsula's college towns, particularly at Northern Michigan University in Marquette. Another popular venue is the Calumet Theatre in Calumet, which offers a variety of entertainment options during the summer months.

Native American Gaming

Gaming is a popular form of entertainment in the Upper Peninsula. As sovereign lands, Native American reservations are often able

Festivals and Events

The Upper Peninsula offers a wide range of events held annually. While many are listed in the destination chapters, these are the most popular:

Fort Mackinac Memorial Day Observance

Fort Mackinac on Mackinac Island, early morning on Memorial Day

- Soldiers march from the fort to the nearby cemetery to perform a short ceremony.

Fort Wilkins Memorial Day Program

Fort Wilkins near Copper Harbor, Memorial Day

- This event celebrates the fort's history while honoring all service members who have died for our nation.

Baraga County Lake Trout Festival

L'Anse, second weekend in June

- This is a classic small-town summer festival, complete with a pie-eating contest, a beach volleyball tournament, and, of course, the Keweenaw Classic Fishing Tournament.

Mackinac Island Lilac Festival

Mackinac Island, 10 days in mid-June

- This charming festival celebrates life on the island, including a 10k run, concerts, wine tastings, the Grande Parade, and much more.

Annual Antiques on the Bay Classic and Antique Car Show

Downtown St. Ignace, third weekend in June

- This urbane affair displays elegant machines from the golden era of the automobile.

Les Cheneaux Boat Fest

Hessel, second weekend in August

- This show offers a rare glimpse at an array of classic nautical beauties.

to offer high-stakes gambling that is not legally allowed elsewhere in the state (except Detroit). Michigan's first Native American casino opened near Sault Ste. Marie in 1984. The Bay Mills Blackjack Casino originally had just 15 blackjack tables and one dice table in a 2,400-square-foot room located in the tribal center.

Over the decades since, several Native American casinos have opened throughout Michigan, many in the Upper Peninsula. Most are open 24 hours a day, seven days a week, and have become considerable tourism draws.

They range from small gambling halls to sumptuous showplaces. The Sault Ste. Marie Kewadin complex, for example, has added an art gallery that displays paintings, jewelry, and crafts made by Native Americans. The venture has proven quite lucrative, as visitors have consistently shown their love of gambling, pouring tens of millions of dollars into casino coffers.

By the early 1990s, the state government decided to enter the picture. In 1993 the state legislature passed and Governor John Engler signed the Tribal State Gaming Compact, giving the state 8 percent of net income derived from games of chance. The added revenue to the state continues to yield hundreds of millions of dollars annually. While providing the state government with an additional source of funds, the success of Native American gaming has also brought tribal governments greater power and influence.

While the pros and cons of gambling remain a matter of political and ethical debate, there's no arguing the positive spinoffs that gaming provides to the reservations' overall economies. Within these communities, revenue from gambling has provided jobs while funding schools, health care facilities, cultural centers, and other essential needs. Additionally, the gaming industry has yielded economic benefits outside Native American communities by creating jobs in the building trades and tourism industries. By all appearances, Michigan residents and visitors will never lose their desire to pursue Lady Luck.

Essentials

Transportation

GETTING THERE
Car

The only route to the Upper Peninsula from the Lower Peninsula by car or bus is via the Mackinac Bridge on I-75—an exhilarating experience for most but deathly frightening for some. Since 2015 the toll has been $4 per passenger car, with no increases currently planned. From Wisconsin, US 41 runs north of Green Bay into Menominee, while US 141/US 8 enters Michigan near Norway and Iron Mountain. Moving west, US 45 connects with US 2 at Watersmeet, and both US 51 from the south and US 2 from the west meet in Ironwood.

Travelers coming from Canada may take King's Highway 17 (the Trans-Canada Highway) to Sault Ste. Marie, Ontario, and cross the St. Mary's River via the International Bridge into the United States. Passenger cars are currently charged a toll of $4 (C$5.10). Go to www.saultbridge.com/toll-rates-auto for the latest information. For the latest currency exchange rates, check www.xe.com/ucc.

Bus

Indian Trails (800/292-3831, www.indiantrails.com), a Michigan-based company, runs regularly scheduled bus routes throughout Michigan, including the Upper Peninsula. Main routes go between Calumet and Milwaukee via Marquette and to St. Ignace and Ironwood via Escanaba.

Air

Detroit Metropolitan Airport (DTW, 800/642-1978) is the area hub for **Delta Airlines** (888/750-3284, www.delta.com), which allows you fly to Detroit from anywhere in the United States and overseas, connecting to several of the Upper Peninsula's commercial airports, including Escanaba, Marquette, Pellston/Mackinac Island, and Sault Ste. Marie. Houghton is accessible only via Chicago.

Flights from Detroit are rather limited, with only one or two arrivals and departures per day at regional airports. The major airports for U.P. destinations are:

- **Pellston Regional Airport (PLN):** US 31, Pellston, 231/539-8441, www.pellston airport.com

- **Chippewa County International Airport (CIU):** 119 Airport Dr., Kincheloe, 906/495-2522, www.airciu.com

- **Delta County Airport (ESC):** 3300

Airport Rd., Escanaba, 906/786-4902, www.deltacountymi.org

- **Sawyer International Airport (MQT):** 225 Airport Ave., Gwinn, 906/346-3308, www.sawyerairport.com

- **Houghton County Memorial Airport (CMX):** 23810 Airpark Blvd., Calumet, 906/482-3970, www.houghtoncounty.org

Boat

Surrounded by hundreds of miles of shoreline, Michigan's Upper Peninsula is easy to access via the Great Lakes, and visitors who do will find a high concentration of marinas. The Parks and Recreation Division of the state Department of Natural Resources (DNR) has established a network of protected **public mooring facilities** along the Great Lakes, a "marine highway" that ensures that boaters are never far from a safe harbor. More facilities are being added every year, with the ultimate goal of ensuring that a boater is never more than 15 shoreline miles (22 km) from a protected public mooring. Mooring fees vary. For more information or a free *Michigan Harbors Guide,* contact the **DNR Parks and Recreation Division** (P.O. Box 30257, Lansing, MI 48909, 517/373-9900, www.michigan.gov/dnr).

GETTING AROUND
Car

Roads in the Upper Peninsula are plentiful, and most major arteries are in good condition. Along with interstate and federal highways, the state is honeycombed with numerous state highways, marked on road maps by a number surrounded by a circle, oval, or occasionally a diamond. On road signs state highways are identified by their official insignia, which is the number of the road centered within a white diamond. In conversation, they are described with an "M," as in, "Follow M-28 west to Marquette." County roads are marked with squares on most road maps, and may be designated "CR."

Two routes traverse the peninsula from east to west: M-28 is the northern route, passing through Marquette; US 2 is the southern route, passing through Escanaba. If you're traveling from the eastern end of the U.P. all the way to Ironwood, M-28 is usually faster. Several state and federal highways running north-south link M-28 and US 2. These include, from east to west, I-75, M-123, M-77, US 41, US 145, and US 45, among others.

When planning a route in the Upper Peninsula, consult your map legend regarding road surfaces. Roads you might assume are paved may be gravel or dirt, which can make for very slow going. All state and federal highways are paved and well maintained, as are most county and secondary roads. For construction updates, see https://mdotjboss.state.mi.us/MiDrive/construction, or call the Michigan Department of Transportation's road construction hotline (800/641-6368).

The speed limit on interstate highways in Michigan is 70 mph (113 kph), unless otherwise posted. Most four-lane highways and many two-lane highways now have limits of 65 mph (105 kph). Expressways in urban areas often have a posted limit of 55 mph (89 kph). Complete and current information regarding Michigan speed limits can be found by visiting www.michigan.gov/speedlimits.

For first-time visitors to Michigan, one of the most confusing aspects of driving the state's major roads is a type of turn only found here: the Michigan left. Ordinarily, direct left turns are prohibited at intersections where a Michigan left is in place. In these cases, to turn left onto an intersecting road, it's necessary to continue past the intersection and make a U-turn at the median crossover, double back to your intended street, and turn right. To turn left onto a major crossing road, turn right, then make a U-turn at the median and continue on your way. According to the Department of Transportation, these turns serve to relieve congestion and reduce both the number and

the severity of crashes. Crash rates at intersections with a Michigan left are considerably lower than traditional interchanges, enough to make one wonder why other states haven't adopted the idea. Since these turns are usually installed at high-traffic intersections (and can only be used when at least one of the roads is a divided highway), there are relatively few in the Upper Peninsula, but they are present in some of the larger cities, particularly along US 41/M-28 near Marquette.

There's a long-standing joke about Michigan roads that goes: "Michigan has four seasons: winter, winter, winter, and road construction." While certainly an exaggeration, the quip does refer to a perennial problem caused by the state's weather. Temperatures swing from below freezing to a thaw and then back to freezing. When the refreezing occurs, water absorbed into the pavement (especially the porous asphalt) expands and creates potholes. In addition, heavy snowfalls require the use of snowplows, sand, and salt, causing stress and pavement deterioration. Michigan Department of Transportation (MDOT) works constantly from spring through autumn to correct these problems.

Winter Driving

Michigan roads are generally well maintained in winter, plowed free of snow and then salted or sanded. While salt is more effective at melting, sand is less destructive to the pavement and the environment. During and immediately after a storm, however, difficult or even dangerous conditions can occur as road crews strive to keep up with conditions. County and city crews prioritize their attention by well-established protocols; first preference goes to federal and state highways, major thoroughfares, and roads to schools and hospitals, followed by less vital routes. Minor roads are handled differently, especially in the Upper Peninsula. A sign reading "Seasonal Road: Not Maintained in Winter" indicates the route is neither plowed nor patrolled during the winter months. To check driving conditions

Driving Distances and Times

From Chicago to:

- Escanaba: 315 miles (507 km), 6.5 hours
- Houghton: 421 miles (678 km), 6.75 hours
- Ironwood: 403 miles (649 km), 7.75 hours
- Marquette: 386 miles (621 km), 8.25 hours
- Sault Ste. Marie: 509 miles (819 km), 7.75 hours
- St. Ignace: 458 miles (767 km), 7 hours

From Detroit to:

- Escanaba: 435 miles (700 km), 8.25 hours
- Houghton: 554 miles (892 km), 11.5 hours
- Ironwood: 694 miles (1,117 km), 13 hours
- Marquette: 456 miles (734 km), 9 hours
- Sault Ste. Marie: 345 miles (555 km), 5.25 hours
- St. Ignace: 295 miles (475 km), 4.5 hours

From Grand Rapids to:

- Escanaba: 393 miles (632 km), 8 hours
- Houghton: 513 miles (826 km), 11.5 hours
- Ironwood: 585 miles (941 km), 10.5 hours
- Marquette: 415 miles (668 km), 8.75 hours
- Sault Ste. Marie: 304 miles (489 km), 5 hours
- St. Ignace: 254 miles (409 km), 4.25 hours

From Milwaukee to:

- Escanaba: 295 miles (475 km), 5 hours
- Houghton: 332 miles (534 km), 5 hours
- Ironwood: 320 miles (515 km), 6.5 hours
- Marquette: 296 miles (476 km), 6.75 hours
- Sault Ste. Marie: 417 miles (671 km), 9.75 hours
- St. Ignace: 366 miles (589 km), 8.75 hours

before you travel, call the AAA road conditions number (800/337-1334).

If you're unfamiliar with driving in snow, exercise special caution; allow ample extra room between you and the car in front, and remember that stopping distances can be considerably longer. If your car isn't equipped with antilock brakes, tap your brake pedal lightly in rapid succession to come to a stop. Do not stomp on them, or you'll lose control of your vehicle. If your car does have ABS antilock brakes, apply steady pressure, and the system's computer will do the work. A four-wheel-drive vehicle will provide better traction but not greater stopping ability.

Chains and studded snow tires are not permitted on Michigan roads. For winter, many residents do switch to snow tires, which have a heavier tread. If you have a rear-wheel-drive car, adding weight to the back end can greatly improve traction. Bags of water-softener salt or sand work well. Sand is also useful for getting a vehicle unstuck.

Bear in mind that ice is considerably more dangerous than snow, since it significantly limits traction and stopping ability. Be especially aware of black ice, which is pavement that appears wet but is actually covered with of glaze of ice. Watch for icy roads as rain turns to snow (called "freezing rain"), especially on bridges, which freeze first due to the cold air circulating above and below the road deck. Ice also forms after a number of cars travel over a snowy surface, compressing it into a slick, hard pack. This often happens on heavily traveled federal and state highways. On four-lane roads, the lesser-used left lane usually looks snowier but may actually be less dangerous.

Equip your vehicle with a shovel, sand (kitty litter works even better), and boots in case you get stuck. Throw the sand or kitty litter under the front tires for a front-wheel-drive car, the rear tires on a rear-wheel drive. Keep the tires straight and *slowly* apply the gas—doing so excessively will only make the problem worse. Gently rocking the car forward and back, especially if you have someone who can push, works best.

Keep a flashlight, flares, blankets, and extra clothing in your vehicle in case you have to spend the night in your car. It could save your life. In remote areas, help may not always arrive promptly. If you see a car stuck on a snow bank or in a ditch, be a Good Samaritan and offer the stranded driver a push or a ride to town.

Driving and Deer

Michigan is inhabited by some 1.8 million deer, which pose a significant threat to drivers. Several thousand car collisions with deer occur each year, some of which are fatal to drivers. In the U.P. alone, some 2,700 such accidents are reported annually, though many go unreported. Deer can appear suddenly, darting in front of your car with little to no warning, emerging from woods or a roadside ditch. Be especially alert at dawn and dusk, when they tend to be more active. Another time to be on guard is during firearm deer hunting season in November. Yellow and black "leaping deer" signs warn motorists of routes where deer crossings are more common, but keep in mind that they can happen anywhere.

If you see deer by the side of the road, slow down and prepare to stop. If you see a deer cross ahead of you, be especially cautious. Where there's one deer, there are usually several. If you do hit a deer, notify the nearest law enforcement office immediately.

Car Rentals

Rental cars are available at most commercial airports around the peninsula. In the U.P.'s larger cities, you'll have access to the major companies like **National** (800/227-7368), **Budget** (800/527-0700), **Hertz** (800/654-3131), **Enterprise** (855/266-9565), and **Avis** (800/831-2847). Quality local operators are mentioned in the *Getting There and Around* sections. It is strongly recommended that you reserve a car in advance, as small locations have limited inventory. If you plan to do any exploring in the Upper Peninsula, ask about the rental company's policies regarding off-road driving. Many forbid you to leave pavement, which can curtail your access to many U.P. sights.

BORDER CROSSINGS

Due to heightened national security after 9/11, the formerly lax rules at Canadian-U.S. border crossings were made considerably more stringent. Since 2009 a passport or enhanced driver's license (available to residents of Michigan, Minnesota, New York, Vermont, and Washington) is required for crossing the international border. See the U.S. Department of State's travel website (http://travel.state.gov) for more information. Upon arrival to the international border, each vehicle is stopped at the customs checkpoint, where all of the passengers will have to present proper ID and answer questions regarding citizenship and the reason for visiting. If you're traveling with a minor for whom you aren't the parent or legal guardian, you'll need a signed letter from the parent or legal guardian that grants permission for the child to leave the country and that includes a contact phone number. Pets require proof of proper vaccinations; plants are not permitted and will be confiscated.

All foreign visitors, including Canadians, must have a passport to enter the United States. Visit www.usa.gov/visitors/arriving.shtml for current information and requirements.

For visitors arriving by car, the bridge connecting Michigan's Upper Peninsula to Ontario is the International Bridge from Sault Ste. Marie, Michigan, to Sault Ste. Marie, Ontario ($4/C$5.10 for a passenger car). If arriving by boat, visitors must check in at the nearest customs station immediately upon arrival.

Any goods purchased abroad must be declared, and the proper duty must be paid on certain items, including alcohol and cigarettes beyond personal-use limits. Transporting firearms across the border for lawful sporting purposes, such as hunting, requires declaring the weapon at customs and having the necessary paperwork in hand. Failure to declare a weapon may result in arrest.

Recreation

NATIONAL PARKS AND FORESTS

Michigan's Upper Peninsula is home to a national park, a national lakeshore, and two national forests. **Isle Royale National Park** is virtually a world of its own, a 45-mile-long (72-km) wilderness surrounded by the waters of Lake Superior. **Pictured Rocks National Lakeshore** extends along 42 miles (68 km) of Lake Superior shore. The **Ottawa National Forest** in the western Upper Peninsula covers nearly 1 million acres (over 400,000 hectares); the **Hiawatha National Forest** in the eastern U.P. adds another 860,000 acres (350,000 hectares). In addition, the **Seney National Wildlife Refuge** occupies 95,000 acres (38,500 hectares) of cutover logging land in the eastern Upper Peninsula.

In the Upper Peninsula, most parks, with the exception of a few key attractions such as noteworthy waterfalls and beaches, are secluded while still offering a remarkable amount of quality outdoor activities. **Hiking** trails tend to be uncrowded. **Campsites** are isolated, rustic, and are also seldom used. **Mountain biking** is permitted on most federal forest lands but prohibited in national and state parks. Inland lakes are often difficult to reach with a boat trailer, so they tend to be ideal for those looking for a quiet **paddling** experience.

For information on hiking, camping, paddling, and other activities in the national forests, please contact their respective headquarters: **Ottawa National Forest** (E6248 US 2, Ironwood, 906/932-1330, www.fs.fed. us/r9/ottawa); **Hiawatha National Forest** (2727 N. Lincoln Rd., Escanaba, 906/786-4062, www.fs.fed.us/r9/forests/hiawatha).

STATE FORESTS

Like national forests, state forests are hidden gems for anyone seeking a quiet corner of woods or water. Much of the state's forestland was actually acquired by default, picked up during the Depression when landowners were unable to pay their property taxes. Their loss was certainly the public's gain. Much of the land is exceptional, consisting of rivers, waterfalls, lakes, beaches, and forest. Collectively, state forestland in the U.P. amounts to 3.9 million acres (1.6 million hectares), the largest such holding in any state east of the Rocky Mountains.

To receive maps and information on Upper Peninsula state forest camping, hiking, and more, visit the **Michigan Department of Natural Resources (DNR)** website (www.michigan.gov/dnr) or contact **Copper Country State Forest** (Baraga, 906/353-6651), **Escanaba River State Forest** (Escanaba, 906/786-2351), and **Lake Superior State Forest** (Newberry, 906/293-5131).

STATE PARKS

You'll see it scores of times in this guide: Michigan's Upper Peninsula has an outstanding state park system. They are well planned, well maintained, and showcase some of the state's most diverse and beautiful land. Some state parks were clearly set aside for public access, such as the state park beaches along the Lake Michigan shore, while others preserve historical sites and natural jewels like the Porcupine Mountains or Mackinac Island.

The U.P. has 21 state parks and nearly 60 state forest campgrounds. The **DNR Parks and Recreation Division** (517/373-9900, www.michigan.gov/dnr) publishes a handy *State Parks Guide* that includes a map, a short profile of each park, and a chart listing each park's amenities. You can get much of the same information from the website.

Since 2010 Michigan no longer charges daily entry fees for state parks. In lieu of this, the state has introduced the **Recreation Passport** program, where any driver with a

"Take Nothing but Pictures— Leave Nothing but Footprints..."

"And kill nothing but time." Although the precise authorship of this quote is disputed, it's generally attributed to the Baltimore Grotto (local chapter) of the National Speleological Society, a national organization dedicated to exploration and conservation of caves in the United States. The saying, or at least the first part of it, is often displayed in state parks and forests throughout Michigan to emphasize the most essential responsibility of any visitor—the obligation to leave the environment as undisturbed as possible, and to allow future visitors to experience nature unsullied.

Today's conservation movement reflects a tradition of thought that goes back to the late 19th century, when future president Theodore Roosevelt noticed the threat posed to natural resources in the western United States by timber and hunting interests. The experience inspired Roosevelt to take proactive steps toward conservation after he assumed office. As president, he created the National Forest Service, established 51 bird reserves and 4 game preserves, and signed legislation creating the first national parks.

In the 1960s, as First Lady of the United States, Lady Bird Johnson took a strong interest in protecting the environment by promoting the Highway Beautification Act of 1965, which limited roadside billboards and promoted the planting of flowers along roadways. In 1970 President Richard Nixon signed legislation establishing the Environmental Protection Agency to enforce a series of new laws aimed at limiting pollution.

But for today's visitor, honoring the motto of the Baltimore Grotto is simple. Make certain that your stopover includes removing refuse—paper, trash, and plastic bags. Respect native plants and animals. Above all, be a friend to the earth.

car licensed in Michigan can purchase an annual pass for $13 ($35 for nonresidents), regardless of the number of passengers in the vehicle. The annual Recreation Passport, issued in the form of a sticker placed on either the license plate or on the inside passenger-side windshield, is valid for all Michigan state parks.

Camping requires an additional fee. Rates range $16-45 per night depending on the specific location selected, time of year, and whether the campsite is rustic or more modern, with flush toilets, showers, and electricity. Some parks also rent "mini cabins," tiny shelters that offer a roof and walls to protect you from the elements, but little more, for around $30 per night. These book up fast, so be sure to reserve well ahead. A few parks, including Porcupine Mountains Wilderness State Park and Craig Lake State Park, rent out rustic cabins equipped with bunks and a stove or other cooking facility for $50-70 per night. They're great if you have a group or if you're visiting

when the bugs are particularly fierce. These are extremely popular; calling to reserve as early as January is advised.

For a $2 fee, you can make a camping reservation at any park in advance by calling 800/447-2757 or reserving online at www. midnrreservations.com. You can request a specific site, but it will not be guaranteed. Camping reservations are strongly recommended in summer months at many state parks. This guide indicates if a park is particularly popular.

HIKING

Because of its many national and state parks, national and state forests, national lakeshores, and publicly accessible private land, Michigan's Upper Peninsula offers almost unlimited options for hikers. Where you go depends on your taste, and this guide provides you with a number of ideas.

For backpackers, Isle Royale National Park in Lake Superior is an outstanding choice, free of roads and other development. Evenly spaced rustic campsites allow you to hike the length of this 45-mile-long (72-km) archipelago, while water taxi services can provide transit back to your starting point. Slightly less remote, Porcupine Mountains Wilderness State Park in the western Upper Peninsula also offers great backpacking in a rugged backcountry environment not typical of state parks.

Michigan also has hundreds of miles of linear hiking trails, such as the Bay de Noc/ Grand Island Trail, which bisects the Upper Peninsula. And for those really looking for an adventure, the **North Country National Scenic Trail** (www.nps.gov/noco) traverses the Upper Peninsula as part of a national trail that, when complete, will stretch from North Dakota to New York. Many long segments of the trail crossing national forest land are already open to hikers in Michigan. Check with national forest officials for more information.

BICYCLING

Michigan's Upper Peninsula is noteworthy for its rolling topography, miles of shorelines, and ample country roads, all of which make for a great bicycling destination. Examples for road cycling include the quiet backroads near Les Cheneaux and the winding byways of the Garden Peninsula. Check with local visitors bureaus for suggested routes.

Michigan leads the nation in its number of "rails-to-trails" sites. The term refers to a dormant railroad path with the rails removed and everything else left as-is, sometimes including railroad ties and sharp old mining rock. Currently, 55 such trails crisscross the Upper Peninsula. Some of these more primitive trails are appropriate only for snowmobiles and all-terrain vehicles, although most, especially the Bill Nichols Trail, are great for mountain bikes and pass through wonderful wilderness terrain.

Michigan is kind to mountain bikers, with an abundance of opportunities in many state and national forests. Off-road riding in places like the Keweenaw and the Huron Mountains is perhaps the best between the Rockies and the Appalachians, with an added Michigan perk—stunning Great Lakes views.

SKIING

Each winter the upper Great Lakes produce a number of lake-effect snows, which fall onto some of the Midwest's hilliest terrain. That convenient marriage has made the Upper Peninsula the top ski destination in the Midwest. Strictly speaking, while the area isn't *truly* mountainous, the resorts do an admirable job of working creatively with the terrain—carving out 600-foot (185-meter) vertical drops and runs that wind through the pines or offer spectacular views of the Great Lakes.

Though downhill ski areas can be found throughout the peninsula, most are concentrated in the western U.P. from Ironwood to the Porcupine Mountains.

Cross-country skiers have even more to choose from. Though they don't all offer lodging, the U.P. has several privately run cross-country trail systems. Many of the downhill resorts, such as Big Powderhorn Mountain in Bessemer, also have notable cross-country trails. The national lakeshores and many state parks groom trails for skiing, and the state and national forests offer virtually limitless opportunity for backcountry skiing.

For information on both downhill and cross-country skiing, contact **Pure Michigan** (800/644-2489, www.michigan.org/skiing).

GOLF

The U.P. has plenty of top-tier courses, many which feature a diverse terrain of hills and water views that make for an extraordinary golfing experience. Drummond Island, Mackinac Island, and Marquette are home to some of the U.P.'s finest courses. Here you'll find award-winners like The Rock at the Drummond Island Resort and Conference Center, The Jewel at the Grand Hotel on Mackinac Island, and Greywalls at the Marquette Golf Club. You'll also find plenty of well-kept and challenging courses elsewhere on the peninsula. For more information, consult the destination chapters or contact **Pure Michigan** (800/644-2489, www.michigan.org/golfing).

BOATING AND FISHING

Michigan is home to over one million registered boats, more than any state except California. There are also an estimated 200,000 to 300,000 unregistered boats in the state. Michigan boaters cruise from port to port on the Great Lakes, sail along scenic shorelines like Pictured Rocks and along island chains, as well as water ski on thousands of inland lakes, paddle white-water rivers and quiet waters, and fish just about everywhere.

Small watercraft such as day sailors, fishing boats, and canoes are readily available to rent in many U.P. communities. Contact the local chamber of commerce or visitors bureau in the area you plan to visit for more information. For larger sailboats or powerboats, contact the **Michigan Charter Boat Association** (800/622-2971, www.michigancharterboats.com). The **Pure Michigan** website (www.michigan.org) also has an interactive travel planner that can provide you with a list of charter operations in any given region.

If you'll be hauling your own boat by trailer, the **Michigan DNR** (517/373-9900, www.michigan.gov/dnr) publishes a list of public launch sites. If you'll be arriving by water, see the *Getting There* section earlier in this chapter for information on Great Lakes public mooring facilities. A Coast Guard-approved lifejacket—known as a PFD, or personal flotation device—is required for each person on any kind of boat.

Michigan's Upper Peninsula is a paddler's dream. You can canoe or run white water down several nationally designated Wild and Scenic Rivers, surf waves along Lake Michigan's shoreline, or sea kayak along Pictured Rocks or Isle Royale National Park. For a more peaceful experience, the Sturgeon River is a favorite. The U.P. also has several notable white-water rivers, including the beautiful Presque Isle River and the Ontonagon. For more information on paddling destinations and liveries, contact the **Michigan Association of Paddle Sports Providers** (www.michigan.org).

Fishing has long been popular in Michigan. It's a highly versatile sport with different styles suited for various seasons: summertime fly-fishing along a pristine stream or winter ice-fishing from a shanty. Michigan's quantity of blue-ribbon trout streams is unrivaled anywhere east of Montana. Most of the best streams are in the eastern U.P., including the Fox, the Chocolay, and the Carp Rivers.

"Deep-sea" charters on the Great Lakes go after the big chinook and coho salmon, as well as lake trout. Lake Michigan's Little and Big Bay de Noc arguably offer the finest walleye fishing in the state, if not all the Great Lakes. Inland, thousands of lakes harbor walleye, northern pike, muskie, bass, and panfish. Some of the most popular spots are the Manistique Lakes chain and huge Lake Gogebic.

The ultimate level of solitude can be found in the dozens of small lakes in the Ottawa and Hiawatha National Forests, which are peaceful, harder to get to, and lightly used. As a result, these waterways teem with fish. Some, like the Sylvania Wilderness, have special fishing regulations, so check with authorities. All Michigan waters require a valid Michigan fishing license. For specific fishing information, contact the **DNR Fisheries Division** (517/373-1204, www.michigan.gov/dnr).

HUNTING

With its abundance of wildlife, forests, and undeveloped land, Michigan's tradition of hunting continues today, with white-tailed deer being the most sought-after game. There are some 270,000 deer in the Upper Peninsula. Of these, hunters take several thousand each year; in 2021, U.P. hunters harvested some 34,200 deer.

While the sentiment and sympathies of many people tend toward the deer, this annual culling of the herd helps prevent much larger problems, chief among them being deer-vehicle accidents and fatalities. When the statewide deer population peaked in the 1980s at about two million animals, signs of distress were seen in the herd. Animals were perilously underweight and in some places as many as 6 of 10 fawns died. Some 125,000 animals starved to death during a single hard winter. Deer-vehicle accidents increased to 40,000 each year, killing an average of 5 people and injuring an additional 1,500 annually. Crop damage appeared and threatened significant economic damage as the urban and suburban deer population grew. Fencing, trapping, and birth control have proved far less effective in controlling the population than recreational hunting, which is the most efficient means of balancing the population and encouraging healthy cohabitation with human interests and the economy.

The DNR has spent many years trying to strike a balance between scientific herd management and other considerations to maintain a healthy deer population, working with hunters and members of the agricultural industry to develop a mutually beneficial situation. The ideal herd size is around 1.5 million animals, with a buck population of approximately 35 percent. Michigan's hunting rules and regulations change frequently as management needs vary. Special hunting seasons are declared and canceled as needed, and specific rules balance the number of antlerless and antlered deer that can be taken by each hunter. There are also a number of general regulations, in addition to season-specific rules that often change from season to season.

Hunting Licenses

No one can hunt in Michigan without the proper license. Licensing is a two-tier process, in that hunters must first purchase a Base License, which allows the holder to hunt small game (rabbits, hares, crows, pheasant, quail, grouse, and squirrels) and to purchase the advanced specialty license required for other prey. For state residents, an annual Base License costs $11, while nonresidents will have to pay considerably more: $151. Deer licenses

run an additional $20 for both Michigan and out-of-state residents. Separate licenses are required for both firearm and archery seasons. While the nonresident rate is much steeper, given the abundance of deer and the quality of Michigan hunting, it's worth it.

Other specialty licenses are needed for hunting elk (Michigan residents only), bears, turkeys, and waterfowl. Specific licenses required for hunting these species are limited and are distributed by lottery. In addition, specially licensed fur harvesters and trappers may hunt foxes, coyotes, badgers, beavers, bobcats, muskrat, and mink.

To apply for a license, residents need a valid driver's license or a State of Michigan ID card. Nonresidents need to obtain an MDNR Sport card, a type of Michigan ID allowing you to hunt, fish, and trap in the state. The cost is only $1, and it can be ordered online (www.mdnr-elicense.com). Both residents and nonresidents born on or after January 1, 1960, must present either a hunter safety certificate or a previous hunting license, or must sign their license in the presence of a license agent. Hunters are required to carry the signed license and ID whenever they're in the field.

There are also various discounts for veterans and active duty military. Visit www.michigan.gov/dnr for complete details.

What type of license you get depends on how you like to hunt and when or where you do it. Buck hunting regulations are different in the U.P. than in the rest of the state and vary depending on the type of license purchased, so take your time and make sure you're buying precisely what you need. Note that any deer that has at least one antler extending 3 or more inches (7.6 cm) above its skull is considered "antlered." Any deer without antlers or with the longest antler extending less than 3 inches (7.6 cm) above the skull is considered "antlerless."

Separate licenses are required for both archery and firearm season, which will limit you to only one antlered deer in the U.P. for all seasons combined. You can also use the archery license to tag an antlerless deer during archery season. The Michigan DNR also sells combination deer hunting licenses, which consist of a regular and a restricted license. In the Upper Peninsula, both the restricted and regular license have antler point restrictions. With the restricted license, hunters can take a deer that has at least one antler with four or more antler points, each at least 1 inch (2.5 cm) in length. The regular license can be used on deer with at least one antler with three or more antler points, each at least 1 inch (2.5 cm) in length. Both the regular and combination license can be used for antlerless deer in the Upper Peninsula.

Hunting Safety

It goes without saying that firearms and bows are deadly, so carry and use them with the utmost care. As a means of reducing hunting accidents, the state has a clothing requirement: "You may not hunt with any device, or trap with any firearm, on any lands during daylight hunting hours from August 15-April 30, unless you wear a hat, cap, vest, jacket, or rain gear of highly visible orange color, commonly referred to as Hunter Orange." The Hunter Orange garment must be the outermost garment and visible from all sides. Camouflage items that have at least 50 percent or more of the surface in Hunter Orange are legal. This rule is strictly enforced, except for archery deer hunters. Waterfowl, crow, wild turkey, and archery bear hunters are also exempt.

The above information explains only the highlights of Michigan's complex hunting regulations. For complete information, visit www.michigan.gov/dnr and click "Hunting" on the home page. From this page, scroll down to "Rules and Regulations" and click "Hunting Digests" for documents containing all pertinent information.

Public and Private Land

The Upper Peninsula has seemingly endless acres of public land accessible to hunters; consult www.michigan.gov/dnr for a comprehensive list of locations. In addition to public land, the state has purchased public hunting rights to selected tracts of privately owned land, as well as more than 2 million acres (800,000 hectares) of commercial forests statewide. Hunters can also ask permission to hunt on private land. A verbal agreement from the landowner is all that's necessary. A few tips for asking: obtain permission in advance, and approach the door alone or with one other person. Be certain to leave your firearm behind. If you can't visit the landowner, write a letter or email asking to meet in person or make arrangements by phone. Provide your name and contact information, the dates and times you'd like to hunt, and exactly where on the land you'd prefer to hunt. Ask if there are any prohibited areas, and respect any additional requests from the landowner, including party size limits, ORV limits, and safety zones. Leave the property exactly as you found it or better. Be certain to thank the landowner when finished.

BEACHES

The beaches of the Upper Peninsula have a decidedly different feel than most of their Lower Peninsula counterparts. Often wild and windswept, rocky and remote, these coastlines are a reminder that you're in "the other Michigan." Striped cliffs rise directly from Lake Superior at **Pictured Rocks National Lakeshore,** while nearby, the **Grand Sable Dunes** and **Twelvemile Beach** provide enough sand to thrill even the most devoted beachcomber. You probably won't see many people along Twelvemile Beach, but you may catch a glimpse of a deer, or even a black bear, headed to the water's edge for a drink. While perfect for long, sandy walks, only a hardy few actually swim in Lake Superior, as the water temperatures rarely climb out of the 40s (4-9°C).

Lake Michigan's northern coast forms the southern shoreline of the Upper Peninsula, a winding path filled with secluded bays and inlets. A favorite of anglers, it also offers some quality beaches. Some may be hard to find, as public access can be difficult. The best spots are along US 2 from Naubinway to the Straits of Mackinac, where rest stops and county parks point you toward nice sandy beaches hidden behind the pines. You'll find another good sandy stretch along Green Bay between Menominee and Escanaba, where **J. W. Wells State Park** and several county parks offer inviting beaches.

DIVING

A century ago, the Great Lakes were the superhighways of their era, offering the fastest and most efficient mode of transport. Lumber, copper, iron ore, and other commodities were hauled from the forests and mines to Great Lakes ports; passengers traveled on steamships from urban areas around the southern Great Lakes to breath in the fresh cool air of northern resorts.

Unfortunately, the Great Lakes were also known for shallow reefs and violent storms, which led to hundreds of shipwrecks. But the fresh cold lake water—free of barnacles and worms—kept those shipwrecks from decaying. Today, many sit on the lake floor, undisturbed and virtually unchanged.

A century later, these freshwater time capsules are an unending source of delight for divers. Michigan has set aside nine areas where shipwrecks were particularly prevalent as **underwater preserves,** protecting their historic significance and mapping and marking them for divers. Together they cover 1,900 square miles (4,900 sq km) of Great Lakes bottomland—an area roughly the size of Delaware. Along the Lake Superior shore of the Upper Peninsula, underwater preserves are located off of the Keweenaw Peninsula and at Marquette, Munising, and Whitefish Point, as well as around the Straits of Mackinac in Lake Huron.

Most of the popular dive sites are marked with buoys in summer by volunteers of the Michigan Underwater Preserve Council. All the preserves are served by dive charters. For more information, request the booklet that describes each preserve and provides a list of dive charters and other services from the **Michigan Underwater Preserve Council** (560 N. State St., St. Ignace, MI 49781, 800/970-8717, www.michiganpreserves.org). You can also contact the chamber of commerce or visitors bureau nearest the preserve you want to visit, and consult the appropriate chapters in this guide.

Food and Accommodations

FOOD AND DRINK

Throughout the Upper Peninsula, many Main Street cafés and bakeries serve up the pasty, a potpie creation of beef, potatoes, onions, rutabagas, and other vegetables. (Pronounce it PASS-tee, not PACE-tee.) Brought to the U.P. by Cornish miners, the pasty made for a hearty and filling meal that was easy to transport deep into the mine and warm up later with their candles. The same concept works well today if you're headed from town to your campfire.

Another Michigan food well worth tasting is its abundant fresh fish, from brook trout to Great Lakes whitefish. In Great Lakes ports, you'll often be able to find a commercial fishery operating a small retail store, usually down by the docks. They often sell both fresh catch and smoked fish. The latter is absolutely superb with a bottle of wine and a Great Lakes sunset.

Wine and Beer

While wineries in the Upper Peninsula are not plentiful, there are some standouts. **Threefold Vine Winery** (S232 Menominee St., Stephenson, 906/753-6000, www.exploringthenorth.com/threefold/vine.html) near Menominee is an example. Due to its fortuitous location, which offers mild winters and temperate weather, the locale is excellent for growing grapes. Another worthwhile destination is **Northern Sun Winery** (983 10th Rd., Bark River, 906/399-9212, www. northernsunwinery.com).

Beer is the most popular craft beverage in the U.P., at which a number of microbreweries excel. Among the best breweries are the **Keweenaw Brewing Company** (408 Shelden Ave., Houghton, 906/482-5596, www. keweenawbrewing.com), **The Library** (62 N. Isle Royale St., Houghton, 906/481-2665, www. thelibraryhoughton.com), and **Hereford and Hops** (624 Ludington St., Escanaba, 906/789-1945, www.herefordandhops.com).

LODGING OPTIONS

Michigan's Upper Peninsula is well served by most of the moderately priced national chains, but it lacks the higher-end hotel groups such as Hilton or Westin. If you prefer staying in a chain establishment, pick up a copy of its national directory or consult its website to find current locations, rates, and services for its properties in Michigan. There's nothing wrong with chains, but there are several alternatives. All Michigan lodgings charge a 6 percent "use tax," similar to a sales tax. Many counties also have additional room taxes, ranging 2-5 percent, to fund their visitors bureaus and other tourism-related services.

Camping

Camping in Michigan's Upper Peninsula means different things to different people. You can park an RV next to a pool with a waterslide, or pitch a tent in backcountry so remote you could go weeks without seeing another soul. With tens of thousands of varied campsites throughout the state, you'll have no problem finding the option best for you.

This guide lists many campgrounds, intentionally omitting highly developed RV-type properties. State park campgrounds are included since they are almost universally good and often the best option in a particular area. Almost all campgrounds become very busy during the summer months. You can reserve ahead of time and (though it's not guaranteed) even request a specific site

by calling 800/447-2757 or by visiting www. midnrreservations.com.

State and national forests also have excellent camping facilities, which are generally more rustic and located in appealing isolated places. A directory of Upper Peninsula campgrounds is available from the **Michigan DNR** (517/373-9900, www.michigan.gov/dnr). Backcountry camping is also permitted in many forests and on commercial lands owned by paper and mining companies.

For a complete list of private campgrounds, view a free *Michigan Campground Directory* at the **Association of RV Parks and Campgrounds of Michigan** website (9700 M-37 S., Buckley, MI 49620, 231/269-2267, www.michcampgrounds.com) or order a print copy for $3. You can also order a free *RV and Campsite Guide* from the **Michigan Association of Recreational Vehicles and Campgrounds** (2222 Association Dr., Okemos, MI 48864, 517/349-8881, www. marvac.org).

For help in selecting public or private campgrounds geared to your tastes and destination, check out the interactive Travel Planner on the **Pure Michigan** website (www.michigan.org).

Independent Motels

Over the past few decades, the combination of interstate highways and chain motels proved fatal to hundreds of independently owned motels, as Americans professed their love for efficiency and predictability. Recently, however, the pendulum seems to be swinging back the other way, as interesting inns and distinctive lodges are appearing in the most unlikely of places.

Many of these are traditional old mom-and-pop motels reminiscent of the 1960s—places with a neon vacancy sign and lawn chairs out front, the kind of places now romanticized along Route 66.

The good news is that this form of lodging never entirely left the Upper Peninsula. Too out-of-the-way to attract the big chains, many U.P. towns still have several independent

Baking Pasties

Prepare your favorite pie-crust recipe, making enough for four nine-inch pans. Then mix together:

- 2 pounds cooked pork and/or beef, cut into half-inch cubes

- 2 cups onion, diced

- 1 cup rutabaga, diced

- 1 cup potatoes, diced

- Salt and pepper to taste

Roll pastry out and cut four circles, using a nine-inch plate as a pattern. On one-half of the dough, layer meat, then onion, rutabaga, potatoes, and more meat. Fold pastry in half, then roll and crimp edges tightly together. Prick with a fork three times. Bake on a cookie sheet for one hour at 400°F. Yields four large pasties.

motels. Most are not fancy, and in some cases can appear tired and unappealing. But on the other hand, many mom-and-pop motels are clean, tidy, and remarkably inexpensive, and sometimes offer perks most national chains don't—allowing pets, for example. Additionally, they're often pedestrian-friendly, located in town or along a waterfront, rather than stranded out along a highway. Be aware that some do not accept credit cards, but if they don't, they will almost always take a personal check. Many are listed in this guide, and you may discover many more. Don't be afraid to try.

Bed-and-Breakfasts

The Upper Peninsula has dozens of bed-and-breakfast inns. Some are the traditional old-fashioned variety—a spare room or two in someone's quaint old farmhouse—but those have become the exception rather than the norm. Today's B&Bs run the gamut from large inns with amenities like pools and tennis courts to renovated lighthouses and other quaint historical buildings. For a Michigan bed-and-breakfast directory, contact the **Michigan Lake to Lake Bed and Breakfast Association** (888/575-1610, www. laketolake.com).

Ski and Golf Resorts

Several of the U.P.'s ski resorts double as golf resorts in summer, ringed with lodgings that range from motel-style rooms to condo units and townhouses with kitchens, which allow you to save money by eating in. Many also offer other amenities, such as pools, game rooms, and fitness centers, so they can be a particularly good choice for families with active kids. While golf resorts tend to be pricey, ski resorts that don't have the summer golf draw can be great bargains. For information on golf resorts and ski resorts with lodging open in the off-season, consult **Pure Michigan** (800/644-2489, www.michigan.org).

Travel Tips

TRAVELERS WITH DISABILITIES

Thanks to the implementation of the Americans with Disabilities Act, Michigan is very accessible for those with physical limitations. Most welcome centers and rest areas are equipped with features that can accommodate wheelchairs, such as convenient parking spaces, entrance ramps, wide passages, automatic doors, and spacious restrooms. The same can be said for major retail chains, hotel chains, and key attractions, such as the football stadium at the University of Michigan and the Michigan's Adventure amusement park in Muskegon. When in doubt about the possibility of access, call the establishment in question.

TRAVELING WITH CHILDREN

With its multitude of beaches, state parks, museums, and other amusements, Michigan is a very kid-friendly destination. Traveling with children, you'll find lots for them to do. Many restaurants and hotels go out of their way to accommodate young travelers. A great kid (and pet) friendly destination is the **Holiday Inn Express in Munising,** which offers an indoor pool. Nearby, **Pictured Rocks National Lakeshore** has sandy beaches, crystal-clear lakes, and hikes suitable for all ages.

When traveling with children, supervise them at all times, both to keep them safe and to minimize the possibility of disturbing others. If you decide to venture into Canada, you must have proper identification for them as well as yourself.

TRAVELING WITH PETS

Although pets are prohibited in much of Michigan's national parkland and in most of the state's hotels, restaurants, and stores, many places do welcome them, including highway rest areas. In locations where pets are allowed, it's crucial to understand the relevant rules. Typically you are asked to keep your pets on a leash at all times, walk them in designated areas only, control their behavior so as not to disturb or endanger others, and always pick up after them. When in doubt, call ahead to verify the pet policies.

WOMEN TRAVELING ALONE

It's important to take precautions, especially in urban centers. Tell someone back home about your intended travel plans, limit driving to the daytime, and keep close to busy attractions, streets, and campgrounds. Try to stow your money, credit cards, and identification close to your person; large purses make for easy targets. If you feel someone is stalking you, find a public place such as a store, tourism bureau, or police station, and don't hesitate to alert the police. Keep the doors to your lodging and vehicle locked at all times.

Before heading out on your trip, be sure to have a cell phone, which can be useful in an emergency. Do remember, however, that cell service is limited or nonexistent in the state's more remote areas, especially parts of the Upper Peninsula.

SENIOR TRAVELERS

Senior travelers should have little trouble getting assistance. For help with directions, there are welcome centers and tourism bureaus throughout the state, plus plenty of locals able to point you in the right direction. In addition, many establishments, especially restaurants, offer discounts to senior travelers. The **National Park Service** (www.nps. gov) offers a lifetime pass ($80) for U.S. citizens and permanent residents over age 61, allowing them and up to four adults free access to national parks and federal lands that charge entrance fees, including national lakeshores.

LGBTQ+ TRAVELERS

Michigan has traditionally been one of the more liberal Midwestern states, and has evolved with the rest of the nation in recent years in greater tolerance of its gay and lesbian citizens. This courtesy is extended to visitors, although in more conservative areas, including some Upper Peninsula communities, old biases persist.

Gradually, however, even conservative areas have become more enlightened. In the Upper Peninsula, Mackinac Island has become a friendly location for LGBTQ+ travelers. Both the Grand Hotel and Mission Point Resort host weddings for couples of any orientation. A great way to enjoy the straits is on a **Sip 'n Sail** cruise (off Main Street between the Seabiscuit café and the taxi office, 844/906-9006, www.puremichiganboatcruises.com). Sip 'n Sail is a sponsor of **Straits Pride** (www.straitspride.org), a local advocacy organization that seeks to promote awareness of and respect for the LGBTQ+ community.

Many U.P. communities are home to LGBTQ+-friendly businesses. Please check **Upper Peninsula Rainbow Pride** (www.uprainbowpride.org) for additional details and information.

For more information about related issues, events, and establishments in Michigan, contact the **Pride Source Media Group** (20222 Farmington Rd., Livonia, 734/293-7200, www.pridesource.com), which produces an annual business directory for the state's LGBTQ+ residents and also puts out a free weekly newspaper, *Between the Lines*, which serves the LGBTQ+ community.

TRAVELERS OF COLOR

In terms of diversity, Michigan represents something of a paradox. Despite having a widely varied population representing a wide swath of racial and ethnic backgrounds, segregation remains a problem. While strides have been made in recent years, Michigan's percentage of Black residents stands at 14.1 percent, only slightly above the national average of 12.6 percent, with most living in urban areas of Detroit, Flint, and Benton Harbor. Likewise, Michigan's Latino community (which is comparatively small) largely dwells in southwest Detroit and Pontiac.

However, physical separation does not translate to racial hostility. According to the Michigan State Police, of 48,052 violent crimes committed in Michigan in 2020, only 556, or approximately 1.2 percent, were classified as "hate crimes"—crimes motivated by the victim's racial, ethnic, sexual, or religious identification. Tolerance and acceptance have established a firm anchor in Michigan, a trend which will no doubt continue. While the Upper Peninsula's mostly rural population is heavily white, the state is known for a high level of tolerance and acceptance of people from all backgrounds.

The fruits of decades of social progress show themselves in the cultural and economic framework of Michigan. Today, Black Michiganders are the proud owner/operators of a wide variety of businesses in all corners of the state, ranging from microbreweries to clothing manufacturers to retailers.

Health and Safety

HAZARDS
Contaminated Water

Even the most pristine Michigan waters may be tainted with *Giardia lamblia,* a microscopic organism most commonly transmitted in the feces of beavers, moose, and other mammals. It is present in many lakes and streams in the Upper Peninsula. **Giardiasis** can result in severe stomach cramps, vomiting, and diarrhea. As one Isle Royale ranger says, "It won't kill you, but it may make you wish you were dead." Neither chemical treatment with halazone nor a water filter will make water safe from giardia; the safe alternative is a water purifier capable of filtering down to 0.4 microns or less. Boiling is also effective, but make certain to get the water to a full rolling boil for five minutes. Isle Royale water may also be infected with the **hydatid tapeworm,** also requiring purifying or boiling. For short hikes, carrying bottled water may be the best alternative.

Mosquitoes and Blackflies

Michigan's Upper Peninsula has its share of insects. The first hatch of **mosquitoes** usually occurs in early June, depending on local weather conditions. Their bite causes little or no pain but will leave a small lump and an itchy reaction. Be aware that some mosquitoes can carry communicable diseases. Malaria is nonexistent this far north, but mosquito-borne diseases such as West Nile virus have made national headlines, so it's best to take measures against bites. Mosquitoes can persist all summer but tend to be less of a problem as the season wears on, especially if conditions are dry. Mosquitoes are most common in low-lying wet areas and woods. Unfortunately, this accounts for a vast portion of the Upper Peninsula. They tend to be most active at dusk. The best way to avoid them is to stay in a breeze and wear pants and long sleeves. While many people will endorse repellent as an effective measure, with those containing DEET the best, studies have linked it to several health risks. If you choose to use repellent, be sure to wash your hands carefully before eating and to read the label warnings, especially before applying it to small children.

Blackflies can be an equally bothersome travel companion. They pose less of a health risk than mosquitoes but have a far more painful bite—somewhere between a mosquito bite and a bee sting on the pain scale. Blackflies resemble houseflies, only larger. They tend to be worst in the deep woods and during the early summer. U.P. blackflies can be the stuff of legend; anyone planning time in the backcountry should carry the strongest repellent available and pack a head net. Even if you're not in the backcountry, blackflies can make their presence known. If you come prepared, they're more irritating than problematic.

Ticks

Wood ticks and **deer ticks** are found in U.P. woods and grasslands. The larger wood tick, which is about 0.25 inches (0.6 cm) long, can attach itself to the skin and suck the blood of its victim. But despite this, the insect is relatively harmless. If you find a wood tick on you, your companion, or your pet, grasp it as close to the head as possible and yank. Don't leave a piece of the insect embedded in your skin, as it can lead to infection. Ticks prefer warm areas of the body (human or canine)—the scalp, neck, armpits, or genitals. Check under your dog's collar and around its ears.

Deer ticks are considerably more dangerous. They may transmit **Lyme disease,** a potentially debilitating condition. Lyme disease shows up as a temporary red rash that often resembles a ring, which slowly expands outward. Other symptoms as the disease progresses include sore joints, fatigue, and nausea. If left untreated, it can lead to arthritis and severe neurological and cardiac problems. Caught early, antibiotics can treat it effectively.

Additionally, deer ticks are tiny—often no larger than the head of a pin. Like wood ticks, they burrow into the skin, especially on warm areas of the body. After hiking, check yourself and your hiking partners carefully. If it's large enough, grasp the tick and pull it like you would a wood tick, or use tweezers. If you've been in a tick-infested area, watch for a rash within the next week, and have anything suspicious looked at promptly by a doctor. Your best defense against ticks is to wear long pants and long sleeves and to spray yourself liberally with an effective repellent, such as those containing DEET.

Dogs are highly susceptible to Lyme disease. Check your pet carefully and thoroughly for deer ticks by slowly running your fingers or a comb through her coat to get a look at the skin—a task that requires considerable patience from both you and your dog. Again, ears, necks, bellies, and genitals are areas most preferred by ticks. Signs that your dog may have acquired Lyme disease include nausea, fatigue, and lameness that may come and go from different joints. If you see potential symptoms, take your pet to a veterinarian immediately. Like humans, dogs respond well to antibiotics if the disease is caught early enough.

There is a canine vaccine for Lyme disease, but veterinarians disagree as to its effectiveness. There are some very good tick repellent sprays on the market intended for dogs.

Black Bears

When it comes to bigger animals, deer pose the greatest danger, as they cause thousands of accidents each year on Michigan roads. But **black bears** certainly seem more frightening, especially when you're deep in the woods. Black bears are found throughout northern Michigan, with the Upper Peninsula having an especially large population. They usually live in heavily forested areas, but will routinely wander into open spaces, especially for berries and other food sources. They're

beautiful animals, and you should consider yourself lucky if you observe one.

Black bears are generally shy creatures that would prefer to have nothing to do with you. If they hear you coming down the trail, they'll likely run the other way. If you happen to see one before it sees you, make sure you've left it an escape route, then clap, yell, or bang pans. Give especially wide berth to a mother with cubs. There are very few documented cases of black bear aggression against humans, and theories vary on what to do if you should ever find yourself in such a situation. Most behaviorists believe that, unlike the grizzlies of the western United States, black bears will be intimidated by dominant behaviors such as arm waving and shouting.

The worst situations occur when bears are lured into populated areas by human carelessness. It's always sad to see a bear relocated away from its home territory, but it happens frequently near campgrounds when humans don't properly store food or dispose of garbage. If you're car camping, keep all foodstuffs in your car (with the doors and windows closed and locked!). If you're tent camping, keep everything in airtight storage containers if possible, and suspend the containers on a line between two trees, high enough off the ground and far enough apart to be out of a bear's reach. Latched coolers placed under a picnic table are insufficient to keep bears out.

Clean pans and utensils right away, dumping the water well away from camp, and store them with the food. Never, ever keep any food (even gum) in your tent. Bears have an extremely good sense of smell and may be tempted to join you. Some say cosmetics also can attract them, so play it safe and store all soap and toothpaste with the food. It's also a good idea to leave your tent unzipped during the day while you're gone. Bears are curious, and if they want to look inside your tent, they'll make their own entrance if they can't find one.

If you're at a campground, deposit garbage in the animal-proof refuse containers provided. If you're backcountry camping, pack it out. Never, ever attempt to feed a bear, no matter how "tame" it may seem.

CORONAVIRUS

At the time of this writing in April 2023, Michigan's Upper Peninsula was moderately impacted by the effects of the coronavirus, but the situation is constantly evolving. Since the onset of the pandemic, cases have spiked in the U.P. due to the large number of visitors during the summer months. Throughout the course of the pandemic, the region's vaccination rate among adults aged 18-45 lagged below the national average. Common mitigation efforts, such as distancing and mask wearing, were widely observed early on but, as in many other places in the nation, have decreased due to "COVID fatigue." That said, the entire state of Michigan, including the Upper Peninsula, has experienced a dramatic drop in the number of positive tests and the total number of diagnosed cases, a positive harbinger for the future.

Now more than ever, Moon encourages readers to be courteous and ethical in their travel. Be respectful to residents and mindful of the evolving situation in your chosen destination when planning your trip. Get vaccinated if your health allows, and if possible, test regularly before, during, and after your trip to ensure you continue to test negative for COVID-19.

Resources

- CDC: www.cdc.gov/coronavirus/2019-ncov/travelers
- State of Michigan: https://michigan.gov/coronavirus/stats

EMERGENCIES

All of Michigan's Upper Peninsula is tied into the 911 emergency system. Dial 911 for free from any telephone (including pay phones) to reach an operator who can quickly dispatch local police, fire, or ambulance services. To locate a pay phone, visit Google Maps and enter "payphones near me." Cellular devices can also access the 911 system, but be aware that cell towers can be few and far between in rural areas. Much of the Upper Peninsula remains without reliable cellular or digital wireless service, but this can vary from carrier to carrier.

Hospitals

Every major city in the sparsely populated Upper Peninsula has a hospital, so you likely won't be too far away from quality medical care, unless you're deep in the woods.

Major hospitals include **Mackinac Straits Hospital** (1140 N. State St., St. Ignace, 906/643-8585, www.mackinacstraitshealth.org), **UP Health System Marquette** (580 W. College Ave., Marquette, 906/449-3000 www.mgh.org), and **War Memorial Hospital** (500 Osborn Blvd., Sault St. Marie, 906/635-4460, www.warmemorialhospital.org).

Information and Services

VISITOR INFORMATION

For general information on traveling in Michigan, your best source is the state-run **Pure Michigan** (800/644-2489, www.michigan.org, 9am-5pm Mon.-Fri.). Your call is answered by a real person who can send or fax brochures and consult a vast database to field your questions about festivals, lodgings, and a myriad of other topics. It's a much more helpful service than many tourism hotlines.

You may find it even more convenient to access the state tourism database directly at www.michigan.org. This comprehensive website with an interactive menu provides specific information tailored to the parameters you set. Tell it you want to go charter fishing on Lake Superior in fall, and it will display a list of appropriate charters; click on each for a detailed description, rates, and directions. Currently the site has categories for accommodations, attractions, camping, charter boats, communities, events, golf, restaurants, shopping, and skiing.

For information specific to the Upper Peninsula, contact the **Upper Peninsula Travel and Recreation Association** (P.O. Box 400, Iron Mountain, 906/774-5480 or 800/562-7134, www.uptravel.com).

The Michigan Department of Transportation operates seven **Welcome Centers** throughout the state. These facilities are stocked with travel literature and staffed with "travel counselors" who are quite knowledgeable about the state in general and their region in particular. The Welcome Centers are open year-round.

You'll find Welcome Centers at major gateways to the peninsula and at a few other "interior" locations. They're marked on the state highway map and with signs on the nearest highway. Hours vary.

MAPS

Michigan's official state road map is one of the few maps of the state that doesn't parcel the Upper Peninsula into frustrating and impossible to follow pieces. You can pick one up at a Michigan Welcome Center or request one from Pure Michigan.

The DeLorme *Michigan Atlas and Gazetteer* provides great detail, with the state portrayed in 102 large-scale maps. Though the 15-inch-long format is unwieldy for hikers, it's a great resource for planning your trip, and even identifies lighthouses, historic sites, waterfalls, industrial tours, and other points of interest. You can find it in many Midwestern bookstores or by visiting www.mapszu.com.

If you'll be exploring the backcountry, you're best off with an official topographic map produced by the U.S. Geological Survey. Michigan's national forests and lakeshores have topographic maps for sale at their visitors centers and ranger stations. Outside federal lands, many local outfitter shops carry them in addition to other highly detailed maps. If you can, buy one ahead of time at an outfitter or map store that carries topographic maps. If the store doesn't have the one you need, they can usually help you look up its number and possibly order it for you. You also can contact the **U.S. Geological Survey** (800/872-6277, www.usgs.gov) for a free map index and order form.

TIME AND MONEY

The Upper Peninsula is located in the eastern time zone, with the exception of the four Upper Peninsula counties that border Wisconsin: Gogebic, Iron, Dickinson, and Menominee Counties, all of which are in the central time zone.

Visa and MasterCard are accepted throughout the peninsula, except in some of the smallest towns. ATMs are plentiful, most of which are tied to the national Cirrus network. That said, there may be some mom-and-pop motels that accept only cash or checks. You might be surprised at how many small establishments are willing to take personal and out-of-town checks, which they often prefer over credit cards. Cash is required at self-registration campgrounds. Never count on getting by with only plastic.

If you're traveling to or from Canada, you'll find currency exchanges at the border and at nearby banks in both countries. In the past, Canadian and U.S. funds were accepted on reciprocal sides of the border, especially coins. In recent years, however, exchange rates have varied considerably, and it's therefore best to exchange currencies when traveling in either direction.

If you're a U.S. resident with Canadian currency left over at the end of a trip, it's best to have bills, not coins. Most American banks (especially away from border areas) will exchange only paper money.

Resources

Suggested Reading

ATLASES

DeLorme. *Michigan Atlas and Gazetteer*. Yarmouth, ME: DeLorme, 2022. Covering everything from major highways and byways to the back roads, this is one of the most detailed atlases you can find. Topographical maps and GPS grids are included (www.mapscompany.com).

Sportsman's Connection. *Northern Michigan All-Outdoors Atlas and Field Guide*. Superior, WI: Sportsman's Connection, 2023. Detailed maps, supplemental information, and helpful advice make this a must-have atlas for anyone who wants to spend any amount of time in Michigan's outdoors (https://scmaps.com).

FICTION

Harrison, Jim. *True North*. New York: Grove, 2004. Best known as the author of *Legends of the Fall*, Michigan native Harrison tells the story of a wealthy, dysfunctional family with the Upper Peninsula's harsh landscape as the backdrop. A tragedy, the book can be shocking and dark, but filled with beauty.

Hemingway, Ernest. *The Nick Adams Stories*. New York: Scribner, 1981. Hemingway's semiautobiographical account tells the story of Nick Adams as his life progresses from soldier to veteran, writer, and parent.

Monson, Ander. *Other Electricities: Stories*. Louisville, KY: Sarabande, 2005. Raised in the U.P., Monson presents a melancholic vision of his native peninsula through this critically acclaimed collection of stories and lists.

Traver, Robert. *Anatomy of a Murder*. New York: St. Martin's Griffin; 25th Anniversary Edition, 2005. This popular historical novel was written under a pseudonym by state Supreme Court justice John Voelker about a love-triangle murder that took place at the Lumberjack Tavern in Big Bay. The gripping novel was made into a feature-length movie in 1959, filmed on location in Marquette and Big Bay, by legendary director Otto Preminger. Highly recommended.

GENERAL INTEREST

Emerick, Lon L. *The Superior Peninsula: Seasons in the Upper Peninsula of Michigan*. Skandia, MI: North Country Publishing, 1996. A collection of essays about and "love letters" to the big lake and its peninsula, categorized by season.

Peterson, Carolyn C. *A View From the Wolf's Eye*. Calumet, MI: Copper Island Printing, 2008. The personal account of a woman who worked on Isle Royale with her husband for 37 summers conducting the ongoing study of the moose-wolf relationship while raising a family. An intimate account of nature from the perspective of one of its custodians.

Peterson, Rolf O. *The Wolves of Isle Royale: A Broken Balance*. Ann Arbor, MI: University of Michigan Press, 2007. Internationally known wolf researcher Peterson has compiled a firsthand account of Isle Royale National Park's ongoing wolf study. A delightful, informative book, it's filled with personal stories and powerful images.

Stonehouse, Frederick. *The Wreck of the Edmund Fitzgerald.* Gwinn, MI: Avery Color Studios, 2006. A thorough and thoughtful analysis of one of the most tragic disasters to occur on the Great Lakes. While offering no firm opinion as to the cause of the tragedy, the author discusses the events leading up to this famous shipwreck and the various theories of what caused its demise.

Traver, Robert. *Trout Magic.* New York: Touchstone, 1989. Personal reflections on the pleasures and solitude of trout fishing from accomplished author Robert Traver, better known as Justice John Voelker.

NATURAL HISTORY

Gostomski, Ted, et al. *Island Life: An Isle Royale Nature Guide.* Hancock, MI: Book Concern Printers, 2007. A comprehensive reference to the flora and fauna of Isle Royale in small paperback form. Excellent companion for a fishing or camping trip.

Grady, Wayne. *The Great Lakes: The Natural History of a Changing Region.* Vancouver: Greystone, 2011. A wonderfully illustrated natural history of the lakes with fascinating information on their formation as well as their present-day ecology and biology. Part written history, part photographic record, this book would be a beautiful and informative addition to any coffee table.

Kershaw, Linda. *Trees of Michigan: Including Tall Shrubs.* Auburn, WA: Lone Pine Publishing, 2006. This is *the* guide for tree identification in Michigan. Nearly 300 species of trees are referenced here, with color photographs and illustrations of the bark,

leaves, flowers, and overall shape of each tree. Tips are included for distinguishing among similar species.

Tekiela, Stan. *Birds of Michigan Field Guide,* 3rd Edition, Cambridge, MI: Adventure Publications, 2019. In this handy pocket-size guide, the author separates the wheat from the chaff, providing 118 concise yet informative summaries of the most common of Michigan's 800 bird species. Written in nontechnical language with vibrant, pleasing images.

OUTDOOR RECREATION

DuFresne, Jim. *Isle Royale National Park: Foot Trails and Water Routes,* 4th ed. Petoskey, MI: Michigantrailmaps.com, 2020. The definitive guide to Isle Royale, filled with practical information about campsites, portages, fishing spots, and more. Small enough to carry along, and an indispensable resource.

DuFresne, Jim. *Porcupine Mountains Wilderness State Park: A Backcountry Guide for Hikers, Backpackers, Campers, and Winter Visitors.* San Diego: Thunder Bay Press, 2022. An indispensable guide to this mammoth wild and beautiful park, with extensive coverage of the park's trail system for both day hikers and backpackers.

Hansen, Eric. *Hiking Michigan's Upper Peninsula.* Guilford, CT: FalconGuides, 2015. Hansen set out to hike and map 50 of the Upper Peninsula's finest trails, many of them little-known gems. His work is magnificently displayed in this book through compelling images.

Hillstrom, Kevin, and Laurie Collier Hillstrom. *Paddling Michigan.* Guilford, CT: FalconGuides, 2001. This extensive paddling guide predominantly covers routes and rivers in the Upper Peninsula but does include some Lower Peninsula waterways.

Suggested Movies and Music

MOVIES

Anatomy of a Murder, 1959. Based on the novel by Michigan Supreme Court justice and Ishpeming native John Voelker, this movie is based on an actual 1952 murder case in which Voelker, then a private attorney, was defense counsel. Filmed in Big Bay and Marquette, it stars Jimmy Stewart and George C. Scott and was directed by Otto Preminger.

Escanaba in da Moonlight, 2001. Starring, written, and directed by Jeff Daniels, this offbeat comedy has taken some heat for its stereotypical portrayal of the residents of Escanaba. Some claim, however, that the depiction is spot-on. With a quirky plot and a good deal of off-color humor, this film isn't for everyone.

Somewhere in Time, 1980. While not a classic, this film has acquired a cult following and a reputation as a timeless love story. Its stars, Jane Seymour and Christopher Reeve, are overshadowed only by the magnificent Grand Hotel and the Mackinac Island setting.

MUSIC

Lightfoot, Gordon. "The Wreck of the *Edmund Fitzgerald,*" 1976. From the album *Summertime Dream,* Gordon Lightfoot's folk retelling of the tragic sinking of the *Edmund Fitzgerald* during a Lake Superior storm immortalized the event in popular memory.

Murdock, Lee. "The Great Lakes Song," 1998. A heartwarming folk tribute to the five inland seas. It makes mention of the lakes heritage of commercial fishing, iron ore transit, and simple contemplation. The most popular recording is by singer Pat Dailey.

Stevens, Sufjan. *Greetings from Michigan: The Great Lakes State,* 2003. When Michigan native Sufjan Stevens released his indie ode to Michigan, people took note. Pay special attention to songs set in the Upper Peninsula. Includes "For the Widows in Paradise, For the Fatherless in Ypsilanti," "The Upper Peninsula," "Tahquamenon Falls," "Sleeping Bear, Sault Saint Marie," and "Oh God, Where Are You Now? (In Pickerel Lake? Pigeon? Marquette? Mackinaw?)."

Internet Resources

STATEWIDE INFORMATION

Travel Michigan
www.michigan.org
Michigan's official travel website is an integral part of the state's Pure Michigan tourism campaign. It's the most visited state tourism site in the United States, and is frequently updated.

Upper Peninsula Travel and Recreation Association
www.uptravel.com

Upper Peninsula-specific tourism information and numerous helpful links. Request the free travel planner.

OUTDOOR RECREATION AND CAMPING

Michigan Department of Natural Resources
www.michigan.gov/dnr
The site for state park info, campground reservations, and information on all sorts of

outdoor recreation, including fishing, hunting, and snowmobile registration.

Michigan Interactive
www.fishweb.com

A great resource for all sorts of outdoor activities in Michigan, including interactive maps for fishing, hiking, and snowmobile and off-road vehicle trails.

National Park Service
www.nps.gov

Official one-stop shopping for all of the national parks and lakeshores in Michigan—Isle Royale, Keweenaw, and Pictured Rocks—plus Sleeping Bear Dunes in the Lower Peninsula

as well as the North Country National Scenic Trail.

U.S. Forest Service
www.fs.fed.us

A site that provides valuable information about both the Hiawatha and Ottawa National Forests.

TRANSPORTATION

Michigan Department of Transportation
www.michigan.gov/mdot

The best, most up-to-date source for information on major road construction projects and various public transportation options.

Index

A

accessibility: 326
Active Backwoods Retreat: 145
Adventure Copper Mine: 149
A. E. Seaman Mineral Museum: 162
Agate Beach: 176, 178
Agate Falls: 137
air travel: 313
Alberta: 160
Alger County Heritage Center: 233
Alger Falls: 237
Alger Underwater Preserve: 14, 237–238
Algonquin Falls: 137
Algonquin Pathway: 279, 281
Al Quaal Recreation Area: 216
Anatomy of a Murder: 230
Anderson Lake Pathway: 216
animals: 300–302
Anna River: 239
Annual Antiques on the Bay: 65
Annual End of Summer Blues Fest: 133
Annual Grand Marais Music and Arts Festival: 247
Annual Mackinac Bridge Walk: 65, 78
Annual Manistique Folkfest: 89
Annual Marquette Blues Fest: 212
Arch Rock: 50
Art for All: 112
Art on the Rocks: 212
arts: 309–311
Astor House Antique Doll and Indian Artifact Museum: 178
ATMs: 331
Aune-Osborn Park: 283
Aurora Borealis Forecaster: 37
Au Sable Light Station: 246
auto shows: 65, 77
auto travel: 312–316

B

backpacking: Marquette and Lake Superior 247–248; Superior Upland 149
Badwater Ski-Ters Water Ski Show: 124
Bailey Park: 113
Balloons on the Bay and Pioneer Days: 103
Baraga State Park: 176
Bare Bluff Trail: 183
Bass Lake: 125
Bass Lake Motorcycle Trail: 215
Bay City Lake Trail: 291
Bay de Noc/Grand Island Trail: 103

Bay Furnace: 240
Bay Mills Casino: 279
Bays de Noc: 96
Bayshore Park: 233
beaches: general discussion 91, 322–323; Escanaba and Lake Michigan 86, 96, 100, 105, 113; Keweenaw Peninsula and Isle Royale 176, 178, 180, 184, 189; Marquette and Lake Superior 215, 228, 232–233, 235, 244, 246, 248–249; Straits of Mackinac 67, 78; Superior Upland 132, 140, 141, 146, 152; Whitefish and Lake Huron 281, 283, 287, 293
Beaver Basin Loop Trail: 247
Beaver Lake: 244, 246
beer/breweries: general discussion 15, 220–221, 323–324; Escanaba and Lake Michigan 107; Keweenaw Peninsula and Isle Royale 169, 181; Marquette and Lake Superior 210–211, 218, 234, 250; Straits of Mackinac 78; Superior Upland 141; Whitefish and Lake Huron 271, 282
Benjamin Blacksmith Shop: 46
Bewabic State Park: 133–134, 136
bicycling: general discussion 319; Escanaba and Lake Michigan 89, 91, 95, 103–104, 110, 112; Keweenaw Peninsula and Isle Royale 170–171, 181, 183–184; Marquette and Lake Superior 213–214, 225, 227, 232, 233, 234–235, 246, 247, 254, 255–256, 257; Straits of Mackinac 50, 52, 53, 55, 56; Superior Upland 125, 133–134, 141, 143, 150, 152; Whitefish and Lake Huron 279–280, 289
Biddle House: 46
Big Bay: 222
Big Bay de Noc: 96, 113
Big Bay Harbor of Refuge: 228
Big Bay Pathway: 225, 228
Big Bay Point Lighthouse: 224
Big Carp River Trail: 150
Big Island Lake Canoeing Area: 105
Big Manistique Lake: 84
Big Pine Picnic Grounds: 273
Big Powderhorn Mountain: 144
Big Pup Falls: 228
Big Snow Resort: 145
Bill Nichols Trail: 172
Bimbo's Wine Press: 33, 128
Birch Hill Trail: 291
birds and wildlife: general discussion 17, 39, 300–302, 316, 329–330; Escanaba and Lake Michigan 89, 103, 104, 112; Keweenaw Peninsula and Isle Royale 171–172, 179, 189,

List of Maps

Photo Credits

All photos © Paul Vachon except page 6 © Jason P Ross | Dreamstime.com; page 8 © Michigannut | Dreamstime.com; page 10 © Adeliepenguin |Dreamstime.com; page 12 © (top) Michigannut | Dreamstime.com; (bottom) Luke Wendling | Dreamstime.com; page 14 © (top) Ethan Daniels | Dreamstime.com; (bottom) Bobbypalosaari | Dreamstime.com; page 15 © Susan Sheldon | Dreamstime.com; page 16 © Michigannut | Dreamstime.com; page 17 © (top) Snehitdesign | Dreamstime.com; page 18 © Ehrlif | Dreamstime.com; page 23 © Michael Smith | Dreamstime.com; page 24 © (top) Cindy Dixon | Dreamstime.com; page 29 © Michigannut | Dreamstime.com; page 30 © Snehitdesign | Dreamstime.com; page 34 © (top) Beautynature | Dreamstime.com; (bottom) Qube002 | Dreamstime.com; page 36 © Steven Pepple | Dreamstime.com; page 38 © (bottom) Steve Lagreca | Dreamstime.com; page 39 © Paul Sparks | Dreamstime.com; page 40 © Bain25 | Dreamstime.com; page 41 © Gerald D. Tang | Dreamstime.com; page 51 © (left middle) Jabell5 | Dreamstime.com; page 56 © (top left) Bexcellent | Dreamstime.com; (top right) Dennis Caskey | Dreamstime.com; page 61 © Dennis Caskey | Dreamstime.com; page 68 © (top) Ehrlif | Dreamstime.com; (left middle) Ehrlif | Dreamstime.com; (right middle) Ehrlif | Dreamstime.com; (bottom) Paul Lemke | Dreamstime.com; page 77 © (top) Picturemakersllc | Dreamstime.com; page 84 © (top left) Alexey Stiop | Dreamstime.com; (top right) Dean Pennala | Dreamstime.com; page 88 © Hannah Babiak | Dreamstime.com; page 90 © (top right) Ehrlif | Dreamstime.com; (bottom) Kenneth Keifer | Dreamstime.com; page 108 © Gerald D. Tang | Dreamstime.com; page 117 © (top) Tony Savino | Dreamstime.com; (bottom) Gerald D. Tang | Dreamstime.com; page 120 © Ehrlif | Dreamstime.com; page 137 © (top) Steven Prorak | Dreamstime.com; page 144 © (bottom) Ehrlif | Dreamstime.com; page 153 © (left middle) Jason P Ross | Dreamstime.com; page 158 © Greg Kretovic | Dreamstime.com; page 159 © (top right) Bonita Cheshier | Dreamstime.com; page 165 © (top) Snehitdesign | Dreamstime.com; (left middle) James Pintar | Dreamstime.com; page 168 © (top) Gerald D. Tang | Dreamstime.com; (bottom) Steve Lagreca | Dreamstime.com; page 175 © (top left) Bonita Cheshier | Dreamstime.com; (top right) Craig Sterken | Dreamstime.com; (bottom) Will Emmert | Dreamstime.com; page 184 © (right middle) Ehrlif | Dreamstime.com; (bottom) Paul Lemke | Dreamstime.com; page 200 © Heather Mcardle | Dreamstime.com; page 204 © (top right) James Phelps | Dreamstime.com; page 211 © (top) Ehrlif | Dreamstime.com; (bottom) Snehitdesign | Dreamstime.com; page 214 © Jim Roberts | Dreamstime.com; page 219 © (top left) Alicia Hess | Dreamstime.com; (top right) Baluzek | Dreamstime.com; (bottom) Leppekmatthew | Dreamstime.com; page 222 © Kristen Prahl | Dreamstime.com; page 226 © Tmsotirin | Dreamstime.com; page 228 © (bottom) Paul Lemke | Dreamstime.com; page 238 © (top left) Craig Sterken | Dreamstime.com; (top right) Gerald D. Tang | Dreamstime.com; (bottom) Le Thuy Do | Dreamstime.com; page 257 © Gerald D. Tang | Dreamstime.com; page 262 © (top left) Joseph Mercier | Dreamstime.com; page 270 © (right middle) Joseph Mercier | Dreamstime.com; page 279 © (bottom) Ehrlif | Dreamstime.com; page 290 © (top) Schneidersimages | Dreamstime.com; (right middle) Joshua West | Dreamstime.com; (bottom) Marysue Ryan | Dreamstime.com; page 292 © Manon Ringuette | Dreamstime.com

ROAD TRIP GUIDES

MOON

SOUTH FLORIDA & THE KEYS
Road Trip

WITH MIAMI, WALT DISNEY WORLD, TAMPA & THE EVERGLADES

JASON FERGUSON

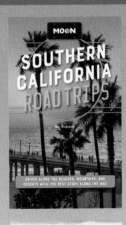

MOON

SOUTHERN CALIFORNIA
ROAD TRIPS

DRIVES ALONG THE BEACHES, MOUNTAINS, AND DESERTS WITH THE BEST STOPS ALONG THE WAY

MOON

SOUTHWEST ROAD TRIP

Tim Hull

DRIVE THE LOOP FROM LAS VEGAS TO SANTA FE, VISITING 5 NATIONAL PARKS ALONG THE WAY

MOON

U.S. & CANADIAN ROCKY MOUNTAINS
Road Trip

DRIVE THE CONTINENTAL DIVIDE AND EXPLORE 8 NATIONAL PARKS

BECKY LOMAX

MOON

VANCOUVER & CANADIAN ROCKIES
ROAD TRIP

ADVENTURES FROM THE COAST TO THE MOUNTAINS

with Victoria & the Sea-to-Sky Highway

MOON

YELLOWSTONE TO GLACIER NATIONAL PARK
ROAD TRIP

Carter G. Walker

CONNECT MONTANA & WYOMING'S 3 NATIONAL PARKS, WITH THE BEST STOPS ALONG THE WAY

MOON

BASEBALL Road Trips

TIMOTHY MALCOLM

THE COMPLETE GUIDE TO ALL THE BALLPARKS, WITH BEER, BITES, AND SIGHTS NEARBY

MOON

the OPEN ROAD

50 BEST ROAD TRIPS in the USA

From Weekend Getaways to Cross-Country Adventures

JESSICA DUNHAM

MOON

Road Trip USA

CROSS-COUNTRY ADVENTURES ON AMERICA'S TWO-LANE HIGHWAYS

Jamie Jensen

MAP SYMBOLS

═══════ Expressway	○ City/Town	ⓘ Information Center	♠ Park
═══════ Primary Road	◉ State Capital	ⓟ Parking Area	↓ Golf Course
═══════ Secondary Road	✸ National Capital	♠ Church	✛ Unique Feature
═ ═ ═ ═ Unpaved Road	✪ Highlight	✿ Winery/Vineyard	⟲ Waterfall
---------- Trail	★ Point of Interest	ⓣ Trailhead	Ⓐ Camping
············· Ferry	● Accommodation	ⓡ Train Station	▲ Mountain
⊶⊶⊶⊶ Railroad	▼ Restaurant/Bar	✕ Airport	⛷ Ski Area
▨▨▨▨ Pedestrian Walkway	■ Other Location	✗ Airfield	⬡ Glacier
▥▥▥▥ Stairs			

CONVERSION TABLES

$°C = (°F - 32) / 1.8$
$°F = (°C \times 1.8) + 32$
1 inch = 2.54 centimeters (cm)
1 foot = 0.304 meters (m)
1 yard = 0.914 meters
1 mile = 1.6093 kilometers (km)
1 km = 0.6214 miles
1 fathom = 1.8288 m
1 chain = 20.1168 m
1 furlong = 201.168 m
1 acre = 0.4047 hectares
1 sq km = 100 hectares
1 sq mile = 2.59 square km
1 ounce = 28.35 grams
1 pound = 0.4536 kilograms
1 short ton = 0.90718 metric ton
1 short ton = 2,000 pounds
1 long ton = 1.016 metric tons
1 long ton = 2,240 pounds
1 metric ton = 1,000 kilograms
1 quart = 0.94635 liters
1 US gallon = 3.7854 liters
1 Imperial gallon = 4.5459 liters
1 nautical mile = 1.852 km

MOON MICHIGAN'S UPPER PENINSULA

Avalon Travel
Hachette Book Group
555 12th Street, Suite 1850
Oakland, CA 94607 USA
www.moon.com

Editor: Rachael Sablik
Managing Editor: Courtney Packard
Copy Editor: Deana Shields
Graphics Coordinator: Darren Alessi
Production Coordinator: Darren Alessi
Cover Design: Toni Tajima
Interior Design: Avalon Travel
Map Editor: Karin Dahl
Cartographers: Jack Moorehead, John Culp
Proofreader: Brett Keener
Indexer: Greg Jewett

ISBN-13: 9781640499966

Printing History
1st Edition — 2009
6th Edition — March 2024
5 4 3 2

Front cover photo: Kitch-iti-kipi Freshwater Spring
© Trace Hudson / Getty Images
Back cover photo: Lovers Leap rock formation at
Pictured Rocks National Lakeshore © Alexey Stiop
| Dreamstime.com

Printed in China by APS